WILLIAM BICKERTON

William Bickerton the year he died, 1905. Photograph by W. R. Gray, who worked in his St. John studio from 1905 to 1947. *Courtesy Gray Studio Glass Plate Negative Collection, Stafford County Museum and Forsyth Digital Library*

WILLIAM BICKERTON

FORGOTTEN LATTER DAY PROPHET

BY DANIEL P. STONE

SIGNATURE BOOKS | 2018 | SALT LAKE CITY

for Laura & Lily,
Keith, Angie & Jared,
Emil & Yvonne
also in loving memory of John Genaro

www.signaturebooks.com. Printed in the USA on paper certified by the Sustainable Forestry Initiative.

Jacket design by Aaron Fisher.

FIRST EDITION | 2018

LIBRARY OF CONGRESS CATALOGING-IN-PUBLICATION DATA

Names: Stone, Daniel P., author.

Title: William Bickerton : forgotten latter day prophet / Daniel P. Stone.

Description: First edition. | Salt Lake City : Signature Books, 2018. | Includes bibliographical references and index.

Identifiers: LCCN 2018002855 (print) | LCCN 2018003990 (ebook) | ISBN 9781560853374 (e-book) | ISBN 9781560852681 (hardcover : alk. paper)

Subjects: LCSH: Bickerton, William, 1815–1905. | Church of Jesus Christ (Bickertonites)

Classification: LCC BX8680.B53 (ebook) | LCC BX8680.B53 S76 2018 (print) | DDC 289.3092 [B] —dc23

LC record available at https://lccn.loc.gov/2018002855

CONTENTS

INTRODUCTION

> *"My kinsfolk have failed, and my familiar friends have forgotten me. … Oh that my words were now written! oh that they were printed in a book! That they were graven with an iron pen and lead in the rock for ever!"*
>
> —Job 19:14–24

Prior to his death in 1905, the deposed prophet of the Church of Jesus Christ, William Bickerton, left a final message to the world when he asked apostle Allen Wright to read the nineteenth chapter of Job at his funeral. There was, of course, bitterness in this request. The onetime church president had been marginalized, his reputation tarnished by men he had mentored, who had assumed the leadership and cast him aside. Bickerton had been one of the major claimants to Joseph Smith's position as president and prophet of the Latter Day Saint church. He had led the Pennsylvania Saints, and those of surrounding areas, by prophecy and revelation, and he had overseen a hundred-fold increase in the membership from the time he assumed responsibility. And yet, there had been a power play and he had lost. After investing everything, temporally and spiritually in the church, he saw nearly everything taken away, leaving him with an affinity for Job in the Bible and the belief that, like Job, eventually someone would set the record straight or at least attempt to tell the whole story. Over a century has passed, and his achievements and trials are still rarely spoken of among the some 23,000 adherents to the church that popularly bears his name.

That no one has previously written a book-length biography is surprising. The church Bickerton founded remains the third-largest of the Restoration movement, and although its numbers are dwarfed by the Utah-based LDS Church with almost sixteen million members and Missouri-based Community of Christ with a quarter-million members, one sees more written about James Jesse Strang of Wisconsin and Granville Hedrick of Missouri, let alone Brigham Young and Joseph Smith III, than about Bickerton. What is the reason? It is certainly not because his story lacks drama. His people lived through the Civil War, and a good number of them moved from Pennsylvania to the middle of Kansas, with all the hardships an overland migration involved and the setbacks of scraping by in an area where people had previously not lived. For a time Bickerton maintained a communal society that was awaiting the gathering of the lost tribes of Israel and Jesus's second coming. He became an opponent of polygamy. At the same time, he himself was suspected of adultery, and although the accusation was probably false, Bickerton had fraternized with female church members (walks in parks) more than common custom allowed. He made some bold theological moves, admitting African Americans and women in the ministry. He looked forward to a Native American prophet. With a life filled with unexpected twists and turns, progressive theological innovations, miracles, prophecies—even scandal—why has he been largely relegated to footnotes within Latter Day Saint history?

There are several reasons. The first is because his own followers rejected him. They came to see him the way they saw Joseph Smith and Sidney Rigdon, as human beings who were susceptible to temptation, especially in uttering contrived, self-serving revelations alongside genuine ones. Theirs was not a rejection of real-life accomplishments or shared visions, but of leaders as role models when their behavior became suspect. In the case of Bickerton's church, its history was written by his rivals. It contains fragments of his life, the official historian, William H. Cadman, a son of Bickerton's successor, deciding that rather than dig up complicated details and engender strife, it would be better to leave the incidents in Bickerton's life alone, thereby almost entirely removing the founder from history.

Another reason we seldom hear about Bickerton is because he did not keep a diary or leave behind other personal records for posterity, at least that are extant. We have some of his correspondence, the minutes of church meetings, and his official church writings—all invaluable in perceiving his worldview. It is, however, a tragedy that there is not more material. For example, it appears that he did not have much of a life outside of the church. That may be a false impression due to the limitations of available information. The matter is further complicated by the fact that much of the information is unavailable to the public. Only lately has the church archive been organized, and most of its holdings are restricted to church members. Because my affiliation allowed me to see documents that have not been scrutinized previously, I was introduced to aspects of the church's wonderfully rich history and insight into the founder's personal thoughts in the context of events as they happened. Most members would not have the academic training or interest to sort through random pieces of evidence to piece together a coherent narrative.

An attempt was made in 1999 when Gary R. Entz completed his doctoral dissertation, "Paradise on the Plains: The Development of Cooperative Alternatives in Kansas, 1850–1900," in which he took the first in-depth look at Bickerton and the Church of Jesus Christ in Kansas. He also published two journal articles on the topic in 2001 and 2006, and that research became a springboard for my own study. Not a church member, Entz nevertheless showed me how to write with both sympathy and scholarship, convincing me that it was possible to unravel the details of Bickerton's life for a biography. In fact, he influenced my desire to pursue a career in history.

Another model for me, especially in terms of balancing faith with the historian's obligation to rely on available evidence, was Richard L. Bushman's landmark biography, *Joseph Smith: Rough Stone Rolling*, in which he wrote about "facing up to [Smith's] mistakes and flaws." Bushman believed that "covering up errors makes no sense. … Most readers do not believe in, nor are they interested in, perfection. Flawless characters are neither attractive nor useful. We want to meet a real person."

It is certainly true that Bickerton had flaws and strengths, also that he was very much a product of his time. Born fifteen years into the nineteenth century, and living to see the beginning of the twentieth, he saw unimaginable changes in the world. I have examined his statements and actions in context, and in doing so I have had a few basic questions in mind, such as how he understood and explained his prophetic calling and what role he imagined the converts played in fulfilling that calling. What lay behind the theological concepts he introduced? What about his family life and finances—his occupation as a coal miner? What did he think about the overall changes in the world—the political and military conflicts, mass migrations of people, discoveries, technological advances, and societal norms?

To answer these questions, I realized soon enough that I would have to get more than a superficial understanding of Bickerton's theology, which was challenging because it changed over time, and not always methodically. Most of Bickerton's views were based on his reading of the Bible and Book of Mormon, although not always in line with conventional thinking about the passages he drew from. He also occasionally drew from the Doctrine and Covenants and from other revelations of Joseph Smith, alternating between acceptance and rejection of various texts. In retrospect, this should not be surprising. Smith's revelations underwent, and continue to undergo, varied interpretations at different times by various Latter Day Saint denominations. In the hierarchy of authoritative texts, however, Bickerton held his own prophecies to be the most reliable (in tandem with the Bible and Book of Mormon). Bickerton's revelations were current and therefore most relevant, less ambiguous because they were delivered in the current idiom, and subject to subsequent clarification. It was axiomatic that the more recent the revelation, the more authoritative. Through his dialogue with the Almighty, Bickerton saw himself as elucidating and correcting Mormon doctrine. He saw it as a partly democratic process because members were often allowed to vote on whether they accepted or rejected a given revelation and were encouraged to utter their own prophecies and interpretations. This added another level of complexity to the matter of doctrine. All the while, national, local, and personal circumstances continued to impact Bickerton's ideas and decisions. I am aware that piecing together these moving parts involves the possibility of misunderstanding them. Although I kept my conclusions close to what is more or less obvious from the available documents, I have also offered qualifiers like *maybe* whenever I have speculated.

Some historians encounter a dilemma in writing about religion and deciding whether, even in their word choices, to credit a prophet's revelations to God. It is an easier task in a biography, to the extent that a biography should more or less reflect the views of the subject. Even so, I do point out contradictions whenever Bickerton's behavior seems self-interested, reminding readers of what the church members themselves were well aware of, that no one is infallible. The members believed in revelation and received revelations themselves, so they understood the play that existed between speaking in tongues and interpreting the message, and if others felt inspired they stood or shouted their acclamation or spoke in tongues themselves. At other times they rejected a revelation. To a certain extent, one feels the same liberty today, especially with the benefit of hindsight, while simultaneously feeling impressed on many levels.

Bickerton had to contend with skeptics from outside and inside. I try to allow the detractors to speak for themselves and acknowledge a valid point or an error where appropriate. Both Bickerton and his opponents engaged in exaggeration and were guilty of incongruity. This study is not intended to determine who was right, but rather to see what the world looked like to them. In doing so, I understand that my interpretations may be challenged by believers and outsiders, including scholars, based on different criteria, no doubt. Knowing that is humbling—and certainly intimidating. Because this is the first book-length biography, and because I cite documents not previously seen, I am burdened with having to offer interpretations without the benefit of previous comments on many of the topics by other historians. For that reason I quote liberally from the sources, giving readers a chance to better judge the validity of my perspective. As others formulate opinions contrary to mine, that will create useful dialogue, which is, after all, what makes history so interesting.

The book could not have been written without the help of Alexander Robinson. His wealth of knowledge, along with his copies of many primary documents, was indispensable in putting me on the right path at the beginning of this project. I am equally grateful to the general historian of the Church of Jesus Christ for access to the archive in Greensburg, Pennsylvania. As I searched through uncatalogued material, I found documents—the church revelation book, for instance—that were thought to have been lost, and that provided perspective I otherwise would not have had. My appreciation to John E. Mancini and the Lamb Foundation for providing invaluable digital files of photos and documents, including typescripts of minutes. I could not have begun to go into depth about the Kansas period without these resources.

I want to thank the staff of the Detre Library and Archives at the Senator John Heinz History Center in Pittsburgh, the Ida Long Goodman Memorial Library in St. John, the state archives at the Kansas Historical Society in Topeka, and the LDS Church History Library in Salt Lake City. In each case, the librarians and archivists helped me find material and patiently answered my many questions. Richard Scaglione Sr., H. Michael Marquardt, and James and Deanna McKay similarly provided me with direction and assistance throughout this project. My gratitude to members of the Church of Jesus Christ Detroit Branch #2 Ladies Circle and others who read chapters and offered criticism: John Genaro, Judy Salerno, Richard and Lani Moore, Jan Bork, Gary Coppa, Anne Johns, Teresa Pandone, and John Straccia. My appreciation to Jason Francis of Signature Books and Kevin Coppa for enhancing the photographs. My employers, Mary Ellen Sanko and Anne Johns, gave me ample time to finish this project, for which I am indebted. John Hatch of Signature Books and Joe Geisner led the way to get this book published, and Ron Priddis was the best editor one could have asked for.

Most importantly, my deepest gratitude goes to my wife, Laura, and my parents, Angie and Keith Stone, as well as Yvonne and Emil Lambert, all of whom endured with stoic patience my constant (and sometimes unbearable) questions about sentence structure and grammar. They read and reread chapters and remarkably never complained. My wife traveled across the country with me as I conducted research and tolerated my seclusion at home while writing the book. Through all this, as she and I developed an intimacy with William Bickerton, we grew closer together ourselves. It has been the journey of a lifetime.

Lastly, I want to thank the God to whom Bickerton gave reverence. Without him, Bickerton may never have lived the life that made this biography possible.

ONE

A BEGINNING

1815–44

"I was born in Northumberland England and was a coal miner and a hard working man all my life."

—Jan. 20, 1905

It took about five weeks for sixteen-year-old William Bickerton to reach New York City in 1831, where he arrived at the beginning of summer.[1] One can imagine how warm and humid it must have been below deck and how happy he must have been to emerge into the open air in his new country, even though the culture was foreign and his future uncertain. To cross the Atlantic Ocean in those days required courage. In wishing his family and friends goodbye, he wondered if he would ever see them again, traveling hundreds of miles from his hometown to London, apparently alone, and boarding the *Cambria*,[2] no doubt knowing he risked contracting typhus or cholera onboard the ship.[3]

English emigrant William Smith recalled from his 1850 passage to America "scenes I witnessed daily [that] were awful … [children] dying, leaving their aged parents without means of support in their declining years. … I saw the tear of sympathy run down the cheek of many a hardened sailor." As sea sickness ravaged the passengers, the deck turned filthy. As Benjamin Millward penned in 1854, "The people are lying about in all directions, sick in scores. … It is a pitiful

1. He arrived on June 20, one day before the summer solstice.
2. *Registers of Vessels*, M237/14.
3. Van Vugt, *Britain to America*, 13–14.

sight." Another emigrant, Joseph Hurst, wrote in his diary, "The ship roll'd & tottered & her timbers creaked & shivered ... the roaring of the waves together with the rolling of the shipe made it almost impossible to keep ourselves in our berths." One Irishman joked that "for the first quarter of an hour you feel afraid the ship is going down, and for the next quarter of an hour you feel afraid that it will not go down."[4]

Bickerton may have left England because his world was in transition as his county of Northumberland transformed itself into a coal-mining center during the Industrial Revolution. Bickerton's life began on January 15, 1815, in the town of Kyloe on the far northeast coast, not far from Scotland.[5] Many of his peers, no doubt, had already chosen to leave town and cast their lot with the men operating the mines sixty miles to the south where excavations on either side of the River Tyne extended twenty miles inland, producing large quantities of the black rock they shipped on the North Sea to points along England's eastern coast, 300 miles distant to London.[6]

For a time, Bickerton's father, Thomas, raised sheep in the nearby Cheviot Hills, the same way his forefathers had, as he and his wife, Isabella Hope, raised eleven children. William was the seventh.[7] When Thomas died in 1828, he left Isabella with six youngsters under the age of fifteen, among them William. It is not known when, but eventually the rest of the family would follow William's lead in traveling to America.[8]

When William stepped off the ship in 1831, the United States was undergoing its own technological, social, and political transformation with the populist hero of the War of 1812, Andrew Jackson, in the

4. Smith, *Emigrant's Narrative*, 14; Burnley, *Two Sides*, 19; Van Vugt, *Britain to America*, 14–15.

5. Pilgrim, "Descendants of Thomas Bickerton," 1. More specifically, Bickerton was born in Ancroft Parish, bordering Kyloe.

6. Freese, *Coal: Human History*, 21–22; Ashton, *Industrial Revolution*, 1–17.

7. The children were James, born 1804; John, 1806; Eleanor, 1807; Ann, 1810; Mary, 1812; Thomas, 1814; William, 1815; Isabelle, 1817; Arthur, 1820; Alexander, 1823; Robert, 1824 (Pilgrim, "Descendants of Thomas Bickerton," 1).

8. Pilgrim, 1–6; Jordan, *Genealogical and Personal History,* 2:1028.

White House. Before and after Jackson's administration, voting privileges were extended across the country to nearly every white male, which changed the status quo of most states that had previously allowed only property owners to vote. Factories were blossoming in urban areas, and canals, roads, and railways were spreading across the land. The growth of cities surpassed the increase of population in rural America due to the emigration each year of about 200,000 people from Ireland, England, and Germany, whose presence, and competition for work, sparked nativist resentment—the anti-Catholic activism, for instance.

These changes were accompanied by a spiritual awakening. Baptists and Methodists led the crusade to win souls for an emotional and supernatural engagement with religion. People looked back to a simpler, biblical form of Christianity and forward to the second coming of Christ and the end of the world. Men like Alexander Campbell and Joseph Smith contributed to this reshaping of Christianity, which brought disharmony as Protestant denominations splintered into a variety of sects. Class and racial conflicts persisted. Friction between the North and South, white and black, rich and poor, divided people. The federal government began forcibly removing indigenous people to territory west of the Mississippi River. All the while, Americans tore at each other and debated what would become of them in the midst of a new social structure and new technologies, as they confronted anesthesia, mechanical crop reapers, photography, sewing machines, steam travel, and the telegraph for the first time. Literature was also taking root through the ability of Nathaniel Hawthorne, Edgar Allan Poe, and others to give voice to common people.[9]

Sometime after his arrival to New York City, Bickerton moved to the upper edge of Virginia on the west side of the Allegheny Mountains (now West Virginia) where the Cumberland Road was built in 1818 to link the city of Cumberland, Maryland, on the Potomac River to Wheeling, 150 miles to the west, on the Ohio River, sixty

9. Reynolds, *Waking Giant*, 1–4.

miles south of Pittsburgh. The construction of a federally subsidized gravel road that connected two major river systems made trans-Appalachian travel possible. On both ends of the 150-mile road, steamships docked. Wheeling, which in 1810 had about 100 houses and eleven stores, became a national commercial hub by 1822 that counted 4,681 wagonloads of goods passing through that year, each carrying 3,500 pounds of merchandise. That was probably only a fraction of the actual total traffic from immigrants and merchants passing through the town that year.[10]

Bickerton found work mining coal on the outskirts of Wheeling. He might have learned of the opportunity through one of the networks of immigrants who kept each other apprised of such job openings. It is possible Bickerton knew about Wheeling before he left England. In any case, the coal mines fueled the factories that now dotted the city: ironworks, foundries, paper mills, glass factories, distilleries, cotton mills, and woolen factories that required a million bushels of coal each year to keep running. Flatboat construction also prospered.[11]

Bickerton may have been satisfied with his surroundings when he was a bachelor, but not so in the early 1840s after marrying Dorothy Breminger and having their first son, James, born in 1844. Now Bickerton's eyes turned to the northeast, to Pittsburgh, an even larger manufacturing base. Already in 1817, with the city boasting a population of 6,000 and over 250 factories, people were calling it the "Birmingham of America."[12] Pittsburgh was one of the largest cities west of the Alleghenies, its principal hallmark the smoke that rose over the city due to the industrialization. In 1816 a traveler, David Thomas, described "a hovering cloud of this vapour … [that] rendered [the city] singularly gloomy." Richard Mason agreed that the cloud of "smoke and dust … almost [turns day] to night," that it created a "melancholy"

10. Howe, *What Hath God Wrought*, 212; Rice, *West Virginia*, 87–88. By 1834 the city had 500 houses and the population had risen from under 1,000 to 8,000. Martin, *New and Comprehensive Gazetteer*, 406.

11. Van Vugt, 93; Rice, 84–85; Jordan, 2:1029.

12. Pilgrim, 2; US Census, 1850; Freese, 106–08.

mood.[13] Despite the fact that smog was considered unpleasant, it advertised the city's success. It was a city not without its charms.

The family found housing fifteen miles southeast of the city in the borough of West Elizabeth, a ferry town along the Monongahela River where William was able to find work, again in the coal mines.[14] It seems he was always able to find employment, maybe due to his self-confidence and large calloused hands that showed experience. He was tall; moderately handsome; wore simple, ordinary suits; and kept a trimmed beard that sometimes grew a little long. He had gentle but penetrating eyes framed by large ears, tight cheeks, and a round-tipped nose.

His friends knew he was humble and honest, hardworking, loyal, maybe too pious. But his adversaries said he was headstrong, domineering, and unconcerned about other people, and that he would lose his temper over perceived affronts. That seems to have been the exception rather than the rule, however. He enjoyed singing; an observer mentioned how he sang with "legs crossed, looking toward heaven." When he visited friends, he never left without kneeling with them in prayer.[15] As smart as he was, he did not have much formal education. First and foremost, he was independent, happy to challenge traditional assumptions that did not make sense to him, despite not having been trained at a theological seminary. Theology consumed his mind, though, to the extent that for a time he held no standing in the community outside of his congregation.

By all standards, he was one more poor English emigrant who did not have the requisite background to lead a religious sect. Even after joining the Latter Day Saint movement, he was one of many such leaders at the local level who had discovered Joseph Smith through their stubborn refusal to make peace with mainstream Protestantism.

---

13. Thomas, *Travels through Western Country*, 50; Mason, *Narrative of Richard Lee Mason*, 19–20.

14. Pilgrim, 2; US Census, 1850.

15. "Octogenarian Recalls Knowing Wm. Bickerton," *Gospel News*, Jan. 1968, 11.

In 1852 Bickerton would demonstrate the independence of thought which drew him to Mormonism in the first place by taking a bold stand against Brigham Young. With that act, his life would change forever.[16]

16. Cadman, *History of the Church*, 1:6.

TWO

THE CHURCH OF CHRIST

1845–47

"The Nucleus, that the Lord showed us we should form in this city, has been organized, around which all the righteous of the earth, according to the promise, should centre, and our eyes are beholding the promise verified, the sound has gone forth, the righteous are gathering, and the saints are rejoicing, in the hope set before them, and though it has been but two months since the organizing of the kingdom, hundreds have entered in and are entering continually."

—Sidney Rigdon, June 1845

Bickerton's journey as an American religious figure began when he joined Sidney Rigdon's Church of Christ in June 1845. He had moved from Wheeling, Virginia, to a town fifteen miles southeast of Pittsburgh, West Elizabeth, and this transformed his life. For one thing, he encountered more news about Mormons than he had seen before, including the newspaper reports of Joseph Smith's murder and ensuing power struggle among Latter-day Saint leaders. Journalists were stirred to comment on the strange new faith and what they saw as the consequences of theological fanaticism. When Rigdon, a member of the church's First Presidency, arrived in Pittsburgh on the very day of Smith's assassination in Illinois, June 27, 1844, and when Rigdon left town five days later (but returned to Pittsburgh another three months after that), reporters tried to discern his intentions, drawing curious locals into the drama.

Enlivened reports about this new breakoff from mainstream Protestantism were not new. Occasionally stories had appeared about Joseph Smith's "golden bible" and his church.[1] In fact, it might be useful to review the events that brought Rigdon to Pittsburgh and his influence on Bickerton. The story of Mormonism itself might be said to begin the day in 1832 that Smith wrote in a personal notebook about an event twelve years earlier when he had sought forgiveness of sins. He wrote that "a pillar of light above the brightness of the sun at noon day come down from above and rested upon me ... and I saw the Lord and he spake unto me saying Joseph my Son thy sins are forgiven thee." That was the beginning of what came to be known as the Restoration Movement, with the implication that Jesus himself restored the purest teachings and organizational structure of original Christianity. Jesus told Smith that "the world lieth in Sin ... and mine anger is kindling against the inhabitants of the earth to visit them according to their ungodliness ... and lo I come quickly as it [is] written of me in the cloud clothed in the glory of my Father." Smith took from this that the existing churches of Christendom were in apostasy and that the Second Coming of Jesus was imminent.[2]

While Smith prayed in his room in Palmyra, New York, during the fall of 1823, he received another visitation from the spiritual world, this time a heavenly messenger who told Smith his name "should be had for good and evil among all nations, kindreds, and tongues." The reason, Smith was told, was that an ancient record, buried on the side of a nearby hill, would be transcribed and published by Smith. After translating the artifact with the help of rocks called seer stones (also referred to as interpreters or the Urim and Thummim), which allowed him to read the text in English by the power of God, he gave the golden-hued

1. Joseph Smith said that he uncovered a record from a nearby hill that was written on golden plates in an ancient script known as Reformed Egyptian, and with God's help he translated it, the result being the Book of Mormon. The heavenly messenger who had directed Smith's activities was referred to as the angel Moroni. For more information, see Bushman, *Rough Stone Rolling*, 30–108.

2. Bushman, *Rough Stone Rolling*, 39; Jessee, *Papers of Joseph Smith*, 1:3, 6–7.

leaves of the book, or "golden plates," back to the messenger. In March 1830 a Palmyra printer published Smith's manuscript with financing from local farmer Martin Harris.[3]

The book relates how some ancient inhabitants of Jerusalem, beginning with an Israelite prophet, Lehi, fled the city preceding the Babylonian captivity, thereafter sailing with his family to the New World.[4] It also contains a short history of the Jaredites, who were said to have escaped the Tower of Babel for the Americas in about 2300 BCE.[5] The significance of the book's message was its millennialism and promise that the American Indians, descendants of Lehi, would be converted to Christianity and restored to their former cultural and spiritual status. This would happen through the help of a "choice seer" named Joseph, presumed to be Joseph Smith, who would gather them to a new city called the New Jerusalem.[6]

One week after the book's publication, the *Rochester Daily Advertiser* published a review:

> Blasphemy—Book of Mormon, Alias the Golden Bible
>
> The Book of Mormon has been placed in our hands. A viler imposition was never practiced. It is an evidence of fraud, blasphemy, and credulity, shocking both to Christians and moralists. The author and proprietor is Joseph Smith, Jr., a fellow who by some hocus pocus acquired such influence over a wealthy farmer of Wayne county that the latter mortgaged his farm for $3,000, which he paid for printing and binding five thousand copies of the blasphemous work.[7]

The next month Smith and his followers established what they called the Church of Christ, saying it was a restoration of the original or "primitive" Christian church. He announced that God had

3. Smith, *History of the Church*, 1:11.

4. Historian Daniel Walker Howe summarizes the book as one of "human struggle and conflict, of divine intervention, heroic good and atrocious evil, of prophecy, morality, and law." Howe, *What Hath God Wrought*, 314.

5. Ether 3:21–28 & 4:1–7, Book of Mormon.

6. 1 Ne. 22:7–31, 2 Ne. 3:5–25, 3 Ne. 21:1–29, Book of Mormon.

7. *Daily Advertiser*, Apr. 2, 1830.

appointed him an elder and apostle.[8] While proselytizing their message near Cleveland, four of Smith's followers met with prominent Campbellite Baptist minister Sidney Rigdon in a town called Mentor. At first Rigdon called the Book of Mormon a "silly fabrication," but one night, as he continued to read the book, he became convinced of its authenticity.[9] One of the missionaries who had introduced the book to Rigdon, Parley Pratt, related that Rigdon "had a great struggle of mind before he fully believed and embraced it." Rigdon's Baptist training caused him to seek confirmation of his belief, and it came in the form of a vision that came to his eyes of "that little man who bro't me the Book of Mormon," a man whose heart was "pure as an angel; and this was a testimony from God; that the Book of Mormon, was a Divine Revelation."[10]

Rigdon's conversion enthralled Joseph Smith. Up to this point in 1830, the converts had been mostly uneducated farmers and small-town working-class people. Now Smith had in his company someone of theological prominence, whom he esteemed from their first meeting. He soon appointed Rigdon to be his counselor. It was the two of them working together, not Joseph Smith alone, who established the church's organization and procedures, prophesied, received revelations, and revised lost books from the Bible. Rigdon helped Smith transcribe what was called the Book of Moses and a good portion of the Doctrine and Covenants, compilations of Smith's revelations. To Mormons, the Book of Moses introduced the concept of an eternal afterlife in which resurrected individuals are given multiple earths and heavens to preside over. A central character is Enoch, the Old Testament figure who is said to have ascended to heaven without dying, his holy city, known as Zion, having been "taken up into heaven." The Doctrine and Covenants was a collection of the day-to-day revelations Joseph Smith received, occasionally in conjunction with Rigdon, often

8. Brodie, *No Man Knows*, 84.

9. Howe, *Mormonism Unvailed*, 103; Hayden, *Early History*, 210–11.

10. Howe, 217.

to resolve practical problems. It was canonized in 1835. Both works helped Smith and Rigdon establish a new religious society.[11]

The church moved its headquarters from New York to Ohio in January 1831. There the church formed a communitarian society, and under the direction of Smith and Rigdon changed the name of the organization in 1834 from the Church of Christ to the Church of the Latter-day Saints. By 1835 the community had four thousand converts. Despite its success, the communal enterprise suffered after the president and his counselor established a financial institution, the Kirtland Safety Society bank, that was intended to enrich its investors. A land bank, it differed from other banks that issued notes redeemable in U.S.-minted coins. By contrast, the Kirtland establishment offered a means for cash-poor farmers to obtain loans, presumably allowing them to also partake in commercial exchanges while the bank's investors made a profit. The problem was that the bank had insufficient liquid capital to back its notes, as reported in the *Cleveland Daily Gazette*. "During the past two days an emission of bills from the society of Mormons, has been showered upon us," the newspaper reported. "As far as we can learn there is no property bound for their redemption, no coin on hand to redeem them with, and no responsible individuals whose honor or whose honesty is pledged for their payment … we consider this whole affair a deception." A run on the bank ended in some 300 converts losing their money and leaving the church, and Smith and Rigdon were forced to escape the area on horseback in the middle of the night. They escaped to Far West, Missouri, in September 1838, where they intended to establish another church headquarters.[12]

Fifty miles south of Far West, the town of Independence, Missouri, had been identified by Smith as the site of the future New Jerusalem. However, two years after Mormons began moving there in 1831, they

11. Van Wagoner, *Sidney Rigdon*, 71; Moses 1:39; 7:23.

12. Bushman, *Rough Stone Rolling*, 330; Howe, *What Hath God Wrought*, 315; *Cleveland Daily Gazette*, Jan. 12, 1837.

were expelled and had to move to the northern half of the state. Conflicts with neighbors continued. In the Missouri Compromise of 1820, the territory became a slave state in return for Maine's admission to the Union as a free state. Mormons were mostly anti-slavery Yankees, so they posed a threat to slaveholders. Eventually Mormons organized a militia against hostile native Missourians and squared off against state troops, with bloodshed on both sides and an order from the governor that Mormons leave the state.[13] To avoid further violence, Mormons agreed to turn Smith over to government authorities. Five months later, the leader escaped custody and joined his followers camped along the Illinois bank of the Mississippi River.

In the 1840s it seemed that the Latter-day Saints had founded a safe haven, midway between St. Louis and Dubuque, as the population of the city of Nauvoo grew to rival Chicago and Smith ran for US president in 1844, Rigdon his vice-presidential running mate. But soon there were rumors of polygamy, an attempt by the city to silence an opposition newspaper, and before it was over, Smith and his brother Hyrum had been assassinated in mid-1844. Unfortunately, Joseph had left no clear instructions about what to do if something happened to him.[14]

In the same month of June, Rigdon and his family arrived in Pittsburgh, apparently to establish residency as Smith's running mate in their bid for the US presidency, to give the impression of wide support from more than one state and to fulfill a prophecy that Rigdon would "sooner or later" end up there. Born and raised in Western Pennsylvania, Rigdon was comfortable in Pittsburgh, where he had pastored one of the largest Baptist churches in the city from 1822 to 1823, prior to his move to the Kirtland area.[15] As he returned in 1844, he brought a much different message this time. The *People's Organ*

13. Jessee, *Joseph Smith Papers*, 1:473.

14. *Times and Seasons*, Jan. 15, 1841, 273–74.

15. Keller, "I Never Knew a Time," 21; David Whitmer to Joseph Smith III, Dec. 9, 1886, cited in *Saints' Herald*, Feb. 5, 1887.

speculated that he was there to deny having plagiarized the Book of Mormon from a manuscript by the late Ohio minister Solomon Spaulding. In any case, before Rigdon could settle in and determine how to build up a new congregation, he received news from a Mormon convert, Jedediah Grant, of Smith's assassination. Grant had a copy of the *Nauvoo Neighbor* reporting the news. It compelled Rigdon to return immediately to Illinois. As the only remaining member of the First Presidency, he assumed he would secure the church's organizational and prophetic leadership.[16]

In Pennsylvania, meanwhile, conflicting reports spiraled into the newspapers about the circumstances of Joseph Smith's death. The July 8 *Pittsburgh Morning Post* reported accurately that Smith and others had been held in a jail in Carthage, twenty miles southeast of Nauvoo, but added a misconstrued scenario of a Mormon posse trying to assist the prisoners in a jailbreak and prompting the violence. The prisoners were portrayed as vigilantes with their own weapons, firing the first shots with pistols "through the windows and doors of the jail and … wounding, it is supposed, mortally, four of the old citizens of Hancock!" None of that was true. It stated that the Saints presented an ongoing danger because they wanted vengeance. A reporter from the *Pittsburgh Christian Advocate* assumed that the Mormons wanted to assassinate the Illinois governor. Some articles were more sympathetic. The *Pittsburgh Morning Post* editorialized on July 9 that the assassinations gave "evidence of the rapid progress that mob law is making in our country," calling for "the strong arm of the civil authorities" to protect "citizens of every shade of opinion. … The religious freedom of which we boast will soon be trampled under the feet of the mob" unless something was done, the *Post* feared.[17]

It may seem odd that Joseph Smith had not previously established

16. "Elder Sidney Rigdon Arrived," *The People's Organ*, June 29, 1844. For information regarding Rigdon and Book of Mormon authorship, see Bush, "Spaulding Theory," 40–69.

17. "Death of Joe Smith and Others"; "The Progress of Mob Law," *Pittsburgh Morning Post*, July 8, 9, 1844; "Death of Joe and Hiram Smith," *Pittsburgh Christian Advocate*, July 10, 1844.

a clear procedure for succession. This may have been because an 1843 revelation suggested the possibility that he would see the Millennium.[18] In any case, Rigdon arrived in Nauvoo on Saturday, August 3, 1844, and found the Saints entangled in administrative confusion. He delivered an eloquent, if verbose, discourse the following Sunday informing the church that in Pittsburgh he had received a vision of Smith's ascent to heaven, taking with him "the keys of the kingdom." It led Rigdon to believe that "no man could ever take [Smith's] place, neither have power to build up the kingdom to any other creature or being but to Joseph Smith." As Smith's assistant, Rigdon believed the Lord had appointed him as a guardian to "build the Church up to Joseph" until the millennial dawn arrived. He proceeded to issue an ominous prophecy about the leading role he would play in a violent run-up to Christ's second coming, which only created second thoughts about his leadership:

> I am going to fight a real bloody battle with sword and with gun ... I will fight the battles of the Lord. I will also cross the Atlantic, encounter the queen's forces, and overcome them—plant the American standard on English ground, and then march to the palace of her majesty, and demand a portion of her riches and dominions, which if she refuse, I will take the little madam by the nose and lead her out, and she shall have no power to help herself. If I do not do this, the Lord never spake by mortal.[19]

Rigdon's view of the apocalypse reflects much of his time and place in his desire to overthrow the British monarchy and imperialism. In Nauvoo, people would have sensed the inappropriateness of celebrating Smith's legacy with talk of "bloody battle[s] with sword and with gun," if not the irony of preparing for a future 1,000-year reign of peace by beating the British on their own soil.

---

18. On April 2, 1843, Smith wrote that he "heard a voice repeat the following: Joseph, my son, if thou livest until thou art eighty-five years old, thou shalt see the face of the Son of Man; therefore let this suffice, and trouble me no more on this matter." Doctrine and Covenants 130:14–15; hereafter D&C.

19. Hyde, *Speech of Elder Orson Hyde,* 12, 16.

Not realizing the damage he had done, Rigdon called for a special assembly on Thursday, August 8, at which he expected to be confirmed as the church's leader. This caught the attention of the Quorum of Twelve Apostles, who were concerned he was moving too fast. On August 7, the Twelve, the high council, and the high priests quorum invited him to meet with them to clarify his Pittsburgh revelation. Was he saying he was the rightful successor or not? they wanted to know. Rigdon answered that as the church's ordained spokesman and last surviving member of the presidency, he was the one who would speak for the martyred prophet until he "shall descend as a mighty angel, lay his hand on [my] head & ordain [me] & say, 'Come up & act for me." Rigdon said he had "discharged my duty, & done what God commanded me. … The people could please themselves whether they accepted [me] or not."[20] In other words, he was offering his service, take it or leave it.

As president of the Twelve, Brigham Young agreed that no one could replace Joseph Smith, but he disagreed that Rigdon was the protector of the church. The Holy Spirit, he later said, had convinced him "that the Twelve constituted an interim church presidency from which a First Presidency would eventually rise." He already "had it in [his] mind all the time that there would have to be a Presidency of three Appointed but I knew the people Could not bear it at the time."[21] Rigdon does not appear to have foreseen this challenge to his authority. In his thinking, God had made his will known by preserving Rigdon for this time of need.

On August 8, approximately five thousand members convened at the grove near the Nauvoo temple to hear Rigdon speak. Because of his oratorical capability and canny intellect, he should have had little trouble consolidating his grasp on the leadership. On the other hand, about one-third of the attendant congregants were British emigrants who had known Brigham Young during his overseas mission and would have

20. See Van Wagoner, *Sidney Rigdon*, 338.

21. Miscellaneous Minutes, Feb. 12, 1849, Brigham Young Collection, cited in Van Wagoner, *Sidney Rigdon*, 338; Kenney, *Wilford Woodruff's Journal*, 5:478.

found in him a familiar voice. Young himself had a subtle discernment and strong will, if not political savvy. After Rigdon expounded for an hour and a half and was going to ask the congregation for their support, Young stood up and interrupted, startling the audience. He then shrewdly dismissed the assembly and requested that everyone reconvene at 2:00 p.m., saying he was the "child" who would tend the "flock" that afternoon as they selected a shepherd.

Recounting this event in 1860, Young said "when I went to meet Sidney Rigdon on the meeting ground I went alone, and was ready alone to face and drive the dogs from the flock."[22] Everything was calculated to assure he was not alone, however, as he asked the men to sit according to priesthood quorums and spoke pastorally, with such sage advice that the *Times and Seasons* perceived "Elijah's mantle ha[ving] truly fallen upon the Twelve."[23] He acknowledged Rigdon's appointment as Joseph Smith's spokesman, but wondered what it meant. "If he wants now to be a spokesman to the Prophet, he must go to the other side of the veil, for the Prophet is there, but Elder Rigdon is here." As far as Young could tell, "no man has a right to counsel the Twelve but Joseph Smith." He asked the congregation to "think on these things. You cannot appoint a prophet; but if you let the Twelve remain and act in their place, the keys of the kingdom are with them and they can manage the affairs of the church and direct all things aright."[24]

Assuming he had given them enough time to think about it, Young called for a vote to support either Rigdon or the Twelve, and the crowd was nearly unanimous in its support of the Twelve. In that moment Rigdon lost the presidency. Young addressed his opponent directly, claiming "Rig[don] is … one with us—we want such men as Bro[ther] R[igdon]. He has been sent away to build a K[ingdom][;] let him keep the instruct[io]n [and] calling[,] let him raise up a k[ingdom]

22. Journal History, Oct. 6, 1860, a multi-volume daily history compiled by church historians, cited in Van Wagoner, *Sidney Rigdon*, 339.

23. Little, *Jacob Hamblin*, 20–21; *Times and Seasons*, Sept. 2, 1844, 637.

24. Young, in Smith, *History of the Church*, 7:231–35.

in Pittsburgh [and] we will lift up his hand. I guess we'll have a printing office [and] gathering there." The crowd perceived this as an act of brotherly affection. Rigdon however, silently fumed. This was one more example of the Twelve's insubordination, he thought, and he was unable to control them. As far as he was concerned, the apostles were driving the gospel train off the tracks with their secret practice of polygamy. His suppressed anger and desperation would begin to show over the next few days as he prepared to leave.[25]

A group of supporters began to coalesce around Rigdon—members who desired to travel with him to Pittsburgh. Unknown to the Twelve, Rigdon ordained several of them as "prophets, priests, and kings," deciding that if the Twelve could grant men such offices, so could he.[26] The precedent for this came from Joseph Smith forming a theocratic organization known as the Council of Fifty in March 1844. Influenced by his millennial expectations and the church's explorations into America's western territories, Smith had hoped to prepare a political government to oversee the kingdom of God. In the *Times and Seasons*, Rigdon seems to have described the secret Council of Fifty when he wrote that "when God sets up a system of salvation, he sets up a system of government; when I speak of a government I mean what I say; I mean a government that shall rule over temporal and spiritual affairs."[27] Rigdon saw his group of followers in terms of what John had prophesied in the New Testament about Christ's disciples becoming "kings and priests" to reign with the Savior a thousand years.[28] By performing these ordinations, Rigdon sincerely believed he was establishing the earthly dominion of Jesus, for the Lord's return to earth. To the Twelve, Rigdon's acts signaled that despite the Twelve's August 8 victory, Rigdon assumed he was still the rightful successor

---

25. Aug. 8, 1844, minutes in Thomas Bullock's handwriting, cited in Van Wagoner, *Sidney Rigdon*, 341; Keller, "I Never Knew," 39n57.

26. Van Wagoner, *Sidney Rigdon*, 353.

27. Bushman, *Rough Stone Rolling*, 519; *Times and Seasons*, May 1, 1844, 524. For more information, see Grow, et al., *Council of Fifty Minutes*.

28. Rev. 1:6; 5:10; 20:6.

to prepare the new Zion. As the last "prophet, seer, and revelator" of Joseph Smith's church presidency, he believed he held authority to appoint theocratic leaders for the Millennium, and as a final blow to the Twelve he divulged to his adherents that the apostles had secretly taken multiple wives and indulged in other alleged heretical practices.[29] Despite the apostles' public denial, Rigdon's confirmation that they were secretly involved with other women sent a shock through the church.

Then Rigdon delivered his last sermon in Nauvoo on September 1. In it, he prophesied again of military battles, along with the collapse of Nauvoo and a premature end to the town's temple construction, followed by the second coming of Christ in Pittsburgh. Increasingly annoyed by such prophecies, the Twelve held a trial of Rigdon for having ordained men without the Twelve's approval. Rigdon chose not to attend the hearing, a public event staged before a large audience. It was ostensibly run by the high council, but Brigham Young took over and presented the question of Rigdon's membership to the audience for a vote, which chose to deny him fellowship. Young then called for "all those who h[e]ld up their hands to support Rigdon as Prophet and Revelator to this people" to be disfellowshipped.[30] The audience agreed. Afterward, the Twelve requested Rigdon's ministerial license. He responded: "I have sat and laughed in my sleeve at the proceedings of the Twelve this evening, for they have been fulfilling in this last act, the vision I had in Pittsburg[h]. I knew you would withdraw fellowship from me, I knew you would oppose me, in all my movements. It was shown to me in the vision before I left Pittsburg[h]." He even threatened to disclose the Twelve's polygamy to the news media.[31] The *Times and Seasons* reported that along with Rigdon, ten of his supporters had been summarily disfellowshipped, or had been "delivered up to the buffetings of Satan," as it was phrased.[32]

Aboard the steamboat *Osprey*, Rigdon retreated from Nauvoo

---

29. Van Wagoner, *Sidney Rigdon*, 353.

30. Dinger, *Nauvoo City and High Council Minutes*, 505–08, 523–24.

31. Van Wagoner, *Sidney Rigdon*, 354; *Times and Seasons*, Sept. 15, 1844, 650.

32. *Times and Seasons*, Oct. 15, 1844; see also Jordan, *A History of the Church of Jesus Christ*, 2:32.

under much different circumstances than his earlier departure in the spring of 1844 when Joseph Smith and "all the [other] dignitaries," according to Rigdon's son John, "came to the boat to bid us goodbye." This time there was only a warning from apostle Orson Hyde that he should "be careful how you put pen to paper in this time of your excitement ... Wait a few months and then see how you feel."[33] Rigdon felt just the opposite, that since the prophetic mantle had descended upon him, it was his duty to expose the Twelve's apostasy. His duty was to establish the kingdom of God in Pennsylvania and guide the members to it.[34] A few weeks earlier, his arrival in Nauvoo was reported by the *Pittsburgh Morning Post*, which predicted that Rigdon "will be chosen Patriarch of the Mormon flock. He is their master spirit, and will make a shrewd and energetic leader." A week later the newspaper corrected itself: "Sidney Rigdon, who claimed the leadership of the church, on the ground of his being the only survivor of the First Presidency, and also, on the ground of his having been named by Joe at one time, as his successor, has had his claims rejected by the Twelve."[35] In two weeks the *Post* could announce Rigdon's return to Pittsburgh, a disappointment to those who thought their city had been purged of an eccentric religious figure.

If it was not enough for Rigdon to be criticized by outsiders, he was also denounced by church members who were loyal to the Twelve, as well as by the Twelve themselves. Apostle John E. Page wrote to the *Commercial Journal and Spirit of the Age* to caution people against associating with "Mr. Sidney Rigdon, Esq., or any of his adherents, thinking to attach themselves to the Church of Jesus Christ of Latter Day Saints—for Mr. S. Rigdon is at this time expelled from the aforesaid Church, and all his adherents are suspended from the performance or administration

---

33. Keller, "I Never Knew a Time," 39; Orson Hyde to Brethren, Sept. 12, 1844, Brigham Young Collection, cited in Van Wagoner, *Sidney Rigdon*, 359.

34. For more on this, see Quinn, "Mormon Succession Crisis," 187–233.

35. "From Nauvoo," "Items from Nauvoo," *Pittsburgh Morning Post*, Aug. 29, Sept. 5, 1844.

of any ordinance whatever."[36] Page asserted that Rigdon had no right to claim spiritual authority in Pittsburgh. The historical record does not indicate what William Bickerton thought of these attempts to discredit Rigdon, although he obviously disregarded them when he joined Rigdon's new Church of Christ in 1845.

The opposition Rigdon encountered would have reminded him of the Savior's words, "Blessed are ye, when men shall revile you, and persecute you, and shall say all manner of evil against you falsely, for my sake … for so persecuted they the prophets which were before you" (Matt. 5:11–12). He felt an alliance with the prophets of old, with one distinction. They had foretold what would transpire in the last days, but Rigdon felt he was a fulfillment of those prophecies. He was the latter-day prophet whose labors would consummate their prophetic work. John A. Forgeus, a member of Rigdon's church, confirmed that God had given Rigdon "a greater calling" than that of a prophet, in his appointment as "a spokesman before the Lord's face. … Recollect that Nephi [in the Book of Mormon] says, that a spokesman will the Lord raise up unto Joseph, who shall be mighty in word and writing, and who shall carry the word of the Lord." God, Forgeus believed, had appointed Rigdon to "lift up his voice" in the "mountains of Pennsylvania" to gather the righteous gentiles and tribes of Israel, meaning Jews and American Indians, to create an earthly heaven.[37]

To explain and validate his divine calling, Rigdon started a publication entitled *The Latter Day Saint's Messenger and Advocate*. In the first issue, he declared that he would teach the same principles as had occupied the pages of Joseph Smith's similarly named newspaper of the mid-1830s, the *Messenger and Advocate* of Kirtland, Ohio.[38] Rigdon remembered the glory days when he and Smith had built a temple in Kirtland and collected thousands of converts. Now he wanted to

36. "Ho! The Mormons," *Commercial Journal*, Oct. 10, 1844; see also "Schism among the Mormons," *Pittsburgh Daily Gazette and Advertiser*, Oct. 11, 1844.

37. John A. Forgeus to Samuel Forgeus, *Latter Day Saint's Messenger and Advocate*, Oct. 15, 1844; hereafter *Messenger and Advocate* (but not to be confused with the prior newspaper of that name). Since most of Rigdon's personal papers have been lost, most of his extant writings are from his newspaper.

38. Sidney Rigdon, "Prospectus," *Messenger and Advocate*, Oct. 15, 1844.

reinvent the church and bring it back to an earlier form. One of his followers, Samuel Bennett, expressed in a December 1844 editorial that without a prophet they could not receive God's law, and Rigdon was the single remaining prophet in the Restoration movement.[39]

In the fall of 1844, Rigdon found in the Bible what he believed was a prediction of Joseph Smith's fall from grace. "And in that day seven women shall take hold of one man," Isaiah 4:1 reads, the women "saying, we will eat our bread, and wear our own apparel; only let us be called by thy name, to take away our reproach." Rigdon interpreted the "daughters of Zion" (Isa. 3:16–17, 4:4) not as ancient Hebrews, but as the women who lived in polygamy in Nauvoo where Rigdon learned of the practice when Smith propositioned his daughter, Nancy. Rigdon believed Isaiah's words had come to pass through Rigdon's excommunication, because "in that day shall the branch of the Lord" become the "escaped of Israel," remaining undefiled (Isa. 4:2).[40]

The Pittsburgh congregation, Rigdon taught, were God's chosen people, the new Israel. Through sin, the "choice seer," who many thought was Joseph Smith, had not been allowed to finish his mission of founding the place where the Lord's people could receive Jesus. The Isaiah prophecy confirmed Smith's defection, Rigdon believed. Smith was removed so Rigdon could assume his place at the head of the "escaped branch" in the promised land of Pennsylvania. As the new choice seer, he would complete the interrupted task of establishing Zion. A song penned by Rigdon illustrated his pursuit:

> A Song of Zion.
> By S. Rigdon.
>
> The time is now coming the day is at hand,
> When Zion in strength and in beauty shall stand;
> Awake from her slumbers, in glory arise,
> And send her loud anthems to God in the skies ...

---

39. Samuel Bennett, "The First Presidency," ibid., Dec. 2, 1844.

40. Sidney Rigdon to James M. Grieg, ibid., Nov. 1, 1844; Keller, "I Never Knew a Time, 39n57.

From time immemorial, in prophetic lore,
She's been mark'd as the object of heav'n's kind care,
Her triumph and victory, the prophet's reward,
And Jesus her head, her king, and her Lord …

Thy peace like a river, in righteousness flow
Thy streams of salvation—all nations shall know;
The prince, and the peasant, the noble and mean;
Find salvation in thee forever, amen.[41]

An interesting aspect of Rigdon's church was its progressive view of gender, as indicated by a March 1845 editorial condemning the chauvinistic assumptions that made polygamy possible. Its origin, the writer explained, was a revelation Smith received regarding unborn spirits needing mortal bodies to inhabit. Christ would not return to earth until these unborn spirits had a "tabernacle of clay," the teaching went, and so through intercourse these spirits could enter mortality. The women willing to participate in this plan did so because they were promised exaltation in the next life. The Rigdonites despised the idea that a woman could not enter heaven unless she married a man, and thought the idea of a man marrying several women barbaric. In their view, the subordination of a woman's salvation to a man was one of the most grotesque teachings of the Twelve. "Is this a doctrine to be countenanced by men whom human nature has left with one spark of honesty or common sense?" the editorialist asked. "Forbid it Nature's God! Whilst I have an arm to raise, a voice to speak, or a pen to write, I will not see my fellow beings swindled, deluded, brow-beat, slandered, abused, by villains under the mask of religion."[42]

On the fifteenth anniversary of Joseph Smith's establishment

41. Sidney Rigdon, "A Song of Zion," *Messenger and Advocate*, Feb. 15, 1845. Currently, a Church of Jesus Christ hymnal, *The Songs of Zion*, consists of hymns received by revelation to Arlene Buffington, a woman with no musical training. Similar to Rigdon's hymn, the songs proclaim Zion's imminent arrival and admonish listeners to remain righteous.

42. Henry Rowe, "Mormonism—The Spiritual Wife Doctrine," *Messenger and Advocate*, Mar. 1, 1845. For more on eternal spiritual marriage, see D&C 132:18–19; Richards, *Marvelous Work*, 193–206.

of the Church of Christ, Rigdon organized his new denomination during a six-day conference beginning April 6, 1845. For the morning sermon, he drew on 1 Peter 2:9, rousing the crowd with characteristic passion. "But ye are a chosen generation," he told them, "a royal priesthood, an holy nation, a peculiar people; that ye should shew forth the praises of him who hath called you out of darkness into his marvelous light."[43]

The next day all those who had been ordained prophets, priests, and kings were asked to sit in front. The seventy-two men and boys whom he called the Grand Council received a blessing from their president. "I lay it upon you in the name of Jesus," he told them, "that you shall be the kings over whom the Son of God shall reign as King of kings and Lord of lords. I lay it upon you to be crowned in the presence of God when Jesus shall come with all the hosts of heaven; when heaven and earth shall be redeemed." He then asked the congregation what position they desired him to hold in the church, and the crowd unanimously appointed him "first president of this kingdom and church, and to stand as prophet, seer, revelator and translator, to this church and kingdom of Christ of the last days." Then the Grand Council, with "their hearts overflowing with gratitude and thanksgiving towards God," promised to uphold the president. Having spent the recent months struggling with pen and paper to avenge his honor, he received the acknowledgments with appreciation.

On Tuesday, April 8, the congregation endorsed the original name Joseph Smith had given the movement, the Church of Christ. On Wednesday before leaving the house, Rigdon drew on another innovation of Smith's, assembling a few male members of his church and consecrating them through a ritual washing and anointing, for which Smith's inspiration had been the Old Testament. While kneeling in prayer,

43. "Minutes of a Conference of the Church of Christ," *Messenger and Advocate*, May 1, 1845; 1 Pet. 2:9.

> there appeared over our heads, in the room, a ray of light forming a hollow square, inside of which, stood a company of heavenly messengers, each with a banner in his hand, with their eyes looking downward upon us, their countenances expressive of the deep interest they felt in what was then passing on the earth; there also appeared heavenly messengers on horseback with crowns upon their heads, and plumes floating in the air, dressed in glorious attire until, like Elisha, we cried in our hearts, "the chariots of Israel, and the horsemen thereof;" even my little son of fourteen years of age saw the vision; and gazed with great astonishment, saying, that he thought his imagination was running away with him, after which we arose and lifted our hands to heaven in holy convocation to God, at which time, it was shown an angel in heaven registering the acceptance of our work, and the decrees of the Great God, that the kingdom is ours, and we shall prevail; my anxieties therefore, in relation to our work in organizing the kingdom, and the acceptance of that organization, by our heavenly Father, is now forever at rest.[44]

The following day Rigdon confirmed the correctness of Joseph Smith's teaching about proxy ordinances for the deceased who had not had the opportunity of becoming baptized. The Twelve no longer had the authority to perform baptisms for the dead, he stated, because of unworthiness. It was still necessary to perform the baptisms before Christ's second advent when the dead would rise in the First Resurrection. As the conference came closer to its conclusion on April 10, the congregants were alarmed to hear cries of terror in the streets—"Our friends and neighbors in the midst of sorrow, distress and confusion, were flying for their lives," the minutes reported. Known later as the Great Conflagration of 1845, the fire was "vast and awful, and in some points so inconceivably grand and terrific, as to defy all our feeble powers of description," the *Protestant Unionist* explained. Rigdon closed the meeting early and petitioned the Lord to spare the city. Some of the congregants said they saw "an escort of heavenly messengers … leaving the room," upon which "the course of the wind was instantly changed,

44. Ibid.

and the violence of the flames were stayed, and our city saved from an entire overthrow."[45]

When the story of Rigdon saving the city reached the secular press, people were repulsed. "These fanatics quietly pursued their mummeries while the city was consuming," the *Pittsburgh Daily Gazette and Advertiser* huffed. "Our citizens would have thanked them to have sent their 'escort of heavenly messengers' a little sooner, and not have waited until the fairest part of our city was laid in ashes, and many lives had fallen a sacrifice to the devouring element." Rigdon's newspaper contained other "strange things," the writer claimed, and promoted as many absurdities "in this enlightened age as ever took place in the darkest eras."[46]

As astonishing as Rigdon's claims were, they instilled in some people curiosity to prompt further investigation, so that the congregation was soon visited by journalists, investigators, and onlookers who learned the difference between the Pennsylvania denomination and the followers of Brigham Young. The Pittsburgh group, for instance, had renounced "the 'spiritual wife system,'" the *Daily Gazette* reported, and believed in civil law. They planned on establishing a utopia in Pennsylvania rather than settling the West, the way the Illinois branch of Mormonism did, and therefore posed no challenge to the government's alleged right to Manifest Destiny.[47]

Seeing that "hundreds have entered in and are entering [the congregation] continually," Rigdon wrote in mid-1845 it was clear to him that the Millennium was imminent.[48] In reality, the church membership would never exceed four hundred, but it was a decent size for a congregation, if not for a denomination. One of those drawn to Rigdon

45. "Terrible Visitation," *Protestant Unionist*, Apr. 11, 1845; "Minutes," *Messenger and Advocate*, May 1, 1845.

46. "More Mormon Fanaticism," *Pittsburgh Daily Gazette and Advertiser*, May 7, 1845.

47. "Pittsburgh Mormonism," ibid., May 8, 1845. The Twelve had sent emissaries to California and Oregon to explore the establishment of colonies there. Grow, et al., "Council of Fifty Minutes," introduction.

48. "History of Facts," *Messenger and Advocate*, June 15, 1845.

was William Bickerton, who heard the prophet speak in mid-1845. Bickerton wanted a better life. He was still employed as a coal miner, working the deposits along the Monongahela River, and lacked formal education. His income was limited to the point that his wife, Dorothy, and infant son, James, probably struggled to get by.[49] He had not yet received American citizenship either. When he encountered prejudice against immigrants, he may have found support among those connected to the local Methodist church.[50]

Rather than being put off by local reports of Rigdon's revelations and miracles, he must have found them intriguing. Rigdon spoke in Limetown (Coal Bluff), Pennsylvania, six miles from West Elizabeth, and the coal miner decided to hear the famous preacher. Recalling this in 1903, Bickerton remarked that "Sidney Rigdon was the best orator I have ever heard in classing the scriptures together." After only one worship service, Bickerton concluded that the man he had heard speak "had the power of God."[51] The subject of the first sermon enthralled him, and he said enthusiastically that he was previously "never taught such a Gospel." Rigdon preached that "there is but one Holy Spirit, and whether Jew or Gentile, bond or free, we have been all made to drink of the same spirit." Bickerton felt thunderstruck by this, along with the claim that converts could speak in tongues and heal the sick.[52]

Although Bickerton had never heard such a gospel preached, he was prepared for it by the Methodism he had become acquainted with. Like Mormons, Methodists did not require formal education for the ministry. Both denominations followed the Arminian view that individuals have free will and autonomy in deciding matters of religion and life. Both held out the promise of personal revelation for people

49. William Bickerton, "Testimony, June 1903," 1; US Census, 1850.

50. He filed for citizenship on August 5, 1848. Naturalization Petitions, NAI 3, M1537; Humphrey, "Biography of William Bickerton."

51. "A Letter," *St. John Sun*, Aug. 4, 1887; Bickerton, "Testimony, June 1903," 1.

52. Bickerton, *Ensign*, 5.

in need of moral instruction.[53] And both expected to see the Second Advent. Unlike Methodism, Rigdon's church was still evolving, not a vested organization, and afforded its members the opportunity to mature along with the church.

Bickerton resigned "as a good standing member" of the Methodist faith in June and received baptism at the hands of John Frazier, one of Rigdon's high councilors.[54] It is not certain whether Dorothy was baptized at that time. Bickerton's baptism was followed by "the gift of the Holy Spirit at the laying on of hands." Since then, he later summarized, "I have spoken in new tongues, have had the interpretation, I have seen the sick healed and I have been healed myself, so that I [k]now that the Gospel is the power of God." He marveled at the spiritual gifts he witnessed and that Rigdon promised him. Shortly thereafter, he "was called by the Holy Spirit to be an Elder," he reported. At his ordination, as with his baptism, "the power of God came down and sealed the office upon me."

There was actually more to his ordination than the laying on of hands. It involved Rigdon's practice of "washing and annointing" those whom God had called to the work,[55] continuing Joseph Smith's 1836 ritual at a priesthood meeting in the Kirtland temple. The washings consisted of men bathing their bodies to symbolize a natural and spiritual cleansing, and anointings conducted by pouring oil on members' heads, followed by the laying on of hands for prayer.[56] The symbolism drew on the sanctification of Moses and Aaron from the book of Exodus, wherein God instructed Moses to "bring Aaron and his sons unto the door of the tabernacle of the congregation, and wash them with water," then "put upon Aaron the holy garments, and anoint him, and sanctify him; that he may minister unto me in the priest's office." Bickerton had not graduated from a seminary, nor did his desire to preach

53. Howe, *What Hath God Wrought?* 179; Butler, *Awash in a Sea of Faith*, 239–41; however, Methodists began retreating from charismatic personal revelations in the 1820s.

54. Bickerton, *Ensign*, 5.

55. Ibid., 5; Bickerton, "Testimony June 1903," 1.

56. Bushman, *Rough Stone Rolling*, 308–12; Jessee, et al., *Joseph Smith Papers*, 1:461, 473.

the gospel give him divine authority. Instead, his ordination came by way of a ritual performed for the holiest men of ancient Israel. As he recalled in 1863, he felt emboldened by this consecration to go forth "preaching to all that would hear."[57]

Not long after, Bickerton received additional callings as a seventy and then as a "prophet, priest, and king," equal in authority to Rigdon, in title at least. His acceptance of this spiritual path, veering ever farther from his secular occupation, was not out of ambition or boredom but because of the transforming sense of peace and joy he had received.[58] Like Rigdon, he thought the Savior's imminent return necessitated his evangelism. For that reason, he began studying in Rigdon's School of the Prophets, or the "solemn assemblies," as they were sometimes called, based on the ministerial school founded by Joseph Smith in December 1832. The reference to prophets came from Samuel's students, Elijah and others, in the Old Testament.[59] The original charge in Kirtland had been to study "things both in heaven, and in earth, and under the earth; things which have been; things which are; things which must shortly come to pass."[60] That was, in fact, what Bickerton and others engaged in: a course of study of church doctrine and history, national politics, and foreign languages, all done in an environment in which they sanctified themselves through military-like discipline and monastic-like spirituality, refraining from levity or idleness, or even from sleeping too long.

In imitation of Smith's school, the president of Rigdon's School of the Prophets apparently greeted his students at the beginning of each meeting with his hands uplifted, at which he would recite the following covenant: "Art thou a brother or brethren? I salute you in the name of the Lord Jesus Christ, in token, or remembrance of the everlasting covenant, in which covenant I receive you to fellowship in

57. Exod. 40:10–12; Bickerton, *Ensign*, 5.

58. Bickerton, "Testimony, June 1903," 1.

59. There was a "company of the prophets ... Samuel standing as appointed over them." 1 Sam. 19:18–24.

60. D&C 88:77–81, 125–35.

a determination that is fixed, immovable and unchangeable, to be your friend and brother through the grace of God, in the bonds of love." The members, in turn, would lift their hands to the president and recite the same promise. A March 1845 editorial noted that the organization would see the priesthood "perfected in their ministry for the salvation of Zion, and of the nations of Israel, and of the Gentiles, as many as will believe." The Rigdonites, like the other Mormons, believed their primary responsibility was to convert the world prior to Jesus's return. For men like Bickerton, whose backgrounds were in the trades and crafts, it was an opportunity to be trained in theology and liberal arts in an environment of cooperation and high purpose.[61]

Bickerton had been a member only two months when Rigdon decided to start building the New Jerusalem, although Rigdon was not yet sure where and so he and apostle William McLellin traveled by horseback to the southern end of the Cumberland Valley looking for a suitable spot. Stopping on a stone bridge about a mile west of Greencastle to take in the scenery, they saw a 390-acre farm owned by Andrew McLanahan, called Adventure Farm, and were impressed by the spanning hillsides and winding creek. Rigdon at once recognized "the place the Lord has shown us in visions to be the site of the city of the New Jerusalem." In gathering more information about the area, they won "friends in the neighborhood," in part "by their quaint manners and 'solemn converse.'" They also learned that the farm's owner was willing to sell.[62]

With help from Rigdon's brother-in-law Peter Boyer, a well-to-do farmer of Allegheny County and high councilor in the church, a contract was signed for $14,700, with a down payment of $6,000 that he and two others, church patriarch Carvel Rigdon and high councilor Charles Beck, paid. The balance was to be due in April 1847, two years distant. A follower of Brigham Young with contacts in Pittsburgh, Amos Fielding, kept Young abreast of Rigdon's progress:

61. D&C 90:8, cited in "For the Messenger and Advocate," *Messenger and Advocate*, Mar. 1, 1845.

62. Bates, *History of Franklin County*, 563; Nead, "History of Mormonism," 9:424.

> Mr. Rigdon is about to move on to the East, and there purchase lands and settle.[63] He has a revelation to this effect that all his followers must sell all their goods and houses, and lands or the Lord will not bless them. … His main Revelation is this, that they must go eastward and purchase lands, and stay there till they shall be called upon by the rulers of this nation, who will have viewed their good works and conduct. Mr. Rigdon states that the war will commence in the West, and move eastward, and that they, the Rigdonites, will be prepared with power to join the great army, and so continue to move eastward till they shall arrive in England, where I suppose he intends fulfilling his prophecy: that is, making his hands serve instead of a hankerchief to Victoria's Nose![64]

For his part, Rigdon believed Nauvoo would soon be destroyed due to the dishonesty of the leaders. In a December 1845 circular, he predicted that when the destruction commenced, the judgements of God would continue from Nauvoo until the rest of the world was destroyed. Mormons began their exodus from the city in the winter of 1845–46, and he thought his prediction was coming true just in time to move to Adventure Farm and recreate the communitarian community that had failed in Ohio.[65]

Rather than find inspiration in Rigdon's plan, though, Bickerton thought it was a mistake, that Rigdon "went wrong" in "wanting to make a gathering in the … Allegheny Mountains." He had forgotten that Rigdon's eye was on the Cumberland Valley, not the Allegheny Mountains, but in Pennsylvania nonetheless. The acolyte's sentiment was clear enough. He thought their leader had faltered, so he and others decided to stay put in Pittsburgh. At the School of the Prophets, the students learned to discern whether things were right. In response, Rigdon sent "two of his apostles to stop our assembly of the school of the prophets," where discontent was fomenting. It was not just the

63. Greencastle is halfway between Pittsburgh and Philadelphia, so not quite the East Coast, but less than 100 miles from Baltimore and Washington, DC.

64. Bates, *History of Franklin County*, 564; Conrad, *Conococheague*, 26; Van Wagoner, *Sidney Rigdon*, 380; Amos Fielding to Brigham Young, *New York Messenger*, Sept. 20, 1845.

65. "Tour East," *Messenger and Advocate*, Dec. 1845.

idea of removing to the wilderness, whether a mountain top or remote valley, but Rigdon had become "so extreme in his ideas," his son later remembered, that "at times [he was] perfectly wild."[66]

For instance, one night Rigdon instructed followers to prepare for the visitation of seven Old Testament luminaries: Abraham, Daniel, Elijah, Isaac, Jacob, Malachi, and Noah. These spirits were going to appear to members individually in their own homes, he said. When the spirits did not appear, Rigdon received another revelation that the vision "would be confined exclusively to those, who freely gave up all their property to the Lord." Twenty of his followers complied with the stipulation and waited for the event, which again did not come. Rigdon determined that "it would be inconvenient for the angels to call at the different houses," so the twenty men were to gather at his house for this glorious experience. When they met, two of the men perceived the divine spirits transporting themselves to earth, at which point Rigdon abruptly called off the meeting, sending everyone home in confusion.[67]

Bickerton was disappointed when he heard Rigdon try to smooth over his failed prophecies and explain away discrepancies in his predictions. One sticking point may have been the prophecy published in the February 15, 1845, issue of the *Messenger and Advocate*, agreeing with Joseph Smith that the end would begin with civil war in the United States:

> This nation will, at a period now future, divide into parties, and these parties will go to war one with the other, and increase in violence until the government will loose its power, and the country be a scene of confusion and bloodshed. Party against party, and district against district, until all peace and good order will depart to return no more until the God of heaven shall take the power into his own hands. ... This republic has a nation [of Native Americans] laying on her western border, with whom no very good feelings exist, and that nation only wants an opportunity to avenge themselves of injuries they claim to have sustained. In addition,

---

66. Bickerton, "Testimony, June 1903," 1; Keller, "I Never Knew a Time," 40.
67. "Another Mormon Humbug," *Washington Reporter*, Mar. 14, 1846.

> there is yet another nation of colored people in the south, who would gladly deliver themselves from their present condition.[68]

When Joseph Smith hinted of civil war, and prophesied that it would begin with South Carolina's secession from the Union, it was no doubt over the state's rejection of the federal tariffs of 1828 and 1832, prompting President Jackson to consider dispatching federal troops to force compliance.[69] Smith's 1832 prediction was that "slaves shall rise up against their masters" and that American Indians "will marshal themselves, and shall become exceeding angry, and shall vex" the nation, and war would spread "until the consumption decreed hath made a full end of all nations! ... Wherefore, stand ye in holy places, and be not moved, until the day of the Lord come; for behold it cometh quickly, saith the Lord. Amen."[70]

How could one reconcile the promised defection of South Carolina, which had not yet occurred; the defeat of Great Britain, a country that had only risen higher in power; and the idea that world-wide war would begin at Nauvoo as the Twelve retreated to the great western desert? As frustrated as Bickerton was, Rigdon could not understand why some followers failed to comprehend the divine origin of his plan for a millennial city in the Cumberland Valley. He decided to make one more pitch for his venture at the 1846 April conference, the last general conference of the Church of Christ in Pittsburgh.

As Rigdon spoke, Bickerton sat behind him on the stand, having been added to the Grand Council to replace former apostle William McLellin after McLellin defected in December 1845.[71] Bickerton would have listened particularly closely as his leader related a "vision" in which he saw "thousands" of "the honorable men of the city" of Pittsburgh contributing financially to Zion, while "many" of the old

68. "The Purposes of God," *Messenger and Advocate*, Feb. 15, 1845.
69. Howe, *What Hath God Wrought?* 395–410.
70. D&C 87:1–8; cf. "Prophecy by Joseph Smith," 1.
71. Shipps, *Journals of William E. McLellin*, 337–38.

Mormon adherents of the city, "among whom he recognised the faces of several," would not be among the elect. Rigdon continued:

> There seemed to have been a struggle between the Lord and satan, between the powers of light and the powers of darkness. The devil had sought to overthrow this kingdom—some of those whom we once loved as brethren had left us, or fallen by transgression, and by circulating the most base and malicious slanders against us, had shown the corruption of their own hearts. In the midst of this conflict, interposition of providence had placed it beyond their reach to do us harm. There could be no doubt now in what relation we stand to the heavens, and by whose wisdom power we are guided—no man in this kingdom could rise up and say he had had no evidence for in the gloomiest hour of our history, when human wisdom was of no avail, the great God had clearly shown us that he was our guardian and protector. I feel as if we stand on "terra firma."[72]

After the sermon, H. G. Whitlock presented a call from the financial committee in the form of a revelation to give "all that can be spared, from the widow's mite to him that has thousands," in order to establish "a perpetual home for my saints," meaning (without naming it) Adventure Farm. After Whitlock read the revelation, the Grand Council was asked for its endorsement, and it voted unanimously in the affirmative. Rigdon declared, according to the minutes, "that he was treading upon ground unexplored by man, for he had no predecessor ... His enemies had been aiming a death blow at the kingdom, but the Lord had stretched forth his hand in its deliverance from their reach, and covered its opposers with eternal shame."

Even though Bickerton and others suspected that Rigdon was leading the church in the wrong direction, they hesitated to oppose him openly. Besides, Rigdon spoke with such power and inspiration, it caused Bickerton to feel "what it meant by being baptised with the Holy Ghost." But doubts returned after the conference. Rigdon's

72. "Minutes of a Conference," *Messenger and Advocate*, June 1846.

closing of the School of the Prophets strengthened Bickerton's resolve to oppose moving the church to a cow pasture.[73]

When Rigdon and his followers traveled to the Cumberland Valley in May, it looked to the 150–200 settlers like a good investment. The land was beautiful, the natural resources abundant. Timber dotted the landscape; quarries of limestone, clay, and sand rested under the earth; and the soil was rich in nutrients. The farm consisted of materials perfect for the establishment of a prosperous city. "Here then, is to be prepared a rest, a repose for the children of God; such a rest, as his people have never known," announced the August *Messenger and Advocate*.[74]

One of the barns was transformed into a meeting house where neighbors began attending services too. The locals were "generous, kind, and hospitable—willing that all people should enjoy their religious faith without molestation—and we find ourselves ... treated with that kindness and respect due one citizen from another," Rigdon's newspaper editorialized in June. Among the parishioners were farmers, mechanics, and businessmen. If the group had not gotten caught up in planning a grand city, rather than just getting by at first, they may have done well, but their discussions turned to "laying out avenues and streets, building glass works, cotton mills, &c." Everything would be taken care of when Christ arrived, anyway, they thought. Rigdon visited a communal group of German sectarians in the eastern part of the county several times, hoping to gain converts and combine assets, but to no avail.[75]

In early 1847, only months away from defaulting on the mortgage, the believers gathered in the evening, clothed in "ascension robes," and knelt down in a meadow behind the barn to pray fervently for the Savior's return. The following morning, shivering from the cold, they retreated to their homes to ponder what their next plan should be.[76] In short, they would soon lose $6,000 in their attempt to build the New

73. Ibid.; Bickerton, "Testimony, June 1903," 1

74. "Adventure Farm," *Messenger and Advocate*, Aug. 1846.

75. Editorial, *Messenger and Advocate*, June 1846; McCauley, *Historical Sketch*, 192; Nead, "History of Mormonism," 9:424.

76. Van Wagoner, *Sidney Rigdon*, 391; Nead, 423.

Jerusalem in Franklin County. In writing about this later, Rigdon tried to put the situation in a positive light but betrayed his loose grip on reality, saying that

> a messenger stood before me, not on earth but in the air who said some thing which let me know that I must leave this place, but how to get away I knew not; ... While I was pondering on this subject there came a strange woman there, some 50 years of age, saying the Lord had sent her there but she knew not what for. The day arrived that I must go. I mentioned in her presence that I wanted to leave but had no means to help myself; ... she put her hand into her pocket and took from thence a roll of bank bills and handed them to me saying now get ready and go home with me. I found the spirit pressing me to make no delay; accordingly I made all possible exertions; and that same day I found myself in possession of a car[r]iage and horses harnessed for the journey, and the messenger [our driver], my eldest son, a lad of [18] years, and myself in it and all of us on the road, and after a journey of some 400 miles we reached her house."[77]

Rather than admit his failure, Rigdon relied on the comfort of the miraculous. His farewell comment to onlookers was a strange epithet, "If any ask to know where I am gone, tell them I am gone to Hell on a thousand years' mission." The deed to Adventure Farm was returned to McLanahan in August at a sheriff's auction.[78] From then on, Rigdon is said to have vacillated between fits of hysteria, anger, and despair. His son recalled that he was "sane upon every subject except religion. When he got on that subject, he seemed to lose himself."[79] At the same time, his contributions to the theology of all branches of the Restoration Movement was as large and lasting as that of Joseph Smith himself. He was a charismatic speaker, an earnest minister, and an enigma.[80] He lived the rest of his life in the care of his family, mostly aloof from his followers.

---

77. Rigdon to Stephen Post, Jan. 23, 1856, Post Collection, cited in Van Wagoner, *Sidney Rigdon*, 392.

78. Journal History, Nov. 14, 1849, 4, cited in Van Wagoner, *Sidney Rigdon*, 392–93.

79. Keller, "I Never Knew a Time," 40.

80. Van Wagoner, *Sidney Rigdon*, viii.

The remaining Rigdonites had to eke out whatever existence they could, many of them migrating back to Pittsburgh to accept charity from the dissenters. Bickerton remembered that he felt "alone, seeking to know what course to pursue. My house was a resting place for many of those who had followed Sidney Rigdon." It is difficult to comprehend how the shattered members felt. As the Church of Christ faded away, other adherents began to coalesce around the coal miner. One later convert saw in him the new "prophet to lead this people."[81] Bickerton reminded himself that it was the restored gospel he was committed to, not to Rigdon, and that he had received a divine calling even though the man who had converted him had himself stumbled. Bickerton was intent on not losing track of the path he was meant to follow, now that he had found it.

81. Charles Brown, quoted in Bickerton, "Testimony, June 1903," 1, 9.

THREE

YOUNG'S LATTER-DAY SAINTS

1847–52

"If the approval of God were to come to [me] by accepting the doctrine of polygamy, [I would] prefer the displeasure of God."
—early 1852

The disappearance of Sidney Rigdon and collapse of his church in August 1847 confirmed a premonition. The extent of William Bickerton's displeasure may have mirrored John Wickliffe Rigdon's opinion of his father: "I do not think the [Nauvoo] Church made any mistake in placing the leadership on Brigham Young ... Sidney Rigdon had no executive ability, was broken down with sickness, and could not have taken charge of the Church at that time. ... I have no fault to find with the Church with doing what they did. It was the best thing they could have done under the circumstances."[1] Bickerton saw firsthand Rigdon's erratic behavior. How many of the original adherents gravitated around Bickerton when Rigdon left Pennsylvania is unknown, but it is known that Bickerton hesitated at that time from picking up the torch. Like many others, he decided to wait and see. For stability though, Brigham Young was looking like a more viable option.

Rigdon lived with his daughter Athalia in Friendship, New York, not far from the Pennsylvania border. Her husband, George W. Robinson, had allowed his father-in-law a room as long as he agreed to never again "open his mouth about religion,"[2] and remarkably Rigdon conceded

1. Keller, "I Never Knew a Time," 40.
2. Journal History, Apr. 6, 1848, 4, cited in Van Wagoner, *Sidney Rigdon*, 399.

to those terms. Knowing this, Bickerton and others stayed away. Another factional leader, James Jesse Strang, had claimed the presidency after Joseph Smith's death, and attention had shifted to him. Thousands of Latter-day Saints traveled to Wisconsin, believing what Strang said about an angel appearing and anointing his head with oil and ordaining him to the leadership of the church. In 1848 Strang led his adherents to Beaver Island at the top of Lake Michigan, and two years later had himself coronated king of the church.[3] Bickerton may have thought that was too presumptuous to deserve serious consideration.

The ordinations the Pennsylvania coal miner received from Rigdon empowered him to head a congregation, so he decided that, with confirmation from the Holy Spirit, he would lead the little group in the Pittsburgh area even though the larger denomination no longer existed. As he examined himself, he must have concluded that, unlike Rigdon, he had never uttered false prophecies and had never led people astray. During his short affiliation with Rigdon, he had upheld his responsibilities without over-reaching, simply delivering sermons, baptizing, and performing marriages.[4] Another man's apostasy should not impact his spiritual calling, he decided. Still, he felt exposed as an uneducated immigrant. If he was going to lead a congregation, he would at least need the legal protection of naturalization, since the anti-immigrant sentiment had gotten worse, especially for those who gave allegiance to a royal family or belonged to something other than mainstream Protestantism.[5] In August 1848 he swore to "abstain forever all allegiance and fidelity to the Queen of Great Britain … whereof I was heretofore a subject,"[6] and tried to embrace wholly the American political system. His citizenship was granted in 1856.[7]

While waiting to be naturalized, he did his best to lead his West

3. Van Noord, *Assassination of a Michigan King*, 4, 97.

4. He married William Brothers and Mary Walker on May 4, 1846, according to the Brothers Family Register, LDS Church History Library.

5. Cohn, *Mass Migration*, 215–16.

6. Nationalization Petitions, *Ancestry.com*.

7. *List of Immigrants*, 3:6.

Elizabeth congregation and give comfort to the members while maintaining his own family. He was working at the mines six days a week and on Sundays transforming himself into a minister. In 1850 he and his wife, Dorothy, cared for four children: their own six-year-old James, four-year-old Eliza Ann, and one-year-old Josephine, and fifteen-year-old Margaret, whom they had taken in. It is estimated that a family of four needed at least $600 annually to get by. As a coal foreman, he might have earned about $500. From 1841 to 1855, wages dropped nearly 10 percent, and cost increases meant that the same amount of income had less buying power. The reason employers paid less was because of mechanization and immigration, which created a buyer's market.[8]

If that was not bleak enough, coal miners were not able to work the entire year. The water level of the Monongahela River dropped enough during the summer that barges could not find passage. In the winter when there was ice in the river, the mines closed again. Therefore miners worked eleven hours a day when they could. It was grueling, tedious work, with frequent accidents and the risk of contracting black lung disease. When the Mexican–American War ended in 1848 and gold was discovered in California, miners were tempted to leave coal behind and try their hand at something more valuable out west.[9] Bickerton's brother-in-law John Douglass, whose wife, Eleanor, died around 1847, did so. After he disappeared to the gold fields, he was never heard from again.[10]

Bickerton's socio-economic circumstances explain why he considered uniting with Brigham Young. As he struggled to support his family, let alone a small parish, one can surmise the degree of hardship he endured. His attraction to Young did not mean he had been blind to the criticisms Rigdon's newspaper had lodged against the Nauvoo apostles. A committee of five had been formed "to expose the false doctrines of

8. US Census, 1850; Cohn, *Mass Migration*, 212–13.

9. Roy, *History of Coal Miners*, 45; Howe, *What Hath God Wrought*, 815.

10. Jordan, *Genealogical and Personal History*, 2:1029, Eleanor's name is incorrectly listed as Margaret; Pilgrim, "Descendants of Thomas Bickerton," 1.

Brigham Young, P. P. Pratt, and Orson Pratt," and their findings were published. What they discovered was that in Young's church "a woman had no eternal salvation unless she had a husband; and they appointed Mothers in Israel to teach young women to be married into the Priesthood; and they succeeded in their undertaking to a great extent. Thus," Bickerton knew "they took advantage of" their positions of trust to deviate from "the gospel in its purity."[11] He agreed with Rigdon that the teaching of celestial marriage, meaning that marriage would continue into the next life, denigrated women by conflating matrimony and salvation. He thought this meant that women were being taken advantage of, especially when he learned from Rigdon that the Twelve were practicing polygamy. Rigdon persuaded Bickerton that Young had wrongfully usurped the church presidency. However, Rigdon did not prove himself to be the new "choice seer" either, having fallen into delusions of conquering the world, fancying the destruction of Queen Victoria's armies as a way of promoting the peaceful teachings of Jesus Christ. He coerced his converts to invest in the New Jerusalem in the Cumberland Valley, bankrupted the members, and abandoned them when the enterprise failed. For all his accusations against the Twelve, Rigdon had demonstrated he could not lead a church either.

Bickerton faced serious questions. Were Rigdon's claims a ploy to garner support for his pride? Maybe Rigdon's allegations against the Twelve had been exaggerated. It might have been just rivalry, and Brigham Young may have spared his followers Rigdon's volatility. After all, the Twelve publicly denied polygamy. As the year 1850 approached, Bickerton's prejudice dissipated, his thoughts paralleling those of Joseph Smith's youngest son, David Hyrum Smith, in a poem Smith penned in the mid-1860s: "The remedy I now will tell, / Apply it, it will answer well, / Turn right about upon your track, / Shake mister Sidney from your back. / And then you will imitate Joseph Smith / And make the matter plain. / Or kick the bucket and perish with, /

11. Bickerton, "Testimony, June 1903," 1.

Your Sidney on the brain."[12] Bickerton decided not to dwell on the past, nor did he want to fall into the same fanaticism Rigdon had, blaming his failures on others. He determined to prepare himself for the future and make a fresh start.

After the war in Mexico, the United States expanded by 20 percent, adding what became the states of Arizona, California, Nevada, New Mexico, Utah, and parts of Colorado and Wyoming, enticing adventurers and innovators—miners and yeoman farmers—to move to the mountains and coast. There were significant issues to resolve, among them whether California, New Mexico, and Texas would be slave states, and one more time Senator Henry Clay of Kentucky, the architect of the 1820 Missouri Compromise, suggested in what became known as the Compromise of 1850 that California be free and settlers in the remaining region determine their own fate on the question of slavery. The compromise granted a portion of Texas to New Mexico, provided federal funds to pay Texas's state debt, abolished the slave trade in the nation's capital, and required cooperation in returning fugitive slaves.[13]

Abolitionists disliked the thought of a compromise, and secessionists like Robert Barnwell Rhett thought it would only convince Northerners "we value a union with them more than we value the institution of slavery," and that it would make them appear weak.[14] Bickerton would have seen this strife in the light of Joseph Smith's Civil War prophecy, Smith's dim view of the country's ability to hold together being one reason Bickerton probably considered investigating Young's oasis in the desert. It seemed to him that Young was establishing a refuge from the prophesied calamities. From all appearances, Young was succeeding, at least in the physical trappings of a society apart from the world. Bickerton was later interested to learn that US President Millard Fillmore was appointing the pioneer prophet

12. David Hyrum Smith, "Sidney on the Brain," Wilford Wood Museum, Bountiful, Utah, cited in Van Wagoner, *Sidney Rigdon*, 471–72.

13. Walther, *Shattering of the Union*, xvii.

14. Ibid., xvii–xix.

territorial governor. Thousands of beleaguered onetime followers of Joseph Smith had already settled in the Salt Lake Valley and in outlying areas, and the city itself was becoming a flourishing commercial center as westward travelers, gold seekers, and religious pioneers stopped or settled there. The Brighamites were prospering, and part of their triumphant march to the Rocky Mountains had been their willingness to be flexible in meeting tough challenges with new resolutions. Young's Mormonism had evolved since his people were expelled from Nauvoo.[15]

Bickerton also may have been impressed that when riots broke out among the Mormons' neighbors in and around Nauvoo in September 1845 and vigilantes tried to expel the Latter-day Saints from the city at that time, the Mormons had patiently finished constructing their temple through October, even though they knew they were about to abandon it. Young allowed all church members to partake in the endowment ceremony that was previously available only to the elite. Now Bickerton wondered if the pioneer Saints were a new Israel emulating the Hebrew refugees in the Bible fleeing Egypt. Young had planned on leaving the country and entering the northern territory of Mexico, thereby delivering his people from the clutches of the gentiles, symbolically performing an exodus to a promised land.[16]

In February 1846 the first wagon parties started west to the Oregon Trail on the far side of Iowa. On February 19, a cold blinding storm halted the companies for a week. While huddling in tents, Young's secret plural wife Eliza R. Snow composed a hymn to invigorate the Saints. "Altho' in woods and tents we dwell / Shout, shout, O Camp of Israel," the first verse proclaimed. When Young arrived, he stood on top of a wagon and from there divided the five hundred Saints into groups of hundreds, fifties, and tens, then instructed them to cross to the far side of the state where the Missouri River divides it from Nebraska Territory, on their way to Zion.[17]

15. Turner, *Brigham Young*, 199.

16. Bowman, *Mormon People*, 94.

17. Beecher, *Personal Writings of Eliza Roxcy Snow*, 114, cited in ibid., 98.

The trail across Iowa presented perilous hazards. Frigid air and rain were constant companions, afflicting the refugees with diphtheria, dysentery, malaria, typhoid, and whooping cough. When the weather dried, rattlesnakes swarmed the ground. Those with guns kept them close in case of snakes or Indian attacks. Along the way, men planted crops, built log houses, and dug wells for the wagon trains that would follow, hoping to alleviate their hardships. The gravestones of those who died served as trail markers. The muddy ground made it difficult for the wagons, and most companies only made a few miles a day. Food and water were scarce. When Young preached, he often spoke in aggravation about those who stole supplies or fought with local settlers.

After five months of hard travel, Young's camp had only journeyed three hundred miles and was still in Iowa. At the eastern bank of the Missouri River, a temporary town was built across the river on Potawatomi Indian land. They spent the summer founding what would become Winter Quarters, not just for themselves but for ten thousand more pilgrims scattered behind them. They lived in wagon boxes until they could build cabins or pitch tents or construct prairie-style sod houses. Contracting malaria in summer and pneumonia in winter, about six hundred died.[18]

In May they learned that the United States had declared war on Mexico. Young had a strong aversion to Washington and had wanted to settle outside of the U.S., but these new circumstances presented an opportunity for the church when James Allen of the US Army arrived in June to recruit men, offering to pay each volunteer an advance of $42 (over $1,000 today) and monthly wage of between $7 and $50 (nearly $1,500). When Young encouraged the young men to sign up, five hundred did. He recognized the irony of aiding the country that had just expelled them, and his intent remained the same, to establish a theocratic kingdom in the West. However, he was not above improvising from day to day or taking money from the country that had evicted them. The funds the men of the Mormon Battalion received

18. Bowman, *Mormon People*, 100.

would help facilitate the mass migration to the Great Basin the following spring.[19]

To purify the people for their trek west, Young called for a two-week season of repentance. "You must stop your back biteings speaking evil of the Twelve speaking evil of me," he said, "or you will be damned." The mood changed. People felt an impulse to conform, and soon to praise God in song and dance. It was a happy time despite travails. Young had a dream in which he saw Joseph Smith ask his mother, Lucy Mack Smith (who had remained in Nauvoo), what she was reading. "Have you got the Word of God there?" he asked. When she said yes, he responded, "I think you will be sick of that pretty soon." The interpretation, Young decided, was that he himself would soon be the conduit for more counsel from heaven, and that the revelations to come would freshen those that had come before.[20]

On January 14, Young penned "the Word and Will of the Lord" to organize the camp. The order came in the form of the promised revelation. "I am he who led the children of Israel out of the land of Egypt," it read, "and my arm is stretched out in the last days, to save my people Israel."[21] This voice from heaven enhanced Young's position as Smith's successor, so that when spring arrived and Young literally followed the revelation's instructions and led an advance party of 148 men and a few women to the unknown mountains and lakes of the far West, the people followed him. On April 5 the company began journeying through what are now Nebraska and Wyoming, with a brief stop at Fort Bridger, where they met members of the Mormon Battalion who were returning from Mexico by way of California and Nevada. They greeted Young's group with shouts of "Hosanna!" Some of Young's group had fallen ill to "mountain fever" from tick bites, Young included, and for

19. "Epistle from the Quorum of the Twelve Apostles," *Latter-day Saints' Millennial Star*, Mar. 15, 1848, 82.

20. Kenney, *Wilford Woodruff's Journal,* 3:100–01; Turner, *Brigham Young*, 162–63, citing the journals of Willard Richards and Erastus Snow, Aug. 8, 11, 14, 1846, LDS Church History Library.

21. D&C 136:22.

the remaining ten days of the trip, he left the company in the hands of the other apostles, who reached the Salt Lake Valley ahead of him on July 22. Two days later "President Young expressed his full satisfaction in the Appearance of the valley as A resting place for the Saints" and happily proclaimed it "the Promised Land." A few days later, he and six other apostles baptized each other in one of the streams that flowed from the Wasatch Mountains, entering, "as it were, … a new world," and prompting them "to renew our covenants & commence in newness of life," according to Erastus Snow. On August 8 the entire Mormon camp followed suit. For them, the renewal of becoming born again through baptism separated them from their past and was a way to dedicate themselves to a revitalized future, which again would not have been lost on Bickerton.[22]

As expected, the Great Basin was not vacant. The Shoshone tribe lived to the north of the valley and Utes were situated to the south. At first Young discouraged extended commerce and interaction with them, even though he expected eventually to convert the Indians to produce a "white & delightsome people" in fulfillment of what he considered a Book of Mormon promise. In that day, Young said, people would "live to the age of a tree & be visited & hold communion with the Angels; & bring in the millennium."[23] Young never gave up his dream of converting the "Lamanites," as the Book of Mormon called the Indians, even though a protracted seven-year war involving casualties in the hundreds on all sides dampened his belief that it would happen anytime soon.[24]

Young was not officially recognized as president of the church until December 27, 1847, at a conference to the east of Winter Quarters, when Orson Pratt suggested to the assembly that a presidency be

---

22. Kenney, *Wilford Woodruff's Journal*, 3:233–34; Turner, *Brigham Young*, 168–70, citing the Horace K. Whitney Journal, July 25 1847, BYU Special Collections.

23. Bagley, *Pioneer Camp*, 243–44.

24. See Peterson, *Utah's Black Hawk War*. Mormons killed several hundred Indians, and nearly 80 Mormons were killed.

formed with Heber Kimball and Willard Richards as first and second counselors. The congregation agreed and shouted, "Hosanna! Hosanna! Hosanna! To God and the Lamb! Amen! Amen! and Amen!" At the close of the meeting, three violinists played "God save the king," the symbolism being intentional. Young had just obtained power over the church and region, and with that authority he intended to erect God's kingdom on the shores of the Great Salt Lake.[25]

In leaving the Salt Lake Valley to attend the conference in Iowa in 1847, Young left behind perhaps two hundred Latter-day Saints. By the fall of the next year, the valley contained over four thousand residents. For a while the political future of the region was uncertain and the secretive Council of Fifty made important policy decisions. In 1849 when the council petitioned the US Congress for statehood, it referred to itself as the Provisional State of Deseret, a Book of Mormon term (deseret) for honeybee and metaphor for the collaborative nature of the Saints. The Mormons proposed governing a vast territory including today's Arizona, Nevada, Utah, and portions of California, Colorado, New Mexico, and Oregon.[26]

One of the sticking points between Young and the federal government was that he did not want them appointing territorial officials. "There is no difference in reality between a monarchy, despot, and republicanism," he said. The purpose of all governments was to enforce laws, he said, so the priesthood was as good as any other governing institution. Since the Saints adhered to God and to a higher law than civil ordinances, federal law was nothing to them. "If this people will do right as they say they will, they can trample on all laws under their feet," he affirmed.[27]

As houses were being erected in the Salt Lake Valley in early 1848, members of the Mormon Battalion in California, under the

25. General Church Minutes, Dec. 27, 1847, Box 1, Folder 61, CR 100 318, LDS Church History Library, cited in Turner, *Brigham Young*, 174; Turner, 173–74.

26. Rogers, *Council of Fifty*, 225n170; Turner, 175, 195–96.

27. Ibid., 184, citing the General Church Minutes, Oct. 22, 1848; Oct. 14, 1849, LDS Church History Library.

supervision of John Marshall in the mountains east of Sacramento, were constructing a sawmill for local businessman Johann Sutter when gold was discovered.[28] Young felt ambivalent about this. "To talk of going away from this valley for anything is like vinegar to my eyes," he declared. He warned the men that "gold will sink a man to hell." Not that Young ignored the benefits of the money that flowed back to Salt Lake City, the western junction for argonauts and merchants. Young gathered what gold he could and minted coins with it, believing that if the church supervised its use, gold was not a problem. He sent "gold missionaries" to California to pan for metal and send what they collected back to the church.[29]

With avarice afoot and the arrival of outsiders in the heretofore isolated territory, there was an inevitable increase in vice. Some veterans of the Mormon Battalion acted licentiously and gambled and drank. Young threatened to dispatch such men to the next life, invoking the Law of God. One such man, Ira West, was tried by the Salt Lake City high council on allegations of fraud and indebtedness in March 1849. When the Council of Fifty discussed the case, Young referenced the doctrine of blood atonement, by which it was occasionally better to execute a man than allow him to live in sin. This gave him a clean slate in the next life, Young said, since the execution was a way for him to pay for what he had done. The doctrine instilled fear and ensured obedience to the church's influential leader.[30]

Although the US Congress created a territory instead of a state and granted the Mormons less land than they had requested, it was still a vast expanse including all of present-day Nevada and Utah, half of Colorado, and a corner of Wyoming. They had apparently found grace in some politicians' eyes, their hardships having elicited

28. Howe, *What Hath God Wrought*, 813.

29. Turner, *Brigham Young*, 180, citing General Church Minutes, Oct. 1, 1848; Aug. 12, 1849.

30. Turner, 187–89. The Council of Fifty had previously considered "the case of Ira E. West" and "the council all agreed that he had forfeited his Head, but the difficulty was how he should be disposed of," whether privately or publicly. Rogers, *Council of Fifty*, 164–66.

empathy. This left an impression on William Bickerton. To him, the pioneer prophet appeared to have been touched by heaven, where Rigdon had failed. It was a courageous act to lead people into the unknown and establish a thriving commercial center. Strict enforcement of rules in the absence of other law-keeping infrastructure was necessary. As the church expanded, its coffers filled with gold. As early as 1847 the *Pittsburgh Gazette* commented with admiration about the Mormon journey to Mexico, which is said surpassed any other hegira in American history. "We have noticed for several weeks past, various parties of emigrants to the West passing thro' this city," the editorial offered. "An unusual portion of them are well dressed, intelligent persons, from the Eastern States. We think they are the most substantial persons who have gone West for a long time. We have noticed none, apparently, in better circumstances. To our surprise a gentleman who has every opportunity of knowing, assures us the great majority of them are *Mormons.*"[31] The astonished locals must have struggled to reconcile this information with the simultaneous collapse of Rigdon's New Jerusalem.

Bickerton himself was at a crossroads. In 1850 he decided to send an inquiry to Kanesville (Council Bluffs), situated on the Iowa side of the Missouri River opposite Winter Quarters, requesting information about the church. The town had been named by Mormons for Thomas L. Kane, a political ally who had helped gain federal approval for their occupancy of Indian lands along the Missouri River.[32] Kanesville was the last commercial hub before emigrants reached the Great Salt Lake City, and Bickerton probably felt confident his letter would reach someone there, whereas sending it to the Rocky Mountains would be less sure of success. He explained that he wanted to discuss the possibility of joining the Latter-day Saints.

His congregation at the time had nine members. It resembled the

---

31. "Mormons," *Pittsburgh Gazette*, May 6, 1847, reprinted in the *Washington Reporter*, May 22, 1847.

32. Linn, *Story of Mormons*, 393.

School of the Prophets in that the members met in his home, taught each other the scriptures, and conducted a few religious ordinances, probably baptisms, communion, anointings, and the laying on of hands to comfort the sick. In 1849 the word of the Lord came to Charles Brown, a member of the congregation, confirming Bickerton's role as a prophet, and he anointed Bickerton's head with oil and declared that under his leadership "this people should go in and out and find pasture."[33] This gave the leader confidence that he was pursuing the right course, just that it required an excessive amount of emotional and financial health to do it alone, without a denominational affiliation. Bickerton decided he could use some help.

Instead of receiving a reply directly from the authorities in Kanesville or Salt Lake City, Bickerton was visited by two Brighamite missionaries, John Murray and David James Ross, who were sent to West Elizabeth in 1851. The missionaries exchanged beliefs, concerns, and questions with the Pennsylvania group, probably withholding criticisms or ultimatums until they had assessed Bickerton's concerns. They understood that he had been taught by Sidney Rigdon and probably displayed sensitivity to the hardship Bickerton had suffered as a result, maybe even identifying with him since Bickerton had soured on Rigdon's excesses.[34] The two parties shared important similarities. The missionaries insisted that Mormons were not guilty of polygamy, which put everyone at ease.[35] The two groups believed in the same scriptures, including the Book of Mormon, Book of Moses, and Doctrine and Covenants. They believed in proxy baptisms for the dead. Both groups believed that worthy individuals could receive personal revelation, that God was an approachable being who intervened in human affairs. They may have even agreed on the divine potential of mortal beings, the doctrine of deification in the next life having been

33. Bickerton, "Testimony, June 1903," 9.

34. "News from the Elders," "News from the Traveling Elders," *Frontier Guardian*, July 25, Aug. 22, 1851; Bean and Allen to Palmer, Dec. 14, 1885, Lamb Foundation Archive.

35. Bean and Allen to Palmer, Dec. 14, 1885; William Bickerton, *St. John Weekly News*, Aug. 16, 1889; Cadman, *History of the Church of Jesus Christ*, 1:5–6; Entz, "Zion Valley," 101.

taught by Joseph Smith in 1844. Paramount to both group's eschatology was Jesus Christ's imminent return.[36] Bickerton agreed with the Mormons that God's judgment would soon fall on the United States.

Despite all the similarities, there were differences in their theologies and practices. At this time, Bickerton may not have considered Joseph Smith the "choice seer" who would gather the tribes of Israel and usher in the Millennium (2 Ne. 3:6–24), principally because Smith had died without accomplishing those feats. Mormons, on the other hand, had considered Smith to be that prophesied seer,[37] and Sidney Rigdon's followers had thought their leader was the "choice seer." After Smith's death, Latter-day Saints began to think the gathering of Israel would come about by baptizing new members rather than by means of physical relocation, and church patriarchs were called to bestow a blessing on novices assigning them a tribe of Israel—proclaiming them Israelites by adoption or blood. Bickerton may not have approved of this, and he would eventually consider lineage irrelevant to salvation, which required repentance, baptism, and acceptance of the divinity of Christ for anyone, regardless of their past. If one had the desire, one was entitled to participate in the establishment of Zion, he believed. Out of this line of thinking, Bickerton would become convinced that the Choice Seer would be an American Indian.

He concluded this after reading the prophet Lehi's words in the Book of Mormon, "Joseph [of Egypt] truly said: Thus saith the Lord unto me: A choice seer will I raise up out of the fruit of thy loins." The survivors in the Book of Mormon account were Native Americans, and they were originally from Jerusalem, according to the Book of Mormon. Furthermore, the preface to the Book of Mormon stated that the book would come forth "in due time by the way of Gentile." As Bickerton saw it, the book came forth by means of Joseph Smith, thus disqualifying him from consideration as the Choice Seer. The Israelite

36. Smith, *History of the Church*, 2:182; D&C 130:14–15.

37. Bushman, *Rough Stone Rolling*, 122–23, 165, 415–16; Richards, *Marvelous Work*, 207–42.

seer would be a deliverer who would lead his people from bondage like Moses. Overall, Bickerton concluded, Joseph Smith did not fulfill any of these Book of Mormon prophecies.[38] Few people in Mormon history had ever envisioned such a concept as Bickerton developed, but it appeared so logical to him that he would not be dissuaded.[39]

He had other variances in belief from Young's church. On two occasions Bickerton had been told he had the spiritual mantle of a prophet. Both Rigdon and Brown had confirmed this. The missionaries, Ross and Murray, would have considered Brigham Young and the Quorum of the Twelve to hold exclusive claim to that title. With respect to blood atonement, Bickerton had probably not learned of it, but it was not something he would have condoned. Nor did he believe a woman's salvation hinged on her husband's priesthood rank. Her faith and piety alone would dictate her salvation. Even so, after discussing variances, Ross and Murray saw no reason not to accept Bickerton into the Utah fold, concluding that their differences were reconcilable. Even though they would have thought Bickerton had peculiar ideas about the Millennium, the man accepted Smith and Young as God's leaders, which was the most important thing. If he held alternative ideas about Zion, members of the Utah church did as well. Ross and Murray primarily needed Bickerton to accept the transfer of priesthood authority from Joseph Smith to Brigham Young; all else was a matter of details. When he affirmed that concept, they welcomed him.[40]

The missionaries baptized Bickerton, his wife, Dorothy, and eight other members of the congregation, mirroring what the Saints had done in renewing their covenants when they entered the Salt Lake Valley.[41] On Sunday, May 25, 1851, the missionaries organized the branch at the home of William Thews. Ross and Murray confirmed each baptized member by laying hands on their heads and offering a prayer. In

38. 2 Ne. 3:6; preface, Book of Mormon, 1830 edition.

39. For more information regarding his beliefs about the apocalypse, Zion, the Choice Seer, and Jesus Christ's Second Coming, see Bickerton, *Ensign*, 11–12, 15–17.

40. Bickerton, "Testimony, June 1903," 1; Entz, "Zion Valley," 101.

41. Bean and Allen to Palmer, Dec. 14, 1885.

their supplication, they asked the Lord to give each convert the Holy Ghost. The duo understood that some members were dependent on Bickerton as their leader, so during the meeting they ordained him an elder and appointed him presiding minister. They also ordained William Thews a priest and ordained George Rain a teacher, and called the two to be Bickerton's first and second counselors. Joining with the Brighamites was not something Bickerton had foreseen, but he was relieved to realize he would not have to carry the weight of the congregation's future on his shoulders alone.[42]

As branch leader, he continued to emphasize that Jesus, as quoted in the Book of Mormon, accepted everyone: men and women, bond and free. Taking the Book of Mormon literally, his views would have shocked the average neighbor if they knew he thought the day would come when American Indians would teach white people the true gospel. Americans considered Indians savages. Under Andrew Jackson, Indians had been pushed out of the eastern and southern states to the edge of civilization. If Americans did not "serve the God of the land, who is Jesus Christ," Bickerton would have warned the branch, the Lord would destroy them and allow the Indians to repossess the continent.[43]

To the extent that he shared such thoughts with people outside of the congregation, whose ancestors had endured Indian attacks in settling Western Pennsylvania, he would not have been popular in the community. Nonetheless, some people listened and liked what they heard. They may have liked the idea that America had a special purpose; that it was a promised land possessing a faith that could stand up to the "great and abominable church" in Rome (1 Ne. 13:25), in keeping with the anti-Catholic sentiment of the Book of Mormon. They might have agreed that over the years many "plain and precious" teachings of the Bible had been lost (13:25–28). The Book of Mormon held that the eucharist was representational rather than the actual body and blood of Jesus (3 Nephi 18:1–13), and that infants did not require

42. Martin and Mancini, "History," 2.

43. 3 Ne. 21:4; Ether 2:12, Book of Mormon.

baptism (Moro. 8:5–23), teachings that were popular in America. The book told of a king named Mosiah who relinquished his throne in favor of a government of elected judges (Mosiah 29:1–37). With a character similar to George Washington, Mosiah renounced monarchical rule and ensured that the government would operate "by the voice of the people." The book's republican undertones may have tempered the opposition to the heretical concept of extra-canonical scripture.[44]

Bickerton's branch grew. In July William Thews became an elder and four others, Thomas Innes, George Rain, Robert Russell, and Martin Wardell, were ordained priests. By September the branch had tripled in membership to twenty-seven members, some of whom attended a district conference in conjunction with members from the McKeesport branch, eight miles distant, and Youghiogheny branch, six miles from West Elizabeth. Bickerton felt euphoric—secure that this was God's kingdom, Brigham Young leading the way. In the district meeting, he led the motion to sustain Young and his counselors and the Twelve Apostles in their offices. John Murray spoke on the "rise and prosperity of the church, in spite of all opposition." The conference was impressive enough that the members decided to send the minutes to the *Frontier Guardian* in Kanesville. Bickerton thanked the elders who had converted him and his congregants. For a brief moment, he had found peace, his ministerial troubles solved, although that feeling would not last.[45]

Young shocked many outsiders when he admitted in 1851 that he had more than one wife, and when in 1852 he and apostle Orson Pratt publicly declared polygamy an official tenet of the church. Polygamy had been receiving more and more publicity, and it had forced a response from Salt Lake City. For instance, in 1851 a Mormon named Frederick Cox was charged with bigamy in Iowa and ordered to abandon the latest two of his three wives. In early 1852 an exposé

44. See Butler, *Awash in a Sea of Faith*, 285; Cohn, *Mass Migration*, 217–18.

45. Martin and Mancini, "History of the Church,"3–4; "News from the Traveling Elders," *Frontier Guardian*, Aug. 22, 1851.

by an ex-Mormon appeared in the *Lehigh [Pennsylvania] Register* about "licentiousness run mad" in Utah. Young withheld official acknowledgment until a special conference in August 1852, but missionaries were sent out in advance to privately prepare members across the country for the announcement.[46]

When Bickerton heard the news, he was attending a church leadership meeting in Allegheny City (north side of Pittsburgh). If they rejected the doctrine, they would reap damnation, they were told. This astounded the branch leaders, but Bickerton was particularly dumbfounded. The missionaries had previously assured him that this was not the case. *Did a man's word mean nothing?* he must have thought. He rose from his seat and said, "If the approval of God were to come to [me] by accepting the doctrine of polygamy, I would prefer the displeasure of God." He then walked out of the meeting, never to return.[47]

He informed the West Elizabeth branch on Wednesday, March 10, 1852. Standing in front of the congregation, he declared that he would forsake the Mormons and asked them to sign an affidavit he had penned stating, "We the undersigned have left off all connection whatsoever with Brigham Young and the Twelve, whose headquarters or home is the Valley of the Great Salt Lake, because of their adultery and general wickedness."[48] When he invited the others to join him, however, no one immediately stepped forward to sign the statement,

46. Turner, *Brigham Young*, 204; Bowman, *Mormon People*, 125; "Mormonism Exposed, by a Mormon," *Lehigh Register*, Mar. 25, 1852.

47. Cadman, *History of the Church of Jesus Christ*, 6; Watson, *History of the Church of Jesus Christ*, 2:36. Cadman remembered hearing about Bickerton's departure from the Allegheny City meeting from his father, William Cadman Sr.; the quotation might be considered a paraphrase. Ergo Cadman's recount, at first glance, may seem a little dubious. Cadman even wrote, "I have not pretended to relate this incident in my Father's exact words, but the thought conveyed is the same." However, several primary documents demonstrate that Bickerton abhorred polygamy and that he was quite vocal about his disgust. In addition, primary documents confirm that the doctrine of polygamy was the reason why Bickerton abandoned Brigham Young. So in the end, Bickerton's sarcastic declaration about preferring God's displeasure rather than accepting polygamy is likely accurate.

48. Martin and Mancini, "History of the Church," 5.

probably wanting to investigate the claim themselves and have time to think it over.

At the special conference on August 29 in Salt Lake City, apostle Orson Pratt gave a stunning defense of what he called an "essential doctrine." All people, he declared, had existed as spirits before they received a body on earth. When a couple conceived, a pre-existent spirit entered the baby's body. The spirit was an entity that had been fathered by God, who in heaven was surrounded by his wives and spirit children waiting to be born into mortality. Through procreation, Pratt said, human beings acted in partnership with God and increased their glory in the next life. The more babies, the greater exaltation. The more marriages, the more children were given the opportunity to accept salvation.[49]

Pratt argued that plural marriage mirrored the ancient custom of the Israelites and was therefore a divine law. Orson Spencer, a British convert and pamphleteer, supported this in 1853, writing that the "family order which God established with Abraham and the Patriarchs, was the order observed among celestial beings in the celestial world." In other words, polygamy was the order of heaven. Pratt and Spencer, like Joseph Smith, believed that God had a history, was not unbegotten, had been a man who died and was resurrected. In the flesh, God had married several women who were sealed to him for eternity. When they rose to the heavens, God and his wives conceived spirit children. Therefore, Abraham's multiple marriages emulated God's familial relationships. Women had a special role in that they had the opportunity to become plural wives and mothers in heaven, to give birth to spirits in the next life who would one day inhabit earthly bodies in other worlds. Without the women, procreation, and families, the plan of salvation

49. *Journal of Discourses*, Aug. 29, 1852, 1:53–66. Pratt said "there are more Gods than one" and that in heaven there will be "many fathers" and "many families" (56–57). Young too had recently said that a faithful Latter-day Saint, after the resurrection, would "organize an Earth, People it, redeem it, and sanctify it." Discourse of Aug. 8, 1852, LDS Church History Library, cited in Turner, *Brigham Young*, 205.

could not continue. Therefore, polygamy was good for women and a virtuous practice.[50]

Pratt's argument had theological concepts that wove the Mormon scriptures, Joseph Smith's prophecies, and biblical history into a social code. Polygamy was said to trump Victorian monogamy. It offered an avenue where a "numerous and faithful posterity can be raised up, and taught in the principles of righteousness and truth." Plural marriage gave couples an opportunity to raise children in devout households. It kept families united where they might otherwise lead lives of isolation. As the country industrialized, immigrant fathers and mothers worked long days, returning home exhausted. To help stave off poverty, working-class households often took in other relatives and boarders. The hard daily routines of industrialized life fragmented the immigrant family. Pratt believed that middle- and upper-class families did not fare much better. Wives and children grew apart from the work environment, creating what historians termed the "cult of domesticity." Although the culture promoted piety among women, it relegated mothers to a lonely life. Housebound females had the responsibility to create a refuge for the husband, a man who often did not understand the needs or personalities of his own household. The American family was therefore being destroyed, Pratt asserted, and in its place were prostitution and orphaned children living on the streets. Plural marriage kept families intact, under the protection of a religion founded on principles of God's love.[51]

After the August conference, Young sent missionaries out to further familiarize the branches with the principles and protocols of celestial marriage. Expecting the federal government to object, he prepared a defense he thought Washington could not dispute, that polygamy was founded in religion and therefore protected by the First Amendment. "There is not a constitution [or] law in any state in the union that forbids a man having two wives," he said. Nor could there be if practiced

50. Spencer, *Letters*, 192; cited in Bowman, *Mormon People*, 126.

51. Bowman, *Mormon People*, 127–28.

as a "principal of faith." In addition, if the question of slavery was left to the western territories to decide as a matter of popular sovereignty, then certainly the same states ought to be allowed to decide the question of plural marriage. "As for Congress they might as well abolish slavery in the South as plurality in Utah."[52]

Despite this shrewd defense, Bickerton was unable to shake his convictions about sexuality. His religious background in Methodism and early Mormonism taught him that the fall of Adam and Eve brought on carnal desires, and God established the institution of marriage so that a man and a woman could have sexual relations within the confines of matrimony. Physical love bound a couple together. The greatest sin against the marriage covenant was adultery. Simply put, sex had limits. In his mind, the scriptures were clear on this.[53]

By contrast, Young and Pratt pointed out that polygamous sex was within the marriage contract. Bickerton considered that to be a self-serving farce—nothing more than an attempt to justify sin—because the Book of Mormon prophet Jacob condemned the people for wanting to "excuse themselves in committing whoredoms, because of the things which were written concerning David, and Solomon his son." Jacob continued, saying

> Behold, David and Solomon truly had many wives and concubines, which thing was abominable before me, saith the Lord. … Wherefore, my brethren, hear me, and hearken to the word of the Lord: For there shall not any man among you have save it be one wife; and concubines he shall have none; For I, the Lord God, delight in the chastity of women. And whoredoms are an abomination before me; thus saith the Lord of Hosts. (Jacob 2:22–28)

Taking this a step farther, Bickerton proposed that Jacob was also speaking to people in the modern age, not just to those of the sixth

52. Discourse of Aug. 1, 1852; Young to John Milton Bernhisel, Sept. 14, 1852, LDS Church History Library, cited in Turner, *Brigham Young*, 204.

53. Hansen, *Mormonism*, 150–54; Matt. 5:31–32.

century BCE. He was speaking to people of the new covenant in the nineteenth century for whom the Book of Mormon was intended.[54]

If Young and Pratt had had the opportunity to counter Bickerton's argument, they might have quoted the verse a few lines ahead where God stated that if needed to "raise up seed unto me, I will command my people; otherwise they shall hearken unto these things" (2:30). To which Bickerton would have said that if there were a need for more procreation, it could be done within traditional marriage.

As progressive as Bickerton's views towards women were, he held the Victorian ethic that women should be decorous and virtuous, isolated from the corruptions of society, and provide a comfortable home for their husbands. Unlike Victorianism, which limited married couples to sex for the purpose of procreation, Bickerton's religious heritage taught him that an intimate relationship provided a healthy moral life. He also believed in large families. In 1852 he had three small children and another, Clara Virginia, on the way, and he believed that men should be as decorous and virtuous as women.[55]

After ten months of affiliation with the Utah Latter-day Saints, Bickerton felt as violated and deceived, just as he had when Sidney Rigdon left Pittsburgh for the Cumberland Valley. Again Bickerton stood at a personal juncture and felt somewhat unsure how to proceed. It is remarkable that he did not return to Methodism, and the reason he did not was because he retained the firm belief that his calling was from heaven.[56] The way he saw it, his spiritual dedication had preserved him from sophistry, and despite the failures of Rigdon and others, he could not denounce what he knew was true. The Book of Mormon opened his eyes to the glorious potential of the American Indians and the foretold peaceful onset of the Second Coming. He was determined to take part in it, somehow.

It is not certain how many members from the West Elizabeth

54. Bickerton, *Ensign*, 3.

55. Langland, *Nobody's Angels*, 25–28; US Census, 1860.

56. Bickerton, *Ensign*, 5.

branch followed Bickerton's exit from the Utah denomination, but we know several of them did. He retained his congregation, in any case, and that gave him hope. As he "paused to know what course to follow," one certainty remained: plural marriage would transform the perception of Mormonism. He would need to find a way of distinguishing himself from them. "The people of Salt Lake are gone astray," he would testify, "and if the Lord had not left us a seed we should have been as Sodom and like unto Gommorah." If his followers were to be free of debauchery, someone needed to assume the role of leadership. There would have to be a prophet who could stand "in the room and stead of Joseph Smith to lead forth his people." After thinking about it, he concluded that "that man is William Bickerton."[57]

57. Ibid., 4–5.

FOUR

LEFT ALONE

1852–55

"But the Lord did not leave me. No, he showed me a vision, and in the vision I was on the highest mountain on the earth: he told me if I did not preach the Gospel, I would fall into a dreadful chasm below, the sight there was awful."

—1863

After William Bickerton abandoned the LDS Church, he found himself deserted even by his West Elizabeth congregation as it awaited Brigham Young's announcement of plural marriage. He may have wondered, having gained in popularity as a minister and tripled the number of people attending services, if he had acted too quickly in denouncing the Twelve. To his congregants, his renunciation may have appeared to be based on a misunderstanding or perhaps temperament, since he had a history of disagreeing with ecclesiastical authority.

It is not certain that his own wife shared his secessionist impulse at the time, so he was really left to his own counsel. What should he do? Should he organize a new church? What if he returned to the Methodist faith? Either way, he would have to make a decision about the Book of Mormon, whether to give it up or detach it somehow from mainstream Mormonism. He would probably appear to people to be an apostate or hypocrite. By now the American public considered the Book of Mormon to be inextricably linked to Brigham Young, who for a while held such political power and financing that Bickerton must have been envious. Now, as Mormons were becoming increasingly unpopular nationally, the more people became familiar with their antinomian ways, any perceived association would tar Bickerton with the same brush. That meant that there were many reasons to retire his minister's calling and few reasons to continue. Only a divine manifestation could persuade him to persist.

One result of Young's August 1852 announcement was that it incited Bickerton to review the Utah church's theology to see what else he might agree or disagree with. Without a clear explanation of how he reevaluated it, we can see by correlating his conclusions with the Bible and Book of Mormon how he might have come to a new understanding. According to apostle Orson Pratt, plural marriage increased a man's exaltation in the afterlife. All men of the priesthood, when they died and resurrected, became gods to the planets they and their male children created, the more kingdoms the better. That was the rationale for why it would benefit men to have several wives on earth, and therefore more children, and thereby more pre-existent spirits inhabiting mortal bodies and going on to become gods or mothers in heaven. Within polygamy, the familial order was an eternal cycle of progression to godhood.[1] Bickerton considered whether he believed this. Surprisingly, the concept could be defended by relying on the New Testament.

The apostle Paul explained that Jesus died for sins so people would be sanctified and resurrected with a new body, full of glory and presumably occupying the same heavenly home as the Savior (Heb. 2:11; 1 Cor. 15:49). By reverse logic, Bickerton decided that in rejecting plural marriage, the theological pillars supporting it crumbled, including exaltation to godhood. As he read the scriptures, he concluded that worthy individuals would become joint-heirs with Jesus in his eternal kingdom but would not be granted omnipotence. Theologically, he began retreating to his Protestant roots.

Then he wrestled with the Book of Moses and Doctrine and

1. Turner, *Brigham Young*, 204; Bowman, *Mormon People*, 126–27; Bushman, *Rough Stone Rolling*, 533–37.

Covenants because of their support of the doctrine of deification, as in the following words God was said to have spoken to Moses:

> The heavens, they are many, and they cannot be numbered unto man; but they are numbered unto me, for they are mine. And as one earth shall pass away, and the heavens thereof, even so shall another come; and there is no end to my works, neither to my words. For behold, this is my work and my glory—to bring to pass the immortality and eternal life of man. (Moses 1:35–39)

God had created and populated other worlds, so Joseph Smith's Book of Moses said, and the implication was that by mimicking what had gone before, men could reach equal status. They would raise God to a higher divine level as well. In the Doctrine and Covenants, Joseph Smith explained even more explicitly the characteristics of those who achieved godhood:

> They are they who received the testimony of Jesus, and believed on his name and were baptized … that by keeping the commandments they might be washed and cleansed from all their sins, … and who overcome by faith, and are sealed by the Holy Spirit of promise, which the Father sheds forth upon all those who are just and true. … Wherefore, as it is written, they are gods, even the sons of God—Wherefore, all things are theirs, whether life or death, or things present, or things to come, all are theirs and they are Christ's, and Christ is God's. (D&C 76:51–59)

Smith recorded the Book of Moses in 1830 and followed up with the revelation in the Doctrine and Covenants in 1832. This was two decades before the Twelve publicly affirmed the doctrine of plural marriage and defended it by explaining its connection to godhood. On one hand, these ideas about achieving exaltation corresponded with Paul's epistles about celestial glory. Men would one day resurrect, receive a heavenly body, and become the brethren of Jesus. Bickerton himself accepted this but had never considered that it would be a justification for plural marriage. Now he could see that the Utah church's theology would evolve to produce ever more harmonization through new revelations. He worked backward from that premise and found that it cast doubt, for him, on the meaning and reliability of the early revelations. The Book of Moses and Doctrine and Covenants were the catalysts for the new doctrines and therefore, at least in part, suspect.

Baptism for the dead was a doctrine Bickerton had endorsed, but it was likewise interconnected with family salvation, plural marriage, and godhood. The practice was supposed to help connect families together, bringing one's relatives from past generations into the fold who had not accepted Christ. Joseph Smith explained in a letter to the apostles that "the Saints have the privilege of being baptized, for those of their relatives who are dead, who they believe would have embraced the gospel if they had been privileged with hearing it, and who have received the gospel in the spirit, through the instrumentality of those who have been commissioned to preach to them while in [spirit] prison."[2] For Mormons, baptism for the dead fulfilled what the prophet Malachi wrote in the Old Testament, "And [God] shall turn the heart of the fathers to the children, and the heart of the children to their fathers" (Mal. 4:6). Those who were deceased were dependent on this rite of salvation, according to Joseph Smith, who said that "they without us, cannot be made perfect." Mortals could become partners with Christ in the salvation of the dead. When everyone who had lived on earth was linked together as one large family and given an opportunity to receive the vicarious ordinances, Latter-day Saints would present a redeemed earth to Christ, and another earth will have fulfilled its mission, lifting Christ to a higher level of righteousness and, in turn, adding exaltation to those who helped accomplish the task.[3] The culmination of these three doctrines—plural marriage, baptism for the dead, and godhood—fulfilled the Lord's stated intent in the Book of Moses, which was to immortalize man.

The revelations given to Joseph Smith allowed for this reinterpretation. Bickerton considered the Book of Mormon, like the New

2. Quoted in Bushman, *Rough Stone Rolling*, 422.
3. Ibid., 423.

Testament, to be ancient, and they both forbade polygamy. What about the scripture where Paul asks, "Else what shall they do which are baptized for the dead, if the dead rise not at all? Why are they then baptized for the dead?" (1 Cor. 15:29)? To Mormons, this was rhetorical, but to Bickerton's thinking it was probably a criticism of a heretical ritual by some group that was unsure of the resurrection to begin with. In the Book of Mormon, Bickerton could find no mention of the practice. He began to see a pattern whereby unresolved biblical questions, unanswered in the Book of Mormon, were given unambiguous treatment in the revelations of Joseph Smith.[4]

He now faced a conundrum. He had felt the influence of the Holy Spirit confirming his authority in the Rigdon and Young churches. Could he now say the teachings of those churches were flawed? Bickerton had trusted Rigdon, who taught that Joseph Smith had fallen into sin through plural marriage, exacerbated by Young's promotion of it. Yet Rigdon himself had promised a utopian society in the Cumberland Valley based on revelations that had left his followers bankrupt. Was Bickerton's belief in the Restoration therefore unfounded? He concluded that the founding prophet, Joseph Smith, had—despite unorthodox teachings—fulfilled some of God's plans. "The Lord in his wisdom passed by all the great men of learning and refinement and revealed himself unto that obscure young man name[d] Joseph Smith," Bickerton wrote, "who was honored of God with the visitation and ministry of angels, was made instrumental in the hands of the Lord of translating the Book of Mormon from Egyptian hieroglyphics … and was entrusted with the Holy priesthood of Jesus Christ." Despite his failings, Smith had received priesthood authority and the gift of prophecy, had translated the Book of Mormon, and had accepted the mandate to warn people of the world's imminent end. He "suffered persecutions, and at last, death at the hands of a ruthless mob." The Book of Mormon made him, in the eyes of the world, a heretic. Everything had been fine until the seer became comfortable in Illinois.

4. For more information about his doctrinal views, see Bickerton, *Ensign*, 9–14.

His circumstances improved, his political clout increased, and he introduced unconventional doctrines Bickerton could not accept. Yet it was because of the Book of Mormon that Joseph Smith was assassinated, Bickerton assumed, and because of the book's purity. "The wisdom of God in every generation has been foolishness with men, yet on earth [Smith] was not suffered to live in his own land and enjoy the privilege of worshiping God according to the dictates of his own conscience."[5] He died as a result of preaching the restored gospel.

Sidney Rigdon presented similar issues and explanations. Bickerton could not deny that when he saw Rigdon preach, the power of God was manifested. When Rigdon proved himself incompetent, Bickerton ceased to believe him. Only after joining Young's church did Bickerton realize that Rigdon's accusations against the apostles were correct. What about Rigdon's divine authority? Bickerton remained convinced that the succession to Joseph Smith rightfully belonged to Rigdon, who, as the prophet's first counselor, should have received the appointment. When Bickerton received baptism in 1845, Rigdon still held priesthood authority, as Bickerton wrote in his autobiographical sketch:

> I entered the Church under Elder Sidney Rigdon's organization. I was called by the Holy Spirit to be an Elder. I received ordination and the power of God came down and sealed the office upon me. I went preaching to all that would hear. I was afterwards called into the Quorum of seventies. I received the ordination the second time, but the Church became disorganized.[6]

Rigdon defected after he ordained Bickerton, who felt confident in his claim to have received priesthood authority from his mentor; this is why he experienced the gift of the Holy Ghost in both Rigdon's and Young's churches.

Reviewing the leaders' spiritual paths, Bickerton found the most fault with Brigham Young, for having corrupted the church, Bickerton

5. Ibid., 3.
6. Ibid., 5.

came to think. "They do not follow Joseph Smith nor yet the Book of Mormon," he said of the Twelve. "They have sunk into adultery and lasciviousness, they had the way of truth, but they have departed from it." How could Young deny polygamy and then proclaim it? For eight years, Young had lied about his marital status, even while simultaneously adding additional wives to his family. The more Bickerton thought about it, the more disgusted he became. Joseph Smith deserved respect despite his errors because he was the person whom God had chosen to restore the priesthood. It must not have been Smith, he came to believe, but Young who had introduced polygamy in Nauvoo. He thought of Peter's words in a paraphrase of 2 Peter 2:10–12: "They walk after the flesh in the lust of uncleanness and despise government, they are presumptuous and selfwilled, and speak evil of the things that they understand not, and shall utterly perish in their own corruption." At his core, Bickerton felt the Protestant agitators were right that polygamy was an affront to God's law and an indignity to women and needed to be stopped.

After sorting out what he believed, he had to decide what to do about it. There was not another Mormon sect that did not esteem Joseph Smith's later teachings about family in the celestial realm. This weighed on his mind. "I paused to know what course to follow," believing that "a man cannot build up the Church of Christ without divin[e] command from the Lord, for it would only be sectarianism and man's authority." In the midst of his contemplation, a vision opened to him, in which the Lord took him to "the highest mountain on the earth: he told me if I did not preach the Gospel, I would fall into a dreadful chasm below, the sight there[of] was awful."[7] Astonished, Bickerton interpreted being alone on the world's highest mountain to indicate that he was the last man willing to preserve the restoration of true Christianity. He had two options. He could continue to preach, or he could go the way of others before him who had stumbled. It was his

7. Ibid.

choice, but he had been chosen for the work. "I moved with fear," he said, "having the Holy Spirit with me."[8]

He first mentioned his vision in the 1863 *Ensign*. With this tract, he hoped to publicize the history and doctrine of his new church, the Church of Jesus Christ of Latter Day Saints, sometimes shortened to the Church of Jesus Christ. Bickerton preferred the full name, perhaps because it signified apostolic authority and the Second Coming. In 1903 he recorded the vision in his autobiography with a minor addendum that when he "was carried away in the spirit and placed on a high mountain," there was "just room enough for me to stand." If he did not preach the gospel, the Lord had told him, he would "fall and be torn into bits."[9] An interesting omission from both accounts is any mention of the ten months he spent with Brigham Young's church, only saying that he received the revelation sometime after leaving Rigdon's Church of Christ. His reluctance to mention his conversion to Young's church indicated the degree of repugnance he felt toward polygamy, and he regretted his association with the LDS Church so much he wanted to place as wide a gulf between the two of them as possible.

A year before Bickerton published *The Ensign*, the US Congress passed the Morrill Anti-Bigamy Act prohibiting plural marriage in the territories and limiting church ownership of real estate to $50,000.[10] President Abraham Lincoln signed the bill but chose not to enforce it, saying with usual candor that Mormons were like a log that was "too hard to split, too wet to burn, and too heavy to move."[11] They were, in fact, numerous and distant, and therefore difficult to control. Confirming this, Governor Young responded defiantly by saying he would not suspend plural marriages and continuing to meet with his own ghost legislature in disregard for federal authority.[12]

Bickerton still wanted to be sure people understood the difference

8. Bickerton, "Testimony, June 1903," 2.

9. Ibid.

10. Bushman and Bushman, *Building the Kingdom*, 66–67.

11. Ibid., 67.

12. Turner, *Brigham Young*, 323.

between his church and Young's. "Here I was," he declared in the *Ensign*, "without learning, popular opinion against me, and the Salt Lake Mormons stood in the way." He hoped to show that he was as opposed to Utah Mormons as any other Christian would be, although his obsession with this was a kind of nod to his former affiliation with the Utah denomination. When Pratt officially acknowledged polygamy in 1852, the congregation in West Elizabeth finally came around to Bickerton's side. By then, he had decided to move forward, one way or the other. "I could not turn back unto Methodism again, no, I know they had not the Gospel. I stood in contemplation. The chasm was before me, no other alternative but to do my duty to God and man."[13]

His duty to God was to preach, as he saw it, and his duty to man was to oppose Brigham Young, bringing him back to where he started with a congregation and little money. He and Dorothy personally had three small children. Their youngest, Josephine, would die at age three in September.[14] Clara Virginia would be born the next year. William's out-of-body revelation anchored his faith during this time of stress. At least there had been a transformation in the coal industry that stabilized his wages.[15]

Elizabeth, and its sister town of West Elizabeth on the opposite bank of the Monongahela River, were sustained by steamboat construction before coal mining became the predominant industry. Once the mines were established, their proximity to the river allowed the mining companies to transport coal on barges to the Ohio and Mississippi Rivers. A local directory estimated that the deposit near Elizabeth contained about 300 million tons of coal, or about 8 billion bushels, a bushel at the time costing 4½ cents. That meant there was a vein of coal worth $370 million, about $11 billion today. It was significant enough to justify building an incline railroad to transport the product downhill to the river, where it was then loaded onto barges by

13. Bickerton, *Ensign*, 5.
14. "Record of Church," vol. 1, strip 3.
15. US Census, 1860.

horse-pulled cars. Other companies that supplied the miners thrived, for instance those that constructed and repaired river barges. Some of the product was shipped to Pittsburgh, and some traveled as far as Cincinnati, Louisville, St. Louis, Memphis, and New Orleans. By the 1880s Elizabeth was known as the regional coal capital,[16] meaning that Bickerton had job security.

It was at the mines that leaders of the new West Elizabeth denomination met most of the men who converted to the Church of Jesus Christ. "I went ahead preaching repentance toward God, and faith in the Lord Jesus Christ," Bickerton wrote, converting four men who worked under him at the mine.[17] Technically he had already converted his workmate, Charles Brown, but more miners converted, William Bacon and Daniel Davidson, along with Bickerton's older brother, Thomas, who joined the faith after following his brother-in-law to California. Unlike most treasure seekers, Thomas found success and returned only to retrieve his family. His wife refused to travel west, so he and Eliza and the children moved to West Elizabeth to work under his younger brother's supervision.[18]

Not that miners were the only converts. On days off, "I held outdoor meetings," Bickerton explained, "sometimes in the market place, sometime[s] in public houses, on streets or any other available place."[19] By marketplace he meant the wharfs where the steamboats docked on Market Street on both sides of the river. The ferries brought passengers, goods for stores, supplies for the industries, and daily newspapers. As a steamboat announced its arrival by blowing its whistle, it drew the bustling crowds that congregated at the riverfront to meet arrivals, read daily headlines, and socialize, the ferries being Elizabeth's connection to the outside world.[20] Along the waterfront, Bickerton declared his

16. Wiley, *Elizabeth and Her Neighbors*, 136–39.

17. *Ensign*, 5.

18. Martin and Mancini, "History of the Church," 2; Jordan, *Genealogical and Personal History*, 2:1029; Robinson, "Passing of the Torch," 13.

19. Bickerton, "Testimony, June 1903," 2.

20. Wiley, *Elizabeth and Her Neighbors*, 116. The ferries arrived at noon and dusk.

gospel message, hoping to gain new converts. As he recalled, on one occasion he held an impromptu service "beside the ferry, at a store house door," and a woman walking by stopped to hear him, "testified to the gospel," and soon received baptism.[21]

He had almost no apprehension about preaching in public. "I held these outdoor meetings and many were convinced, and several were baptized," he reported matter-of-factly. Unlike most ministers in the United States, whose salaries and reputations were derived from attracting congregants to established church buildings, Bickerton still lacked a physical church. So he walked the streets, talking directly to people as they conducted their daily lives. He received no salary, nor did he expect his converts to support his family, following the admonition of Jesus, "Freely ye have received, freely give" (Matt. 10:8). Yet he traveled. "I then went to Allegheny City," he wrote, and "had good meetings there." Next he "baptized a family, on the hills opposite Pittsburgh, and also baptized a good many at Six-Mile Ferry; and had a good many members at Pine Run." By the end of 1852, he had rebaptized his one-time Mormon congregation and attracted enough converts from the surrounding Pittsburgh area that it was beginning to look like a real church.[22]

To bring everyone together from the outlying areas, he held a church conference at his home that was blessed by a "rainbow form that stood over me at that Conference," confirmation that this was God's church. "I felt by the Power of God that I was as a rock, and if a cannon ball would strike me it would not affect me, being protected by the Power of God."[23] In his autobiography he referenced the New Testament metaphor of Peter being a rock (John 1:42), which was apropos since he too had received a commission to convert the world. "We met together and the Lord met with us," he wrote, "and we could many times sing with the poet: 'The Spirit of God like a fire is burning,

21. Bickerton, "Testimony, June 1903," 2.
22. Ibid.; Bean, Journals, 4:3–4.
23. Bickerton, 7.

The latter day glory begins to come forth, The visions and blessings of old are returning, The Angels are coming to visit the earth.'"[24]

About the same time, in September 1852, Utah apostle Orson Pratt traveled to Washington, DC, with a commission to defend polygamy. His approach was to publish a monthly newspaper entitled *The Seer*, which nevertheless incited more people than it converted. Not only was it a political miscalculation for Pratt to boast that Mormons would soon "flourish over the whole Earth," he reprimanded those who rejected polygamy. "About four-fifths of the population of the globe, believe and practice, according to their respective laws, the doctrine of a Plurality of Wives," he editorialized, and "if the popularity of a doctrine is in proportion to the numbers who believe in it, then it follows that the Plurality system is four times more popular among the inhabitants of the earth, than the one wife system." In the United States, he argued, marriage was a states' rights issue. The Constitution allowed territories and states to enact the kind of matrimonial laws that were appropriate to their region. Moreover, any Mormon who "refused to obey this command," he stated, would be "damned." At least, they could not reject the principle and retain good standing in the church. "Have any of the States or Territories a constitutional right to pass laws 'prohibiting the free exercise of the religion' which the church of the Saints conscientiously and sincerely believe to be essential to their salvation?" he asked. "No: they have no such right."[25] Perhaps this kind of rhetoric was beneficial for Pratt himself, but it was not persuasive to the public, let alone the legislators.

When news of the periodical reached Bickerton, he obtained a copy and called a meeting to discuss it, at which it was decided that it should not go without refutation. This was an opportunity to differentiate between the Utah Mormons and the Church of Jesus Christ, which adhered to the New Testament's teachings on marriage. Pratt's periodical was an affront to righteousness, Bickerton argued. He

24. Bickerton, *Ensign*, 5. The poet was Joseph Smith's scribe, William W. Phelps.
25. Orson Pratt, *The Seer*, Jan. 1853, 12–13.

countered it, in part, by relating the experience of "a Latter Day Saint that was on his way to Nawvan [Nauvoo], but was delayed on account of the river freezing and did not reach his destination," and after traveling 100 miles came to stop in front of Bickerton's home. "He did not know there was a Latter Day Saint anywhere near" but had found his way by the Holy Spirit, Bickerton wrote.[26] This was how the scattered flock would be gathered. They would be led, not by threats or political pressure, but by the Spirit.

Aside from the provocation Pratt's writings provided, Bickerton was optimistic. "The sick are often healed in our midst by following the instruction of James (5th ch.): [If there is] any sick among you let him call for the Elders of the Church, and let them pray over him anointing him with oil in the name of the Lord, and the prayer of faith shall save the sick and the Lord will raise him up." Some of the congregation had "unknowingly dr[u]nk poison and it has not hurt them," he reported. Others had been "healed of deafness, and devils have been cast out, and the power of God is made manifest amoungst us according to our faith." These developments gave the members reason to "rejoice in the everlasting gospel, in all its power and glory, by the angel of God's presence in these last days."[27]

Although the records are scant, in September 1854 at another conference in West Elizabeth, Martin Wardell received an ordination to be an elder. At the same conference, three women were baptized. By the end of the year, the church could report a membership of sixty members.[28] At a spring 1855 conference, Bickerton reported that he saw the prophecies becoming fulfilled. The US Congress had passed the Kansas–Nebraska Act opening the way for slavery in the western territories. It "will not be long," he reported. The act nullified the 1820 Missouri Compromise and the Compromise of 1850 by opening up most of the western half of the continent to popular sovereignty, allowing settlers

26. Bickerton, "Testimony, June 1903," 7.
27. Bickerton, *Ensign*, 4.
28. Martin and Mancini, "History of the Church," 7.

to vote for themselves whether they wanted to allow or prohibit slavery. The bill was created by Senator Stephen Douglas of Illinois, who wanted to see the West settled quickly, a railroad built to the Pacific. However, the bill split his party, half of the northern Democrats voting against it. Senator Charles Sumner of Massachusetts correctly summed up the passage of the bill: "Thus it puts Freedom and Slavery face to face, and bids them grapple."[29]

The new Republican Party opposed this as a matter of labor equity. Slaveholders would absorb the best lands and slaves would compete with wage-laborers, ultimately hindering the commercial potential of the region. Abraham Lincoln was an ex-Whig[30] who joined the Republicans and detested the Kansas–Nebraska bill. "Near eighty years ago we began by declaring that all men are created equal," he commented, but from then on "we have run down the other direction, that for some men to enslave others is a 'sacred right of self-government.' These principles cannot stand together."[31] On March 30, 1855, the day before Bickerton held his spring conference, Kansas elected its territorial legislature in an environment of thousands of armed antislavery and proslavery militia swarming through the region. The proslavery candidates won the most seats, making Kansas a slave territory, and before long the legislature made it illegal to speak against the institution of slavery. Bickerton's view, by contrast, was that the land should not only be free but should be given back to the Indians.

Bickerton may have looked like an abolitionist to his contemporaries as someone who advocated unlawful resistance to slaveholders. The lawful thing, the advocates of slavery argued, was to follow the Bible and US Constitution, both of which endorsed slave-holding. The Constitution counted a slave as three-fifths of a person for the sake of allocating congressional seats. In the Old Testament, there were rules

29. Walther, *Shattering of the Union*, 46.

30. The Whigs had become less relevant in the North and were failing in the South due to their lack of protection for slavery.

31. Ibid., 51.

governing a slave's behavior and treatment. King David enslaved the Canaanites; apostle Paul returned a fugitive slave to his owner, Philemon, a Christian. Even in the Northern states, many of the opponents of slavery accepted these historical precedents and considered blacks inferior to whites. Bickerton offered blacks priesthood offices, but without being an insurrectionist.[32] In Utah blacks were kept at arm's length, ostensibly based on Joseph Smith's Book of Abraham. That pseudepigraphal book identified the pharaoh of Egypt as a descendant of Noah's cursed son Ham, the Canaanites as an ethnic group that was "despised among all people," possibly implying a racial division.[33]

Bickerton's sympathy with black-skinned Africans derived from three possible reasons. The Bible and Book of Mormon called for all people to be treated fairly. "Inequality should be no more in this land, especially among this my people," King Benjamin is reported to have said in the Book of Mormon. Despite being a king, he offers his "desire" that "this land be a land of liberty, and [that] every man may enjoy his rights and privileges alike" (Mosiah 29:32). The apostle Paul himself wrote to the Galatians, "There is neither Jew nor Greek, there is neither bond nor free, there is neither male nor female: for ye are all one in Christ Jesus" (Gal. 3:28). The second reason may have been because he could imagine himself and fellow mine workers competing poorly against slave labor. "The difference between us," said US Senator James Henry Hammond of South Carolina in his famous 1858 "Cotton is King" speech,

> is that our slaves are hired for life and well compensated; there is no starvation, no begging, no want of employment among our people, and not too much employment either. Yours are hired by the day, not cared for, and scantily compensated, which may be proved in the most painful manner, at any hour, in any street in any of your large towns. Why, you

32. "Redstone Valley Branch," 8–9; William Bickerton, "Saints vs. Mormons," *St. John Weekly News*, June 28, 1889; Watson, "Church of Jesus Christ (Headquartered in Monongahela)," 204.

33. Bushman, *Rough Stone Rolling*, 288. According to the book of Genesis, Ham had a son named Canaan, who became the father of the Canaanites, see Genesis 9:18–27.

> meet more beggars in one day, in any single street of the city of New York, than you would meet in a lifetime in the whole South.[34]

Although biased, the senator's viewpoint was partly true. In most lower-class American households, fathers, mothers, and children all worked. If a laborer fell ill or was maimed, they generally lost their employment. People employed to do identical work were paid differently: adults more than children, men more than women, whites more than free blacks, skilled more than unskilled, native-born more than foreign-born, and Protestants more than Catholics or Jews. Bickerton, however, would have seen the reality of slavery in Virginia and the contrast between the decrepit slave quarters there, compared to the better living conditions for Africans in Pennsylvania, a free state. In any case, the fact that the nation was being torn apart was evidence to Bickerton that God was displeased with slavery, even though topics like these were not without controversy in his own denomination. Even polygamy was disputed despite Bickerton's strong opposition to it.

In 1855 some of his congregants decided they preferred Brigham Young's theology. A council meeting was called and it was determined that

> as some individuals ha[ve] been inclining to the people of Salt Lake and their doctrine of Polygamy and other false and abominable doctrines, we have felt it our duty while sitting in Counsil before the Lord, that all who holds such doctrines, after due examination before witnesses, shall be cut off from the Church of Jesus Christ of Latter Day Saints, as the spirit may direct, and shall have no fellowship with the Saints.[35]

Some of those who had been familiar with the Utah church must have found it difficult to give up the idea of a society in heaven that paralleled the order on earth. They found Bickerton's more traditional Christian doctrine less satisfying than the Utah church's doctrines of family salvation and racial purity.

---

34. "Speech of Hon. J. H. Hammond, of South Carolina, in the Senate, March 4, 1858," *Congressional Globe*, 35th Congress, 1st session, appendix, 70–71.

35. Martin and Mancini, "History of the Church," 6. Present at the hearing were Thomas Bickerton, William Bickerton, Charles Brown, and Jacob Stranger.

During the same year, another member of the Bickerton denomination, Charles Brown, separated from the church and began persuading people to join him in Bissell, Pennsylvania—a shock to Bickerton, whose relationship with Brown had been quite close. For nearly a decade, they had worked and preached together. At a special conference, three men—Thomas Bickerton, John Robinson, and William Thews—were asked to meet with Brown and determine the reason. "After trying somewhat to justify himself," the trio reported, "he said he would submit himself into the hands of the Elders, to do what they felt to do by the Spirit, if it was to be baptized again." Brown's resolve softened, and he was rebaptized on April 23. Eventually he was reinstated as an elder.[36]

Brown's decision to rejoin Bickerton was partly influenced by Bickerton's healing of "a woman who had been confined to her bed for five years." As Bickerton summarized the event, he and a few other elders "carried her down to Peters Creek in her bed, and it took four of us to baptize her, and when we brought her up out of the water the blood flowed from her mouth. We carried her home, confirmed her a member of the Church and attended the ordinance on her, and she was healed sound and well. She also bore children afterwards." Brown thought the "credit for healing her" belonged to Bickerton and the other men of the congregation.[37]

It had been four years since Bickerton had cut his ties with Brigham Young, and in that time he had managed to keep his congregation together without the support of other ecclesiastical leaders. He had followed his heart and mind and promptings of the Holy Spirit as far as he could, preaching in the streets and traveling miles to baptize new converts. The dire circumstances he was returned to may have been a blessing in that, with limited education and leadership experience, he underwent an apprenticeship in church leadership. People disagreed with him, congregants disavowed their allegiance, friends became distant, and, step by step, he learned how to deal with these kinds of

36. Martin and Mancini, 8.
37. Bickerton, "Testimony, June 1903," 8.

developments. The way forward, he had learned, was to rely on the scriptures and let people feel the Holy Spirit themselves so they could judge whether they were on the right path or not. In the end, he was learning right along with them.

FIVE

REVIVAL

1856–58

"Try me and prove me, and see if I will not open unto you the windows of Heaven and pour you out a blessing so that there shall not be room enough to contain it."

—revelation, William Bacon, October 7, 1857

After dealing with two serious challenges to his leadership in 1855, Bickerton still had a pressing concern. Some of the members had become apathetic and treated the gospel as a Sunday-only matter, without committing fully to the guidance of the Holy Spirit as true disciples. Some of them had indulged in worldly pleasures or succumbed to sectarian arguments. It was clear that a spiritual revival was needed.

When Bickerton addressed a church conference on July 4, 1856, on the anniversary of America's independence, he departed from the usual speech about political freedom and, as Thomas Redpath recorded in the minutes, spoke for two hours on relying on whatever "the Holy Spirit might dictate and direct." The church had a "special theology" that was as much the result of revelation as biblical exegesis. The problem with the Bible, we can imagine him explaining, was that it had not been properly transmitted through history, so that the pure teachings of Jesus had become corrupted.[1] The ancient church had fallen into apostasy, the Book of Mormon advocated, and "many plain

1. Martin and Mancini, "History of the Church," 9.

and precious things" had been lost "from the book ... of the Lamb of God," and because of that many had "stumble[d]" (1 Ne. 13:28–29).

Protestants of the day would have agreed that the Roman Catholic Church had altered some of the Bible's foundational principles involving the mode of baptism, the eucharist, and the ecclesiastical structure of the church. The apostle Paul had warned the Saints "that in the latter times, some shall depart from the faith, giving heed to seducing spirits and doctrines of devils; speaking lies in hypocrisy; having their conscience seared with a hot iron; forbidding to marry, and commanding to abstain from meats which God hath created to be received with thanksgiving of them which believe and know the truth" (1 Tim. 4:1–3). Protestants pointed to celibacy, the pope's request that people abstain from eating meat on days of penance, and the sale of indulgences for the remission of sins as fulfillment of Paul's prophecy.[2]

Like the Mormons, Bickerton saw the Reformation as God's precursor to Joseph Smith's full restoration of the gospel. Even with all its zeal, the Reformation had not retrieved the complete original gospel message, he believed. "Because of the greatness of their stumbling block," the Book of Mormon continued, "they have built up many churches; nevertheless, they put down the power and miracles of God, and preach up unto themselves their own wisdom and their own learning, that they may get gain and grind upon the face of the poor" (2 Ne. 26:20). However, as God told Nephi, "I will be merciful unto the Gentiles in that day, insomuch that I will bring forth unto them, in mine own power, much of my gospel, which shall be plain and precious, saith the Lamb" (1 Ne. 13:34).

The purpose of the Book of Mormon was to restore the "plain and precious" doctrines that were missing from the Bible, to clear up any ambiguity within the Bible. The Book of Mormon spoke in greater clarity about baptism, the Holy Ghost, the state of the soul after death, administration of communion, the gathering of Israel, and church organization and governance. It did not take long, after the Book of

2. Bickerton, *Ensign*, 2.

Mormon was published, for men to distort the simplicity of the gospel once more, Bickerton perceived, so that Joseph Smith, Sidney Rigdon, and Brigham Young preached contrasting interpretations. That is why the prophetic mantle had fallen to Bickerton.

The conference was a success. It included one baptism. Three men, George Rain, George Swards, and James Wagoner, were ordained elders. The Spirit was so powerful, according to Thomas Redpath, that everyone's heart was filled with "joy and gladness, as a precious fortaste of a more precious future, when [God] shall pour out His spirit upon all flesh, when He shall reign Jehovah King over all the Earth."[3] Redpath thought the conference had demonstrated what an Old Testament prophet predicted about the latter days, when God would pour out His Spirit "upon all flesh; and your sons and your daughters shall prophesy, your old men shall dream dreams, your young men shall see visions" (Joel 2:28). Bickerton felt that the revival he had longed for had been launched.

Two days later, on Sunday July 6, there were five more baptisms. In another two days, two more individuals testified after their baptisms to their "heartfelt satisfaction" and thankfulness "to the giver of all good, for His kindly care, for His everlasting unvarying love." At that service Hannah Rain said she felt the "soft balmy soul-absorbing influence" of the Spirit, and Redpath was so overcome, he added his own prayer in the minutes. "O Lord, My God, Thou King of Saints," he wrote, "prepare our Hearts to make the room, that thou mayest use us for thy honor in saving and reconciling many souls to thee." The testimonies and prayer captured the feeling Bickerton had hoped to convey to his converts, that they would realize the time had come to know the love of the Savior.[4]

Bickerton understood the limits of his church, considering that most of the members were working-class people with little education. He himself had no formal training. However, he believed his congregation had unmatched zeal that would carry them through. The more

3. Martin and Mancini, "History of the Church," 9.
4. Ibid., 9–10.

devout members considered themselves to be like the original apostles whom the elite had wanted to prevent from spreading Christianity throughout the world. The following Sunday, July 13, Redpath was so impressed with the sermon Bickerton delivered, he recorded it in its entirety, it being one of the few early sermons that was transcribed. Redpath prefaced the transcription by noting that "Brother William Bickerton came filled with the spirit of God. Opened the meeting and showed the infinatly rich provision made for the Saints, and that all things are, and shall work together, both for their present and future, everlasting good." Bickerton spoke of the light of the gospel, which he said the medieval clergy had all but extinguished, "yet Our Father in his infinite goodness, wisdom, and love, had again lighted up our souls with the true light, not so much in books, as with the spirit, on and in our hearts, giving us each the needful assurance with in our selves that what we teach is veritably true, is the will of our Father, and that we are building up the Kingdom of God with the materials." The Spirit, Bickerton proclaimed, "is all sufficient for instruction, reproof, [and] correction," and to provide "all that is needful … to go out to meet with the great Bridegroom." He added that "error must fall" in the presence of truth.[5]

It appeared to the congregation that God's words to the prophet Isaiah had come to pass: "Behold, I will proceed to do a marvellous work among this people, even a marvellous work and a wonder: for the wisdom of their wise men shall perish, and the understanding of their prudent men shall be hid" (29:14). While meditating on this during the following months, Bickerton might have visualized Jesus beckoning a child and telling his disciples that "whosoever therefore shall humble himself as this little child, the same is greatest in the kingdom of heaven" (Matt. 18:4). Bickerton might have had children on his mind, since Dorothy had recently given birth,[6] and he began

5. Ibid., 10.

6. Dorothy gave birth to a new daughter, Angeline Ann, earlier in the year. See US Census, 1860.

wondering whether they should be allowed to partake of the Lord's supper. When he prayed about it, "the word of the Lord came upon me and did manifest, by His Holy Spirit, that it was His will that children have the sacrement administered to them." This was not expected at the time. In fact, Bickerton hesitated, and Jesus's voice came to him, saying, "If my word offend, they will be offended by my presence, such can never enter into my rest." He concluded that if his congregants saw innocent children partake of the sacrament, it would persuade them to be more humble themselves, and in turn the Lord would find pleasure in the church and bestow more of his blessings on it.

He called a council meeting on October 22, 1856, to consider the revelation. As the elders discussed it, one of them suddenly said, "The Lord He is God, The Lord He is God, The Lord He is God and not Man, that He should repent, nor the Son of Man that He should lie, therefore, saith the Lord, Ye are accepted before me as a Church, for ye are not those that turn unto Satan, nor those that follow the wages of Balaam." The message was taken to be a sign of approval, so the church began including children in the Lord's Supper. Interestingly, this would later be discontinued when they decided that if children did not need baptism, being without sin, they could not renew their covenant or go through repentance to prepare to partake of the sacrament.[7]

Many people, on hearing Bickerton and his followers talk about religion, were unimpressed, especially when the congregation lapsed into biblical language and spoke in tongues. On occasion, however, the same discourse could affect someone deeply, as something they had been longing for. That was the case of William Cadman, an Englishman who arrived in the United States in the fall of 1856 and was staying at a West Elizabeth tavern with friends when he overheard a conversation. Specifically, it was the bartender defending religious

7. Martin and Mancini, "History of the Church," 2–3, 94. During the time the sacrament was offered to children, those who had reached an undefined "age of accountability" were no longer allowed to participate without being baptized. Children were considered members of the church until they reached this age. Joseph Smith defined the age of accountability as eight (D&C 68:27).

points against the ripostes of rude customers. "Every point that the man raised … he proved by Scripture," wrote Cadman, who found this "astonishing." The drinkers "answered him only with laughter and ridicule and frequent expressions of the word Mormonism." When the bar closed, Cadman asked the tender "what in the world" he was doing "in a barroom dishing out liquor" with his grasp of scripture, and apparently having found his spiritual home in a church whose doctrine he considered worth defending. The man replied that his membership with the Bickerton church had been revoked because he had committed a serious sin, but he still believed the tenets. Cadman asked where he could find this church.

A few days later, "I was wonderfully affected whilst" at the worship service, he wrote, "more than I ever had been in any meeting before in my life." The feeling surprised him. After leaving, he wondered about this and decided his emotions had deceived him. It had been a long time since he had attended a church service, he concluded, so the feeling must have sneaked up on him. On the other hand, he had found the people to his liking and decided to continue visiting the services later on when he and his family moved to West Elizabeth. As a young man, Cadman had been suspicious of ministers who could not answer his theological questions and were more pastoral than intellectual. True religion, he thought, had disappeared. He expected Bickerton's church to similarly disappoint; but instead, he found himself spending hours "compar[ing] their teachings with the Scriptures as earnestly and seriously as I was able" in order to prove them wrong, but was unable to.

The confidence of Bickerton's members that they could receive direct revelation from God was one thing that greatly puzzled Cadman. "They must be wrong or else the whole religious wor[l]d was wrong," he thought. When the topic of the Book of Mormon came up, and he heard about the gold plates, angels, and prophets, he wondered how this could be real. "The religious world, as far as I understood, upheld that there would be no revelation from God to man later than the Bible." It was shocking to hear people refer to a modern book with the same reverence they afforded the Bible. If it were from God, then he had been in error his whole life.

"I remember one night I was so earnest" in trying to disprove the promise of personal revelation, he stayed up "reading the Bible all night" and was "forced to conclude that it teaches no such thing"—that there was no condemnation of God speaking directly to average individuals. Other teachings appeared to be equally unbiblical, so he would "express myself to that affect, but was almost always worsted." For a while he thought it was his lack of training that was the problem, that divinity graduates must be able to answer these people in West Elizabeth and "prove them wrong," even while his confidence in that proposition waned.

His brash, competitive personality got him into arguments, as happened one day on a steamboat when he overheard a minister talking and could not help joining in the conversation "for the purpose of introducing some of these points of Mormon doctrine that I had been trying to disprove and could not." He took "the Mormons side of each of these questions," and to his surprise he found the minister was confounded. The trained theologian was "as helpless in opposing me on these points of Mormon doctrine as I was in opposing them." This "amused me considerably." Cadman was becoming converted. He would soon become convinced that there was not a "minister on earth that can prove" the Mormon gospel wrong.[8]

He came to see God's guiding hand in his own life as the very reason he had left England, for instance, and arrived at the doorstep of the Bickerton group. He and his wife, Elizabeth, had emigrated from Liverpool as newlyweds when he was twenty-two and she was twenty. At first they boarded a ship and disembarked because they were overcome by a sense of panic. A few days later they tried again and found a ship to their liking. At the end of a thirty-two-day trip on calm water the entire way, they were caught in a storm just off the coast that lasted three days and destroyed the vessel's main mast. The ship dropped

8. Cadman, *Faith and Doctrines*, 2:10–12.

anchor the third night of the storm around midnight. The next morning a vessel appeared next to theirs selling supplies. Cadman purchased a newspaper and learned that the first ship they had boarded in Liverpool had sunk in the storm and there were no survivors. He believed his fear of boarding that ship had been "providential," saying that "no person could make me believe the contrary." As often happens in such situations, he wondered why God spared him and his wife and not the passengers of the other ship.

They next boarded a train and traveled over 700 miles to Alliance, Ohio, where they waited a few hours to transfer to Pittsburgh. The night was cold, they were exhausted from the trip. He lay down on a bench and fell asleep, but was awakened by his wife's screams when the heating stove next to them fell over. He grabbed his wife with one hand and ran into another room, trying with his other hand to keep their luggage "from getting afire." When he returned to investigate the cause of this mishap, he found to his horror that the stove had toppled because a railroad car had crashed into the waiting room. It was apparent that he and his wife were the only ones who were not seriously injured or killed. Being spared twice caused him and his wife to reflect that they were "under the special care of the Almighty and [had been] preserved marvelously both by sea and by land."[9]

Bickerton asked his members to share such convictions with other Christians who had not felt the influence of the Holy Spirit. At the April 1857 conference, he suggested that they also share such experiences with each other, that "if all those who had been healed by the laying on of hands would bear their testimonies to what the Lord had done for them, it might have a good effect." These experiences were what made them different from "all other people because we stand for the faith and promises of the Gospel." One could read the scriptures for one's own edification, but it was important to go out into the world and experience miracles like in the Bible and share these experiences with others.

9. Ibid., 9–10.

Charles Marks rose to his feet and testified that both he and his daughter had been healed. He became didactic and suggested that if the men who chewed, smoked, and sniffed tobacco refrained from doing such "detestable things," God would heal them. "The Lord require[s] us to cleanse ourselves from all filthiness of the flesh," he reminded them.[10]

Bickerton organized another conference in July to discuss their intended missionary outreach. The men who would be sent out needed first to sanctify themselves, much like the member who opposed tobacco had said, because "the Gospel comes not by word only, but by power and the Holy Ghost." They continued to bear testimony of spiritual events. Charles Cowan said he was converted after hearing only one sermon. A compelling testimony came from a woman known as Sister Harniham, who converted in 1832 in Kirtland, Ohio. When she was confirmed, she said, she was promised she would "live to see Zion flourish." Well, she said, she had seen that happen in West Elizabeth; she had experienced visions, healings, and the gift of tongues, and the promise given to her twenty-five years ago had been fulfilled.[11]

If Bickerton was satisfied that the spiritual seeds he had planted in early 1857 had begun to sprout, the harvest would come the next October at another church conference. Although there was one excommunication, the rest of the meeting went smoothly. Thomas Bickerton commented on the "extraordinary degree of Peace" he felt during the meeting, adding that while he and Charles Brown were walking home he felt so energized by the Spirit that he wanted the church to schedule another service for the following day. Turning in the direction of William Bacon's home, Thomas and Charles pitched the idea without success. They tried the same with William Bickerton, with the same result. Ironically, the next morning everyone encountered either obstacles in getting to work or when they arrived at the mines they had to turn around because of some technical difficulty.

10. Martin and Mancini, "History of the Church," 11.
11. Ibid., 12.

Bickerton decided the two brethren must have received a premonition about the need to hold another service.

At 10 a.m. a few people arrived and enjoyed a stimulating church meeting, so much so that another service was announced for that afternoon. It went so well that two people requested baptism, and more worshipers continued to arrive through the late afternoon and into the evening, prompting the scheduling of yet another service three days later on Tuesday, October 6. When Bickerton's wife fell ill and was disappointed at having to miss the meeting, being "racked in pain," the elders poured a little oil on her head, laid their hands on her, and asked God to take away the pain. Immediately she was healed.[12]

On Wednesday the members had a rare experience when William Bickerton stood up and declared the word of the Lord. "I accept of you this day as my Church," he said, referring to the church in the ancient city of Philadelphia (now Alasehir, about 100 miles east of Izmir, Turkey), recorded by the apostle John in Revelation 3:7–13. "I know thy works," he continued, "for thou hast a little strength, and has[t] kept my word, and has[t] not denied my name." The next evening the members gathered yet another time, and once more Bickerton spoke in a first-person voice for the Savior, saying: "The Lord I am God, the Lord I am God, therefore you are of them that will not turn aside, therefore will I bless you." To that, William Bacon added, "Try me and prove me, and see if I will not open unto you the windows of Heaven and pour you out a blessing so that there shall not be room enough to contain it" (Mal. 3:10). The congregation must have marveled at this revelatory repartee.[13]

There would be one more Sunday service to conclude the fall conference, at which this time Bickerton spoke in tongues and two women, Elizabeth Carney and Charlotte Hibbs, offered as the interpretation, "Fear not my little flock for it is your Fathers good pleasure to give you the kingdom." When Dorothy Bickerton heard this, she testified that "the spirit ran through her like lightning." George Rain

12. Ibid., 13–16.

13. "Book of Record," 1–2.

was equally convinced, with "as clear a knowledge of it being the Word of the Lord as he ha[d] of his own existence." Sister Hambelton said she would rather die than doubt it.[14] One man reported a vision of "the road … the saints were traveling on, the foot of which … was in the waters, and ascended gradually up to Heaven." It was a "straight and narrow" road, he said, and "on each side … was all manner of beautiful flowers to tempt the saints to pluck them." Yet the road was so firm "that many cannon balls that were fired at the road, could not even as much as make a mark upon it."[15] The six-day conference ended with everyone in awe.

Sometime in 1857 a Mormon elder, Samuel A. Woolley, arrived to impart the news that Bickerton had been excommunicated from the Utah church. Bickerton said it meant nothing to him, that he had received a higher calling.[16] His own church was ready to expand, he believed. Two new branches opened in 1858 in Allegheny, Pennsylvania, and Wheeling, Virginia, and the membership was growing every year. For Bickerton, this was proof enough that God had ordained his ministry. In April 1858, he proudly declared, "God is amoungst us and blesses us and especially to prepare a people for his second coming of the Messiah, and we are under the renewed covenant and we are thankful that God is with us indeed." He was convinced his church could save the country, and the world, from total disaster.[17]

They could avert the bulk of prophesied calamities, he believed, having been given the keys of peace and prosperity. The passage from the Book of Revelation mentioned the "Key of David" and city of peace, the New Jerusalem. "I have set before thee an open door, and no man can shut it," the passage read (Rev. 3:8–12).[18] When overcome by the Spirit once more in July 1858, Bickerton uttered in a prophetic

14. Martin and Mancini, "History of the Church," 14, 16.

15. Bickerton, *Ensign*, 6–7.

16. Eli Kendall, "The Other Side," *St. John Weekly News*, July 19, 1889.

17. Martin and Mancini, "History of the Church," 17; Cadman, *History of the Church of Jesus Christ*, 1:28.

18. "Book of Record," 1–2;

voice, "For unto you is given the keys of this last Ministry and the last warning voice to the world, therefore be faithful to the end of your calling." Peace was an unexpected goal to strive for in the midst of the sectional conflict in the United States that was becoming more heated than ever, the nation moving ever closer to civil war. Seemingly unconcerned, the instructions to the members of Bickerton's church were to "feed the flock of God over which I have made you overseers."[19] Abraham Lincoln, having just accepted the Republican Party's endorsement for the US Senate campaign, presaged the future in the rousing speech he gave in which he famously predicted that "a house divided against itself cannot stand. I believe this government cannot endure, permanently half slave and half free."[20]

Lincoln's speech and Bickerton's prophecy both conveyed a sense of urgency, although with different priorities. In West Elizabeth, the concern was to expand the radius of influence of the church. At the October conference, a traveling quorum of five elders had been formed, commissioning William Bacon, William Bickerton, Charles Brown, James Wagoner, and Webster Wagoner to spread the restored gospel to neighboring communities. The members voiced a desire to build a church headquarters. In praying about it, James Wagoner prophesied, "Verily, Verily, thus saith the Lord, go ye forth and build me an house and dedicate it unto me and I will fill it with my glory."[21] A man known as Brother Lloyd said he had previously received confirmation that Green Oak (Greenock), seven miles east of West Elizabeth, was where the headquarters would be.[22] In a vision he had received, he saw a "light come to Green Oak" and "spread from there" in all directions. At that, two men stood with William Bickerton and sang in tongues about the "Trump of Zion," and Bickerton prophesied that the meeting house and headquarters would be built and the missionaries would

19. Martin and Mancini, "History of the Church," 17.
20. McPherson, *Battle Cry of Freedom*, 179.
21. "Book of Record," 3.
22. At the previous conference a new branch in Green Oak was authorized.

find success. Speaking for the Lord, he said "the gates of Hell shall shake before you. … I will bless you, because of your love for one another and because you have set your love upon me."[23]

Once again revealing his expectation to see the Millennium, Bickerton spoke on October 7, 1858, to state the church's beliefs. "We believe in the gathering of Israel, and a thorough renovation of the Earth," he said. "We believe that Christ will come soon in the clouds of Heaven." Revelation and preaching with a warning voice were central to the church. A visitor in the congregation, Mel McLac'lin, responded by asking to become a member.[24]

As God kept talking to Bickerton and others, a new question arose regarding what should be done with the revelations. One night a member saw a book of "great value" in a dream, the book containing "the revelations and other gifts received by us." A church secretary predicted that their "children, and those that shall arise after us," would thank them for preserving the word of God, adding that "this is the mind of the Lord that we keep a record of these things." By doing so, the members would not only demonstrate that they had been "accepted by the Almighty," but that "where the Smiths, Joseph and Hyrum, fell," they would "carry forwards the Kingdom and this Church—i[n] a continuation of the same foundation."[25]

The church was maturing. "Truly the set time to favor Zion was

23. Martin and Mancini, "History of the Church," 19. The two men were Charles Brown and Charles Cowan.

24. Ibid., 20.

25. Ibid. This book of revelations was supposed to serve the Church of Jesus Christ in a similar way the Doctrine and Covenants served the Mormon Church. For Brigham Young's Latter-day Saints, the Doctrine and Covenants was an open scriptural canon that could document the Lord's words over time. The text therefore, was a powerful symbol of prophetic power the Mormons used to prove their church's spiritual authority. Bickerton did not agree with all the revelations recorded in the Doctrine and Covenants, sometimes referencing certain revelations of Joseph Smith, but not accepting the entire book. Yet despite his apprehension, he and his followers understood why the text had such a powerful influence on the Mormons. The Church of Jesus Christ hoped to pick up where Smith and the patriarchs of the early Restoration had allegedly failed, with this new book of revelations helping to serve that purpose.

come," the secretary enthused.[26] The experiences of new converts such as William Cadman indicated that God had a special purpose for the membership. A church headquarters was planned. Missionaries were traveling as far as they could. At home, Bickerton's wife, Dorothy, gave birth to another daughter, Josephine, in 1858, named after the daughter who had died in 1852. The revival was a success, and everything seemed to be looking good.[27] However, the country was headed in another direction. In three years the Civil War would begin. Bickerton would point out that the war was a fulfillment of Joseph Smith's 1832 revelation, and therefore an indication that the other foretold events were about to follow. On the positive side, Bickerton had been tried and proven strong enough to lead the church through any manner of trying times.

26. Ibid., 14.
27. Pilgrim, "Descendants of Thomas Bickerton," 2, 14.

SIX

PROPHET AND SEER

1859–61

"I am the God of Abraham, Isaac, and Jacob, I sent forth my servant Joseph [Smith], with a message of glad tidings to this generation; Him have they slain, saith the Lord; my people they have persecuted, scattered, and driven out, yet once again, I have raised up another like unto Joseph, to lead forth my people; him shall ye hear in all things."

—revelation, Webster Wagoner, Dec. 11, 1859

From 1859 to 1861, Americans watched the final events unfold that would trigger Southern secession. They understood that war was increasingly inevitable. The North had developed armaments that would make the conflict catastrophic. In the South, aside from reliance on cotton as the main cash crop and the plantation culture surrounding it, Southerners worried about their constitutional right to own slaves, their state sovereignty being threatened.

William Bickerton looked beyond the contentiousness to the prophecies in the Book of Mormon promising that in the day of "vengeance and fury," Christ would establish his church in a city of refuge, the New Jerusalem.[1] The prophet felt his commission from God was to be in place to assist in building Zion, seeing himself in the very role the ancient biblical prophets had foretold. If Utah Mormons considered their leader to be a latter-day Moses, then Bickerton

1. 3 Ne. 21:21–23.

was Joshua, succeeding where Moses failed, leading his people to the promised land.

At the January 1859 conference, other biblical parallels were mentioned. Bickerton addressed the congregation to tell them that "we are now acting the part of John the Baptist, to prepare a people for, and a way for, the second coming of Christ, and here we stand, waiting for the glorious appearing of the Son of God."[2] Once again the message would be the same as preached by Jesus's cousin, John: "Repent … for the kingdom of heaven is at hand" (Matt. 3:2). There was significance in other scriptural passages, as well, such as where John the Revelator is given a book by an angel who says, "Take it, and eat it up; and it shall make thy belly bitter, but it shall be in thy mouth sweet as honey" (Rev. 10:9). To Bickerton, this probably addressed how comforting the enlightenment of revelation was, but how depressing it was to realize how dark the future looked. "The people believe anything," he complained. "They listen to anything, [other] than the voice of inspiration in our day and generation. But the time now is, that God does speak to us," he said, "for there is but one Holy Spirit, and you cannot adulterate it."[3]

Ministers were chosen in Bickerton's denomination based on their spiritual gifts, as was Mel McLac'lin after he spoke in tongues at the January 1859 conference. His message was interpreted to mean that he had a special calling. It was God's will, James Wagoner declared, that McLac'lin be ordained an elder. There was "never … clearer evidence," according to the secretary. Nor could there be clearer evidence of the decentralized administration in the church, which would pose a problem going forward. The ministers meeting together the next day concluded that God had indeed called McLac'lin to be an elder, and there was nothing for them to do short of ordaining him.

At the next conference held in April, the elders resisted Bickerton's intent to see the word preached throughout the entire world. When Charles Cowan arose and spoke in tongues, Bickerton took the

2. Martin and Mancini, "History of the Church," 21.

3. Ibid.

opportunity to emphasize the necessity of their outreach to the world, interpreting the message as this:

> Verily, verily, thus saith the Lord, I will not accept of this conference because of the coldness and carelessness of some of you, O ye Elders, and shall I bless you? and ye so indifferent? Nay, verily, nay, But verily, thus saith the Lord, oh ye Elders, say no more that ye have obstacles in the way, say no more that ye have hinderences in the way. For I have commanded you to go forth, and I will sweep away those obstacles, and I will sweep away those stumbling blocks, Amen.[4]

Surprisingly, the elders accepted the rebuke and made an about-face. They began looking into more specific ways to alter their course to be more receptive to God's word. Four people attending the meeting as outsiders were so impressed by the sense of God's presence in the room that they asked for baptism the next day. In a conference session held three months later on July 4, 1859, Bickerton arose and channeled God's voice to say, "Verily, verily, thus saith the Lord, ... my peace shall rest upon you, and ye shall be blessed, for ye shall be led forth by my Spirit in ways of truth and holiness." To reap this reward, the men would have to go out into the streets and preach repentance. Three men spoke in tongues the next day to confirm this message. "Cleanse my church from iniquity and I will bless you," God said through the interpretation.

Taking the message literally to mean that before they went out into the world, they needed to purify the church itself, they began compiling a comprehensive list of members in each branch and making notes about their activity and degree of faithfulness in such areas as attendance. Those who were passive in their devotion or had committed serious sins were to be stricken from the rolls. We can see in this that the church members considered their salvation to be a collective endeavor, the individual's duty being that of following the decisions arrived together. In addition, they were expected to help each other

4. "Book of Record," 4.

by rebuking disobedience and keeping the congregation pure, by removing those who were unworthy of membership. By judging each member, it helped others from falling into idleness or sin, and thereby the whole church benefitted. In one instance when Charles Cowan was overcome by the Spirit, the Lord instructed the elders to first find out why members were being negligent, "then if they will not do their duties, cut them off, and I will bless you, and ye shall be blessed and multiplied, Amen."[5] Eventually the church would determine that a periodic review of individual worthiness was not the best approach to personal righteousness. Instead, it tended toward pharisaical divisions. For the time being, it was assumed that discipline was the best way to keep everyone on the right path.

It is true that their lives became more focused by this kind of single-mindedness, every exertion being made in the direction of personal perfection. Their intent was to be pure enough to survive the societal destruction that was assumed to be imminent. First they looked inward to cleanse themselves, before they attempted to put the nation in order, or to gather the righteous from within the surrounding society. If they were going to be an example to the world, they needed to be perfected through unity, through unequivocal leadership and the imposition of harmony. This is what Charles Brown perceived on July 5 when he declared that God wanted Bickerton to be formally ordained head of the church. Immediately several men seconded the motion, saying "the time was come for the setting in order of the Church" and that "William Bickerton was called of God a Prophet and Seer."[6]

One of the members, William Bacon, channeled the voice of Christ to declare, "Ye shall not have it to be said unto you where is your prophet, or that you have no prophet; For this day, I set him forth before you, and he shall no longer be weak, and leave the church weak and out of Order; For, thus saith the Lord, be it known unto you my people, that from this day forth you shall look unto him as your leader, Amen."

5. Ibid., 5; Martin and Mancini, "History of the Church," 22–23.
6. Martin and Mancini, 23.

And that was that, except for Bacon's clarification "that although it was only now that he [Bickerton] is set forth by the Church, yet, he had the gift of Prophesy since his first ordination." Even in the middle of that thought, Bacon was suddenly interrupted by the Lord speaking through him saying "that ye must acknowledge his [Bickerton's] Authority[,] and those that will not do so will lose the Spirit, Amen."[7]

It is interesting that with so many men speaking the mind of God, Bickerton's gift of prophecy was evidence of his calling, not that his position was a temporary necessity. With their lack of education and wealth, perhaps Bickerton was seen as one among equals or a fulfillment of God's word to Peter in the New Testament (Acts 2:17) that "in the last days, saith God, I will pour out of my Spirit upon all flesh: and your sons and your daughters shall prophesy, and your young men shall see visions, and your old men shall dream dreams." In any case, several men confirmed God's voice to them calling Bickerton as the prophet. What it meant for the men to say by revelation that Bickerton was a prophet may have had to do partly with Bickerton's track record. The evidence is that he was not considered infallible. It may have been a vote of confidence that the Holy Spirit would continue to show him the right direction for the church.

In keeping with other ordinations, Bickerton's feet were washed (not his entire body, as Rigdon would have done) and his head anointed with oil. Then the elders surrounded him, laid their hands on his head, and uttered a prayer, at which the Spirit fell upon them and Bickerton and Charles Brown began speaking in tongues as confirmation that God was "seal[ing] the office upon him," the minutes read.

As someone holding the prophetic office, Bickerton's calling, somewhat distinct from that of the others in the congregation, was to see the future. He had other roles, as well. He was called a seer, with a more specific meaning related to the uncovering of hidden mysteries from the past. He was also thought to be able to perceive God's mind and will for the present. In the Bible, the distinction between prophets and

7. "Book of Record," 6; Martin and Mancini, "History of the Church," 24.

seers was that seers observed and perceived the meaning of prophecies. Sometimes the prophets, speaking under the influence of the Holy Spirit, were unaware of what they were saying or what the meaning was.[8] In the Book of Mormon, this is even more clear. A seer is someone who translates ancient records and "can know of things which are past, and also of things which are to come, and by them shall all things be revealed, or, rather, shall secret things be made manifest, and hidden things shall come to light, and things which are not known shall be made known by them, and also things shall be made known by them which otherwise could not be known" (Mosiah 8:17).

The seers in the Book of Mormon were those who translated ancient texts through devices called the "interpreters," or what Joseph Smith called the Urim and Thummim. Smith had in mind two stones that in the Bible priests used in some manner similar to casting lots to ask questions of God.[9] The angel Moroni told Joseph Smith that "the possession and use of these stones were what constituted 'seers' in ancient or former times."[10] David, for instance, fought the Amalekites and inquired of the Urim and Thummim whether he would "overtake them?" The Urim and Thummim responded, "Pursue: for thou shalt surely overtake them, and without fail recover all" (1 Sam. 30:8). The stones are first mentioned in the second book of the Old Testament, but without mentioning their origin. It is explained in the Book of Mormon by connecting seer stones to the confusion of languages at the Tower of Babel. The Book of Mormon tells that, before sending a man named the "brother of Jared" and his family and friends to the New World in eight ships, Christ appears and gives them two stones, saying, "Wherefore I will cause in my own due time that these stones shall magnify to the eyes of men these things which ye shall write" (Ether 3:23–24). Later in the Book of Mormon, these stones are used by a Nephite king

---

8. See 2 Kings 17:13. The Hebrew words translated as seer (*ra'ah, chazah, choseh*) mean to see, gaze at, or envision.

9. Exod. 28:30; Lev. 16:8; Josh. 18:6–10; 1 Sam. 14:42; 30:8; 1 Chron. 24:31; 25:8; 26:13–14.

10. Recounted in Brodie, *No Man Knows My History*, 39–40.

to translate the records of Jared's people years after their disappearance; the stones are then placed with the Nephite records by one Moroni, in order to be retrieved later by Joseph Smith. Portions of the plates were left untranslated, according to Joseph Smith, including a revelation to the brother of Jared covering the entire history of the world—past, present, and future—including things God did not want to have disclosed. When he had finished the Book of Mormon transcription, Smith gave the plates and interpreters back to the angel.

Like Joseph Smith and Sidney Rigdon before him, Bickerton looked to the day when the angel would bring back the plates, along with the Urim and Thummim. All three men expected to see the return of Jesus in their day, and each one assumed the sealed portion of the plates would be translated prior to the Second Coming. It would, among other things, solidify the status of the translator in helping prepare the way for the Millennium. Calling Bickerton a seer intensified the anticipation that he would be involved with additional ancient texts and that his transcriptions would unlock the history of the world, making plain the scriptural passages that had baffled theologians for centuries.[11]

In the autumn of 1859, the faithful of Bickerton's denomination gathered at their new building in Green Oak, Pennsylvania, to dedicate it as their branch meeting house and as the churchwide headquarters. A year previous they had been told by James Wagoner what to expect at the dedication, Wagoner prophesying that it would be

---

11. Joseph Smith was promised knowledge "that has not been revealed since the world was until now; Which our forefathers have awaited with anxious expectation to be revealed in the last times, which their minds were pointed to by the angels, as held in reserve for the fulness of their glory; A time to come in the which nothing shall be withheld" (D&C 121:26–32). After Smith's death, Sidney Rigdon wrote that God had given Smith "the keys of the mysteries of the things which had been sealed" until Smith had proven himself unworthy. "He [Smith] is gone and Christ has not come, and another [Rigdon] has taken his place as revelator" (Rigdon to Stephen Post, June 1, 1866, Post Collection, box 1, fd. 2; cited in Van Wagoner, *Sidney Rigdon*, 410–11). In 1891 Bickerton said he and his followers "felt by the Spirit of god, that it was the will of god, for us to have the Urim and Thummin" and that "god would Send Moroni to deliver the Sealed Records to Bro William Bickerton." "Cherokee District Conference," Jan. 17–20, 1891, 1–4.

like a day of Pentecost. Bickerton explained that the gates of Hell would shake before them on that day. Green Oak was the place God had chosen, and like King Solomon's temple on Mount Moriah, the Saints would finally have a tabernacle of their own in the foothills of the Allegheny Mountains.

At 8 a.m. on October 2, the members met and prayed for two hours prior to the formal dedication at 10 a.m. Bickerton addressed the congregation and reminded them that God had sent out his apostles in pairs. In remembrance of that fact, he asked the elders to stand together in the aisle and file down to the front two by two, then asked the members to do the same. Then the whole congregation began to march around the building singing the hymn "How Firm a Foundation."[12] Part of the song reads:

> How firm a foundation, ye Saints of the Lord,
> Is laid for your faith in his excellent word!
> What more can he say than to you he hath said,
> Who unto the Savior, who unto the Savior,
> Who unto the Savior for refuge have fled? …
>
> Fear not, I am with thee; oh, be not dismayed,
> For I am thy God and will still give thee aid.
> I'll strengthen thee, help thee, and cause thee to stand,
> Upheld by my righteous, upheld by my righteous,
> Upheld by my righteous, omnipotent hand.[13]

After parading through the chapel, they knelt before the altar and presented themselves to God in prayer. Their demonstration showed Bickerton their "willingness to leave [their] all to go forth in the name of the Lord."[14] They had given of their means, and now they were placing their lives on the altar. Lingering a while in meditation, Henry Bake heard the Lord say, "I will reveal myself unto you my people, in a greater manner than has ever been made known unto this generation:

12. Martin and Mancini, "History of the Church," 24.
13. Hastings, *Songs of Pilgrimage*, 524.
14. Martin and Mancini, "History of the Church," 24.

for I will do greater wonders in this generation than what has ever been done. And I will let them know that I have raised up a man to lead forth my people, to the lost inheritances of my people, Israel[,] and that man is in your midst, Amen."[15]

What followed was the four-day October conference beginning October 3, centered on how they could preach repentance to the entire country. Some apparently thought it would be imprudent to use the Book of Mormon. Bickerton and Charles Brown thought otherwise and drew on the biblical imagery of Ezekiel bringing together "two sticks" that were "written on" (scrolls) to make their point.[16] The biblical context is striking because it occurs as part of a vision Ezekiel has of a valley of bones, and when God tells Ezekiel to speak, the bones rise up and become skeletons that are soon clothed with flesh. Ezekiel is commanded to call on the four winds to breathe life into the figures, but the corpses protest, saying "our bones are dried, and our hope is lost: we are cut off for our parts." God knows otherwise. "Therefore prophesy," he tells Ezekiel, "and say unto them, Thus saith the Lord God; Behold, O my people, I will open your graves, and cause you to come up out of your graves, and bring you into the land of Israel" (Ezek. 37). This, Bickerton and Brown believed, was a vision of what would literally happen during the Millennium.

"Moreover, thou son of man," God continues to speak to Ezekiel, "take thee one stick, and write upon it, For Judah, and for the children of Israel his companions: then take another stick, and write upon it, For Joseph, the stick of Ephraim, and for all the house of Israel his companions: And join them one to another into one stick; and they shall become one in thine hand." Traditionally, this has been interpreted to mean the reunion of the northern and southern kingdoms of Israel. But Bickerton and Brown interpreted the scroll of Judah to be the Bible and the stick of Ephraim to be the Book of Mormon, so that when Ezekiel is told to put both sticks "in thine hand before their

15. "Book of Record," 7.

16. Martin and Mancini, "History of the Church," 25.

eyes. And say unto them, Thus saith the Lord God; Behold, I will take the children of Israel from among the heathen, whither they be gone, and will gather them on every side, and bring them into their own land," it meant to them, in part, that the American Indians would be rescued from oppression by Europeans and returned to their own lands in America.[17]

Several Native American tribes located in present-day Oklahoma during the antebellum period were there because they had been forced to move west from Florida, Georgia, Alabama, and elsewhere by the Indian Removal Act President Andrew Jackson signed in 1830. Jackson thought the Indians occupied land that should belong to the federal government, that under Indian stewardship the land was not meeting its economic potential.[18] It is interesting that this act of Congress and publication of the Book of Mormon occurred within two months of each other. What remained for the prophet and seer to do was to send representatives to show the native people their destiny while the country was preoccupied with its own troubles. At the Green Oak conference, Henry Bake stood up and proposed, as the word of the Lord, that the Saints "humble yourselves in mighty prayer, and I will shower down my blessings as I have declared unto you." The members knelt down and prayed, and Charles Brown responded in the voice of Jesus saying that Bickerton "shall receive the word at my mouth, And he shall lead you forth, and your sound shall go forth to all the earth." Bickerton, Brown, and James Wagoner simultaneously stood up and spoke in tongues, interpreted by Bickerton to be confirmation that the Lord would "set my Angels to guard this House that ye have built unto me, and ye shall go from thence, unto all nations, Amen."[19]

---

17. On October 2, 1859, James Brown prophesied a similar message: "Verily, verily, thus saith the Lord, God, forasmuch as I have revealed unto this generation the Stick of Ephraim; thus saith the Lord, Join the two sticks together; and I will make them mighty to gather my people from the West and also to accomplish, my great purposes in these last days," see "Book of Record," 7.

18. Howe, *What Hath God Wrought*, 347–52.

19. "Book of Record," 7–8.

The modest building that would be the church's headquarters had become a temple in their eyes. It didn't matter that it was a simple wood-frame structure, it had acquired the spiritual beauty of the temple described in the Old Testament. One member, M. Hunter, reported seeing ancient apostles and prophets walking to and fro in the meeting house.[20] These epiphanies occurred while the elders conducted business, such as on October 4 when Bickerton proposed that, considering how often Charles Brown and James Wagoner had joined him in uttering prophecies, they be named his counselors and their gifts given formal recognition. When Brown heard his name mentioned, he said the Holy Spirit "ran through him" and he knew it was of God.[21] The appointments were probably no surprise to the congregation, as many agreed that they were the right men for the positions.

Others were reluctant to endorse this move, knowing that Brown and Wagoner had both defected from the church in the past. In 1855 Brown had attempted to set up his own church, and in October 1857, Wagoner had separated himself from Bickerton, but no details were given.[22] Bickerton had long since forgiven them, but their offenses lingered with some of the other members. While considering these details, Hunter suddenly stood up and related a vision of Brown and Wagoner standing "in the midst of a multitude of people, surrounded with the glory of God." Seven men confirmed that they believed the vision, and Bickerton added that he saw a "cloud of Devine Glory decend into the house." For the moment, the matter seemed resolved.[23]

Bickerton wanted, additionally, that Thomas Bickerton and George Barnes should be called as bishops. The New Testament explained that bishops were expected to visit the branches, offer advice, and settle disputes. It was not to be a rank in the priesthood, but an office one could fill if already ordained as an elder. The presidency may

---

20. Martin and Mancini, "History of the Church," 25.
21. "Book of Record," 8.
22. Martin and Mancini, "History of the Church," 8, 15.
23. Ibid., 25–26.

have referenced the apostle Paul's advice that they "must be blameless, the husband of one wife, vigilant, sober, of good behavior, given to hospitality, apt to teach" (1Tim. 3:2–7), attributes found in abundance in Bickerton and Barnes. "I know that this is the true Church of the living God," Barnes would soon say, "and friends, if there is any among you that wants salvation, come this way and obey the commandments of God," he said in a pastoral voice.[24]

Next the presidency decided to ordain Ralph Marsh as a patriarch. One might think of a father or grandfather with a large family when the word *patriarch* is used, or the Old Testament patriarchs—Abraham, Isaac, and Jacob—who blessed their sons and foretold their futures. It appears that the patriarchs in Bickerton's church bestowed blessings on members, as had been initiated by Joseph Smith in the 1830s in Kirtland, Ohio. This began when Joseph Smith Jr. and his father attended a session of the School of the Prophets. When the son was about to wash his father's feet, the son requested a "father's blessing," and Joseph Sr. told his son the Lord had promised him that he would "continue in his Priests office until Christ come."[25] The son was impressed by the spiritual potential of such a blessing and appointed his father patriarch to the whole church in order to give blessings to individuals outside the Smith family. It was under Brigham Young that patriarchs started assigning converts an Israelite identity, and the patrilineal office became institutionalized. Bickerton did not see the patriarch's role to initiate new members into a tribe of Israel, and he did not consider the office to be one that belonged in the Smith family; nor did he consider patriarchs to be evangelists.[26] Like Joseph Smith, he saw significance in connecting the church to its biblical foundation by giving comfort and direction to an individual and significance to the family unit.

---

24. Ibid.; Cadman, *History of the Church of Jesus Christ,* 1:29.

25. Bushman, *Rough Stone Rolling,* 262.

26. In July 1887, Charles Brown, who was already a prophet, seer, and revelator, was ordained a patriarch. It was a special office held in addition to others. Unlike the Mormon Church, the office of patriarch was not equivalent to the office of evangelist. See J. S. Weeks, "A Letter," *St. John Sun,* Aug. 4, 1887.

As Bickerton, Brown, and Barnes laid their hands on Ralph Marsh, the latter saw a "great cloud of Glory" that was "like the Sun and [had] three links hanging from it," representing the presidency's reliance on the Holy Spirit. The three men then ordained various men to the offices of elder or evangelist. Even though the intention was to close the conference on that high note, people were so moved they believed there was more to experience and convinced the leaders to extend the conference longer.

In keeping with that decision, the elders drafted a statement and when everyone met the next day, October 5, they recited it together. It was a covenant to "give ourselves, our bodies, our souls, our time, our wives, and children, and all we possess … [to] anything, that the Lord shall call us to." The Lord answered their commitment through William Bacon, saying he was "well pleased with you for your diligence and faithfulness before me." On the following day, Brown announced that each member would "receive a gift at the hands of the Lord[.] Therefore, exercise faith[,] for when every man [h]as received his proper gift I will send down the cloven tongues of fire and authority to go forth." Bickerton interjected his approval and began enumerating what spiritual gift each member possessed. James Wagoner had the gift of discernment. Others possessed knowledge, wisdom, healing, the ability to work miracles, and several had the gift of speaking in tongues. In fact, as should be evident, Bickerton's emphasis on spiritual gifts was a primary feature of the church's theology and worship. This was partly due to the origin of the church in the Latter Day Saint movement and partly in keeping with the antebellum environment that included mysticism, the Holiness Movement (a remnant of the Second Great Awakening), personal perfection, public displays of spirituality, and anxiety about the future. "For we wrestle not against flesh and blood," Bickerton would agree with the apostle Paul, "but against principalities, against powers, against the rulers of the darkness of this world, against spiritual wickedness in high places" (Eph. 6:12). The physical battles would be seen soon enough; for the time being, they were engaged in a spiritual battle against temptation, trials, contention spawned by unseen demons—attempts to influence each individual heart.

On this last day of conference, October 6, Satan's influence was felt when a few of the members expressed doubts about the excessive spiritual manifestations. After the regular meetings, some of the members retired to Brother Cookston's house, where Bickerton recited another revelation. It was an unexpected way to quell discontent over too much revelation, but the Lord was unhappy and would not be confined. "For would I own and bless an unholy church?" the spirit protested. "Verily saith the Lord, ye are clean before me, and cursed be they that will say that my church is fallen." If anyone wanted to know what to expect in the future, follow the lead of Bickerton, they were told, and "ye shall see Visions, Dream Dreams, ye shall prophesy, there shall be Tongues, and Interpretations, and all other gifts, the dumb shall speak, the deaf shall hear, the lame shall walk, the sick shall be raised, and the poor shall hear the Gospel, Amen."[27]

It was a strong answer. There was a feeling among the leadership that it was time to prune the gospel tree of members who doubted what their own eyes beheld, who dragged their heels, gossiped, and spread doubt and contention. God, Bickerton knew, would not allow a few to overthrow the work for which he had sacrificed so much. The spiritual gifts would continue. The poor would hear the message and believe it. What Jesus quoted in the temple from the prophet Isaiah was relevant to Bickerton: "The Spirit of the Lord is upon me, because he hath anointed me to preach the gospel to the poor; he hath sent me to heal the brokenhearted, to preach deliverance to the captives, and recovering of sight to the blind, to set at liberty them that are bruised" (Luke 4:18). The church led by Bickerton would work the same miracles and preach the same gospel the Savior had.

The year 1859 stood out for Bickerton as the time he received more than nominal recognition as leader of the movement. Already for ten years, Charles Brown had affirmed Bickerton's prophetic gift, and the

27. Martin and Mancini, "History of the Church," 25–27; "Book of Record," 9–10.

elders finally decided to recognize this by granting their spiritual leader an office bearing the title of prophet, even though there was not much precedent for this. In the early Mormon Church, a few individuals, Joseph Smith and Sidney Rigdon, for instance, were called "prophets, seers, and revelators." They were nevertheless ordained to the high priesthood as elders or high priests. A rare instance in the Bible is when Elijah anointed his disciple, Elisha (1 Kings 19:16), to be a prophet. By creating a priesthood office to accommodate the visionary gift, the church symbolically indicated its acceptance of Bickerton's revelations.

People were drawn to the charismatic nature of the church, even a few who had been part of the larger LDS movement and had concluded that their former leaders had lost their way. As Webster Wagoner said it on December 11, serving as an oracle for God's message, "Hear ye the word of the Lord God of Hosts today. … I decreed that I would set up an Ensign, and raise up a Standard; that Ensign has been lifted, that Standard raised, and now I have called forth my servant William Bickerton to lead forth my people, and they shall go in and out and find pasture, and the world shall know that there is a God in Heaven; therefore, touch not mine anointed, Saith the Lord, Amen."[28]

The message drew upon the prophet Isaiah's vision of a destroyed "land shadowing with wings," which Sidney Rigdon understood to mean the geographical shape of the United States, Florida resembling a bird's head and the northern and southern continents the outstretched wings.[29] This was the land where God would lift up an "ensign on the mountains" (Isa. 18:1–3). The location where the flag would be unfurled, Bickerton had come to believe, was the northern edge of the Allegheny Mountains. It was easy for him to see his followers as the ensign to the world the ancient Hebrew envisioned.[30] Isaiah described a time of peace, when "the wolf also shall dwell with the lamb, and the

28. "Book of Record," 11.

29. John A. Forgeus to Samuel Forgeus, *Messenger and Advocate*, Pittsburgh, May 15, 1845.

30. Bickerton, *Ensign*, 1.

leopard shall lie down with the kid; and the calf and the young lion and the fatling together; and a little child shall lead them." It would be a time, according to Isaiah, when God would "gather together the dispersed of Judah from the four corners of the earth" (Isa. 11:6–12). As Bickerton understood it, God would destroy the United States and replace it with a pastoral Eden.

On New Year's Eve the Saints attended a watch meeting in Green Oak. The end times were so near, they might occur at any moment, especially on a day like New Year's when God's anger was sure to be piqued. If anything was possible, it in fact came to pass, although within the safety of the sanctuary as Brother Fielding experienced a vision of Bickerton standing beneath an arch, "on either side a serephim and a hand held out to him, and a voice, This is he—this is he." They would be visited by angels, Fielding declared, and would become a "society of just men made perfect."[31] The significance of the six-winged seraphim, sometimes referred to as seraphs, was that the creatures served as caretakers of God's throne (Isa. 6:1–3). Their recognition of Bickerton implied that he would have their protection, too, the same way these heavenly beings protected God's throne. It also implied that the millennial reign was near. On New Year's Day, Bickerton followed up with a divine promise that when they went out into the world, they would be "filled with the Holy Ghost and Fire," a favorite theme of the prophet's sermons.[32]

At that, Brother Fielding received another vision, this time of angels sitting around a dining table that was filled with "all manner of delicasies." "I tried twice to get at it," he said, "but failed twice, but at length I gained the point[.] Then I beheld Angels[,] [and] those that sat around the table were united." To Fielding, this indicated the future state of the church. Henry Bake agreed. "Verily thus saith the Lord God," Bake intoned. "Angels shall come down and commission you to go forth, unto all nations, and the power of God shall rest upon you." This prompted Benjamin Meadowcroft to relate that he and another elder had traveled

31. Martin and Mancini, "History of the Church," 27.
32. "Book of Record," 11.

a week ago to visit members in another town. Arriving back at midnight, thirsty from traveling, he grabbed a cup and filled it with water, not knowing his wife had been making soap and had filled the cup with lye. As he drank, he felt an abnormal icy feeling in his throat. He fell on his knees, realizing what he had drunk and assuming he would die. As he pled with God to spare him, he heard a voice say, "Fear not, for I am with thee," and he miraculously escaped any ill effect. The words of Jesus to his apostles came to mind, promising them that "if they drink any deadly thing, it shall not hurt them" (Mark 16:17–18).

Some of the members still doubted whether the revelations were real or contrived, which irritated Bickerton and his counselor, Charles Brown, who spoke in tongues, interpreted by William Bacon to say, "Hear ye the word of the Lord, … deceive not yourselves neither think to deceive this people or I will set you as a monument[,] as Lots wife. Amen."[33] Of course, Lot's wife was turned into a pillar of salt in the Bible (Gen. 19:1–26). The secretary neglected to record what effect this may have had on the scoffers. It would be interesting to know, since they could have seen it as a warning directed at Bickerton, rather than at them, or at anyone else who might embellish the revelations to tailor them to their preconceived expectation. Then again, the detractors would have had to believe the latest communication was from God in order to see it as a vindication of their concerns.

As the January conference continued the following day, sitting in the congregation, Jacob Stranger had not attended for some time and was asking to be readmitted into the church. Bickerton asked God and was told, as he related it to the congregation, "Verily thus saith the Lord ye are all fallible, and ye may transgress[,] therefore tremble and fear before me for I am God and this is my word[:] ye are all fallible therefore hear O my people and watch and pray for ye may fall, Amen." It was, once more, as if the message had been intended to give support to the critics as much as to answer how to treat a former apostate. It seemed to recall Joseph Smith challenging William McLellin to

33. Ibid., 12; Martin and Mancini, "History of the Church," 28.

write a better revelation than Smith, while acknowledging that his own had faults (D&C 62:4–9).[34] George Barnes added that "a man must first believe in the word of God before he can believe in the power of God," which was a rebuke of the doubters.

To the question of how to receive someone back, a woman, H. Harrison, demonstrated that women too could channel Christ's voice, delivering a message that "if any one be cut off by the Authority of this church they must be restored by repentance and Baptism; and in no other way can they be received, Amen." Henry Bake felt inspired to clarify, thereby having the last word. "Thus saith the Lord," he said, "one Baptism is sufficient inasmuch as ye live before me in righteousness. And if ye fall into sin and come and acknowledge it before me and my people ye shall be forgiven." Then he added a condition for which rebaptism was necessary, if someone had committed a serious sin. "But if for those transgressions any has been separated from the Body of Christ, they must be restored by repentance and Baptism, Amen," he said, thereby agreeing with Harrison.[35]

Since it was determined that Stranger needed to be rebaptized, he must have fallen under the condition mentioned. The elders closed the meeting and led the congregation to the river, which became such an emotional moment that it prompted three other individuals, Ann Josephine Bake, Timothy Cadman, and Edward Stokes, to ask to be admitted into the congregation themselves. On that high note, the church launched a missionary outreach the next day, not yet to the world but to the larger region, almost touching Pittsburgh. "It is the will of the Lord," Bickerton said to Charles Brown and George McNeal as he sent them to Limetown (Coal Bluff), while sending William Bacon to travel a few miles up the Youghiogheny River, and Webster Wagoner to travel to McKeesport where the Youghiogheny and Monongahela Rivers combine. Bickerton himself would travel sixty miles southwest to Wheeling, Virginia. "Every man must fill his

34. See Grandstaff, "Having More Learning Than Sense," for an analysis of the episode.
35. "Book of Record," 12–13; Martin and Mancini, "History of the Church," 28–29.

mission," Bickerton said, "or lose it." Before the conference ended, the men ordained Joseph Astin as a minister.[36]

Bickerton was probably concerned about recent developments in Virginia and wanted to have someone visit Wheeling to check on the welfare and dedication of the congregants. In October the white abolitionist John Brown, with eighteen others, including five free blacks, had assaulted and captured the federal arsenal at Harpers Ferry, Virginia. Previously Brown had met with the black abolitionist Frederick Douglass at a quarry near Chambersburg, Pennsylvania, and informed him of his plan, which Douglas dismissed as a suicide mission that would "array the whole country against us." Brown assumed that the attack on the arsenal would spark a revolution among the slaves everywhere. To his dismay, as he and his men carried out their plan on October 16, 1859, no one came to their side. They were soon overrun by troops. Brown was hanged on December 2 on charges of treason, murder, and insurrection. An unexpected result, at least to Frederick Douglass, was that at the moment of Brown's death, churches across the country in the North rang their bells in his honor and town militias fired guns in salute, ministers extolled him as a saint, and thousands of people bowed their heads in a moment of silence. Ralph Waldo Emerson said that Brown would "make the gallows as glorious as the cross," which Henry David Thoreau seconded.[37]

For Southerners, this support for an abolitionist was chilling and simply increased their distrust of Northerners, to the point that in early 1860 at Boggy Swamp, South Carolina, people evicted two school teachers even though "nothing definite is known of their abolitionist or insurrectionary sentiments," the newspaper reported. However, "being from the North, and, therefore, necessarily imbued with doctrines hostile to our institutions, their presence in this section has been obnoxious."[38] If the political climate gave Bickerton reason to worry, he

36. Martin and Mancini, "History of the Church," 29.
37. McPherson, *Battle Cry of Freedom*, 205–10.
38. Ibid., 212–13.

was reassured, prior to his departure, by Benjamin Meadowcroft saying that as Bickerton preached in the Southern state, "sinners shall fall at your feet." James Wagoner seconded this statement with his own prophetic utterance, "Go ye forth[,] for I will be with you and my power shall attend you and souls shall be saved."[39]

Bickerton returned from Wheeling in March and reported that some in the congregation "tremble[d] and f[e]ll under the word[s]" he spoke. It may not have been an unexpected reaction to his revival-style oratory, but it was nevertheless fulfillment of the prophecy Meadowcroft had uttered before his leader's departure. One can imagine, with people fainting and trembling, how forceful the prophet's style of delivery must have been. He baptized nine new converts in Virginia. His message about the imminent collapse of the government had resonated.[40]

In May the country's political rupture grew more acute when the Republicans chose the dark-horse Abraham Lincoln to be their presidential candidate. On the surface he appeared moderate, his platform addressing tariffs and a proposed transcontinental railroad. But it was known that he opposed the expansion of slavery into the West, which in the past had been a conservative plank and now seemed incendiary. "Let the consequences be what they may," a Georgia newspaper editorialized, "whether the Potomac is crimsoned in human gore, and Pennsylvania Avenue is paved ten fathoms deep with mangled bodies, ... the South will never submit to such humiliation and degradation as the inauguration of Abraham Lincoln." The candidate responded that "the people of the South have too much of good sense, and good temper, to attempt the ruin of the government," adding, "at least, so I hope and believe."[41] Kentucky statesman John J. Crittenden predicted that the South would "not submit to the consequences [of Lincoln's election], and therefore, to avoid her fate, will secede from the Union."[42]

39. "Book of Record," 13.
40. Martin and Mancini, "History of the Church," 29.
41. Basler, *Collected Works of Abraham Lincoln*, 4:95.
42. McPherson, *Battle Cry of Freedom,* 230.

In mid-year 1860, a female church member, Charlotte Hibbs, was sweeping the meeting house when she saw "a woman all dressed in white [who] came in with a crown in her hand. In the crown was twelve stars. She laid the crown upon the stand and said 'This crown belongs to this Church,' then disappeared."[43] It was July when she received this preview of the calling of twelve apostles, or perhaps a prediction of the church's mission to the twelve tribes of Israel. The full meaning was not yet known, except that it was auspicious and bore resemblance to a vision of John the Revelator, in which "there appeared a great wonder in heaven; a woman clothed with the sun, and the moon under her feet, and upon her head a crown of twelve stars" (Rev. 12:1). The members were in good spirits three months later when they set out for Wheeling, Virginia, to hold a conference. It was awkward at first, when on October 8, Alexander Bickerton spoke in tongues, and the Wheeling members reacted with laughter. Trying to put a good face on it, or perhaps to record the members' joy and surprise at witnessing spiritual manifestations, a member recorded that "such a glorious feeling was produced by the Holy Spirit that we was all forced to laugh and praise God." Alexander's foreign speech was accompanied by a vision he described of a "beautiful little tree" that was "fresh and healthy" and had been planted in a flower pot. Behind it was "a large old tree with all the branches dead." Amanda Bickerton picked up this narrative and exclaimed that she saw a beautiful train of angels enter the sanctuary and march around with a flower pot in which a sapling had been planted, and that one of the angels placed the pot on the table in front of the congregation. Charlotte Hibbs stood and gave the interpretation in God's voice, stating that the young church would minister to the "honest in heart" rather than to the established hierarchy.[44]

It was reminiscent of the imagery the apostle Paul drew from the landscape of Asia Minor when he compared the Jewish church to an

43. Cadman, *History of the Church of Jesus Christ,* 29; William Bickerton, "Testimony, June 1903," 13.

44. Martin and Mancini, "History of the Church," 30; "Book of Record," 14.

aging olive tree no longer bearing fruit and in need of being pruned. The best results were obtained when the branches of wild olive trees were grafted into it (Rom. 11). This was the message in both Alexander's and Amanda's visions. The small tree had been cared for by angels to replace the larger tree whose fruit had become bad. If the metaphor gave comfort to Bickerton's group, they were also aware that the apostle Peter had said that judgment would begin at home (1 Pet. 4:17–19). To know they were proceeding properly with the fresh young tree, a committee was formed to study the revelations Bickerton and others had received to be sure the members had not neglected any of the covenants they had made with God. This elicited another comment from the Lord through Alexander Bickerton, promising that those who remained faithful would "rise in the morning of the first Resurrection."[45] On the steamboat, while traveling home to Pennsylvania, the committee met on October 10 in a stateroom to pray for guidance and consider how to review the revelations.

When they were back in Pennsylvania, the committee met with Bickerton and he gave them his most startling command yet, advising them in the name of the Lord to remove from the written records any unfulfilled prophecies. "False predictions," he said, should not be retained, because they could make it appear that the prophet's statements had been equivocal or contrary to the divine purpose:

> Verily verily thus saith the Lord God of Israel, unto you my people inasmuch As there are some false predictions in the church Book at Greenock, Blot them out, from among you And you shall know concerning the promises, And you shall know that there is a Prophet among you, and it shall no more be said your Prophet is weak, for you shall know there is a Prophet among you, And at his mouth you shall hear my word; and my blessings shall rest upon you, Amen.[46]

Wanting to obey the instruction to destroy any false prophecies, the committee began reviewing the revelations and covenants, reporting

45. "Book of Record," 15.
46. Ibid.

in one instance, "We the committee do find a solemn covenant, made by us, the Church, at—Greenoak, October 5, 1859, [that] has never been fulfilled." However, they decided the fault was not in the revelation, but in the membership for failing to carry it out. The membership was therefore "under the obligation of confessing before the Lord, our transgressions, that we may not be counted among the covenant breakers when we have to stand before the judgement seat of Christ."[47] The church's work proceeded through the last day of the October conference, at which William Cadman, a onetime skeptic who could not shake the feeling that his life had been protected from shipwreck and train wreck, was ordained an elder. At his baptism the previous year in December, he had come up out of the water realizing that at such a moment he could "appear before God, knowing that I had just done what he commanded me to do." It was "the answer of a good conscience toward God" and trust in Christ that drove him to associate with the church. He wanted to assist others in their search for salvation. He and his wife, Elizabeth, had decided to buy a grocery store in the area and live among the Saints.[48]

Abraham Lincoln won 40 percent of the vote in November. That was because it was a four-way race. In electoral votes he garnered 180, well beyond the 152 needed to win. The candidate in second place was Democrat John C. Breckinridge of Kentucky, who netted only 72 electoral votes. North of the Mason–Dixon line, Lincoln earned 60 percent of the vote. The victor was careful to show humility so as not to inflame the national debate regarding slavery, but to no avail. The *Richmond Examiner* detected that the Republicans were "a party founded on the single sentiment … of hatred of African slavery." Charles Francis Adams, son of John Quincy Adams and grandson of John Adams, commented in his diary that with Lincoln's win, "the great revolution" had begun. The country would "once and for all" throw out slavery.[49]

47. Martin and Mancini, "History of the Church," 30–31.

48. Cadman, *Faith and Doctrines*, 2:12–13; Cadman, *History of the Church of Jesus Christ*, 1:31.

49. McPherson, *Battle Cry of Freedom,* 231–33.

At another council meeting in December in West Elizabeth, William Bacon spoke about a vivid recent dream the church secretary thought was significant enough to mention in detail. "I though[t] in my dream that we were in a meeting," Bacon said. A voice explained some of the "elders present … have the Gift of healing, [and] they are the ones [who should] attend" to the sick.

> I was then shown the order of sitting each man in his place according to their callings before the Lord; The ordination of each calling was then shown unto me[.] There was a man called to be an Evangelist, I saw him sit in a chair[.] When the Prophet arose and said the Brethren will now attend to the laying on of Hands, according to their Order, I saw myself and five young men that had been Ordained for Evangelists, rise six in all, two on each side and two behind[.] They stood with their right Hands on the mans head so that his Head was completely covered[.] The Prophet then came and stood before the man and laid his two hands upon ours And the power of God came down so Powerful that the man shook as if he was sitting upon a Electrifying machine, in fact we all shook. I then was shown the Prophet standing looking, first at one Elder and then at an other to get them to come, As I have often seen him; showing the contrast of unity and order and otherwise.

Next Bacon received instruction on how to conduct ordinances. He was

> told that Apostles should be ordained only by Apostles, Evangelists by the same order, and Elders by Elders, and all by six when that number is present; but in all cases the Prophets Hands was on the top and he pronounced the blessings; … I was shown that while Evangelists or Elders could not ordain Apostles, yet the Prophet had the power and authority fully committed into his hands by the Great High Priest in Heaven to ordain any order according to Revelation or as it should be Revealed to him to do so.

To modern-day Christians, it may seem out of the ordinary for clergymen to be ordained by prophets. In the Old Testament the prophets were poets and critics, standing outside of the priestly orders. It is true that throughout Israel's history prophets anointed kings, sometimes secretly and without any forewarning—appearing out of nowhere to pour oil on someone's head, for instance. There is that precedent, however (2 Kings 9:1–3; 1 Sam. 16:1–13).

Bacon's dream included instructions on preparing men for mission tours: "I was also shown the manner of sending men on Special Missions. It appears as though the two counsellors washed the feet or one washed and the other wiped them, the Prophet then Anointed him with oil in the name of the Lord, and the three then laid their hands upon his Head." There was one more part to the dream, and it had to do with record keeping. Bacon "noticed [in] particular that every Gift or blessing pronounced upon any person's Head was recorded in [a] Book," and that this was how records should be kept in each congregation as well. In the end, Bacon's dream instructed the Saints on how to maintain order and prepare for the calamities expected to come. God, it appeared, wanted a righteous church, free of hypocrisy, before it took on the responsibility of preaching repentance to the nation.[50]

Five hundred miles away, almost directly south of Pittsburgh, the governor and legislature of South Carolina called a special convention at the end of the year to determine how to proceed in the wake of Lincoln's election. On December 20 the delegates voted 169–0 to leave the United States. A Charleston journalist commented that there was "nothing in all the dark caves of human passion so cruel and deadly as the hatred the South Carolinians profess for the Yankees."[51] That passion was equaled by the resentment felt in Pittsburgh, which became a hotbed of antagonism against the South. When Secretary of War John B. Floyd of Virginia ordered 124 cannons sent to two gulf forts in late December, their progress from the Allegheny Arsenal to what is now Fort Pitt Boulevard and the Monongahela Wharf was slowed by protestors through Christmas Eve. Ultimately only a few cannons reached the steamboat *Silver Wave* before the orders were retracted.[52]

50. "Book of Record," 16–18; Martin and Mancini, "History of the Church," 32–33.
51. McPherson, *Battle Cry of Freedom,* 234.
52. Fox, *Pittsburgh during the American Civil War,* 1.

The Bickerton flock closed out the year by braving the cold water of the ever-present nearby river and baptized John Neish and George Profitt. Of the new elders who were ordained, one of them was the recently baptized Neish, and Jacob Stranger was reinstated to the office. Samuel Braddock and Benjamin Meadowcroft were ordained teachers. This all took place in a dramatic setting, for instance with George Barnes declaring, "Hear ye the word of the Lord. Hear ye the word of the Lord. Brother Neish is called to the office of Elder."[53] Another ordination occurred on New Year's Day. James Morgan was ordained a teacher, prior to Bickerton calling on members to testify to their beliefs. They should do so with confidence, he said, speaking for God: "It is my will that you all bare your testimonies to this work and that this is My Church and that ye be not as reeds shaken in the wind for if ye be as reeds shaken with every wind of Doctrine, ye can have no part or lot with me, saith the Lord God Almighty; therefore, bare your testimonies, and I will bless you saith the Lord God of Hosts."[54]

As Americans spent the holiday season gearing for war, the Christian message of peace was forgotten, both sides calling for an end to tyranny. The definition of tyranny differed depending on the region. There is no indication of fear in Bickerton's writings or in the minutes of the meetings, but that does not mean he or the church felt at ease. In 1860 Bickerton's wife, Dorothy, had given birth to their last daughter, Florence, and they faced the prospect of raising five girls and a son in wartime. As both a father and a minister, as someone about to turn forty-six in January, Bickerton faced the future with paternal instincts, devotion to his faith, and the experience of fifteen years since he preached his first sermon.

There may have been some of his followers and acquaintances among the 10,000 people in front of the Monongahela House in Pittsburgh in February when Lincoln stayed there. People arrived in the rain from all over the surrounding countryside to get a glimpse of him.

53. Martin and Mancini, "History of the Church," 35.

54. Ibid., 36.

Lincoln arrived late because of the storm, but stood on the balcony to "address the citizens of Pennsylvania, briefly, this evening, on what is properly styled their peculiar interest," he said, subtly referencing their Christmas Eve protest. "I have a great regard for Allegheny County," he declared. "It is 'the banner county of the Union,' and rolled up an immense majority for what I, at least, consider a good cause. By a mere accident, and not through any merit of mine, it happened that I was the representative of that cause, and I acknowledge with all sincerity the high honor you have conferred on me." The crowd was overjoyed to hear him condone what the *Pittsburgh Dispatch* had described as "interposing bodies of citizens of the U.S. before the timber wheels [of the approaching canon carriages]." "Three cheers for Honest Abe!" shouted someone in the crowd. The people pleaded for him to speak longer, but he said he had promised to deliver his official address the next day.

On February 15 he spoke to another immense crowd, probably many of whom had seen him the night before, once more standing on the balcony overlooking the waterfront. "The condition of the country, fellow-citizens, is an extraordinary one," he declared, "and fills the mind of every patriot with anxiety and solicitude." He pointed over the river in the direction of Virginia. "Notwithstanding the troubles across the river," he said, "there is no real crisis, springing from anything in the government itself. In plain words, there is really no crisis except an artificial one!" "If the great American people will only keep their temper, on both sides of the line," he said, "the troubles will come to an end, and the question which now distracts the country will be settled." At least publicly Lincoln displayed hope that the secessionist fervor would calm down even though in January Mississippi, Florida, Alabama, Georgia, and Louisiana followed South Carolina out of the Union, followed by Texas on February 1. He declined to say more, confessing that "to touch upon it all would involve an elaborate discussion of a great many questions and circumstances and would perhaps unnecessarily commit me upon matters which have not yet fully developed themselves." The audience was pleased by that. Some shouted, "Good." Others cried, "That's right!" Time would tell, he knew, as did the audience.[55]

In his inaugural address, Lincoln showed a pacific bent. "I have no purpose, directly or indirectly, to interfere with the institution of slavery in the States where it exists," he told the country. "I believe I have no lawful right to do so, and I have no inclination to do so." He assured the country he meant what he said. "Those who nominated and elected me did so with full knowledge that I had made this and many similar declarations and had never recanted them." He would not press the issue "unless it be forced upon the national authority," he said.[56] The next day he learned of the movement of Major Robert Anderson and his troops to the security of Fort Sumter in Charleston Bay because they feared attack and were running low on supplies. A few days later, delegates from seven Southern states met in Montgomery, Alabama, and adopted the Constitution of the Confederate States of America. They had previously ratified the U.S. Constitution in 1787, they said, and had just as much right now to reject it.[57]

It was with this backdrop that Bickerton and the other elders met for the April conference at which men from both sides of the Ohio River gathered. "It was found to be the will of God," the secretary wrote, "that we salute one another with a kiss of Charity." That was the greeting recommended by the apostle Paul in the New Testament (2 Cor. 13:11–12). "A most glorious time we had saluting the brethren," the secretary added. "Likewise we found it to be the Will of God, that the Brethren in this place wash the feet of the brethren that came from a distance," meaning in particular those who had arrived from Wheeling, Virginia. When Benjamin Meadowcroft knelt down to wash the feet of one of his Southern brethren, "the love of God flowed freely," the secretary recorded, and again "the brethren rose, one after another

55. Basler, *Collected Works of Abraham Lincoln*, 4:208–11; Fox, *Pittsburgh during the American Civil War,* 1.

56. Basler, *Collected Works of Abraham Lincoln*, 4:250–54.

57. McPherson, *Battle Cry of Freedom,* 246.

and saluted the [visiting] brethren with a Holy Kiss of Charity."[58] Cultural and political differences would not stop them from worshiping together, demonstrating what Lincoln had in mind for the country when he said that "though passion may have strained[,] it must not break our bonds of affection."[59] At least for now, the church was united.

The same could not be said of the country. That same day, Lincoln sent a message to the governor of South Carolina alerting him that Fort Sumter would be resupplied, although with non-lethal provisions, and he hoped this could be done without interference. Confederate President Jefferson Davis found an opportunity to dramatize the severing of their alliance with the North, and so he ordered General P.G.T. Beauregard to attack before help could arrive. The general opened fire on April 12, and Anderson and his men endured thirty-nine hours of bombardment by 4,000 shells that destroyed part of the fort and set the interior on fire before they surrendered. Lincoln responded by calling out 75,000 state militia to put down the insurrection that was obviously "too powerful to be suppressed by the ordinary course of judicial proceedings." The conflict everyone feared had begun.[60]

Bickerton knew it would come to this, having relied on Joseph Smith's prophecy that the conflict would begin in South Carolina.[61] He found support for this in the Book of Mormon where the resurrected Jesus warned the gentiles that "it shall come to pass in that day … that I will cut off thy horses out of the midst of thee, and I will destroy thy chariots. And I will cut off the cities of thy land, and throw down all thy strongholds … And I will pluck up thy groves out of the midst of thee; so will I destroy thy cities" (3 Ne. 21:14–18). The prophet of Pennsylvania felt some urgency now to finish organizing the church the

58. Martin and Mancini, "History of the Church," 36.

59. Basler, *Collected Works of Abraham Lincoln,* 4:261. The new president famously went on to say that "the mystic chords of memory, stretching from every battlefield and patriot grave to every living heart and hearthstone all over this broad land, will yet swell the chorus of the Union, when again touched, as surely they will be, by the better angels of our nature."

60. McPherson, *Battle Cry of Freedom,* 272–74.

61. *A Prophecy by Joseph Smith,* 1; D&C 87.

way Jesus established it some 2,000 years earlier. For instance, Jesus had called twelve apostles and commissioned them to "teach all nations ... to observe all things whatsoever I have commanded you" (Matt. 28:19–20). Some of Bickerton's followers had already asked why they had not ordained apostles. Another issue was how they would fund twelve men, if their calling was to preach abroad—and whether they should go to the Middle East and Mediterranean as in the New Testament or westward to Indian Territory. Should they preach to the gentiles or only to the House of Israel? "But if they [gentiles] will repent," Jesus said in the Book of Mormon, "and hearken unto my words, and harden not their hearts, I will establish my church among them, and they shall come in unto the covenant and be numbered among this the remnant of Jacob [Native Americans], unto whom I have given this land [America] for their inheritance" (3 Ne. 21:22). Both the gentiles and the Indians needed to hear the urgent message, he concluded. In the near future, the Choice Seer named Joseph would make himself known to the church and presumably would be the one to convince the Indians that they were one of the lost tribes of Israel. Together, the Choice Seer and William Bickerton would lead the Saints to Zion. It was a glorious plan, and time was running out.[62]

62. This idea that time was running short was emphasized by Bickerton on January 2, 1861. He shared with the members a revelation he had earlier that morning. "I saw the sun setting with the moon beneath it and underneath them was a watch set," he said, "and the hour of it was a little over half past eleven," see Cadman, *History of the Church of Jesus Christ*, 1:30–31.

SEVEN

ORGANIZATION

1861–62

"[H]ear ye the word of the Lord, O ye Twelve, whom I have chosen and ordained, I commit unto [you] the Keys of the Kingdom, and no weapon that is formed against you shall prosper, until you have finished your work. I shall make you as a bow—and my word shall go from you as an arrow, and many shall cry out 'what shall we do?'"

—revelation, Charles Brown, July 8, 1862

Bickerton and his followers believed they were favored by God to be acting out the ancient prophecies, in some ways like Jesus mentioned to his disciples, "Many prophets and righteous men have desired to see those things which ye see, and have not seen them; and to hear those things which ye hear, and have not heard them" (Matt. 13:17). The remnant of Israel would soon "rend that veil of unbelief," is how the Book of Mormon described the last days (Ether 4:15). Most Christians, and the Bickertonites alike, assumed the Jewish people would convert to Christianity after the final battle of Armageddon, when Jesus would descend from the sky to the Mount of Olives, as the Prophet Zechariah foretold, and convince the stunned onlookers that he had been crucified for their sakes. "What are these wounds in thine hands?" they would ask him. After they accepted him as the son of God, Christ would deliver them from their enemies (Zech. 13:6; 14).

The Civil War was the conflict Latter Day Saints believed would lead to Armageddon. "With the sword and by bloodshed the inhabitants of the earth shall mourn," Joseph Smith said, "and with famine, and plague, and earthquake, and the thunder of heaven, and the fierce and vivid lightning also, shall the inhabitants of the earth be made to feel the wrath, and indignation, and chastening hand of an Almighty God, until the consumption decreed hath made a full end of all nations." What this meant to Bickerton was that there was a need to hurry the church's preparations. If the gentiles were to be saved, now was their chance (D&C 87:6; 3 Ne. 21–22). What Green Oak offered the world was not only spiritual salvation but earthly redemption during the final drama. Then the wolf would lie down with the lamb through the Messiah's thousand-year reign.

Four days after the surrender of Fort Sumter in South Carolina on April 17, 1861, another Southern state, Virginia, seceded from the U.S. and joined the Confederacy. The state had been central in the Revolutionary period in producing such leaders as George Washington, Thomas Jefferson, and James Madison, and it had a large population and industrial capacity. Spurred by the example of Virginia, three more states left the Union in the following weeks: Arkansas, Tennessee, and North Carolina. Another result of Virginia's exit was its contribution to the Confederate leadership of Robert E. Lee, a full colonel in the US Army and graduate of West Point, with experience in the Mexican–American War. President Lincoln offered him the field command of the US forces on April 18, the same day Lee heard of Virginia's secession. "I cannot raise my hand against my birthplace," he decided, opting rather on April 23 to accept the position of commander-in-chief of Virginia's military forces. Three weeks later he became a brigadier general. His dilemma illustrates what many Americans went through. For instance, US General-in-chief Winfield Scott was from Virginia. If everything seemed muddled, as the war progressed the goals of the Confederacy and the Union changed so much that it was difficult for either side to remember what the original point was.

Bickerton's followers, like other Americans, experienced some dissonance due to the religiosity of the Southern leaders and agreed with

General Lee's statement of May 1861, "I foresee that the country will have to pass through a terrible ordeal, a necessary expiation perhaps for our national sins," the very thing Bickerton had been preaching and would be heartily endorsed by members in Wheeling, Virginia, if not in Green Oak, Pennsylvania.[1] Sixty miles upriver from Wheeling, at the head of the Ohio River, and only twenty miles from Green Oak, Pittsburgh was alive with preparations for the Union side as both a manufacturing center and staging ground. It would have been difficult to escape the impact of the state Committee on Troops and Provisions accepting and outfitting twenty-six companies of volunteers beginning April 26. A newspaper publisher, George H. Thurston, described Pittsburgh in the 1860s:

> For quite the entire period of the war, Pittsburgh was literally a camp and an arsenal. Her foundries, her rolling mills, her tanneries, her harness factories, her clothing manufactories, her [places of] production of shot and shell ... infantry and cavalry accoutrements. ... But few hours of the day or night were without the passage of guns or troops, or was the roll of the drum silent. ... Her streets were literally a war path.[2]

Historian Leland Baldwin adds context: "The war years in Pittsburgh were a time of frenzied money-making and unselfish devotion; of high prices and high rents offset by high wages; of mass meetings in the town hall being addressed by fat stay-at-homes and [the] passing [of] grandiloquent resolutions." The city offered incentives of up to $1,000 to enlist for periods of one month to three years.[3] It was a day of "wars and rumors of wars" and "great pollutions upon the face of the earth," just as the Book of Mormon said (Morm. 8:30–31). Before long the appeal of the drums was heard in Green Oak and West Elizabeth, responded to by William Bacon, for one, who enlisted in

1. McPherson, *Battle Cry of Freedom*, 280–81.
2. Thurston, *Pittsburgh and Allegheny*, 26.
3. Fox, *Pittsburgh during the American Civil War*, 3–5.

September and would remain in the service three years until he contracted dysentery and was discharged.[4]

For a while it seemed that every detail of Joseph Smith's prophecy was being fulfilled: "The Southern States will call on other nations, even the nation of Great Britain, as it is called, and they shall also call upon other nations, in order to defend themselves" (D&C 87:3). Britain relied on the South for cotton to supply its textile factories. "What would happen if no cotton was furnished for three years?" the South Carolina politician James Hammond asked in 1858. "England would topple headlong and carry the whole civilized world with her."[5] "If those miserable Yankees try to blockade us," the *London Times* quoted a Charleston merchant, he had no doubt England would "send their ships to the bottom" of the ocean. The predicted blockade elicited a remark from Britain's prime minister, Viscount Palmerston, who wrote to the foreign minister, John Russell, in October 1861 that "we cannot allow some millions of our [factory workers] to perish to please the Northern States." On the other hand, at another time Palmerston quoted the couplet that "they who in quarrels interpose / will often get a bloody nose." Supplies began to dwindle in Europe, and that made the price of cotton rise to the point that it was more attractive to farmers in Egypt and India, who were more than happy to plant more of the crop to meet the demand.[6]

In the spring of 1861, people in the thirty-five western counties of Virginia were sufficiently discontent with the state's betrayal of the country that they sent representatives to a conference in Wheeling to discuss their future. They had little in common with the coastal side of the state. The mountainous terrain was unsuited for plantation crops, and the culture was different. The state legislature preferred the eastern

4. Stevenson, "History of the Pennsylvania Volunteers." He would recover his health and live another forty-four years, dying on Christmas 1908 in McKeesport, a few miles north of Green Oak (Greenock).

5. U.S. Senate, Mar. 4, 1858, in *Congressional Globe* (Washington DC: 1859), 35th Congress, 1st session, appendix p. 70.

6. McPherson, *Battle Cry of Freedom*, 383–86.

lowlands, indicated by the fact that slaves were taxed at a third their market value, while all other property was valued at full price. The need in the West for infrastructure was barely understood in the East. During the recent meetings on secession, twenty-six of thirty-one delegates from northwest Virginia voted against. Now the delegates in the mountains wanted to rejoin the Union. The problem was that the US Constitution required a seceding region within an existing state to receive the blessing of that state's legislature. The delegates in Wheeling well knew that the Confederate government in Richmond would not consent to their separation.

The solution was to declare the existing state government void and appoint alternative officials, as was done on June 20. When news of this reached Lincoln, he extended official recognition, and the new legislature elected two new US senators and three congressmen, all of whom soon took their seats in Washington. By the time the legislature had completed these adjustments, the Union army had invaded western Virginia and defeated a small Confederate force, which gave teeth to the local determination to stand with the Union. West Virginia would be officially admitted to the United States on June 20, 1863.[7]

Even though Bickerton was silent on this development, it must have been a relief to see the nearby national border erased. It was the parting of the Red Sea for the Israelites to cross over, the way it made contact with the Wheeling branch possible. During the run-up to these developments, the Saints were gathered in the house of Richard Bickerton, the prophet's nephew, on July 6 when Charlotte Hibbs saw a heavenly hand holding two crowns that were placed next to William Bickerton and Charles Brown, between whom stood a tree from the spirit world. The two men were illuminated by a pillar of light. While this was occurring, a Sister Davis was approaching the house and saw the same pillar of light, without having communicated with Hibbs or others in the house. As she related this to the congregation, people marveled that she could describe part of the same

7. Ibid., 298–99.

vision, paralleling Isaiah's prophecy, "For Zion's sake will I not hold my peace, and for Jerusalem's sake I will not rest, … thou shalt also be a crown of glory in the hand of the Lord, and a royal diadem in the hand of thy God" (Isa. 62:1–3). As the visions probably were interpreted, the tree represented the House of Israel, a genealogical tree they believed they, as gentiles, were grafted into.

John Dixon shared his own recent vision of "a very large fish" that had "a basket in its mouth. Then I saw Bro Arthur Bickerton standing by," he said, "and [Bickerton] took the basket. His wife Margaret asked what is in the basket? He then took from the basket a book and said, It is a book for John Dixon." Praying to understand what this meant, he was answered by the Lord's voice to his mind: "I have heard thy prayers, My servant John[,] and I have seen thy tears, that thou art sincere, therefore surely thou shalt stand between my people and me. I will give thee my word and thou shalt speak it faithfully, and I will bless thee, both in temporal and spiritual things." At that, Dixon must have remembered that in the Bible Jesus told Peter he would make him a "fisher of men" (Matt. 4:18). The basket was probably a lure to attract the fish. When he had completed his rehearsal of what he had seen, the elders concluded that it meant God had called him to the priesthood.[8]

Dixon had another message to deliver. The church needed to be purged of the unworthy. As he lay in bed, the Lord said to him one night, "These are my people, but there are some among them, who … will not believe my word that I reveal to my servants and handmaids, therefore, thus saith the Lord, I will cause you to cut them off." Bickerton agreed, having endured the brunt of the hostility from members who suspected him of inventing revelations. "Cursed be they that will say that my church is fallen," he declared in God's voice back in 1859. "Cursed be every one, that shall attempt to upset, or overthrow, or destroy my work."[9]

Sister Davis had also experienced a confirmation of Dixon's spirit

8. Martin and Mancini, "History of the Church," 37–38.

9. Ibid.; "Book of Record," 10.

dictation. In a dream, she had seen Charles Cowan carrying a child he said was dead, but who on investigation was still alive. This could only mean that "Charles Cowan has denied the Authority of this church and said that this church was dead, and likewise, that he is not one of us."[10] This must have sent shock waves through the conference because Cowan was an ardent and gifted minister who had often demonstrated spiritual gifts. In October 1858 he, Bickerton, and Charles Brown had sung together in an unknown language.[11] There is no record of Cowan's response, so it is unknown whether he challenged this. Strange as it would seem for him suddenly to denounce the church, the seeds of doubt had spread through the membership. George Barnes started to question whether they should have ever separated themselves from the Utah church. They had lacked "the vocal voice of the Lord" in coming to that decision, he argued.[12]

This opened a wound in Bickerton's heart. In his mind, there had been no question whether to leave Brigham Young's teachings and practice of polygamy. Why had some of the members dragged their feet on that point? This could not have come at a worse time, since Young, also believing the Civil War had apocalyptic significance, had recently sent missionaries out to gather in the members who were still in the Midwest and East. "All Elders should understand that after baptism comes the gathering," Young wrote to two of his apostles, "and that everything which in the least impedes the gathering tends directly to hinder the great work in which we are engaged." Men throughout Utah Territory were asked to donate wagons and oxen to take east for the immigration the following year, to return with not only immigrants, but also needed merchandise and machinery in case it became unavailable in the future.[13] The missionaries arrived in Western Pennsylvania and encountered Bickerton's group, some of whom converted and decided

10. Martin and Mancini, "History of the Church," 37.

11. Ibid., 19.

12. Ibid., 37.

13. Turner, *Brigham Young*, 313.

to move west and avoid the war. This infuriated Bickerton. "The Utah people sent missionaries out and [s]cared a good many away to Salt Lake City," he fumed.[14]

Throughout the remainder of the 1860s, Young's renewed effort would bring in two or three thousand immigrants each year for a kind of hibernation, away from the waking nightmare that was developing in the East.[15] In that context, Barnes's doubts posed a real threat, and the Utah Mormons held a local conference a half mile away at the same time Bickerton was trying to bolster his followers against this new threat. This may explain the stimulus for the Davis and Dixon revelations. Bickerton offered a final word on the matter when he said the Lord told him "that He accepted this Church as the Church of Alma."[16] Drawn from a story in the Book of Mormon, it was a metaphor about a soldier, Zeniff, who led some Nephite settlers into enemy territory in the south and negotiated with their king to allow them to settle in the region. Zeniff became a king, succeeded by a man named Noah, who had multiple wives and concubines. "And he did cause his people to commit sin," the Book of Mormon reads, "and do that which was abominable in the sight of the Lord. Yea, and they did commit whoredoms and all manner of wickedness." The people were taxed heavily for the construction of "elegant and spacious buildings" (Mosiah 11:2–14). Into this milieu stepped a prophet named Abinadi who promised that the people would be delivered into the hands of their Lamanite enemies if they did not repent. A priest named Alma responded to this and eventually led a church of believers in Christ that grew to encompass the entire Nephite civilization.

In this comparison, Joseph Smith was Zeniff, in that his followers settled in the midst of their enemies. Brigham Young was Noah, and Bickerton was Alma. Why did people not recognize this similarity? he wondered. Paraphrasing the apostle Peter, Bickerton said the Utah

---

14. Bickerton, "Testimony, June 1903," 2.
15. Turner, *Brigham Young*, 313.
16. Bickerton, "Testimony, June 1903," 2.

clan "have eyes full of adultery and cannot cease from sin, beguiling unstable souls, and have exercised their hearts with covetous practices." Warming even more to this topic, he continued to say the settlers of the Great Basin were "cursed children who have forgotten the right way and are gone astray … for it had been better for [them] not to have known the way of righteousness than after they had known it to turn from the holy commandment delivered unto them." Although Bickerton had never personally met Young, he believed he and the Western prophet were engaged in an epic battle exactly like Alma and Noah. He referenced this when he wrote that "in the confusion which resulted from Joseph Smith's death, the Lord moved on William Bickerton to [gather] … a body of people … even as in the day of Alma."[17]

The words of Abinadi were as clear in Bickerton's ears as the cannon fire of the Civil War. "It shall come to pass that this generation, because of their iniquities, shall be … slain; and the vultures of the air, and the dogs, yea, and the wild beasts, shall devour their flesh," the Nephite doomsayer had preached (Mosiah 12:2). Bickerton believed his church would be the last haven for the pure in heart, including for Utah Mormons, if only they could see "the stupendous work of the latter days" occurring in his church. Sometimes he saw it in terms of David and Goliath, his membership of 500 pitted against the mammoth Utah church with over 20,000 members. The battle would decide the ultimate leader of God's people, he thought.[18]

The sins of the desert Saints encompassed more than taking multiple wives. Rogue Mormons massacred an immigrant train in the southern part of the territory, and Bickerton was not shy about enumerating the horror of the event. President James Buchanan urged the Utah attorney general in 1859 to find and prosecute those responsible for the slaughter that occurred two years past in September 1857. The victims were members of the Baker–Fancher party, mostly from

17. Bickerton, *Ensign*, 3, 17; Bickerton, "Testimony, June 1903," 2.

18. Bickerton, *Ensign*, 3–4; Mancini, "List of Branches"; Bushman and Bushman, *Building the Kingdom*, 46.

Arkansas, and they had had the misfortune of traveling through the territory to California during the conflict known as the Utah War. Mormons were at that time isolated from the rest of the country and fearful of outsiders. Buchanan had sent a military force to Utah to curb its disloyalty to the federal government.[19]

And so it happened that, with the approach of the US Army, Mormons were conserving supplies and unwilling to sell goods to the members of the Baker–Fancher wagon train on its way to California. Some immigrants may have responded by voicing support for the incoming troops. In any case, local Mormon leaders Isaac C. Haight and John D. Lee mobilized the regional militia to back up a raid by Paiute Indians that would retaliate by stealing some cattle, horses, and gold currency. The raid went badly, and Mormons who were supposed to provide unseen support, seeing the Indians were outgunned by the marksmen among the travelers, followed up with a raid of their own. The party learned the identity of their attackers, leading Haight to wonder what would happen if the travelers told the California newspapers and federal officials what had occurred. A decision was made to eliminate the immigrants, 120 men, women, and young people, sparing only a few of the youngest children who were taken in by nearby families.[20]

Prior to the attorney general's investigation of the massacre, federal judge John J. Cradlebaugh had begun his own proceeding in Provo in March 1859. US soldiers had found "women's hair … hung to the sagebrushes" at Mountain Meadows and reported "parts of little children's dresses and of female costume [that] dangled from the shrubbery. … For at least a mile in the direction of the road, by 2 miles east and west, there gleamed, bleached white by the weather, the skulls and other bones of those who had suffered."[21] Perhaps the militiamen who had participated in the raid thought this neglected evidence would look

19. Turner, *Brigham Young*, 308.

20. Bowman, *Mormon People*, 120–23. See also Walker et al., *Massacre at Mountain Meadows*.

21. Bowman, 120.

like the remains of an Indian attack. As the investigation proceeded, Cradlebaugh ordered the arrest of three local church leaders, but it was soon after this that President Buchanan contacted the attorney general, and Cradlebaugh's investigation was canceled. The new inquiry made little headway beyond where Cradlebaugh had left off.

Through all of this, Young acted defensively, complaining about federal interference when, for instance, a military escort transported children of the Baker–Fancher party to their relatives in the East. In May 1861, Young visited Mountain Meadows and saw the cairn in which a wooden cross was planted, on which the soldiers had written from the New Testament, "Vengeance is mine; I will repay." Young offered his own interpretation of what God had done: "Vengeance is mine and I have taken a little," he said, indicating how little sympathy he felt for the victims. Nor did he blame the local Mormons who had committed the crime, believing that they and the rest of the Mormons had suffered enough from the federal government.[22]

Bickerton, on the other hand, was appalled, and had a theory of his own about what had occurred. "I had a chance to get acquainted with some of the Danite Band," he said in reference to the Mormon guerrillas who had been active during the Mormon War in Missouri in 1838. "The mountain meadow massacre was committed by, or through these false teachers of my acquaintance, as the Elders from that time, on down to the present, must obey the orders of their superior officers."[23] The reason the Danites were formed was because some prominent Mormons had defected and had information that would be damaging to the church. Oliver Cowdery, Joseph Smith's Book of Mormon scribe, and David and John Whitmer, two of the individuals who signed statements saying they had seen the gold plates, were excommunicated for bringing accusations against other church members, Cowdery having accused Joseph Smith of committing adultery. All three had allegedly initiated "vexatious lawsuits." Still loyal to

22. Turner, *Brigham Young*, 309.
23. Bickerton, "Testimony, June 1903," 1–2.

Smith, Sidney Rigdon preached against the dissenters in a fiery address known as the Salt Sermon, quoting the Savior's statement, "Ye are the salt of the earth: but if the salt have lost his savour, wherewith shall it be salted? It is thenceforth good for nothing, but to be cast out, and to be trodden under foot of men."[24] Eighty-three Mormons, including Smith's brother Hyrum, followed up with a letter warning Cowdery, the Whitmers, and others to "depart with your families peaceably" within three days or face "a more fatal calamity." The vigilantes were then formed by Sampson Avard to nudge the dissenters out of the area and frighten them from speaking against the church.[25]

For decades after Mountain Meadows, rumors had circulated that Brigham Young still operated a group of Danites. Bickerton put two and two together based on what he knew of Missouri, concluding that the atrocity must have been conducted on orders from the top. This was not, in fact, a Danite conspiracy, but whatever the behind-the-scenes story was, the publicity surrounding the failed attempt to bring the guilty parties to justice, as interpreted by Bickerton, may have helped quash some budding interest among his members in rejoining the Utah denomination, at least for the time being. At the July 9, 1861, meeting, he directed the members' attention toward something he considered more essential and for which the time had finally come, which was the formation of a Quorum of Twelve Apostles, one of the pillars in the architecture of the church organization. After conferring with the elders, the first seven apostles were named: George Barnes, Charles Brown, Arthur Bickerton, Joseph Astin, Thomas Bickerton, William Bacon, and James Brown. The following day five more were added to the list: Andrew Rattray, Alexander Bickerton, Cummings Cherry, Benjamin Meadowcroft, and John Neish. Confident that these were the right choices, the elders nevertheless wanted to delay the ordinations, perhaps to give them more time to meditate and receive confirmation of the Holy Spirit.[26]

24. Bushman, *Rough Stone Rolling*, 350; Matt. 5:13.
25. Turner, *Brigham Young*, 56–57.
26. Martin and Mancini, "History of the Church," 38.

When an August 3 council meeting opened, the members of the priesthood felt good about their original choices but still wanted more time to think about it, once more probably feeling the need for a stronger spiritual confirmation. On the other hand, they were ready to proceed with the ordination of six evangelists, announced by Bickerton as John Ashton, John Bickerton, William Cadman, Joseph Knox, James Nichols, and John Stevenson. Later in the meeting, Frederick Abling, John Dixon, and Morgan Thomas were added to the evangelists and John Tilford to the elders.[27]

Bickerton returned to the book of Isaiah in October to see what more the prophet had said would occur in the last days. "Go, ye swift messengers," Isaiah penned in his poetic voice, "to a nation scattered and peeled, to a people terrible from their beginning" (Isa. 18:2). Sidney Rigdon had previously established that the land in the shape of a bird was the United States, so it was a small step for Bickerton to interpret "a nation peeled" to imply the current division between North and South. Even some in the North began to wonder if they were worthy of victory, or if they were so terribly unfit "for empire," as the *Richmond Whig* editorialized, as demonstrated by the devastating defeat at Bull Run in Virginia that July when nearly 500 Union soldiers were killed. A Georgian politician, Thomas Cobb, thought it was "one of the decisive battles of the world." Lincoln immediately signed a bill enlisting 500,000 more men for a three-year term, and three days later he increased the number to a million.[28] The Union was defeated again in August at Wilson's Creek in Missouri, resulting in US General John C. Frémont being removed from command. That battle left half of Missouri under the control of the Confederacy, and hundreds of lives had been lost.[29] Bickerton claimed to know why. It was federalism. Each state considered itself sovereign, and that idea had split the United States into what Isaiah had seen as the "scattered" pieces of the Union.

27. Ibid., 38–39.
28. McPherson, *Battle Cry of Freedom*, 347–48.
29. Piston and Hatcher, *Wilson's Creek*, 337–38.

There would be more devastation, Bickerton knew from the scriptures. "For afore the harvest, when the bud is perfect, and the sour grape is ripening in the flower, [the Lord] shall both cut off the sprigs with pruning hooks, and take away and cut down the branches. They shall be left together unto the fowls of the mountains, and to the beasts of the earth: and the fowls shall summer upon them, and all the beasts of the earth shall winter upon them." So it was when two hundred miles away at the Battle of Leesburg, Union forces suffered losses at a ratio of seven to one. At the conclusion of the war, Bickerton believed, a new banner would be unfurled. What kind of flag would it be? "See ye, when [the Lord] lifteth up an ensign on the mountains; and when he bloweth a trumpet, hear ye" (Isa. 18:3). It would be the banner raised in the Allegheny Mountains, the church secretary noting that after Bickerton finished preaching on this and "the evil pronounced against" the United States, "the blessings of God accompanied the whole of the afternoon."[30]

This sermon had a great effect on the congregation. With such drama occurring all around, it would be hard not to see themselves as the people foretold who would endure calamities at the end times. The thought was as terrifying as it was awe-inspiring. Despite the battles being fought on all sides, they decided it was time to begin preaching in urban centers. Maybe because they were less likely to encounter the clash of troops in the cities, or maybe because they felt they had rehearsed their message to small gatherings and were ready to confront larger crowds. Whatever the case, John Neish and Cummings Cherry were sent to Penn Station (Union Station) in the heart of Pittsburgh; John Stevenson and Arthur Bickerton were to go to Allegheny City, a busy railroad juncture; while Joseph Astin and Alexander Bickerton would visit the ferry crossing in Wheeling, Virginia. At the afternoon session, John Ashton walked around the room speaking in tongues, translated by another brother as, "Go ye into the highways and byways and compel them to come in."

30. Martin and Mancini, "History of the Church," 39.

This met the approval of the secretary. "We found it to be the will of the Lord," he wrote, "that we preach the gospel in every place, whether it be on the railroads or on the Steamboats."[31]

The church's history for the year 1862 began with a meeting on January 2 in West Elizabeth, where Charlotte Hibbs interpreted for Joseph Astin's gift of tongues, saying the gospel would be taken "unto every kindred tongues and people." How could such a small church accomplish such a thing? they must have wondered. Maybe that was part of the miracle that would attract the notice of the world, when the Lord demonstrated that "I am able to do mine own work" (2 Ne. 27:21). Feeling overwhelmed by the realization, Bickerton brought out a basin and water and knelt down to wash the feet of twenty-eight men, followed by a special blessing on each one. It was evident that these men were expected to usher in one of the great events in human history, the gathering prior to the Second Coming.

Next he turned his attention to the church records. Often in the early years of the movement, a secretary was randomly selected before a meeting to take notes, and the records were inconsistent. He felt it was time to bring some order to the minutes, in light of the grand events taking place. They therefore "set apart, by the laying on of hands," two men, Joseph Astin and James Brown, and commissioned them to "keep a true and faithful record" of what they observed.[32]

Three days later, William Bacon decided he was not up to the challenge of a wartime mission assignment after all and withdrew his name from consideration as an apostle. He had enlisted in the army, Bickerton told the members. Since 1852, Bacon had been one of the most reliable, gifted, and competent leaders of the church, his spiritual utterance having confirmed Bickerton's calling to the office of a prophet. What was his motivation in joining the Union army? Scholars have written that the main stimulus behind enlistment was a fear for the country's future. "We were born and bred under the stars and

31. Ibid.
32. Ibid., 40–41.

stripes," an editorial in the *Pittsburgh Post* voiced the prevailing sentiment on April 15, 1861. The country had been a nurturing parent and the South was seen as a misbehaving sibling, threatening the harmony and success of the family. Or as Abraham Lincoln said to Congress on July 4, 1861: "Our popular government has often been called an experiment. Two points in it, our people have already settled—the successful establishing, and the successful administering of it. One still remains—its successful maintenance against a formidable internal attempt to overthrow it." This involved some irony: by compelling the South to conform, the same air of freedom and self-determination the country was known for would be preserved. Even so, it was a powerful idea.[33]

There were other reasons. Some had a romantic view of war involving the glamour and pomp of the uniforms and parades and the testing of one's courage. For some church members, patriotism could have been fused with millennial theory.[34] More mature individuals such as William Bacon may have worried about the US Constitution's protection of religious freedom, without which Bickerton would be unable to preach and the zionic community would not be possible. A New Jersey soldier expressed a similar concern that "our glorious institutions are likely to be destroyed. We will be held responsible before God if we don't do our part in helping to transmit this boon of civil & religious liberty down to succeeding generations."[35] Others were motivated by the example of John Brown and the view of the war as a righteous endeavor, although at first the North was fighting to preserve a Constitution that had slavery written into it. Overall, Bacon's enlistment,

33. McPherson, *Battle Cry of Freedom*, 308–09.

34. See, for instance, the promise in the Book of Mormon that the American colonists would be "delivered by the power of God out of the hands of all other nations" (1 Ne. 13:16–19). The resurrected Jesus said, "For it is wisdom in the Father that they [European immigrants] should be established in this land [America], and be set up as a free people by the power of the Father, that these things [gospel] might come forth from them unto a remnant of your seed [Indians], that the covenant of the Father may be fulfilled which he hath covenanted with his people, O house of Israel" (3 Ne. 21:4).

35. McPherson, *Battle Cry of Freedom*, 309.

although it cost him his position as an apostle, could have fulfilled a deep-seated patriotism fused with his spiritual convictions.

The elders replaced him on the list of prospective apostles with Joseph Knox, a recently ordained evangelist. Another question was raised about whether one could serve in two offices at once, and what the difference was between an ordained office and a calling. Specifically, could Charles Brown and George Barnes (Barnes had replaced James Wagoner as one of Bickerton's counselors in January) be apostles since they were already in the presidency. This had been answered in the affirmative in Utah, where at the time the apostleship was held by men called to the church presidency. It had been different under Joseph Smith. In his day members of the presidency did not come from the Quorum of the Twelve.[36] Bickerton decided that his counselors would not serve in the Quorum of the Twelve. It would be the responsibility of the apostles, as in Joseph Smith's time, to preside over the missions. The church presidency would be elected and sustained annually, and the apostles would be in office for life. The presidency was elected, the apostles were ordained.[37]

When that was settled, it was left to replace Charles Brown and George Barnes as prospective members of the Quorum of the Twelve. When Brown nominated William Cadman, Joseph Astin arose and spoke in tongues, interpreted by Mary Astin to mean, "Verily, Verily, thus saith the Lord God, … I am well pleased with what ye are doing, it is according to My Will, therefore ye shall be blessed."[38] William Bickerton nominated James Nichols to replace George Barnes. Charles Brown then told the congregation he felt inspired to acknowledge John Dixon as a prophet like Bickerton for having demonstrated the gift of dreams and visions and thought he should be acknowledged for his gift and allowed to help guide the church. The elders stopped short

36. Bushman, *Rough Stone Rolling*, 283; Richards, *Marvelous Work*, 85.
37. Martin and Mancini, "History of the Church," 40.
38. Ibid., 42.

of formally ordaining Dixon, so that the priesthood office was left to Bickerton alone, but they recognized Dixon's prophetic ability.[39]

The church was assured on January 8 that to the extent they were "faithful in sowing the seeds" of the gospel, their effort "shall not return unto Me void," the interpretation of Joseph Astin's foreign tongue, received by Robert Riley. Later in the day, Astin again spoke in tongues, with George Barnes interpreting it as a paraphrase of Jesus, "Oh Elizabeth town how often would I have gathered you together as a hen gathers her chickens under her wings and you would not."[40]

These two divine messages corresponded with the apocalyptic view of the Old Testament prophet Hosea, "Sow to yourselves in righteousness" because as "ye have plowed wickedness, ye have reaped iniquity; ye have eaten the fruit of lies: because thou didst trust in thy way, in the multitude of thy mighty men. Therefore shall a tumult arise among thy people, and all thy fortresses shall be spoiled" (Hosea 10:12–14). Echoing that theme, the Book of Mormon people lamented their mortality only when reminded by cataclysms: "O that we had repented before this great and terrible day," they cried. Jesus said to them, "Oh ye people of these great cities which have fallen … how oft would I have gathered you as a hen gathereth her chickens under her wings" (3 Ne. 8:24; 10:4–6). Envisioning similar scenarios in the immediate future, Bickerton asked his ministry to institute a new church office, a high priest after the order of Melchizedek. This would be someone who could help prepare the world for the Second Advent.

What did he mean? Melchizedek in the Hebrew Bible is someone whose name meant "king of righteousness," who visited the patriarch Abraham and fed him bread and wine, blessed him, and received tribute of 10 percent (Gen. 14:18–20). In the Christian interpretation of the Old Testament, Melchizedek was a model for Christ, in that he did not come from an established priesthood line and yet would overturn the established religious order, replacing the priesthood that

39. Ibid.

40. Ibid., 43; Matt. 23:37; 3 Ne. 10:4–6.

relied on lineage and protocol with a priesthood of special appointment and spontaneity. In the Psalms, David sang, "The Lord hath sworn, and will not repent, Thou art a priest for ever after the order of Melchizedek. The Lord at thy right hand shall strike through kings in the day of his wrath. He shall judge among the heathen, he shall fill the places with the dead bodies; he shall wound the heads over many countries."[41] This was a reference to Jesus, the apostle Paul concluded (Heb. 7:17).[42]

The man to fill this auspicious office of high priest was Samuel Grimes, as announced on January 8, 1862, and after Grimes accepted the call and was endorsed by the elders he was ordained "after the order of Melchisedek" and given the "gifts of Wisdom and Revelation."[43] Joseph Smith had installed high priests to hold "the key of the mysteries of the kingdom, even the key of the knowledge of God," with "the privilege of receiving the mysteries of the kingdom of heaven, to have the heavens opened unto them, to commune with the general assembly and church of the Firstborn, and to enjoy the communion and presence of God the Father, and Jesus the Mediator of the new covenant" (D&C 84:19; 107:19).[44] Grimes too was authorized to commune with the heavenly realm regarding the Savior's return.[45]

There were two orders of priesthood in Joseph Smith's church. The members of the lower order (Aaronic Priesthood, including deacons, teachers, and priests) were allowed to administer the sacrament; priests could also baptize. Those of the higher order (Melchizedek Priesthood, including elders, seventies, high priests, patriarchs, apostles, prophets)

41. Ps. 110:4–6.

42. More is said about Melchizedek in the Book of Mormon, for instance that he "did establish peace in the land in his days; therefore he was called the prince of peace" (Alma 13:14–18), another parallel to Jesus.

43. Martin and Mancini, "History of the Church," 44.

44. Bushman, *Rough Stone Rolling*, 258.

45. According to the book of Revelation, during the Millennium all believers will become kings and priests and reign alongside the Messiah (Rev. 5:10). Melchizedek had been a clear example of what the Saints would become as resurrected or transfigured personages during the Millennium, ruling as kings and priests over the world when the Savior returned.

conferred the gift of the Holy Ghost.[46] Bickerton did not see the need to separate the priesthood offices in this way. Rather, the prophets, apostles, patriarchs, high priests, evangelists, and elders all held the Melchizedek Priesthood, while priests, teachers and deacons held ancillary positions. Anyone with the Melchizedek Priesthood had authority to baptize and bestow the Holy Ghost. There was not even a concept of a lower priesthood in Bickerton's writings or in the minutes of meetings.[47]

There was now a high priest, but not a quorum of ordained apostles. Bickerton considered apostles to be the capstone in the priesthood architecture. Other religious reformers had imagined a day when men would act in the capacity of Jesus's original twelve. Roger Williams, for instance, the cleric who was exiled in 1635 from the Massachusetts Bay Colony, was among those who thought it would be a positive development, probably in the context of the approaching Millennium.[48] When the revelation finally arrived to confirm the ordination of apostles, it came in the form of a vision to apostle-designate Benjamin Meadowcroft on the evening of May 28, 1862:

> I saw a vision of a man and He stood before me, and in his hands were two pitchers, and he said unto me,—What seest thou? and I said two pitchers, full and running over. And then a voice behind me said, What is in them two pitchers? I said, I know not, but it is pure like unto crystal. The voice then said, Thou hast heard it said, when thou was before the Throne, that out of the servants of the living God (Lord) should flow living water. That is the living water, thou dost see, and the Man that carries it, What is his

46. Bushman, *Rough Stone Rolling*, 74–75, 157–58; Larry C. Porter, "The Restoration of the Aaronic and Melchizedek Priesthoods," *Ensign*, Dec. 1996; Richards, *Marvelous Work*, 93. The evolution of priesthood in the 1830s is confusing. In June 1831 Smith and others were ordained to the high priesthood, which would later be interpreted to mean they were ordained high priests. Elders and others had been ordained in the church since 1830, without reference to a higher or lower priesthood. Richard Bushman explains that "Joseph may not have realized that elders were part of the Melchizedek Priesthood already and were being ordained to the office of high priest rather than receiving the powers of the high priesthood." Bushman, *Rough Stone Rolling*, 157–58; for more, see Prince, *Power from on High*.

47. Martin and Mancini, "History of the Church," 55. Bickerton did ordain some priests (18, 21).

48. Mather, *Magnalia Christi Americana*, 2:498.

> name? I replied Monstan Farneela, and he said, in other words, Melchisdek the Priest of the most High God and the voice said, see whither he goes. I lost sight of him for a little, I saw him again in the meeting, with—our brothern, and he held the pitchers above their heads, and they began to speak with power, and they spoke with words that shook the whole house, There were some in the house that ran to hide themselves, but they could find no place, the voice said again to me, The things that thou hast seen, write them, for this shall be fulfilled in a few days, on your heads, and now prepare yourselves and wait with patience.[49]

What Meadowcroft was saying was that he had seen Melchizedek himself. If the vision were true, the Old Testament king of righteousness would soon visit the congregation in the spirit and bring with him an endowment of authority. There could not have been a more explicit approval to ordain the apostles, at least given the metaphorical nature of visions.

While this was happening in Western Pennsylvania, the tumult across the country was becoming increasingly brutal. Battles raged east and west, on land and sea. In July, General Lee would push back the Union's advance toward Richmond in six engagements leaving more than 5,000 dead.[50] Prior to the Battle of Antietam in September, a Confederate lookout situated in the Blue Ridge Mountains, watched

> the serpentine approach of four Union corps across the [Middletown] valley—twelve divisions with a total of thirty-two infantry brigades, not including one corps which was still beyond the Catoctins—he said later that "the Hebrew poet whose idea of the awe-inspiring is expressed by the phrase, 'terrible as an army with banners,' [doubtless] had his view from the top of a mountain."[51]

In the subsequent engagement at Antietam Creek, near Sharpsburg, Maryland, the number of soldiers killed was 3,675, and an additional

49. Martin and Mancini, "History of the Church," 44–45.
50. McPherson, *Battle Cry of Freedom*, 418, 457, 470–71.
51. Foote, *Civil War*, 1:675.

19,051 wounded. That brought the total casualties for one day's fighting to 22,726.

Back in Western Pennsylvania, two months before the Battle of Antietam, Benjamin Meadowcroft asked the Saints to fast for two days prior to the conference scheduled for July 5–8. When the Saints arrived in Green Oak, they were spiritually invigorated, though hungry. The opening hymn was chosen with purpose. The lyrics to "Come, Let Us Anew, Our Journey Pursue" encouraged the congregants to never rest "till the Master appear," referencing the imminence of "the millennial year." Meadowcroft spoke in tongues on July 7, and the interpretation sounded like a court bailiff announcing the next order of business: "Set apart—Set apart and ordain the twelve. Set apart and ordain."[52] In a cacophony of languages, eight men gave their approval, after which Bickerton invited the twelve selected individuals to the dais, with John Dixon replacing Andrew Rattray (reason unknown); William Cadman and James Nichols replacing Charles Brown and George Barnes of the church presidency; and Joseph Knox replacing military enlistee William Bacon. The rest of the twelve were the three Bickertons (Alexander, Arthur, Thomas), James Brown, Joseph Astin, Cummings Cherry, John Neish, and Meadowcroft. The secretary recorded that "when the ordinations were over," everyone "praise[d] God and g[a]ve G[l]ory to him."[53]

As far as Bickerton was concerned, the church was now fully organized and ready to venture out while there was still time to rescue their fellow gentiles who were pure of heart and to follow the risen Lord's intention that they "assist my people, the remnant of Jacob [American Indians], and also as many of the house of Israel as shall come, that they may build a city, which shall be called the New Jerusalem" (3 Ne. 21:22–23). Later it would be noticed that the ordinations occurred on Tammuz 9 of the Hebrew calendar, the day commemorating the

52. Martin and Mancini, "History of the Church," 44–46; *Hymns of the Church of Jesus Christ of Latter-day Saints*, 217.

53. Martin and Mancini, "History of the Church," 46.

breach of Jerusalem's walls by Babylonian invaders, the scattering of Israel. The prophet Zechariah promised that Tammuz 9, a day of fasting, would one day become "to the house of Judah joy and gladness, and cheerful feasts" (Zech. 8:19).[54]

The next day Bickerton and others of the priesthood washed the apostles' feet and anointed their heads with oil. George Barnes raised his voice and said, "Hear ye the word of the Lord, ye are My Sons and Daughters, and I have committed unto you the Keys of the Kingdom, therefore be faithful." Charles Brown proclaimed, "Hear ye the word of the Lord, O ye Twelve, whom I have chosen and ordained, I commit unto [you] the Keys of the Kingdom, and no weapon that is formed against you shall prosper, until you have finished your work. I shall make you as a bow—and my word shall go from you as an arrow, and many shall cry out [']what shall we do?[']"[55] This paralleled what Jesus quoted to his disciples from Isaiah, that "no weapon that is formed against thee shall prosper, and every tongue that shall rise against thee in judgement thou shalt condemn. This is the heritage of the servants of the Lord, and their righteousness is of me, saith the Lord" (Isa. 54:17; 3 Ne. 22:17).

The members in Green Oak saw these heavenly pronouncements as the ensign Isaiah had mentioned when he said, "All ye inhabitants of the world, and dwellers on the earth, see ye, when he lifteth up an ensign on the mountains; and when he bloweth a trumpet, hear ye. For so the Lord said unto me, I will take my rest, and I will consider in my dwelling place[,] like a clear heat upon herbs, and like a cloud of dew in the heat of harvest."[56] The apostle William Cadman penned poetic verses to celebrate the step forward "to lead the Church, on Earth, to Heaven."[57]

In the midst of this pentecostal fervor and trauma of the Civil War, it would have been difficult to imagine normalcy. In February 1862

54. Jacob ben Asher, Orach Chayim 549, *Arba'ah Turim*, online at www.sefaria.org/Tur.
55. Martin and Mancini, "History of the Church," 47.
56. Isaiah 18:1–4.
57. Cadman, *Personal Observations*, 9.

the poet Julia Ward Howe published in the *Atlantic Monthly* the "Battle Hymn of the Republic" linking Armageddon with the Civil War.[58] "He is trampling out the vintage where the grapes of wrath are stored," she wrote. It was a "sour ripe grape," Isaiah had written of the fruit that would be destroyed by trimming the branches (Isa. 18:5). "He has sounded forth the trumpet that shall never call retreat," Howe's verse continued. "When he bloweth a trumpet, hear ye," Isaiah had warned (18:3). The feeling in the chapel must have been as fervent as any emotion on the battlefield.

58. Florence Howe Hall, *The Story of the Battle Hymn of the Republic*, 56; *Hymns of the Church of Jesus Christ of Latter-day Saints*, 60.

EIGHT

THE ENSIGN

1862–65

"Son of man, Prophesy and say, Thus Saith the Lord, God, unto my people and servants, Fear ye not, . . . for I have chosen you . . . to administer my word unto the people of the nations of the earth and they shall write to you from the East and from the West and from the North and from the South, to know the truth, and the way of Salvation for I have given that knowlege unto you."

—revelation, Benjamin Meadowcroft, Nov. 9, 1863

Now that William Bickerton had put in place a Quorum of Twelve Apostles, he turned his attention to the devastation around him and the need to establish an ensign that the elect could look to and gather around. Some of the bloodiest battles of the Civil War occurred in 1862.[1] As Joseph Smith said in his Civil War prophecy, "Thus with the sword and by bloodshed the inhabitants of the earth shall mourn."[2] In October 1862 photographer Matthew Brady staged an exhibition in Manhattan that brought the carnage of the Civil War to the eyes of the average citizen. A *New York Times* journalist wrote that "if [Brady] has not brought bodies and laid them in our dooryards and along the streets, he has done something very like it."[3] In similar fashion, the followers of the coal-mining prophet in West Elizabeth, Pennsylvania,

1. The major battles and casualties were Fredericksburg (17,000), Second Bull Run (16,000), Shiloh (24,000), and Stones River (25,000).

2. Doctrine and Covenants 87:6.

3. "Brady's Photographs: Pictures of the Dead at Antietam," *New York Times*, Oct. 20, 1862.

believed the banner they were raising in the Allegheny foothills would draw the attention of the entire world.

Already in 1859, Webster Wagoner thought the "Ensign ha[d] been lifted," the "Standard raised." But thus far, it was a metaphorical ensign.[4] They needed something literal—for instance, a publication missionaries could take with them to show what was happening in Pennsylvania. If so, what type of publication? It took two years for the idea to become a reality, but by the end of 1863 they would produce their first pamphlet, printed nearby in Pittsburgh, as a review of the church's history, doctrines, and revelations. It was addressed to "the Right Honorable President elect, and to the Senators, Governors and Representatives of these United States, and likewise to Kings, Potentates and rulers of the whole earth and to all people." Appropriately titled *The Ensign*, the full title, in keeping with the custom of the time, read like a table of contents: *The Ensign: or a Light to Lighten the Gentiles in which the Doctrine of the Church of Jesus Christ of Latter-Day Saints, is Set Forth, and Scripture Evidence Adduced to Establish It. Also, a Brief Treatise upon the Most Important Prophecies Recorded in the Old and New Testaments, which relate to the Great Work of God or the Latter Days.*

More specifically, it contained a personal history written by William Bickerton, a defense of the Book of Mormon, a review of the larger Latter Day Saint movement, and the church's views on marriage and national government. It stated exactly why the Pennsylvania Saints had separated themselves from the Mormon Church in Utah; it indicated why Bickerton was the rightful successor to Joseph Smith. The tract explained that the church adhered to traditional Christian precepts, not the alleged Utah heresies involving polygamy, baptism for the dead, and the plurality of gods. It included this warning: "Therefore the angel [Moroni] has restored the everlasting gospel and it is preached by this people, by way of commandment, declaring the hour of God's judgments is come, and these things will speedily be all

4. "Book of Record," 11.

fulfilled, and, therefore; seeing the calamities which are coming upon the nations of the earth, we feel it to be our bounden duty to present this memorial to all people."[5]

While Bickerton and his two counselors and two of the apostles began thinking about what they should include in the missionary tract, Bickerton was following the progress of the Civil War for the signs of the end of the world "when the choice of God shall rise of the seed of Joseph," meaning the Choice Seer who would emerge among the Native Americans and his following.[6] While everyone else's eyes were on the North and South, the Bickertonites kept at least a peripheral gaze on the West. Nor could Charles Brown, George Barnes, William Cadman, and Joseph Astin devote too much time to writing just yet. In mid-1862, Brown and Cadman were sent to Virginia to preach, right into the heart of the Civil War conflict, the stronghold of the Confederacy. Other missionary assignments indicated that the church was widening its reach, two elders being sent to Ohio and two, Arthur Bickerton and John Stevenson, to West Virginia. A final missionary pair was directed to the areas of Brownsville, Fayette City, and Mt. Pleasant, about thirty miles south of the church's headquarters in Green Oak, where the elders encountered success. To Bickerton's delight, the missionaries in Virginia also baptized thirty people. In addition, while Brown was preaching one day, a man began convulsing, so Brown "left the pulpit, took the man by the hand, raised him up[,] and the fit left him." This confirmed to the onlookers that Brown possessed the gift of healing, increasing their interest in his message. The elders in West Virginia "brought in many souls," Bickerton reported. The two in Pennsylvania converted eighty-four people. On the other hand, the two in Ohio "did not agree with each other and did not do much good," Bickerton was sorry to disclose. Still, the overall results were so good, "I am giving this to show that it was the word of the Lord," he announced, citing "more than two

5. Bickerton, *Ensign*, 5.
6. Ibid., 17.

hundred" people who joined the church as a result of the 1862 outreach.[7] Many more would be converted during the Civil War.

As the war raged through the year, the shock of the number of deaths reminded some people of life's tenuousness and drew them closer to God, while news of one loss after another on the battlefield embittered others. Only a month after the church's July 1862 conference, Union troops were defeated a second time at Bull Run, at the same place they had been forced to retreat from, with heavy losses, a year earlier. Clara Barton, a volunteer with the ladies' aid society of Washington, DC, recorded that wounded men "were brot down from the field and laid on the ground [on beds of hay] beside the train and so back up the hill 'till they covered acres." The scene she described was horrific. "By midnight there must have been three thousand helpless men lying in that hay," she wrote. "All night we made compresses and slings—and bound up and wet wounds when we could get water, fed what we could, travelled miles in that dark over these poor helpless wretches, in terror lest some one's candle fall into the hay and consume them all." Soon after the Second Battle of Bull Run (also known as Second Manassas), word came that Cincinnati, which like Pittsburgh lay on the Ohio River, was also under threat by Confederate cavalry, although the invaders were quickly repelled by Union defenses.[8]

None of this was a surprise to William Bickerton, nor was it welcome news, since his oldest son, James, had enlisted on August 7, 1862, as part of an infantry regiment. When James's term expired, he signed up again, this time with the Pennsylvania 14th Cavalry Regiment.[9] Part of the reason for his enlistment was that "there was no work to be had" in West Elizabeth. "I sent my oldest son, 17 years of age to war," Bickerton grieved.[10] While William tried his best to keep the church united and contributed as much as he could to his family's

7. Bickerton, "Testimony, June 1903," 11.

8. McPherson, *Battle Cry of Freedom*, 532–33.

9. He enlisted for ninety days as a fifer before switching to a two-year enlistment with mounted troops. Bates, *History of Pennsylvania Volunteers,* 4:77, 870.

10. Bickerton, "Testimony, June 1903," 10; James Bickerton was listed as sixteen years

upkeep, he even left for a time to work near Pittsburgh. "I was over age for a soldier, so I went and worked [in a coal mine] at Sawmill Run," he wrote, referring to the creek by that name that feeds into the Ohio River. The Pittsburgh Coal Company had just opened a mine and built an access road from Coal Hill (Mt. Washington) and needed workers. It was twenty miles north of Elizabeth, where, separated from his family, the forty-seven-year-old church leader was still shoveling coal, this time to fuel Union factories, locomotives, and the war effort. His absence placed a burden on his wife and children. "My Brother sent me word that my wife had no provisions, and I sent her ten dollars," he wrote.[11] With the demand for war materiel, prices rose. At the same time, the effects of the Panic of 1857 still lingered. Another market run in 1861, stimulated by the South's secession, kept wages low. Between 1863 and 1864, real wages fell an average of 20 percent, at the same time prices were rising.[12]

Not only were individual households in trouble, the church itself was deeply in debt and had fallen behind in its payments for its headquarters in Green Oak. On August 30, 1862, the last day of the Second Battle of Bull Run, the elders met to decide what to do about their debts. In retrospect many years later, Bickerton realized it had been a mistake to dedicate a chapel before it was paid for. In Green Oak all seemed well for three years until they had to make the final balloon payments, to which Bickerton contributed $200 ($5,000 today) in the final push, and others contributed significant amounts; still, not everyone pitched in, much to Bickerton's irritation. "The money had to be paid to the builders. It was in war time, and as I was the President of the Church, the Sheriff served papers on me, and I was sued." Because the economy was unstable, the builders demanded payment in hard currency. "The builders would take nothing but gold," Bickerton recorded.[13]

old in the 1860 census, likely making him eighteen in 1862. See the United States Census, West Elizabeth, Allegheny County, June 25, 1860.

11. Bickerton, "Testimony, June 1903," 10; Wall, *Second Geological Survey*, 179.

12. McPherson, *Battle Cry of Freedom*, 448–50.

13. Bickerton, "Testimony, June 1903," 9.

Unsure what to do, a committee of seven men[14] was appointed to meet in Green Oak to sketch out a resolution. They did not like carrying debt (the apostle Paul had exhorted the churches in the New Testament to "owe no man anything," Rom. 13:8) and could not imagine defaulting. At the same time, they knew how much all the members were being squeezed by the rising costs and sinking wages. So the seven men meeting on September 6, 1862, decided that, for now, they would simply make one more request for donations from the members, for whatever amount anyone could manage to pay. They also prioritized what the church owed, placing debts owed to members ahead of the building cost. The first in line was George Barnes, the committee chair, who was owed $80, followed by Peter Webb, who was owed $100, and a Sister Lewis who had loaned the church $10.[15] Having come up with a weak plan that lacked urgency, the predictable result was that the church was unable to see an appreciable increase in collections and Bickerton himself would end up having to contribute another $400 in 1863, about a year's earnings for a coal miner.[16]

Seemingly unconcerned about the finances in Green Oak, the members in West Elizabeth were simultaneously clamoring for a building of their own because they were "meeting from house to house" without enough room for everyone, "and many found fault and wished to have the meetings" moved to a building of some sort, if not a chapel. As Bickerton thought about this, he "heard the song of 'Home Sweet Home' being sung [in his head] by voices not visible but far superior to human voices, and it brought such glorious blessings to me," he said, that he interpreted it as a message to obtain a chapel for the West Elizabeth Saints. The song was popular at the time, a show tune composed by Sir Henry Bishop and lyricized by an American-born playwright living in London, John Howard Payne, for *Clari: Or the Maid of Milan*,

14. George Barnes, Joseph Astin, James Brown, Cummings Cherry, Benjamin Meadowcroft, John Neish, and John Tilford.

15. Martin and Mancini, "History of the Church," 47–48.

16. Ibid., 56; Bickerton, "Testimony, June 1903," 9.

which premiered in 1823 at Covent Garden Theatre. The lyrics to the second verse read:

> An exile from home, splendor dazzles in vain:
> Oh! give me my lowly thatched cottage again!
> The birds singing gayly, that come at my call,—
> Give me them, with the peace of mind dearer than all.

The song had tugged at Bickerton's heart. King Solomon was credited with having said, "Withhold not good from them to whom it is due, when it is in the power of thine hand to do it" (Prov. 3:27). Thinking along those lines, Bickerton "went the next day and purchased" a building to use as a church. He paid $250 that was needed by his family, but found the sacrifice made him happy. "About this time I saw a vision of a table spread with no end to it as far as I could see, and I saw the saints feasting on all sides of the table, and all were rejoicing." He said he "never slept that night, on account of the glory of God that I experienced, it lasting the whole night." After "feasting on heavenly food" for an evening, he concluded that "no one knows without the experience. No tongue can express the peace and rest of a soul wrapt in Jesus' love."[17]

The sentimentality on his part was probably due to his wife's unexpected death that year at the age of about thirty-seven, although the exact date and cause of death are unknown. One can imagine Dorothy overextending herself in caring, without sufficient means, for their seven children: James, Eliza Ann, Josephine (who died in 1852), Clara Virginia, Angeline Ann, Josephine, and Florence. Four of the girls were still young—Clara Virginia ten, Angeline Ann seven, Josephine five, and Florence three—and would be helped by their older sister, Eliza Ann, who was fifteen. Dorothy was William's devoted companion for two decades, and the grief at her passing no doubt was acute.[18]

The next development would be humorous if not so tragic, but no sooner had the West Elizabeth congregation moved into its new

17. Bickerton, "Testimony, June 1903," 9–10.

18. Pilgrim, "Descendants of Thomas Bickerton," 2; Bickerton, *St. John Weekly News*, Aug. 16, 1889.

building than the increase in convert baptisms made it too small to accommodate the number of members and they had to look for a larger building. "There was scarcely a week passed without baptisms," Bickerton wrote. Next he paid $150 for a brick schoolhouse and $60 for pews, and "there was not a member that helped me pay for anything," he complained, "except my Brother Furnished two stoves."[19] But in exchange for his charity, he was repaid by the fact that his gospel message continued to resonate with so many new converts.

The country had seemed to be coming around to Bickerton's way of thinking in late September 1862 when Abraham Lincoln met with his cabinet and told them he had made a covenant with God that if the Union drove rebels from Maryland, he would free the slaves in the Confederacy. He had been working on a draft of the Emancipation Proclamation, drawing on his wartime authority to seize the enemy's resources. He wanted to inform the South that any slaves still in captivity on January 1, 1863, would be recognized by the North as liberated. He did not have the authority to free slaves in the North, only in the states that had seceded from the Union, and in practicality only in areas the Union had won back to the country. Nevertheless, it was a first step. "We shout for joy that we live to record this righteous decree," Frederick Douglass exclaimed. Lincoln signed the document on New Year's Day 1863. He simultaneously pushed for the enlistment of blacks. The military responded reluctantly at first by utilizing them only "to garrison forts" and not in the field, but before long there were units of black soldiers at the front lines too. Lincoln confided to Andrew Johnson, governor of the part of Tennessee the Union had won back, that "the bare sight of fifty thousand armed, and drilled black soldiers on the banks of the Mississippi, would end the rebellion at once."[20] In essence, Lincoln had transformed the country's forces into an army of liberation and had invited the slaves to help the effort to win the war. What rang in Bickerton's head, no

19. Bickerton, "Testimony, June 1903," 10–11.
20. McPherson, *Battle Cry of Freedom*, 557–66.

doubt, when he heard this was the prediction that it "will come to pass, after many days, [that] slaves shall rise up against their masters, who shall be marshaled and disciplined for war," a line from Joseph Smith's prophecy (D&C 87:4).

Just as the army felt the need to recruit increasing numbers of soldiers, so did the church in battling forces of darkness with an army of preachers. Bickerton felt he needed to ordain more officers and extend their reach to distribute the burden of maintaining the church. He was not above reworking the church's organizational structure to do so. There was an endless amount of work involved in overseeing church business, including the need to visit all the various branches, interact with the members, and advise the ministry. He began sending others out to the branches, pleased to have Andrew Rattray travel to Wheeling, Virginia, in October 1862, for instance. With the war on everyone's mind, Rattray employed military language as he encouraged the membership. "Stand to your posts," he said. As a word of comfort, channeling the voice of the Lord, he uttered the promise, "Be faithful and I will bless you." Later in the day at the Wheeling conference, Luke Smith and Rebecca Dixon received baptism. When the new members had hands laid on their heads to bestow the Holy Ghost, Luke Smith spoke in tongues. "Sister Rattray" gave the interpretation a more pacifist theme than Andrew's message, admonishing the members to "seek for knowledge" and learn "the mystery of the Kingdom of God." John Stevenson suggested that since the new member had exercised a spiritual gift, they should ordain him. By day's end, Luke Smith had been baptized, confirmed, and ordained, which was fairly atypical.[21]

Much to Bickerton's delight, the ministry called seventeen men as evangelists on January 5, 1863. In addition, Charles Brown suggested that they ordain Bickerton to the office of "prophet, seer, and revelator," which would be a new position in the church. Previously Bickerton had been ordained a prophet only. When the ministry had agreed to the proposition, Brown washed his leader's feet and anointed

21. Martin and Mancini, "History of the Church," 48–49.

his head with oil. This raised the expectation that the time was ripe for the sealed portion of the gold plates of the Book of Mormon to be translated, no doubt the writings of the brother of Jared that the Book of Mormon described as being extraordinary "unto the overpowering of man to read them" (Ether 12:24). After the ordinance, Bickerton and Brown walked around the congregation pronouncing blessings on all the women, not wanting to exclude them after so much focus on the male priesthood.[22]

Later that month, Bickerton reversed himself on whether his counselors could be apostles. Now it occurred to him that Charles Brown and George Barnes, contrary to his previous reasoning, should in fact become "Apostles and Counselors of the Church of Jesus Christ of Latter Day Saints."[23] He no doubt remembered that Joseph Smith and Oliver Cowdery were referred to as apostles in August 1830, four months after they had ordained each other elders on April 6, 1830, the date of the original church's organization. In an August revelation to Joseph Smith, the Lord said he had "ordained you and confirmed you to be apostles, and especial witnesses of my name."[24] It may be that the titles *elder* and *apostle* were considered interchangeable at the time, and not that they referred to separate offices. Whatever the case, the change for Bickerton's counselors had the effect of bestowing more clout. They would not become part of the Quorum of Twelve Apostles, yet would have their authority extended beyond the local areas where the church had congregations to the mission regions as well.

On March 17, 1863, apostle James Nichols shared a dream that confirmed the idea of the twelve dividing their attention between the home and foreign locations:

> I dreamed that I had been to a meeting, but I can't exactly tell where. But I thought that me and some of the brethren was taking a walk in a field

22. Ibid., 50.

23. Ibid.

24. This has been interpreted to refer to the appearance of the spirits of Peter, James, and John to bestow the Melchizedek Priesthood on Joseph Smith and Oliver Cowdery, D&C 27:12; Bushman, *Rough Stone Rolling*; Richards, *Marvelous Work*, 140.

> and we stopped and sung, "Stars of the Morning Shout for Joy" when there was a very bright light appeared in the sky, apparently in the East, and I thought I was sitting on a fence, with my back toward the East, when there was another great light appeared in the East, but my back was to it, but I saw the brightness of it[,] and it appeared to be brighter than the sun, and appeared to come out of a dark cloud. And I looked around and saw a crown of twelve stars in the sky, partly clouded over. A short distance from where the light came out, ... I thought the stars went away one by one, until they all went but five and these five appeared very bright, and there appeared to be an arrow across each one, and the five appeared to form a line, all connected together, so beautiful that I cannot describe, and I clapped my hands and glorified God.[25]

The crown of twelve stars represented the apostles, he realized, similar to the vision Charlotte Hibbs had seen in 1860, only this time five of the apostles would stay in place and seven would travel elsewhere. Drawing on the prophecy of Charles Brown of July 1862, the arrows referred to preaching the word of God. The hymn Nichols referred to included a line in the second verse, "Come ye tribes of every land," with a refrain, "and praise the Lamb." It was a reference to missionary labor and a gathering prior to the Millennium. In the third verse, the kingdom comes to the Savior when he defeats "the man of sin." "Bring the blest millennium," the refrain goes.[26] Apostles Joseph Astin and Benjamin Meadowcroft accepted the dream as revelatory and spoke in tongues, Meadowcroft interpreting it as a message from Christ, "I will give power to my servant Wm Bickerton, to bind the man of Sin, and shut the door and take the key that binds old Satan a Thousand years."[27]

When the spring arrived, Bickerton found the country chastised and uncertain of victory. Abraham Lincoln considered the war to be God's judgment for sin, something Bickerton agreed with wholeheartedly. The president called for a national day of fasting and prayer, saying:

---

25. Martin and Mancini, "History of the Church," 52.
26. *Deseret Sunday School Song Book*, 9.
27. Martin and Mancini, "History of the Church," 52.

> May we not justly fear that the awful calamity of civil war, which now desolates the land, may be but a punishment, inflicted upon us, for our presumptuous sins, to the needful end of our national reformation as a whole People? We have been the recipients of the choicest bounties of Heaven. We have been preserved, these many years, in peace and prosperity. We have grown in numbers, wealth and power, as no other nation has ever grown. But we have forgotten God. We have forgotten the gracious hand which preserved us in peace, and multiplied and enriched and strengthened us; and we have vainly imagined, in the deceitfulness of our hearts, that all these blessings were produced by some superior wisdom and virtue of our own. Intoxicated with unbroken success, we have become too self-sufficient to feel the necessity of redeeming and preserving grace, too proud to pray to the God that made us! It behooves us then, to humble ourselves before the offended Power, to confess our national sins, and to pray for clemency and forgiveness.[28]

The day of national prayer, although earnestly promoted, had another motivation, as well, in diverting attention away from the unpopular Enrollment Act that Lincoln signed on March 3, 1863, requiring every male citizen to enroll for conscription, along with any immigrant who had applied for citizenship between twenty and forty-five years of age.

On April 5, apostle Joseph Astin baptized four new members: Thomas Weld, Jane Robinson, Mary Taylor, and Margaret Barnes. A member who had recently returned back into fellowship, Charles Cowan, spoke in tongues and gave his own interpretation: "Thus Saith the Lord, This is my Church, and these are my servants that you have come to hear tonight. They have authority to adopt you into my church, and there is no other Church that is my church but this Church and these are my servants and I will bless them and be with them."[29] The four new members were treated to this special welcome into the church by God himself through revelation.

An interesting new development on April 6, 1863, was the suggestion that the church should appoint women as deaconesses.

28. Basler, *Collected Works of Abraham Lincoln*, 5:155–57.
29. Martin and Mancini, "History of the Church," 52.

Charles Cowan and Joseph Knox suggested it after they learned the apostle Paul, in his letter to the church at Rome, used the Greek word *diakonia* for what was translated into the English word *servant.* "I commend unto you Phebe our sister, which is a servant [deaconess] of the church which is at Cenchrea," the text reads (Rom. 16:1–2).[30] A deacon was expected to care for widows and orphans and to perform "wonders and miracles" (Acts 6). A woman could do that as well as a man, Cowan and Knox reasoned. Deaconnesses would also be allowed to deliver communion to shut-ins after the elders had blessed it, and they could anoint a woman to be healed if an ordained man was not present. Spurred by this remarkable development, the Saints decided to appoint midwives not only to care for pregnant women but also to look after and treat the sick and afflicted. The church voted to "have nothing to do with the Doctors at all."[31]

Midwives were more competent than doctors in any case in performing births in the antebellum age. On the battlefield, surgeons were employed to saw off limbs, while most of the restorative care was performed by female volunteers. In the face of infectious disease, doctors watched helplessly as one regiment after another was reduced by half through sickness. "Our doctor knows about as much as a ten year old boy," one soldier complained in a letter home. Another described a field hospital near a farm where "about the building you could see the Hogs belonging to the Farm eating [amputated] arms and other portions."[32] The issue for the Bickertonites was, of course, that they would be protected by the miraculous power of faith healing and could see no benefit to crude medical care.

The Saints continued their discussion of Bible translations on April 7, aware that the king's version was beautifully written but not

30. See also Rom. 16:6, 12; Titus 2:3–5; *Strong's Exhaustive Concordance of the Bible*, 940. Greek word *diakonia* found in "Greek Dictionary of the New Testament," 22, reference number 1248.

31. Cadman, *History of the Church of Jesus Christ*, 145; Martin and Mancini, "History of the Church," 51, 145.

32. McPherson, *Battle Cry of Freedom*, 486–87, 477.

as precisely translated as some of the versions that had appeared since 1611. Joseph Smith also thought the King James Version needed to be corrected and made changes to the Bible and the Book of Mormon both. As invigorating and productive as the conversation was, it did not sit well with Bickerton, who saw it as an attack on the source of his interpretations of ancient prophecy. Christ, for whom he served as amanuensis, agreed with him: "Verily thus saith the Lord, seek not to pull down the scriptures, … Preach my word, though there be many wrong translations in it. … And by this the world shall know that I am the Lord. Hear ye this, for this is my Church and I will let nothing pass that is not according to my will—Saith the Lord, God of Heaven."[33]

That put an end for the moment to the exegetical exercises the members had been engaged in. If the texts contained mistakes, the lessons were clear enough, the Bickertonites concluded. Besides that, who knew where the discussion would end if they questioned the provenance of the word of God? The Book of Mormon stated it clearly: "For behold, this [book] is written for the intent that ye may believe" that other book of scripture, the Bible (Morm. 7:8–9). One purpose of scripture was to convince the Saints of the last days to heed the modern prophet. Where would it lead if they questioned the texts Bickerton had relied on?

At the summer conference in Green Oak on July 5, 1863, the Book of Mormon became the topic of preaching. John Stevenson spoke the word of the Lord, that if they failed to take the Book of Mormon with them when they went into the world to preach, "the blood of this generation will rest upon you." At any other time, the warning might have sounded poetic or soteriological, but in the middle of the Civil War, geographically and chronologically, it must have been unsettling. Two days earlier, 180 miles to the southeast, the deadliest battle of the Civil War had taken place in Gettysburg on Pennsylvania soil. It produced 51,000 casualties, including over 3,000 Union dead, and had begun over the pitiable state of Confederate supplies and a rumor that

33. Martin and Mancini, "History of the Church," 53.

Gettysburg had a supply of shoes. The Confederate commander Ambrose Hill authorized a division of soldiers to enter the town and grab the shoes. As they approached, they collided with two Union cavalry brigades. From there, the battle grew into a turning point of the war.[34]

As reinforcements poured in on both sides, the Confederate artillery barrage on the Union positions could be heard as far away as Pittsburgh and presumably in Green Oak. The dust settled, and General Lee found he had lost a third of his Confederate army. The Union had lost more than one quarter of its force. There was better news from Mississippi, although with an equally grisly body count of about 4,000 killed, where on July 4 troops led by US General Ulysses S. Grant captured the fort overlooking the Mississippi River at Vicksburg. Yet even as the North celebrated this victory, a Confederate force of 2,500 cavalry advanced as far north as Steubenville, Ohio, forty miles west of Pittsburgh. And the draft riots in New York City that month left 120 dead and about 2,000 wounded.

The Saints were confident that they would survive the terror surrounding them by waiting it out. Yet their rhetoric, like Andrew Rattray's in Virginia, was being influenced by the harshness of the war. On July 5, George Meadowcroft commanded the members in the name of the Lord that they "go forth and crush all other systems. Rejoice, Rejoice, ye Saints of the Most High." Charles Cowan arose and predicted that anyone who opposed them "shall perish." Bickerton verified the next day that "no one has power to cut you off." On a more gentle note, James McDowell picked up the theme earlier introduced by Sister Rattray and again promised the "key of knowledge." "Not many days hence, in this Valley," he said, speaking for Christ, "I will pour out My Spirit and give unto them the Key of Knowledge, whereby they may open the door of the Church of Jesus Christ and behold the glories of God."[35]

On July 6 the church added personnel to the priesthood and issued

34. McPherson, *Battle Cry of Freedom*, 653.
35. Martin and Mancini, "History of the Church," 54–55.

more mission calls. James McDowell was asked to join Samuel Grimes in the high priest's office. The Lord said of McDowell, "I know him, and I have proved him, therefore I have a great work for him to do." After Andrew Rattray was called to the same office, he and McDowell were ordained. Two days later the ministry called eleven men on mission tours, seven of them from the Quorum of the Twelve—Alexander Bickerton, Arthur Bickerton, James Brown, William Cadman, John Dixon, Joseph Knox, and James Nichols—in fulfillment of the dream Nichols had of the crown of twelve stars, seven of them becoming separated from the rest. As the apostles went out into the world, there was "a tremendous storm," Nichols recalled from his dream. The Civil War qualified as that tempest. The seven would be joined by the two apostle–counselors George Barnes and Charles Brown—and by William Skillen and John Stevenson.[36]

Before their departure, and before the summer conference ended, the church took a recess on July 8 to marry the prophet to Charlotte Hibbs in the Green Oak chapel, James Brown conducting. It was a day of celebration on two counts, since they were also able to rededicate the Green Oak building after having completed payment to the builders. The dedication was accepted by revelation to Bickerton: "Ye shall meet in this house that you built in My name for [now] to fill up the organization, and from thence ye shall go forth unto all nations." The secretary recorded that members "rejoice[d] with joy unspeakable." Charlotte Bickerton, *née* Hibbs, had been a follower of Bickerton since the 1850s and enjoyed similar spiritual gifts, which meant she appreciated him on a level most other women would not have understood. She knew she was wedding not only the prophet but also the church. At forty-four, she would become the instant mother of six, five of whom needed to be raised to maturity. In addition, in July 1865 she would give birth to her own son, William Alma. It was a lot of responsibility to assume over a short period of time.[37]

36. Ibid., 54–56 & 52.

37. Ibid., 56; Pilgrim, "Descendants of Thomas Bickerton," 2.

Despite the wedding, the conference continued to address routine business. The elders appointed three men to get the missionary pamphlet printed. Until then, what should they use on their mission tours? they wondered. The answer from the Lord came through Joseph Astin that for now the Bible and Book of Mormon would suffice. After all, "there is no other records to be given to the Gentiles." Should they begin preaching to the Indians? When would the sealed portion be revealed? As timely as these questions were, the day was coming to a close and they would have to pick up these themes at a more opportune time.[38]

On July 9 apostle Benjamin Meadowcroft and high priest Andrew Rattray began by suggesting that they endorse William Bickerton as their prophet, seer, and revelator, a touching gesture. Bickerton responded by saying he wanted to be assisted by others in the office, and so he proceeded to lay his hands on his counselors, Charles Brown and George Barnes, and ordain them to the same office. He remembered his rival in Utah who claimed the same authority. Suddenly he spoke in God's voice that something should be done about the effrontery in Utah: "Verily, saith the Lord God. It is My Will that they be seperated from the Priesthood." The official minutes read that it was "moved by President Wm Bickerton and seconded by counselor Charles Brown, that the first Presidency of the organization of the Church of Jesus Christ, as organized by Joseph Smith, but has now become poluted, therefore they are, this ninth day, of the Seventh month, in the year of our Lord, 1863, [to] be seperated from the Holy Priesthood." The conference then excommunicated all the ordained officers of the Latter-day Saints in Utah.[39] Bickerton believed the authority held by his ministry was unmatched by any other.

38. Martin and Mancini, "History of the Church," 56–57. Although Joseph Astin declared that God would give no other records to the gentiles, the Saints did not interpret this to mean that the Lord would not give them the sealed record of the gold plates. The Book of Mormon states that when the gentiles exercise faith like the brother of Jared, "then will I manifest unto them the things which the brother of Jared saw, even to the unfolding unto them all my revelations, saith Jesus Christ" (Ether 4:6–7) Therefore, the Saints understood that Astin's message merely referred to the other records that the Choice Seer would translate.

39. Ibid., 57–58.

To understand what drove his resolve, a sermon he gave at the October 4, 1863, conference on the topic of faith is instructive. It gives a flavor of his rhetorical style as he hammers home each point through repetition, posing and answering questions, and appealing to scripture even while advocating contemporary revelation to supplement the existing canon:

> For without faith we cannot receive revelation from God[,] and without revelation from God for ourselves, we cannot know God. For no man can say that Jesus is the Christ but by the Holy spirit, which is the revelation of Jesus Christ in your souls. For instance, the faith that Abel had, came by revelation that his offering pleased God more than his brother Cain's[,] and Abel's faith would not do for Enoch, no he must have faith, and revelation for himself, and his revelation would not do for Noah[;] for except Noah had received revelation from God for himself he would not have had faith to build the Ark, where by he and his household were saved, and again Noah's revelations would never have satisfied Abraham[.] No, unless he had received revelation from God for himself that he must offer up Isaac[,] he would not have offered him. For the Lord had promised unto him that in his seed, all nations of the world would be blessed, therefore he staggered not at the commandment but offered Isaac, knowing that God was able to raise seed to him from the ashes of his son. Therefore in faith, he offered up his son. And what then? The word of the Lord was given to him by an Angel—saying, now I know that thou fearest God, seeing thou hast not with held thine only son from Me. And therefore it was counted unto him for righteousness. And, again Abraham's revelation would not do for Isaac, or Jacob[,] and their revelations would not do for anyone else. No! Every man must have his own revelation for himself or he can never know whether he is acceptable in the sight of God. For no man can say that Jesus is the Christ, but by the revelation of Jesus in his soul, "Hear the word of the Lord," John 7:17. "If any man will do His will, he shall know of the doctrine, whether it be of God, or whether I speak of myself. Verse 18. He that speaketh of himself, seeketh his own glory. But he that seeketh His glory that sent him[,] the same is true, and no unrighteousness is in him." Now how can we know? Why, we must enter the new and everlasting covenant with [the Lord], and then he has promised to put His laws in our minds, and write them in our hearts, and he will be unto

> you a God, and you shall be His people. And ye need not teach every man his neighbor and every man his brother[,] saying "know ye the Lord," for all shall know me from the least to the greatest, for I will be merciful to their unrighteousness, and their sins, and their iniquities will I remember no more. So then we see it is the privilege of all mankind to know the Lord for themselves, and also of His doctrines, as our Lord has said, "Come one come all and obey the doctrines of Him that sent us and you shall be made to rejoice with that Joy unspeakable and full of glory,["] as our savior has said. And now dear brothers and sisters, let us earnestly contend for the faith that was delivered[,] which faith cometh by hearing[,] and hearing by the word of God and the word of the Lord endureth for ever, and this is the word by which the gospel is preached unto you.[40]

The following day, Bickerton's wife shared a vision she had received early that morning. It confirmed the prophetic mission of the church:

> I saw myself in a large and beautiful pasture field, where an angel gave me a[n] [entrance] pass. I went on through the field to a place where there was a large tree standing, and the leaves of the tree were so bright[,] they shined like gold, there was a small gate that I knocked at, it opened, and I went on through. I was then asked for my pass by the angel. I gave it to him[,] and he looked at it[,] and saw a mark on it, and he asked me how the mark came there. I told him, I did not know. He then put his finger on the mark, and it disapeared, he then told me to pass on. I was in the Garden of Paradise ... and everything looked so beautiful. And in the center there stood a small building, it appeared to be all pure gold, and there was written on it in large letters Rest for the Weary take upon you my cross and you shall find rest. The Savior stood on top of the building with His arms out stretched, and the tears were treckling down His cheeks, pleading for sinners. I heard beautiful music but I could not see it, I also saw Angels enjoying themselves. I went on and, behold I did meet the same woman that I saw in Elizabethtown three years and 3 mo. ago, she had the crown of twelve stars upon her head, and two large lights in her hands and she said, These two lights was for the Prophet and that there was a church to be built up as a Standard in this place.[41]

40. Ibid., 58–59.
41. Ibid., 60.

This vision enthralled the Saints. They must have seen Charlotte as a perfect complement to their leader. The next day, October 6, the ministry responded to the vision by calling additional men on mission tours: George Barnes and Joseph Knox to Ohio; Frederick Abling to "preach to his countrymen, the Germans"; and Andrew Rattray and A. (Alexander or Arthur) Bickerton to an undisclosed area. This was done when the Confederate army had besieged Chattanooga, Tennessee, and food and clothing were in short supply, yet the missionaries traveled "without purse, and scrip, and shoes," as the Bible advised (Luke 22:35). Their mood was one of fearlessness, trusting they would be provided for.[42]

To the Saints' surprise in the fall of 1863, they received a visit from an emissary of Sidney Rigdon. The former leader was still living in a rural part of upstate New York. By correspondence, Rigdon had called a missionary named Stephen Post to travel to Pittsburgh and elsewhere in order to gather in the remnants of the church Rigdon had once presided over. Post had previously aligned with James Strang, prior to his correspondence with Rigdon in 1856 to inquire about Rigdon's ministry. His letter had ignited the prophetic fire in the old man's heart, so that on March 17, 1856, Rigdon penned a letter calling Post to an evangelical partnership in which Rigdon would give him directions by mail. His letter said, in part,

> And now I the Lord … call [thee] to a great work in assisting my servant Sidney Rigdon in preparing the way before me, and Elijah which should come, and I say unto thee, as my servant Sidney Rigdon assisted my servant Joseph Smith with all his might mind and strength … I [have] called thee to assist my servant Sidney Rigdon. … Thine eyes shall see mine elect gathered and Zion redeemed, and thou shall shout Hosannahs in the midst of my people while Babylon shall shake and tremble, and the inhabitants thereof shall quake with fear, and howl, and weep, and mourn for anguish of soul, even so, amen.[43]

42. Ibid.

43. Rigdon to Post, Mar. 17, 1856, Post Collection, box 3, fd. 12, LDS Church History Library, cited in Van Wagoner, *Sidney Rigdon*, 403.

Rigdon was also corresponding with a former member in Philadelphia, Joseph H. Newton, guiding him by revelation as well. In the summer of 1863, Rigdon spent more than three weeks in Philadelphia ordaining men to the priesthood and setting up a new organization to be called the Church of Jesus Christ of the Children of Zion. Then he returned to the seclusion of his daughter's home in Friendship, New York. His overall plan was to send followers to Iowa, once he could get a report on conditions there.[44]

In September Rigdon wrote to Post about his time in the City of Brotherly Love:

> The Lord commenced his work in Philadelphia in a way that I could not tell what he was going to do but as it progressed and as it now exists he had let us all see what he was doing. He was bringing together those, however far apart, who had been calling upon him for the delivernce of Zion and forming a provisional government with which to move the cause of Zion. He has called on five persons with whom he has formed this government and by who he will move the cause of Zion namely the three persons [in Philadelphia, as well as] … yourself and myself.

Post was "not to preach the gospel to the world but [e]ntirely with that old church," meaning the former Rigdonites and other Latter Day Saints, including those from Pittsburgh "to the [Great] Lakes and as far west as that people are scattered." Converts were to "dispose of their affairs and go west of the Mississippi quietly as other citizens go" and establish settlements until called for.[45] Post was to carry Rigdon's *An Appeal to the Latter-Day Saints* to discount the claims of Joseph Smith III. Since 1860 the oldest son of Joseph Smith had been leading the Reorganized Church of Jesus Christ of Latter Day Saints (RLDS) from Nauvoo, Illinois. Post was told to visit Joseph Smith III "to warn him of the judgments of God" unless he repented of "his abominations before the Lord." Post chose to travel first to the Pittsburgh area to convert the Bickertonites.

---

44. Van Wagoner, *Sidney Rigdon*, 405–06; Gregory, "Sidney Rigdon: Post Nauvoo," 55–56.

45. Rigdon to Post, Sept. 26, 1863, Post Collection, box 5, fd. 7.

When he arrived at William Bickerton's home in West Elizabeth on the morning of Thursday, October 22, the Saints welcomed their guest. Post recalled the visit in his journal:

> This morning I arrived at the house of Wm Bickerton the founder of a large organization of Latter Day saints who recognize him as their prophet seer & revelator. I was introduced to several elders & also to the prophet during the day[.] Several told me that they had seen me in vision & knew me as soon as they saw me.

It may have appeared to Post at first that Rigdon's prophecy was coming true. Since people had seen him in vision before his arrival, he was sure to convince them of the importance of joining with Rigdon for the ushering in of Zion. Soon enough, though, he realized he had misread the situation. Returning to his journal, he wrote that

> all seemed anxious to teach me and that I should join them[,] several giving me their testimonies in regard to what they knew about the work[,] all affirming that this was the only true church & that all the latter day saints would have to come through this church to have their standing in the great work of the last days[.] Wm Bickerton explained his position to be that this was the true church acknowledged as the church of Alma which was raised up through the preaching of Abinadi. That he had raised it up by revelation and [he] was now sending the gospel to the Gentiles with good success having organized [the church] with apostles councillors &c[.]

Bickerton invited Post to speak to his church that evening.

> A meeting was appointed for this evening and I spoke a while from 2nd Cor 7th c[hapter] [showing] we have this ministry[.] I did not have very good liberty [of speech]. I arose and spoke again confessing that I had not had my usual libierty & said that perhaps their expectations were too great & mine too that we were nothing but men & begged them not to indulge in the belief as though I had come to unite with them &c as these things remained to be seen afterward[.] [The] meeting closed with singing and a good feeling generally.[46]

---

46. Journal, Oct. 22, 1863, MS 1304: Stephen Post Papers, 1835–1921, box 6, fd. 4, LDS Church History Library.

Post quoted the apostle Paul: "Receive us; we have wronged no man, we have corrupted no man, we have defrauded no man. I speak not this to condemn you: for I have said before, that ye are in our hearts to die and live with you. Great is my boldness of speech toward you, great is my glorying of you: I am filled with comfort, I am exceeding joyful in all our tribulation" (2 Cor. 7:2–4). In other words, they were all Latter Day Saints and shared the same general beliefs, and they should overlook each other's failings and unite. But Bickerton, for one, remembered all too well Rigdon's attempt to build a New Jerusalem at Adventure Farm and how he had "wronged" his followers, "corrupted" his adherents, "defrauded" his supporters.

The ministry wanted to talk about it, however, nine days later on October 31. "The afternoon was occupied chiefly by examining Steven Post," according to the secretary, "a man purporting to have been sent with an appeal to all saints scattered abroad; to acknowledge Sidney Rigdon as the man the Lord has chosen to lead His people in these last days. He also wanted them to acknowledge Rigdon as the Spokesman" who was described in the Book of Mormon (2 Ne. 3:18). They concluded that Rigdon could not be the promised spokesman since he, like Joseph Smith, had English ancestry. The man foretold in the Book of Mormon would be a descendant of the biblical Joseph of Egypt, an Israelite. Smith was a seer among the gentiles whose role was to aid the conversion of the American Indians. The important task of translating the rest of the hidden records would fall, not to Rigdon or even Bickerton, the latter came to believe, but to an American Indian Moses and a spokesman who would make themselves known in the future. Bickerton's followers believed they had the spirit of discernment, for which the secretary penned his gratitude: "But we thank God that he has given us His Spirit, yea, even the spirit of truth which will lead and guide us in to all truth, and show us things to come. Yea we do thank our Heavenly Father that we do know His voice[,] and a Stranger—we will not follow."[47]

47. Martin and Mancini, "History of the Church," 61.

After talking with Post and reading Rigdon's *An Appeal to the Latter-Day Saints*, it became apparent the pamphlet the Bickerton church was preparing should respond to the competing succession claims in the framework of an overall history of the movement. Bickerton had been with both Sidney Rigdon and Brigham Young and had forsaken them both, finding them to be fallen prophets. This would have to be explained. The world needed to see their church as unique from the competing Latter Day Saint factions.

On Monday, November 9, 1863, Benjamin Meadowcroft shared the Lord's words, approving the pamphlet that would be published by the end of the year.

> I have chosen you out of the sons of man to be my servants and to administer my word unto the people of the nations of the earth[,] and they shall write to you from the East and from the West and from the North and from the South, to know the truth, and the way of Salvation. … Therefore straighten out the things that remain, and I will bare my Holy arm, and I will keep you in such a way and manner as I never kept a people before. And all the world shall know that I, the Lord, ruleth in the camp of Israel by my power that I will manifest through you my people[,] … [so] that the living may know that the most high hast established His Kingdom among the sons of men. … And now if you will keep my words, I will bend the Heavens and shake the Earth for your sakes.[48]

The Saints believed the country was destroying itself and the opportunity to send out missionaries was short. Adamant that his church was a shelter from the storm, Bickerton knew the same claim was made by Brigham Young, and knowledge of that rankled. Young too believed he had raised an ensign to the nations. In 1860 he ordered his followers to store grain and other provisions to prepare for the end times that would follow the Civil War. "While the waves of commotion are whelming nearly the whole country," Young had said at the end of the year, "Utah in her rocky fortress is biding her time to step in and rescue

48. Ibid., 50–51.

the constitution."[49] Shortly thereafter, he said that "God has come out of his hiding-place, and has commenced to vex the nation that has rejected us, and he will vex it with a sore vexation. It will not be patched up—it never can come together again. … If our present happy form of government is sustained, which I believe it will be, it will be done by the people I am now looking upon, in connection with their brethren and their offspring."[50] Young had decided that nothing could stop the progress of the Civil War and that Joseph Smith's "prediction is being fulfilled, and we cannot help it."[51] On that point, he and Bickerton were of the same mind.

At the start of 1864, the ministry asked each branch to purchase a quantity of the missionary tract, *The Ensign*, to distribute to their neighbors. "Take a dollars worth of pamphlets," the headquarters urged. Responding favorably, the branches soon depleted the supply and it was necessary to reprint the pamphlet that year. The tract was updated with a discussion of the Christian gospel, an essay about the Old Testament, and extracts from three sources: the apostle William Cadman's journal, the Book of Mormon, and the Utah-oriented *Gospel Reflector* published in Philadelphia. The ministry planned a new wave of missionary tours too, following the success of the excursions of 1863 in which Charles Brown and William Cadman converted twenty-seven people and ordained an elder in Smithfield at the southern edge of the state.[52]

Continuing the church's bureaucratization, Bickerton suggested a new limitation on his and others' revelations, requiring that they be submitted to a council for approval. The Lord would "reveal himself in the midst of council," the secretary noted, to keep the church "in purity and not be led away by false revelations." To ease their minds, however, the Lord reassured the Saints in April that they should not

49. Erickson, *Thief in the Night*, 166–68.
50. *Journal of Discourses*, 1861, 8:324.
51. Van Wagoner, *Complete Discourses of Brigham Young*, 4:2092.
52. Martin and Mancini, "History of the Church," 63; *Ensign* (1864), 42.

anticipate false communications from the prophet. Speaking through Joseph Astin and interpreted by Sam Rowly, the "word of the Lord" assured that "William Bickerton and I will be with you always, even unto the end of the World."[53] Bickerton believed, with the apostle Paul, that the church should "despise not prophesyings" but "prove all things" and "hold fast that which is good" (1 Thess. 5:20–21).

His niece, Amanda Bickerton, delivered a revelation in the summer that was a comfort to those facing the military draft: "Any of my servants that are forced into this war, ... I will protect them for I am God. I am strong to deliver, my arm is not short, and therefore put all iniquity away from you and keep in love and unity with each other."[54] William Bacon and James Bickerton had enlisted, rather than having been drafted, but they too were protected during some of the war's worst battles. Bacon's Pennsylvania 100th Infantry fought in the Second Battle of Bull Run, Antietam, and Fredericksburg in 1862; the siege of Vicksburg in 1863; and the Wilderness Campaign and siege of Petersburg in 1864. Bickerton's Pennsylvania 123rd Infantry fought in the Battle of Fredericksburg in 1862 and Chancellorsville in 1863; when he switched to the 14th Cavalry Regiment, he engaged the enemy at Droop Mountain in 1863 and in the battles of Piedmont, Lynchburg, and Rutherford's Farm in 1864. The 100th Infantry lost 409 men to combat and disease, the 123rd Infantry lost 72 men, and the 14th Cavalry lost 395.[55]

Following the revelation to keep unity and love within the church, apostle William Cadman asked at a conference in July to reinstate Joseph Parsons and ask forgiveness for mistreating him. There had been some kind of disagreement and he had been expelled, "contrary to the law of the Lord," the secretary wrote. After considering the case, the elders concluded that "he had a cause for stumbling and denying the

53. Martin and Mancini, "History of the Church," 63–64.

54. Ibid., 64–65.

55. Detailed information is available online from the National Park Service at "Battle Unit Details," *The Civil War*, www.nps.gov/civilwar; also from Bates, *History of Pennsylvania Volunteers*, 77, 870.

Authority" of the elders, and that it was not right for him to have been "openly rebuked in a public meeting"; that had been "entirely out of order, and not according to the spirit of truth." The leadership asked Thomas Bickerton to give "acknowledgement" of the church's mistake in a letter to Parsons and asked Charles Cowan to deliver it and ask personally for forgiveness.[56]

Another difficult situation occurred in October when apostle James Brown asked permission to leave the church. He was expelled from the quorum in January "for denying its authority," but was reinstated later. Now they found him once more out of harmony with the Quorum of Twelve Apostles. Nevertheless, when asked to "give an account of himself," he stood up and "in very few words concluded by requesting to be allowed to withdraw from the Church." A possible ally, James McDiffit, later explained that Brown was not leaving "because he had anything against anyone, or that anyone had done him any wrong, but because he had seen things different." The apostles decided to let him exercise "his choice as it regards withdrawing."

Possibly in response to Brown's withdrawal from the church, William and Alexander Bickerton made four motions to formalize the church's stand on controversial doctrines. Their proposals were accepted:

> 1st.—That we acknowledge no other God but the one, who is from everlasting to everlasting, the Creator and up holder of all things, both visable and un visable. 2nd.—That we as a church reject the doctrine of baptism by proxy. 3rd.—That we also reject the doctrine of lineal Priesthood. 4th.—That God delighteth only in free will offerings and that tithings are contrary to [the] Gospel.[57]

The ministry had been pondering who might replace James Brown in the Quorum of the Twelve when a former candidate for the position, William Bacon, returned from the military. Bacon attended the fall conference in Mingo, ten miles southwest of Elizabeth, to everyone's

56. Martin and Mancini, "History of the Church," 64–65.
57. Ibid., 63–66; Cadman, *History of the Church*, 47–48.

delight. The morning service on October 16 included the baptisms of three converts: Carolyn Edwards, Sarah Ellen Greybill, and Margaret Jane Wilson. In the evening the members met in Monongahela City at the Cumberland Presbyterian Church, which had been rented for the rest of the conference; for some subsequent services the public would be invited to attend. Bickerton introduced the speaker, who most likely captivated the audience with accounts of his tour of duty and reliance on the Lord throughout. "A very good time we had," the secretary recorded.[58] The next day Joseph Astin made a motion to call Bacon back into the Quorum of Twelve Apostles, a suggestion the church received well but chose not to act on immediately, nor was a decision made after a New Year's Eve revelation from Charles Brown that "it is both the word and will of God." Some of the brethren must have thought Bacon needed time to acclimate to civilian life. Midway into the next year, the ordination to the office of apostle took place on July 3, 1865.[59]

Toward the end of 1864, citizens in the Union states went to the polls to re-elect Lincoln. For a while it had looked as if he would lose to his opponent, George B. McClellan, the general Lincoln had fired in 1862 for being slow to act, slow to react, and more interested in spit and polish than engaging the enemy. Now the Democratic candidate was pushing for compromise with the South, to achieve peace through negotiation, while Lincoln wanted peace through military victory. Lincoln knew he would not convince voters to support him unless there was more progress on the battlefield. By now, everyone just wanted the conflict to end. "Unless some great change takes place," he wrote, he would be "badly beaten." Then the change in fortune occurred on September 1 when General William T. Sherman captured Atlanta. The win came in "the very nick of time," the *Richmond Examiner* dolefully commented, "to save the party of Lincoln from irretrievable ruin." The newspaper predicted that the fall of Atlanta would "diffuse gloom over the South." As a South Carolinian,

58. Martin and Mancini, "History of the Church," 66.
59. Ibid., 66, 69.

Mary Boykin Chesnut, penned, "Since Atlanta, I have felt as if all were dead within me, forever. … We are going to be wiped off the earth." Many Southerners thought as much when Lincoln won re-election—a victory at the ballot box to match the victory on the battlefield. A commentator from the *London Daily News* summarized it all, saying he was "astonished" at "the extent and depth of [this] determination … to fight to the last." The North continued on with earnestness, the editorialist noted, "the like of which the world never saw before, silently, calmly, but desperately in earnest."[60]

And so began Sherman's March to the Sea with 62,000 troops cut free of their supply lines, which meant they had to pillage food and supplies. They were expected to torch anything that could be used in war to "divide the Confederacy in two," as Sherman explained. When they reached Savannah, "the whole army [wa]s burning with an insatiable desire to wreak vengeance upon South Carolina," the state most responsible for the war. By February 1865, the soldiers had reached Columbia in the very center of the state and laid it in ruins. Bickerton probably thought of Christ's warning about the last days, recorded in the Book of Mormon, "I will pluck up thy groves out of the midst of thee; so will I destroy thy cities" (3 Ne. 21:18). "All is gloom, despondency, and inactivity," a South Carolinian wrote. "Our army is demoralized and the people panic stricken. … The power to do [anything] has left us. … To fight longer seems to be madness."[61]

"Fondly do we hope … that this mighty scourge of war may speedily pass away," Lincoln intoned at his re-inauguration on March 4, 1865. "Yet, if God wills that it continue … until every drop of blood drawn with the lash shall be paid by another drawn with the sword, as was said three thousand years ago, so still it must be said 'the judgments of the Lord are true and righteous altogether.'"[62] It was a sentiment

60. McPherson, *Battle Cry of Freedom*, 771, 775, 803, 806.

61. Ibid., 808–829.

62. Basler, *Collected Works of Abraham Lincoln*, 8:332–33. The quotation is from Psalm 19:9.

voiced by William Bickerton in *The Ensign* in 1863, although infused with ardent millenarian fervor, "Behold the Lord will come with fire and with his chariots like a whirlwind to render his anger with fury and his rebuke with flames of fire[,] for by fire and by his sword will the Lord plead with all flesh, and the slain of the Lord shall be many."[63]

The soldier–apostle William Bacon agreed with that. In March he delivered his own prophecy at the church's headquarters in Green Oak: "Verrely Verrely Thus saith the Lord, I will sweep the earth as with a broom of distruction and the wicked shall be swept from it. And I will make the earth a fit place for my people." Not everyone would survive, "but others there are that shall live to see the Saviour come in the clouds of Heaven."[64] In *The Ensign*, according to Bickerton, "we read that men's hearts shall fail them for fear, looking for the things which are coming upon the earth. There will be signs in the sun and in the moon and in the stars, and upon the earth distress of nations; and many false prophets shall arise and deceive many, but in this generation when the signs do appear, the Saviour says, the gospel of the kingdom, or the everlasting gospel, shall be preached to all the world for a witness and then shall the end come."[65]

There had been unmistakable astronomical signs. In 1859 a solar storm had lit up the night sky and interrupted electrical circuits. A telegraph manager in Pittsburgh referred to "streams of fire" running through the circuits, so hot he worried the lines would melt. The next year saw a series of comets mentioned by poet Walt Whitman as a "strange huge meteor-procession dazzling and clear shooting over our heads." The next year the country experienced the Great Comet of 1861 that littered the daytime sky with debris for two days and illuminated the nighttime sky as the earth passed through the comet's tail. During the Battle of Fredericksburg in 1862, the Northern Lights suddenly became visible for two days due to solar winds, it has been

63. Bickerton, *Ensign*, 4.
64. "Greenoak Revelations," 1:3–4.
65. Bickerton, *Ensign*, 4–5.

explained, as "first a glimmer, then a spreading glow, as if all the countryside between Fredericksburg and Washington were afire," according to one historian.[66]

If that had not been enough, in the pews of the Bickertonite chapels the prediction was proven that in the last days "your sons and your daughters shall prophesy, and your young men shall see visions, and your old men shall dream dreams" (Acts 2:17). On April 2 an unidentified church member stood and declared in the Lord's voice that "Verily ... ye shall go forth, and my power shall go with you, and ye shall know, and all men shall see my mighty hand ... for I will show to all men that I have a people, therefore, fear not for I will deliver you, and will multiply you in spiritual blessings, and I will establish you, and send Angels to minister unto you—Amen."[67]

William Bickerton knelt that same day to wash some of the men's feet and to pronounce blessings on them. He blessed Joseph Astin to be "a messinger unto the people and a scribe unto the Lord," Benjamin Meadowcroft to know how "to speak the word of the Living God," having been "made an instrument in the Lord's hands to do a great work." He blessed John McPherson "to receive strength from the Lord and in due time to receive his hearing." If Andrew Rattray stayed "faithful ... the Lord shall inspire you and ye shall see a better day." Robert Brown would experience "the voice of inspiration." To show his gratitude, Charles Brown laid his hands on Bickerton and pronounced a blessing to fulfill the members' expectation that he would "bring forth the hidden records," that "angels shall minister unto thee and they shall show thee to lead this people and finish the great work of the Latter Day."

Later on, Bickerton preached a sermon and "showed where he received his Authority, and how anyone can prove [Bickerton's] Authority, by rendering obedience to the Gospel of the Son of God." He

66. "The Great Auroral Exhibition of August 28th to September 4th, 1859," *American Journal of Science and Arts*, May 1860, 97; Walt Whitman, "Year of Meteors"; Foote, *Civil War*, 2:42.

67. Martin and Mancini, "History of the Church," 68.

pleaded with his people to believe him. "I tell you that God has sent me unto you," he said, and unless they followed him by being baptized and confirmed they would be "damned, I say unto you by the Holy Ghost. Ye will be damned. I appeal not to the authority of Noah, Peter or Paul but to the Authority of Jesus Christ who sent me."[68]

On April 3, 1865, General Robert E. Lee abandoned the town of Petersburg, twenty-four miles south of Richmond, relinquishing the Confederate capital and sending his troops west of the city. Union troops pushed forward, followed by Abraham Lincoln, who had arrived by boat on the James River. He was accompanied by a guard of ten sailors. In Richmond he walked through the charred streets, soon surrounded by jubilant black residents shouting "Glory! Glory! Glory!" and "Bless the Lord!" When one man fell to his knees, Lincoln corrected him. "That is not right. You must kneel to God only, and thank Him for [your] liberty." Earlier in the day, he himself had remarked to Admiral David D. Porter, "Thank God I have lived to see this. It seems to me that I have been dreaming a horrid dream for four years, and now the nightmare is gone."[69]

Five days later at Appomattox Courthouse, as General Lee surrendered his sword, his eye caught the dark complexion of Ely Parker, a Seneca Indian who served as General Grant's secretary. "I am glad to see one real American here," Lee remarked. "We are all Americans," Parker replied with confidence.[70] Indian tribes had fought on both sides during the war, even as additional land was being taken from them, resulting in warfare in Colorado Territory and Minnesota. On Good Friday, five days after Lee's capitulation, the war's dramatic conclusion came in the assassination of Lincoln at a theater in Washington, DC. Mary Todd Lincoln recounted her husband's wish to "visit the Holy Land" before he died "and see those places hallowed by the footsteps

68. Ibid., 68–69.
69. McPherson, *Battle Cry of Freedom*, 846–47.
70. Ibid., 849.

of the Savior."[71] One could understand his longing to see where the original promoter of non-violence had walked and to experience some rest for himself away from the war. What Bickerton longed to see was the same city, but under different circumstances. He wanted to see the city's glory after Jesus Christ appeared on earth to "reign in Mount Zion, and in Jerusalem." After that, there would be no more war, a condition he longed for, in common with the rest of the nation.[72]

71. Fehrenbacher and Fehrenbacher, *Recollected Words of Abraham Lincoln,* 297.
72. Bickerton, *Ensign*, 4.

NINE

INTO THE WEST

1865–72

"This people were as unreasonable and unbelieving, at that time, as ever the Hosts of Israel were at any time."

—William Cadman, 1899

After the Civil War, William Bickerton tried to determine what to do next. The Reconstruction Era was chaotic. Freedmen who could not find work were forced back to the very plantations where they had been confined, now to work for wages below what a white person would accept. Many former slaves became sharecroppers, but were usually exploited by their landowners. Corruption in Washington and in the states under military occupation was rife.[1] Bickerton thought the country would not recover and that Americans had become more profane, less believing, more deserving of God's abandonment. It was the day of the American Indian, he declared. The problem was that the evidence on the ground showed a different picture. Indian Territory had once comprised a vast area, and now had been reduced to the current states of Oklahoma and half of Kansas, with a few scattered reservations.[2] There was a gathering, but not along the lines of what Bickerton had expected. The Indians were being pushed farther west to isolated and desolate regions.

He applied a surprising Old Testament verse to the situation, assigning responsibility for the condition of the Indians to the Indians

1. Foner, *Reconstruction*, 124–75.
2. Gibson, *American Indian*, 365.

themselves. "And thou shalt no more be haughty because of mine holy mountain" (Zeph. 3:11), he quoted. From what he knew, it was "a peculiar trait in the character of the Western Indians to be haughty, but they shall be so no more, because God will send his truth unto them."[3] In his mind, what they most needed was the Christianity in the Book of Mormon, along with humility and a willingness to adapt to circumstances. He believed the Indians were descendants of Israel from the tribe of Joseph (and his son Manasseh) and would soon rise up against the country and take back the land, demonstrating by their actions their noble heritage. This was the next element of Joseph Smith's Civil War prophecy, something the risen Jesus Christ had promised the ancestors of the Indians in the Book of Mormon story.[4] In the company of a Choice Seer named Joseph, who would suddenly appear among his people, Bickerton planned to help gather the lost tribes of Israel into the New Jerusalem. All roads appeared to be leading to this climactic event, and it would involve important transitions for everyone.

The church was going through its own period of adapting to change. Apparently, members started to complain that the prophecies drawn from the Book of Mormon and Joseph Smith had not come true. The war had begun as promised, but had not spread to other countries, and things were returning to normal. Joseph Astin spoke in tongues on July 1, 1865, John Tilford interpreting his verbalizing on behalf of an aggrieved Lord: "The man that denies the Book of Mormon denies the work of God, and is in the gall of bitterness, and in the bonds of iniquity and cannot be one of my people but must be separated." It was time to prune the vineyard of disbelief, the elders concluded from that, and so they removed evangelist Enoch Ison from the ministry. Two days later they removed two more individuals from priesthood office: Joseph Knox from his calling as an apostle and John Ashton from his calling as an evangelist. In place of Knox, they ordained William Bacon, and in place of James Brown (who

3. Bickerton, *Ensign*, 16.
4. Doctrine and Covenants 87:5; 3 Nephi 21:11–13.

had left), William Skillen. This pleased the Lord, who said through Robert Brown, "Saith the Lord Jesus Christ, Rectify and set things in order at home in your Branches, and then ye shall have power and Authority to go forth on your missions."[5]

On December 30, 1865, the conference was treated to a letter from a missionary, John Stevenson, who was in Chariton, Iowa, and experiencing success. George Barnes declared that the missionaries would prevail against "the enemies of the cause of Christ … and devils shall tremble" at their presence.[6]

At the summer conference in mid-1866, Bickerton displayed the official seal the church had received authorizing its recent incorporation in Pittsburgh.[7] This was a minor act of business but one that obviously pleased the prophet because his labors for over a decade had been aimed at earning the church a place of respect in the community. Unlike the Mormons, his group possessed a fairly good reputation among their neighbors. A few years earlier, Brigham Young had defied the federal government with a warning to Congress not to "dictate the Almighty in his revelations." It would be another two decades for the issues plaguing Utah to work their way through the courts, but eventually the church would be disincorporated and have its assets seized.[8] Maybe the comparison to the desert-dwelling Mormons made Bickerton think of what Isaiah had said, "I will pour water upon him that is thirsty, and floods upon the dry ground." This was not meant literally, Bickerton probably explained, but had to do with the redemption of the people of Israel. "I will pour my spirit upon thy seed, and my blessing upon thine offspring" (Isa. 44:2–3). He stepped away from the pulpit at that point and circulated through the congregation to

5. Martin and Mancini, "History of the Church," 69–70; Cadman, *History of the Church of Jesus Christ*, 1:48–49.

6. Cadman, *History of the Church of Jesus Christ*, 49.

7. In April 1865, the ministry asked apostle Joseph Astin to file for the church's incorporation in Pittsburgh. Then in July 1865, the church paid fees for its charter. See Martin and Mancini, "History of the Church," 69–71.

8. Bushman and Bushman, *Building the Kingdom*, 66–71; Turner, *Brigham Young*, 322–23.

give male members "a kiss of Charity." Approaching the pulpit after him was Charles Brown, and after Brown, Bickerton returned to deliver yet another sermon, and "while speaking of the gifts and power of God[,] he spoke in another language."[9]

On October 7, 1866, apostle John Dixon related a vision he had received of a woman bearing a child and "a man clothed in white robes ... [who] came to the child and gave it a bow and arrow." It had been determined from previous revelations that an arrow represented the word of God, and a bow indicated proselytizing. Charles Brown's prophecy in July 1862 had been that God would make the apostles "as a bow—and my word shall go from you as an arrow."[10] The bow and arrow were traditional among the American Indian, so the imagery pointed in the direction of the outreach the church should anticipate.

With most of the membership in Allegheny County, they were lucky to have escaped the devastation of the Civil War. It was difficult for Northerners to imagine just how bad the situation was in the South. A Georgian described riding a train in August 1865: "Every village and station we stopped at presented an array of ruined walls and chimneys standing useless and solitary." Someone from South Carolina visiting Baltimore stood mystified by the disparity between conditions in this border state and home. It was "hard to bear ... this exulting, abounding, overrunning wealth of the North [compared to] the utter desolation of the unfortunate South."[11] "With malice toward none," the words of the US president's second inaugural address had read, "with charity for all, with firmness in the right, as God gives us to see the right, let us strive on to finish the work we are in; to bind up the nation's wounds; to care for him who shall have borne the battle, and for his widow, and his orphan—to do all which may achieve and cherish a just, and a lasting peace."[12] The same theme could be heard

9. Martin and Mancini, "History of the Church," 71.

10. Ibid., 47, 72.

11. Foner, *Reconstruction*, 124.

12. Basler, *Collected Works of Abraham Lincoln*, 8:332–33.

echoed in Green Oak. "Look a round you, and gather up the fallan and Stranghten the weak for I have given this power unto you, do this and I will bless you and multeply you Sayth the Lord, Amen," this translation by Benjamin Meadowcroft was voiced after William Bacon spoke in tongues, October 28, 1866.[13]

Among the "weak" who needed uplifting were the Five Civilized Tribes of Native Americans—the Cherokee, Chickasaw, Choctaw, Creek, and Seminole, who had fought on the side of the Confederacy. Federal officials regarded their involvement as treason. Two US senators from Kansas, James Lane and Samuel Pomeroy, proposed that previous treaties with the tribes be suspended and the Indians be removed from their state. Kansas was where the Indians had been placed already after being deported from Alabama, Florida, South Carolina, Mississippi, and portions of other Southern states—Georgia, North Carolina, and Tennessee. Because the tribes occupied some of the best farmland in Kansas, and in their eyes the Indians had not maintained it, Anglos wanted them out. The land looked particularly unkempt in the mid-1860s, the Indians having been forced into refugee camps. They were suffering from malnutrition and disease. The men stayed away for fear of retribution from Union troops. Through loss of life on the battlefield, starvation, and disease, the Indian population in that region was reduced by 25 percent.

The tribes had to sign new treaties ceding more land to the federal government and allowing chartered railroad companies and ranchers to appropriate more land. Troops were stationed in Indian Territory, although so thinly distributed that a measure of lawlessness resulted. Freed slaves ended up in the same area and tried to establish communities from scratch. In doing so, some of them stole corn and chickens, cattle and horses, to which Indians responded by forming vigilante bands. Criminals were attracted to Indian Territory as a hideout after conducting robberies.[14]

13. "Greenoak Revelations," 1:5.
14. Gibson, *American Indian*, 383–86, 398–400.

Whether or not the Bickerton community was aware of these conditions, the members began in the winter of 1867–68 to deliberate about how they could move there. Apostle John Neish thought the Homestead Act of 1862 allowed them to get close to the Indians, granting settlers up to 160 acres of free land as long as they resided on it for five years and made improvements. Before Robert E. Lee's surrender at Appomattox, about 25,000 settlers had moved west and claimed three million acres.[15] Neish felt it was "ridiculous" to remain in Pennsylvania, "where our temporal opportunities were so much restricted," not to mention the fact that their mission to the Indians lay in the West.[16]

A committee formed at the Mingo branch in Monongahela investigated locations and logistics under the direction of William Cadman, assisted by John Neish and others.[17] The first question was whether it was the will of God. The revelations had mentioned that missionaries would be sent out from "this house," meaning the Green Oak headquarters, so would it be wrong to move the headquarters? "We decided, that we had no knowledge ourselves in this, … [of what] would prevent us from moving west, … and [that] therefore we could conscientiously investigate," they concluded. By "investigate," they meant not only through normal channels but through prayer, and at the next meeting Cadman reported that "the Almighty revealed to me to my entire satisfaction that He would provide us a home in the Indian Territory, by the preaching of the Gospel."[18]

The committee chair needed to present the revelation to a conference in West Elizabeth in April 1868 when the conference would have delegates from each congregation, apparently indicating that the membership was large enough that they could no longer meet

15. McPherson, *Battle Cry of Freedom*, 450–51.

16. Cadman, *Religious Experiences*, 1.

17. The committee members were Joseph Astin, William Cadman, James Louttit, John Neish, James Nichols, William Skillen, and Daniel Thompson.

18. Martin and Mancini, "History of the Church," 57; "Book of Record," 3, 7; Cadman, *Religious Experiences*, 1–2.

together at once. Cadman would represent the Mingo branch. At the opening session, he read aloud his report. Benjamin Meadowcroft gave a tepid endorsement, saying, "I feel more of the power of God in that matter, than I expected to." Bickerton was more sure, saying, "Verily, thus saith the Lord God; the time has come for salvation to go to the Lamanites." The ministry endorsed the pronouncements and agreed to organize a team to visit Indian Territory. It was considered fulfillment of the prophecy the former apostle James Brown had uttered in October 1859, when he interpreted the imagery of two scrolls coming together to imply a meeting of East and West, that God would "gather my people from the West … to accomplish my great purposes in these last days."[19]

At the July conference, Felix McCune was moved "by the power of God" to nominate William Cadman and Benjamin Meadowcroft to undertake the "mission to the Lamanites." One after another, various priesthood leaders stood to endorse this, and then Amanda Bickerton "rose by the Spirit of God" and declared that William Bickerton was also intended to accompany them. The Saints pledged to care for the men's families while they were away, to give three dollars a week to each wife and one dollar for every child under the age of twelve. A committee would "raise or lower the allotment as to the necessity of each case." There was excitement in the air as the Saints realized they were fulfilling prophecy from scripture and from their own oracles, including Henry Bake's 1859 pronouncement that William Bickerton would perform "greater wonders in this generation than what has ever been done."[20]

The first trip would be exploratory. They would meet tribal dignitaries, preach, and inspect the region for a location for a colony. One night before they embarked, Cadman said,

> I dreamed that we had arrived there and had entered the Territory (on foot) near the northeast corner, and were traveling along watching for

19. Cadman, *Religious Experiences*, 2; "Book of Record," 7.
20. Martin and Mancini, "History of the Church," 74; "Book of Record," 7.

> an opportunity of opening up meetings. We came to a certain house and Brother Bickerton said to me: "Brother Cadman, you go to that house and make enquiry for a place to hold meetings, and we will wait here 'til you come back." I did so, and soon returned, telling the Brethren, there was no encouragement for us there. William [Bickerton] said, "Oh well; we will have to go forward then."

Cadman thought little of it at the time, saying he "was not very much impressed with [the dream's] importance," but would soon see its prediction become a reality.[21]

The three men boarded a train in late August 1868 and arrived in Ottawa, fifty miles southwest of Kansas City, on September 3. From there, Bickerton, Cadman, and Meadowcroft took a stage coach sixty miles south to Humboldt, which would have presented a sad scene because the government was removing reluctant Indians from that area.[22] After Humboldt, they got lost. Ten miles into their trek, they "encountered a team going directly through the Cherokee nation to the Creek Agency … who cheerfully submitted to convey us to our destination." They soon after arrived at the little town of Erie thirty miles to the southeast, where they camped for the night. As the sun began to rise, Cadman awoke and felt as if he were in a large building,

> apparently as large as the world; its height, breadth, and length seemed all the same, and I could see perfectly, all its extremities; its grandeur was entirely bewildering. I was astonished, exceedingly, and said to myself, "Why, this is not where I lay down." I then said to myself, "This must be a vision." I then thought, that, if it was a vision, I might see through it by looking hard; I looked upward as piercingly as possible for a few moments, when I observed the top becoming thin, and the vision disappeared.

At that moment he heard Bickerton call out to him to wake up. Cadman arose and explained that he had been awake and had seen a vision. Bickerton, to their astonishment, had seen the same thing

21. Cadman, *Religious Experiences*, 2–3.
22. Miner, *Kansas*, 81, 94–95.

himself, the same grand building as large as the world. It was all "very strange," they concluded.[23]

Their arrival at the Cherokee Nation was delayed because of inclement weather. "In the afternoon of Monday the seventh[,] as we traveled down the western side of Neosho river to the eastward," they knew from the "sudden darkness, the thunders [that] roared and lightnings [that] flashed" that they were in for a "terrible drenching." When they asked an Indian man if they could take refuge in his hut, he declined. Favorable weather returned, and they crossed the Grand River on September 8, encountering a black family, the Burgesses, who had apparently become amalgamated into the Cherokee tribe. The family invited the trio into their home and allowed them to refresh themselves and tell why they had traveled to Indian Territory. "Brother Meadowcroft informed them that it was to preach the everlasting Gospel," Cadman related. The Burgess family was pleased to have the missionaries in their company. "They remarked that it was such men as us that was needed in that Country and conversed very freely and intelligently concerning the object of our visit." The family directed the missionaries to the home of Lewis Downing, the newly elected chief of the Cherokee Nation.[24]

Many of the Southern Cherokees who had disliked the previous chief, William Ross, found in Lewis Downing a fresh start. Nevertheless, the split between the two parties ended up producing fist fights at the polls and when the results were announced. At the same time, news of Downing's election lured expatriates back home who had been living in exile in the Choctaw and Chickasaw nations and in Texas.[25] As the three missionaries approached Chief Downing's home, Cadman halted his steps because he "instantly recognized it as the house … in my dream," he said. He knew "very positively, that there was no good for us there," he told the others. "Well, we will have to go anyhow,"

23. Cadman, *Religious Experiences*, 3; Cadman, *History of the Church of Jesus Christ*, 53.
24. Cadman, *History of the Church of Jesus Christ*, 53–54.
25. Woodward, *Cherokees*, 308–09.

Bickerton responded. "Of course, let us go," Cadman replied, "but that is the way it is going to be." When the men reached the door, they inquired if the chief was available. Learning that he would not return until the next day, they asked if they could stay the night and were told they could and were invited to supper.[26]

Before the meal, the men sat on the porch and sang "Who Are These Arrayed in White," a hymn by Charles Wesley, younger brother of the Methodist founder, John Wesley. A verse of the song reads:

> Who are these arrayed in white,
> Brighter than the noon-day sun,
> Foremost of the sons of light,
> Nearest the eternal throne?
> These are they that bore the cross,
> Nobly for their master stood,
> Sufferers in his righteous cause,
> Followers of their dying Lord.[27]

The household enjoyed their singing so much, one of the women who was ill and confined to her bed asked that they sing to her in her room. "We had the grandest spiritual experience possible, at that place, 'til very late that night," Cadman remembered, "which drove away from our minds (for the time being) entirely, the apprehensions occasioned by the aforementioned dream." Later in the night the premonition returned to him "that we were going to pass through hard experience in that country."[28]

In the morning, the three made plans. "Brother Cadman, you stay here until Mr. Downing comes home, and open up to him the object of our mission as comprehensively as you can," Bickerton instructed, "and I and Brother Meadowcroft will go and visit those colored people we passed last evening." They agreed to meet later on. When the chief arrived that afternoon, he was surprised to find a lone white man

26. Cadman, *Religious Experiences*, 3.
27. Daniell, *Hymns Sung at Broad Street Church*, 121.
28. Cadman, *History of the Church of Jesus Christ*, 54; Cadman, *Religious Experiences*, 4.

waiting for him, and gave Cadman a cool reception. Among other things, Downing let the missionary know that he, Downing, was himself a Baptist minister. Cadman had the impression that because of this, the chief would actively oppose them, and that showed "the correctness of my dream."[29]

On the other hand, Bickerton and Meadowcroft established an immediate rapport with the Burgess family, who were delighted that the missionaries had returned to see them again. Charles Burgess, his wife, and Charles Phillip were baptized the next day, and Burgess was ordained an elder. The missionaries advertised that they would hold worship services that Sunday. Three days later, in the morning and afternoon, congregations of curious Cherokees and blacks gathered in the out-of-doors for what Cadman described as "very good meetings." One moment in particular stood out for him. Burgess and Phillip both stood up and said they had seen the missionaries' arrival in dreams "some weeks previous," and as they said this the rest of the people were "nodding assent that they remembered the declaration." The following week the missionaries made acquaintance with others of the Cherokee race and became "convinced" that if it were not for the opposition of the chief, it would be possible to establish a successful branch.[30]

Before deciding anything definitely, they wanted to visit the other tribes. "We accordingly separated ourselves," Cadman stated. "Brother Meadowcroft and myself went down to the Creeks, whilst Brother Bickerton remained with the Cherokees." To their surprise and anguish, though, all three fell seriously ill. The sickness "fastened itself into our systems to no small degree," Cadman wrote. Trudging on despite their weakened condition, the two visiting the Creeks found them, like the Cherokees, divided into two political groups, this time with two separate leaders. "We saw the Chief of one faction in Creek

29. Cadman, *Religious Experiences*, 4.

30. Martin and Mancini, "History of the Church," 75; Cadman, *History of the Church of Jesus Christ*, 54–55.

Agency, named Sanns," but felt no rapport with him, so they traveled back to meet up with Bickerton.[31]

Alone in Cherokee territory, Bickerton had attempted to speak to Chief Downing personally and was rebuffed. The chief "refused to receive us as God's people on mission to the red man." On being told they were not wanted there, Bickerton said he "saw a black cloud come between him and me." He came away assuming that they would need to approach the mission differently. "When the time does come, we shall speak [to them in] their own language," he concluded. That would help eliminate the divide between them. For the moment, they had "run against a rock."

That is not to say that Bickerton gave up. He gave a Book of Mormon to an individual he identified as Chief Naze, who was "fairly well educated," and found he "did not make any objections to the book" and invited the missionaries to dinner.[32] From this they determined that not all Indians of high standing would reject their message out of hand. They "gave out an appointment for Sunday at a little Indian school house" and attracted attendance but not serious interest. One man took pity on them and let them stay the night. Bickerton thought the indifference they encountered was a result of the Indians' previous contact with white people. He comforted himself with the thought that it wasn't going any better in Utah either, after they heard Brigham Young had taken a hard line, campaigning against Indians who had interfered with Mormon expansion or with the overland traffic. Bickerton also knew it was hard for the Indians in the Kansas area to know what to make of missionaries who carried a Book of Mormon in hand with the Bible.[33]

In the end, it was their sickness and depletion of funds that forced them to break off their excursion. "Hitherto, we had fed our souls with the joyful anticipations of a prosperous mission and fortified ourselves

31. Cadman, *History of the Church of Jesus Christ*, 55.

32. Bickerton, "Testimony, June 1903," 5.

33. Ibid., 5–6; Gibson, *American Indian*, 358.

against small calamities by scriptural examples," Cadman reminisced, but "disease had fairly attacked our systems and even our reason we perceived was materially shaken, and the necessity of returning home and leaving our work for the present undone seemed to fasten itself upon us like fate." Traveling "hurriedly toward home," they "dreaded to arrive there, knowing, or at least fearing that our presence and appearance there would strike a dagger to the fair hearts of our brethren and sisters, and blast the joyous hopes which had so recently animated their whole souls." They ran low on funds at Pleasant Hill, Missouri, across the border from Kansas, and decided that Meadowcroft, the healthiest among them, "should proceed home," which he did, and "expressed money to us to convey us also home."[34] Bickerton and Cadman arrived back in Pennsylvania in October after having spent a month in Indian Territory and not having found a location for the church colony. The trip had cost them $420.[35]

In Green Oak the first month of 1869, the missionaries spoke briefly about their trip to a conference crowd, including Bickerton's remark, "Verily thus saith the Lord God, Lewis Downing will be moved out of the way." Cadman dreamed about the Cherokee chief again two years later, this time that they were at his residence and Downing "expressed regret to me." This surprised Cadman, especially when he "received in the news in the *New York Tribune* (which I then took) of his assassination." In fact, the *Tribune* was wrong. Downing was still alive and well, although a year later, in November 1872, he would contract pneumonia and die, presenting a fresh set of circumstances for the Bickerton community to consider regarding the mission to the Indians.[36]

---

34. Money sent by "express" was conveyed by train or stage coach in an iron box, in care of a private courier such as Adams Express Company, whose messengers retrieved the packages at the depot or way station and delivered them to the specified individuals. See, for instance, Stimson, *History of the Express Companies*.

35. Cadman, *History of the Church of Jesus Christ*, 55–56; Martin and Mancini, "History of the Church," 75.

36. Cadman, *History of the Church of Jesus Christ*, 56; Cadman, *Religious Experiences*, 5; Martin and Mancini, "History of the Church," 75. The story, as first reported by the *St.*

The July 1869 conference did not turn out the way Bickerton, Cadman, and Meadowcroft had imagined. The three presented a detailed report of their mission, relating all the important events that had transpired, and Cadman shared a lengthy description of the area's geography, foliage, crop production, and demographics to entice the Saints to settle there. Nevertheless, some of the members were unhappy with the outlay of money and poor results from the trip and did not want to hear anything more about sending missionaries west. "In our General Conference," Cadman wrote, "this Mission was practically laid aside and abandoned; I fought against this step desperately, but was overwhelmingly defeated." He thought the ministry was as bullheaded as the Israelites in the Bible who accepted the reports of ten spies over the information provided by their faithful countrymen Joshua and Caleb.[37] It was not the only sour note at the conference. The apostle Thomas Bickerton sent a letter in lieu of his attendance, giving an excuse the elders found unacceptable, so they "suspended [him] from his Calling." Apparently the apostle had already been neglectful and had been visited in April 1868 by Morgan Thomas to see "if he intends to Reform his Duty."[38]

At a conference held in Wheeling, West Virginia, in January 1870, many of the Saints continued to demonstrate indifference about preaching in the West. Instead, they focused on doubling their efforts to preach to the American people in general, and to that end they solicited "aid from each Branch toward supporting the families of those whom the Lord has chosen, and may choose to go and preach the Gospel." John Stevenson and D. L. Shinn, for instance, had been called to venture out on a new missionary tour.[39]

Louis Republican, was more tentative: "The reported assassination of Lewis Downing, Chief of the Cherokee Nation, if confirmed, . . ." See "Reported Murder of Chief Downing," *Chicago Tribune*, Feb. 1, 1871, from the *St. Louis Republican*, Jan. 30, 1871.

37. Cadman, *History of the Church of Jesus Christ*, 52–57; Cadman, *Religious Experiences*, 5.

38. Martin and Mancini, "History of the Church," 75–76; "West Elizabeth Branch," 1:35. At this same conference, William and Charlotte would transfer to the church the deed of the West Elizabeth meeting house that William had paid for.

39. Cadman, *History of the Church of Jesus Christ*, 58.

On January 4 some of the members knelt down for supplication to God, and afterward D. L. Shinn said,

> I saw while upon our knees in prayer, a man of strange appearance. He was I thought, a Jew of the ancient stamp. I thought it was Peter, the old Apostle; he was standing in the middle of the room facing Bro. William Bickerton. I observed his large head, long dark whiskers, his heavy round features, massive forehead and heavy brows. After I had taken a view thus of him, he turned to me, raised his hands, as if to put them upon my head addressing me thus, "How is thy faith?"

George Barnes interpreted this to mean that Shinn was being called on a mission.[40] A noteworthy element of the vision was Shinn's awareness that the apostle Peter would not have the features of a northern European, the apparent lack of racial preference having been a hallmark of the trip to Indian Territory, too, in the conversion of a black family.

The need to warn Americans rather than Native Americans in particular became even more engrained in the members after they heard Sarah Hercula tell about the vision she received. It was one night when she "went to bed" that the experience overcame her, and she was reminded by it that she should not overlook her own family and friends:

> I was carried away in the spirit into a room where the whole Church was gathered together with their hymn books in their hands singing some of the most lovely and beautiful hymns that I ever heard. I beheld my mother sitting near me (she had been dead for many years) and I was astonished to find myself among the Saints. I asked my mother if this was the true Church of God. She said, "Yes, child, this is the only true Church that will stand at the last day," and she said, "Never stop, until you join it." (Repeating it three times.) "Although I am happy, [her mother said,] I knew nothing about this Church while on earth."[41]

If there were Americans like Hercula's mother who would have converted if they had heard the gospel message, then why should the Saints devote

40. Ibid., 58–59; Martin and Mancini, "History of the Church," 77.
41. Cadman, *History of the Church of Jesus Christ*, 59.

all their attention to preaching in Indian Territory? There was more missionary work to do within the United States generally, it appeared.

Due to his work schedule, apostle John Dixon was unable to attend this lively meeting. His guilt at having missed it made him feel "to condemn myself," and in his humility he heard God confirm to his mind that his "servants" should be "set at liberty that they may go forth to publish glad tidings of great things to the Nations of the earth." He may have understood this to include the Native Americans, but he also interpreted it to mean they should not discontinue their efforts to find other receptive people as well. After all, they had not yet seen "a full end of all nations," as Joseph Smith's prophecy had foreseen (D&C 87:6). The idea that there were others still to convert occurred to Bickerton on January 5 while William Moore was sharing a vision he had received in which he saw Andrew Rattray holding a sword and key. All of a sudden Bickerton felt inspired and said, "Verily thus saith the Lord, It is my will that my servant Andrew Rattray be ordained an Apostle and set apart to gather the Old Saints into my Church," meaning that Rattray should visit members of the rival Latter Day Saint factions. The conference endorsed this, and Rattray was immediately ordained to replace Thomas Bickerton in the Quorum of Twelve Apostles. In the afternoon the Saints determined that if Mormons or others converted after being members of one of the other factions, they would have to "acknowledge the Authority of the Church by baptism."[42]

During the past five years, the Saints had replaced three apostles and lost some of their dissident members. Discipleship had proven to be difficult. Therefore, Bickerton prophesied that God would, in essence, separate the wheat from the chaff (Matt. 3:12) so that when they were sent forth they would "go in faith and the power of the Great Jehovah." The imagery of an adamant Old Testament Jehovah was intentional—the side of deity inclined to "turn and overturn," "tear up and pull down," and "break in pieces" the hearts of those who professed to love the truth. God would then "fit and join together the timbers,"

42. Ibid.; Martin and Mancini, "History of the Church," 77.

in other words gather in the true Saints, including some from the other Latter Day Saint factions. Then the church would be "firm as a rock."[43]

It was decided to send Rattray and Joseph Knox, who had re-committed himself, to Illinois to visit the schismatic Latter Day Saints. John Stevenson was sent to West Virginia to support the congregation there. In April the men gave reports on their travels, but the trips turned out to have been uneventful. Taken aback by the fruitlessness of the effort, the members decided "the brethren had not fulfilled their missions and that [their assignments] still remained to be carried out." Rattray and Knox had barely penetrated the state of Illinois, traveling only a few miles across the border from Indiana to spend most of their time in a rural area around Danville. After debating with a Campbellite preacher and ordaining an elder named David Doop, they returned home. Stevenson went to the area of the Long Drain waterway sixty miles south of Wheeling to see some recent converts. He discovered that the members were not yet grounded in the teachings of the Book of Mormon. This elicited a flurry of responses from members speaking in tongues and interpreting the message to be that, as George Barnes said, no minister could organize a "Church of Latter Day Saints" without "the light and glory that attends the Book of Mormon."[44]

Three months later the ministry renewed its call to Rattray and Knox to return and "fulfill the mission the Lord had given" them. Rattray was called to the front for the laying on of hands, and as he walked forward "the Savior appeared before him and a voice [called] to him saying, 'have I not sent thee?'" Rattray said he was astonished, telling the conference in a rhetorical voice, "Can I then say, I have not been an apostle? Have I not seen Jesus?"[45]

Despite Rattray's and Knox's renewed dedication to preach, the Bickertonites as a whole found themselves once again at variance with

43. Martin and Mancini, "History of the Church," 78; Cadman, *History of the Church of Jesus Christ*, 59–60.

44. Martin and Mancini, "History of the Church," 78.

45. Ibid.

each other about moving into the West. Some wanted instead to move to Tennessee, possibly to convert the remaining Lamanites there rather than in Kansas and Indian Territory. Cadman scoffed at the idea. The Cherokee had been removed from Tennessee. Would they encounter Lewis Downing, he wanted to know, referencing Bickerton's prophecy that Downing would be "moved out of the way." "Certainly not," Cadman chided.[46]

The frustration felt by Cadman and others must have been heightened when Bickerton said one of the brethren would become a Judas: "Thus saith the Lord, unto that man, that will fight against this Church, God will make him of the synagog[ue] of Satan." The next day when Charles Cowan, one of the church's evangelists, was called in, he announced that he did not believe in excommunication and "did not believe in his calling of Evangelist." He had mostly grown tired of the church judging others when he personally believed that only God could judge. Acknowledging his right to his opinion, the ministry removed him from his calling, fulfilling Sister Davis's July 1861 dream of Cowan holding a child he thought was dead, the child representing the church.[47]

"We believe that this Church has a right to deal with its members as the New Testament scriptures direct, on disorderly conduct, or the violation of the commandments of the Lord," Bickerton wrote in *The Ensign*, "but it has no authority to try men on the right of property, of life, or to take from them this world's goods, or to put them in jeopardy, either life or limb, neither to inflict any physical punishment upon them. We can only excommunicate them from this Church and withdraw from their fellowship."[48] According to its established rules, it appears the church was not beyond its rights in disfellowshipping Cowan. His response, though, was to form an alliance with the prophet's older brother Thomas Bickerton, who had been relieved of

46. Cadman, *Religious Experiences*, 5.
47. Martin and Mancini, "History of the Church," 37, 79.
48. Bickerton, *Ensign*, 14.

his apostleship, and the two would thereafter create a division in the church, gathering a small group of sympathizers around them.[49] Attempts to reintroduce harmony in the church went unrealized. George Barnes in October spoke of the Israelites when they "passed through the wilderness [and] God was with them [so that] wheresoever Israel moved, they moved together, and God moved with them." It was an appropriate example, considering the difficulty the Israelites had following Moses. As Barnes spoke, seven men—William Bacon, William Bickerton, Charles Brown, William Cadman, Alexander Cherry, Hugh Scott, and John Stevenson—stood up to show support for what was being said. A suggestion from the Mingo branch to appoint a minister who would visit all the branches during the next year was upheld, and the crowd unanimously chose William Bickerton to do so. The Mingo branch pledged $100 in his support.[50] They knew that something had to be done to help the church heal from its wounds.

Toward the end of the year, November 6, 1870, the Lord made known that Bickerton, unlike Moses, would not be replaced due to unfaithfulness (Num. 20:12). Benjamin Meadowcroft spoke in tongues to the Green Oak branch, interpreted as follows.

> Hear ye the [interpretation][,] O my [people][,] the Lord [has] Suffered Division that my Church may be Clensed from unbleavers, for I have made [a promise] unto you, and the doubtful and [unbelieving] I will [separate] from you, for nether man nor women which speak [evil] of my Servant William Bickerton is of use but is of the devil, therefor I will Strengthen my Servant with wisdom and Knowlage and faith and power and glory and I will arm my Servant [against] all the powers of darkness, there is nether man nor women nor feet of men that lift up arms [against] my Servant William Bickerton [that] Shall prosper, for they shall be a Shamed of themselves and there own words Shall [accuse] them. Therefor be ye Strong O my Servants be ye Strong be ye Strong, in my word, for I will bring in [among] [you] faithful and [determined] men that will

49. See "List of Branches and Members," 98.
50. Martin and Mancini, "History of the Church," 80.

> [assist] you in my work[.] As I am able to Shake the Heavens and Earth I am also able to make you Stand, Amen.[51]

Yet the December conference quickly devolved into infighting. Some of the members disparaged William Cadman's resolution to discuss the Indian mission. The Mingo branch wanted help dealing with the "Cowanites," who were causing "a deal of trouble" in their area. Cadman wrote that he became so distraught, "I remember very well, in going home from that Conference, I was hanging down my head, being grieved and discouraged intensely." He had pushed through a resolution in October to further investigate sending at least some of the Saints west. "I felt delighted, then, and thought … we should discover what had been wrong, and be able to correct ourselves and proceed." Instead of that, "when the time came" for final approval, Cadman continued, "I was grievously disappointed, for instead of the matter being investigated, it was ridiculed severely, and myself too, for supposing there was any cause for investigation." He remembered his vision in Kansas, shared by Bickerton, of the "wonderous beauty" and "glory of Zion," not just on earth, but also in the next life. "We were in a realm beyond our sphere, as poor, degraded mortals here. We can never expect to attain to the heavenly by pursuing the earthly … hence our failure."[52] It was because they had been concentrating too much on the financial feasibility and logistics of the mission, he decided, that they had not considered the spiritual side of it. The spiritual blessings would completely outweigh the material benefits of acquiring land near Indian Territory, Cadman thought. It may be true that more suitable, charming, or fertile lands existed in Tennessee and elsewhere, but Cadman understood that his and Bickerton's vision revealed the glorious spiritual wealth the Saints would achieve by preaching to the descendants of Israel. The Book of Mormon said the Indians would be "nursed by the Gentiles" and "carried in their arms" and "upon their shoulders" (1 Ne. 22:6). They would

51. "Greenoak Revelations," 1:7.

52. Martin and Mancini, "History of the Church," 80; Cadman, *Religious Experiences*, 6.

not all simply convert at once; they needed assistance, both in spiritual matters and in other ways too, he concluded.

He and Bickerton were still unable to dissuade a good number of members from moving to Tennessee in 1871. The members traveled some 600 miles to the southwest and took advantage of the Homestead Act.[53] It was another 600 miles from there to the Indian settlements on the far side of Missouri. Tennessee was 25 percent black and had an active Ku Klux Klan. When Andrew Flowers, a black man, won his election over a white candidate for justice of the peace in Chattanooga in 1870, Flowers was whipped. "They said they had nothing particular against me," he remarked, "but they did not intend any nigger to hold office in the United States."[54] Bickerton and others could not believe their fellow members would cast their lots with people of such a state. "When a number of our people emigrated to Tennessee, in the spring of 1871," Cadman wrote, "was it not an act of unbelief in what had been revealed to this people concerning Indian Territory? Certainly it was. From the time this spirit of unbelief took possession of our people, in the fall of 1868, the course of this Church has been steadily downward."[55]

To make circumstances bleaker, Andrew Rattray's report in April, after returning from Illinois and Missouri, did not impress the Saints any more than his report of his first mission. He had visited members of the Church of Christ (Temple Lot) headquartered in Independence, Missouri, and the Reorganized Church of Jesus Christ of Latter Day Saints (RLDS) headquartered in Plano, Illinois, without results. Both churches had claims and objectives similar to those of Bickerton. The Church of Christ was overseen by Granville Hedrick and occupied land Joseph Smith had designated in 1831 as the site for the New Jerusalem. After being visited by an angel and instructed to gather there, Hedrick had led a sizeable membership to Independence. One of the original members of Joseph Smith's Quorum of Twelve Apostles, John E. Page,

53. Martin and Mancini, "History of the Church," 82.

54. Foner, *Reconstruction*, 426–27.

55. Cadman, *Religious Experiences*, 5–6.

had helped unify the Illinois and Indiana branches of Bloomington, Crow Creek, Eagle Creek, Half Moon Prairie, and Vermillion, and he had ordained Hedrick an apostle and then a "prophet, seer, and revelator," and the members of these branches formed the core of the group that moved to Missouri.[56]

The RLDS church had begun when Jason W. Briggs, onetime follower of James J. Strang and William Smith, received a revelation to "wait for the seed of Joseph," meaning the son of Joseph Smith. With another former follower of Strang, Zenas H. Gurley, the two men established the Reorganized Church and convinced Joseph Smith III to lead them.[57] After approaching the RLDS, Rattray found that despite their appeal to priesthood authority and prophetic gifts, they seemed to be "not better than any other sect." The Hedrickites were similarly "difficult," and, in Rattray's opinion, "deficient in knowlege of the spirit and destitute of all the power of God." Rattray did learn that the "Colored brother" in Kansas, Charles Burgess, was "going about preaching among" the Cherokee and was "considered to be a smart man."[58]

Matters grew less auspicious for an exodus to Kansas when Alexander and Arthur Bickerton were stripped of their apostleship. They were missing from the July conference without explanation and so removed from office until they could explain their absence. John Dixon was "in full expectation that [Alexander] would be here" and had been detained, but that did not prove to be the case. Arthur Bickerton sent a letter to the conference, but the ministry ruled it was insufficient to exonerate him, and he too was suspended.[59]

These were internal matters having to do with faith and devotion. Then on July 6 the unthinkable happened when flames consumed the Green Oak headquarters. The fire began in "the hotel next adjoining,"

56. Addams, "Church of Christ (Temple Lot)," 206–11.

57. Speek, "From Strangites to Reorganized Latter Day Saints," 146–50.

58. Martin and Mancini, "History of the Church," 82. By comparison, Brigham Young forbade the ordination of blacks, a policy that would not change until 1978 (LDS Official Declaration 2).

59. Martin and Mancini, 83.

the *Monongahela Valley Republican* reported. Both buildings were "burned to the ground."[60] Two days later when the ministry met, Cadman saw this as the Lord's punishment for their lack of harmony:

> When the General Conference of 1871 arrived, it found us in this situation; part of our people gone to Tennessee; the rest all unsettled, and confidence largely broken. I returned home as soon as Conference was over. I had only been home a few hours when I received word of our meeting house at Greenoak being burned. I was more grieved than astonished at this occurrence, and expressed astonishment that we were not all burned in it; in view of our conduct in recent years.[61]

The unavoidable conclusion by members was that this disaster contradicted what Bickerton said the Lord told him in 1859, "I will set my Angels to guard this [meeting] House that ye have built unto me." It was a witness against their leader's prophetic authority, they concluded.[62] Bickerton had the support of the majority of delegates, however. The members soon found a lot in nearby Coultersville, across the Youghiogheny River from Green Oak, that could be purchased for $500. But after purchasing the land, the contention was so disruptive that the building would never be finished. The destruction of headquarters was a setback for everyone, regardless of perspective, and contributed to a general indecisiveness for years to come.[63]

Benjamin Meadowcroft remained upbeat. On September 30, 1871, he reported that "two have been baptized [in Green Oak] since last Conference." The ministers agreed to set aside tobacco in order to give a good impression to the public. A decision was made to reconsider the Indian mission and discuss it at the January 1872 conference.[64] If Meadowcroft thought the church would soon be back on track,

60. "Church Burned," *Monongahela Valley Republican*, July 13, 1871. Cadman wrote that the fire occurred on July 4, but the newspaper had it as July 6.

61. Cadman, *Religious Experiences*, 6–7.

62. Martin and Mancini, "History of the Church," 84; "Book of Record," 8.

63. Cadman, *Religious Experiences*, 7.

64. Martin and Mancini, "History of the Church," 85; Cadman, *History of the Church of Jesus Christ*, 62.

though, the reality of the coming year was anything but encouraging. At the January conference, there was disagreement over whether the Indian mission was worth pursuing at all, and they merely decided to lay it over until such time as it might be "brought forward by the Holy Spirit of God."[65] Bickerton was alarmed to learn of another development as well, this time a racist doctrine that had taken hold of the Little Redstone branch, about twenty miles to the south. The ministry asked secretary Joseph Astin to correct the members' misgivings about the African race. It was, perhaps, the kind of issue one would expect during the era of Reconstruction.

> By order of the Conference
> An Epistle unto the Church of Jesus Christ at Little Redstone
>
> Beloved Brethern & Sisters in the Lord[,] the Conference sends greeting.
> It having come to the attention of the conference that there is some feeling insisting in some parts of the Church, that would rather slight the [colored][66] people, therefore the Conference sought after the mind of the Lord upon the subject.
> And it was felt by the Holy Spirit that the Lord looked upon Israel and blessed them yet they, themselves looked upon the Gentiles as unclean, Until God showed unto his Servant Peter that he had clensed the gentiles by his Spirit, by them obeying the Gospel, therefore he was not to call them unclean[.] In like manner have we also been led to look on the Colloured people as being beneath the Gentiles[,] but the Gospel brings them up and makes them have Equal access unto the Supper of the Lord, and Equal Fellowship in the Church of Jesus Christ. Amen.
>
> Joseph Astin[,] Recording Secretary of the Church
> Given January 2, 1872[,] West Elizabeth

On January 25, 1872, the *Monongahela Valley Republican* published a description of the church and its teachings. The editor suggested that "it would be well for our people to study and be informed as to this

65. Martin and Mancini, "History of the Church," 86; Cadman, *History of the Church of Jesus Christ*, 62–63.

66. The letter has "collordrd" people. See "Redstone Valley Branch," 8–9.

sect of Christians who now have a church and a growing congregation in our midst." An anonymous person, presumably a member of Bickerton's church, wrote an accompanying defense of the Book of Mormon.[67] Another anonymous member added a note on February 5 making sure readers understood that the church was not associated with Brigham Young. "You must not confound the rising congregation of the Church of Jesus Christ of L.D.S. of Monongahela City and vicinity with the Salt Lake Mormonry—they have neither lot nor part with them." The member credited the "breach" between the two churches to polygamy. "The church in Monongahela city and vicinity remain[s] true to the Faith once delivered to the Saints, whilst Salt Lake Mormonry by the practice of Polygamy have incorporated that into their system which is alike repugnant to Christian civilization and a pure morality. Truth."[68]

The newspaper coverage was gratifying, yet Bickerton aspired for a more substantive achievement. Members had quarreled over the church's authority, moved to Tennessee, questioned the integrity of his revelations, lapsed into racism in one instance, wondered about the Book of Mormon, and most regrettably opposed the Indian mission. Members were becoming contentious and idle. This had to stop, Bickerton resolved. It bothered him that he and two others had braved the elements and risked life and limb to reach the Native Americans, all for the disapproval of the community of Saints. He was determined, as the others had expected of Andrew Rattray and Joseph Knox, to finish his mission.

A glimmer of hope for a better future did arise at the winter conference in January 1872 when Bickerton volunteered to devote his life to proselytizing, given that the church would reimburse his travel expenses. The conference accepted the proposal. An elder laid his hands on the prophet's head and promised that as he "gather[ed] the sheep of Israel's flock, God shall work by thee in sign[s] and miracles and gifts of the

67. "The Mormons," *Monongahela Valley Republican*, Jan. 25, 1872.
68. "The Mormons," *Monongahela Valley Republican*, Feb. 15, 1872.

Holy Ghost."[69] Bickerton concluded that this meant he would be successful, and that in establishing a stake in the West, he would thereby fulfill the prophecy of Isaiah, "Enlarge the place of thy tent, and let them stretch forth the curtains of thine habitations: spare not, lengthen thy cords, and strengthen thy stakes; For thou shalt break forth on the right hand and on the left; and thy seed shall inherit the Gentiles, and make the desolate cities to be inhabited" (Isa. 54:2–3). The American Indians were exiled to a shrinking area in the West, their numbers depleted, but before long they would prosper and become more numerous than the European Americans, Bickerton believed Isaiah to be saying. They would inhabit the cities of the gentiles and stretch forth the glorious tent of Zion as one of the lost tribes of Israel. Bickerton yearned to take part in the millennial drama and to see it come to fruition at the edge of Indian Territory.

69. Martin and Mancini, "History of the Church," 86.

TEN

ZION VALLEY

1872–79

"While I was at prayer, the whole end of the house seemed open to my view and I saw a multitude of the ancient Fathers above my head looking down upon me. They were waiting for a movement of this Church, the gathering of the Saints and the establishing of Zion."

—June 3, 1874

Even though William Bickerton had faced some discouragement, he pressed on to plan for a migration west, the prophecies being clear enough that Zion would resemble a tent and its stakes would stretch to distant lands. It was logical that one of those stakes would be near the American Indians, a special tribe of Israel who Bickerton believed would help gather the other Israelite tribes together. In the Book of Mormon, the prophet Moroni had longed to see this event: "Put on thy beautiful garments, O daughter of Zion, and strengthen thy stakes and enlarge thy borders forever, that thou mayest no more be confounded, that the covenants of the Eternal Father which he hath made unto thee, O house of Israel, may be fulfilled" (Moro. 10:31).

Eventually Bickerton decided it was not enough just to have a branch near Indian Territory, but that the church headquarters would need to be moved there. The achievement of that goal would prove to be long and difficult, a road paved with contention and dissent rather than common purpose, the first evidence of which occurred at the July 1872 conference. When Bickerton arrived at the assembly, he was prepared to report on his recent examination of the church revelations, as he had been requested to do back in January. It had been a year since the Green Oak branch burned down and some members still clamored for him to admit that his 1859 prophecy had been wrong, because angels had not watched over the headquarters. Bickerton disagreed. The way he saw it, in harmony with William Cadman's view, God had spared the Saints and protected them and their records, so they should be grateful instead of indignant, and see the conflagration for what it was: a warning to repent. In addition, he could find nothing wrong with any of the revelations, he said, except for a few unfulfilled missions that were the fault of the ministry. He convinced the conference to accept a motion that they "humble ourselves before God, by acknowledging that we have come short of the will of God, and that we [should] go to, and build up another house to worship the Lord in."[1]

Having settled that, Bickerton moved on to the theme that was closest to his heart, the establishment of a "stake of Zion" in the West. *Zion* implied that it would be in or near Indian Territory. Recently the ministry had stipulated that no motion would be upheld unless it was "brought forward by the Holy Spirit of God," so in keeping with that, several people stood and attested to their spiritual witness of the importance of the prophet's plan. "Bro. Menzees testified, that it had been brought in by the power of God," and "Bro. Wm Bacon, and Henry Hannah and John Neish all felt that this is the time of the Lord to commence this great work," the secretary recorded. When Charles Brown and William Skillen also agreed, Bickerton must have felt overjoyed to think that after years of waiting, many of the Saints were finally in agreement on this. The apostle Benjamin Meadowcroft declared "that from this time, this doctrine of gathering should be taught to the Sisters, and all the Saints, that as faith comes by hearing, those who have faith in the Lord [should be] performing his word." The secretary recorded that everyone "rejoice[d] in the power of God."

1. Martin and Mancini, "History of the Church," 84, 86–87.

The elders asked that a report of the proceedings be read to all the branches of the church.[2]

Not everyone felt as excited about this proposition. George Barnes, Bickerton's counselor in the presidency, intentionally absented himself from the July conference, as did Joseph Knox and a few others, because of Bickerton's inability to acknowledge his failed revelations. Barnes had harbored doubts before. In 1861 he had openly questioned whether it had been right to separate from Brigham Young, for instance, and thought the prophet needed to have "the vocal voice of the Lord in such matters." After the Green Oak headquarters burned down, the skepticism resurfaced and spread through the Rock Run branch, which he attended, six miles north of Elizabeth. The branch decided not to send anyone to give a report to the October 1872 conference, signaling their dissatisfaction. Unlike other dissenters, the ministry could not be too hasty in dealing with Barnes, a member of the church presidency since 1862. Barnes possessed spiritual gifts and a charisma that people admired. The leaders sent the other counselor in the presidency, Charles Brown, to contact Barnes and invite him and others of his branch to attend a council meeting at West Elizabeth on October 19 following the fall conference.[3]

The council had suspected what was wrong, but it was shocked to hear Andrew Rattray and Joseph Knox, representing the Rock Run branch, "make known their grievances" and announce that they intended to separate from the church and reach out to other Latter Day Saints. Their reason, they said, was an 1870 revelation to Bickerton in which the Lord said he would "turn and overturn and tear up and pull down and break in pieces" the hearts of those who professed to love truth, "and afterwards, fit and join together the timbers, that the building may be firm as a rock, that cannot be moved." The secretary wrote that Rattray and Knox were clearly "guilty of misconstruing the revelation." They

2. Ibid., 87; Cadman, *History of the Church of Jesus Christ*, 1:64.

3. Martin and Mancini, "History of the Church," 37, 87; "The Bickertonite Church," *Deseret News*, May 6, 1933.

wanted to "tear up and pull down and break in pieces" the false revelations recorded by Bickerton and find new truth by searching out other dissident Latter Day Saints. They even presented their own revelation to the council in support of their intention.[4] In any case, the council voted to suspend Rattray and Knox "from all Church privileges" and notify every branch "not to receive them into fellowship." The council felt it necessary to act quickly and decisively. Not so with Barnes, however. In fact, they took advantage of his absence to postpone dealing with his membership for the time being, possibly hoping it would divide the opposition.[5]

If so, Barnes pressed the matter by staying away from the December conference. An embarrassment to the leadership, it had not gone unnoticed by the rest of the church. Something had to be done about this affront. The undiplomatic solution the church came up with was to send William Bickerton with two others, Charles Brown and Benjamin Meadowcroft, to reach out to Barnes, whose disagreement was, of course, with Bickerton himself. The poor choice of ambassadors yielded the unavoidable result of the three returning empty handed. In addition to the division in the church, the attempt to bring the Rock Run branch back into the fold delayed Bickerton's plans to send pioneers west. He organized seven men into a committee to study and report on the feasibility of a settlement to get the project back on track, but there was not much more he could do while other controversies overshadowed the church.[6]

Perhaps to distance himself from the dissension, or just to find work at a better wage, he moved for a few months to Cambridge, Ohio, in late 1872. During the 1870s another economic downturn hurt working-class families. Employers cut back workers' hours and reduced wages as they rode out the recession, leaving coal miners and iron workers with two options: earn less or relocate. Women had few

4. The text of this revelation is not extant.

5. Martin and Mancini, "History of the Church," 78, 88; Cadman, *History of the Church of Jesus Christ*, 64–65.

6. Cadman, *History of the Church of Jesus Christ*, 65; Entz, "Paradise on the Plains," 155; Martin and Mancini, "History of the Church," 89.

opportunities to work.[7] William Oscar Hands, whose father, John Hands, joined the church, said that in late 1872 "trouble again began brewing, and my Father and Bickerton decided to move to Cambridge where they found work in the coal mines."[8] James Cadman accompanied them, and together the three men organized a branch.

Their congregation attracted the attention of a journalist for the *Cambridge News*, who was impressed that coal miners had taken up preaching. The *Monongahela Valley Republican* reprinted the article in which the reporter described "the preachers, elders Cadman and Bigerton, [who] are miners, and work through the week at Scott's mines, ministering to their own and their friends' necessities with their own hands, for they profess to emulate the example of Christ and the Apostles." At the worship service, they "exhibit[ed] a force and vigor of expression which makes one involuntarily refer to the account of the arraignment of Peter and John before the Jewish Sanhedrin … when it was discovered that, although they were illiterate men, they were bold, and powerful in defense of the truth." In fact, "the preachers were so familiar with the Scriptures that they could call up any passage needed, and their tongues were as nimble as if they had been playing gymnastics with Greek verbs instead of digging coal." The reporter implored readers to treat them with respect. "Great injustice has been done to them by connecting them with Mormonism. This they detest no less strongly than orthodox Christians, and it is unjust to attempt to be unfair with men who are so fair with others," the reporter continued.

> Because they are small in numbers and have a poor following, is not a good or sufficient reason why they are not sincere, and possibly better men than some who cast stones at them. They take the Scriptures, pure and simple, and claim that a passage quoted by them, plain men that they are, is as good as the same passage quoted by a learned and fashionable preacher. Who says it is not? Then let them be treated with candor.[9]

---

7. Kleinberg, *Shadow of the Mills*, 26–27; Entz, "Paradise on the Plains," 152.
8. Hands, "Life of William Oscar Hands," n.p.; Entz, "Paradise on the Plains," 155.
9. *Monongahela Valley Republican*, Jan. 16, 1873.

No matter where Bickerton went, a degree of controversy followed. At least in Cambridge he was recognized as being an honest Christian. If George Barnes could see him in the same light, he would be in Kansas rather than Pennsylvania.

The July 1873 conference in Coultersville, across the Youghiogheny River from Green Oak, included an appearance from the church's second counselor, George Barnes, who had emerged from hiding in order to answer questions face-to-face. He confirmed what they knew. "It was false revelations, given to the Church in its rise," he said, that had kept him away. Revelations should not be accepted unless their origin was unequivocal, like hearing the "vocal voice of God." The fact that people had spoken in tongues or seen visions when the revelations were announced made no difference. When he was done speaking, a lengthy discussion followed. When they realized they would not soon come to a consensus, the morning session was adjourned.[10]

At the evening session that started at 7:00 p.m., Bickerton opened by asking for five men to form a council to rule on the Rock Run branch.[11] Five men were chosen, and they withdrew to deliberate. On their return, they issued a straightforward response. The dissenters had made up their minds and would not be convinced otherwise, so "the Rock Run Brethren cannot be one with us." The conference agreed to excommunicate the key agitators, Andrew Rattray and Joseph Knox, "for upholding false revelations against the Church"; George Barnes "for taking part with these who brought false revelations, and denying the Priesthood," and for "his conduct in trying to destroy the Church"; and John Ashton and Peter Ramsey for causes "similar to the others." The conference placed Charles Brown and John Parker in charge of the errant congregation. These two men did their best but were unable to keep the branch from spiraling out of the church's orbit as the members followed the leaders, literally as well as figuratively, when Barnes

10. Martin and Mancini, "History of the Church," 90.

11. The members of the council were John Bickerton, Alexander Cherry, Cummings Cherry, Benjamin Meadowcroft, and William Reader.

led them to a new location in the towns of Coal Valley and New England, Pennsylvania, six miles north of West Elizabeth. In late 1885 they began taking steps to reaffiliate with the Utah church, which they did the next year.[12]

As disappointed as he was, the prophet was now able to refocus on the mission to the American Indians. At the July conference, he asked for a report from the committee he had commissioned in December. "A long conversation" ensued, although without anything concrete being decided. William Cadman and William Menzies were added to the committee.[13] Cadman thought it was not insignificant that in a recent Sunday service in West Elizabeth, Charles Brown shared a dream that "himself and some other brethren heard men rapping in the coal mine there for help … and went to work to accomplish their deliverance." Since they were unable to reach the trapped miners, they "finally ceased their efforts, and left these men to die," but then, "after a considerable time had elapsed, … these brethren heard them rapping again." The second attempt being successful, they "carried these parties out to the light of the day." The rescued miners were "wrapped in blankets, and had the appearance of Indians." One of them "turned out to be a woman, who rose and glorified God; and, almost immediately, was transformed into one of youth and beauty, and richly adorned, entirely beyond description."

Cadman believed the dream's interpretation had to do with the church's first unsuccessful attempt to reach the Indians, with an assurance that their second try would not end in failure. The beautifying of the young woman represented the "adorning of the House of Jacob," Jacob being the biblical father of the twelve tribes of Israel.[14] "Put on thy beautiful garments, O daughter of Zion," the prophecy read. There was one missionary laboring near Indian Territory at the time, John

12. Martin and Mancini, "History of the Church," 90–91; Cadman, *History of the Church of Jesus Christ*, 67–68; "Way Paved for the Honest in Heart," n.p.

13. Martin and Mancini, "History of the Church," 93.

14. Cadman, *Religious Experiences*, 7–8.

Stevenson, whose letter motivated the church to take Cadman's interpretation of the dream seriously.

When Stevenson returned and spoke in person at the church conference in early 1874, he related that while he was laboring in southeastern Kansas, he was the conduit for several miracles that had convinced people of his authority. "I was called on December 8, 1873, to attend to the ordinance upon a child of Lewis Beaston, Neosho County, Kansas, who had a white swelling in its legs," he remarked. "The gift of healing was made manifest." Again "the same month, I was called to attend the ordinance on a child of George Shauver in Wilson County, Kansas, who had been scalded, ... I went forty miles to administer to it and the flesh began to heal right away." He baptized eighteen people. The members were so enthused by this, they took up a collection so he could return to Kansas, with "a blessing ... to the White Man, the Red Man and the Black Man." A prediction was made that Stevenson would be able to "address the Indians in their own language." The man whom Bickerton had once considered an infidel was now able to convince the church of what he had been unable to persuade them, which was the potential for fulfilling prophecies in the West.[15]

At the July 1874 conference, the prophet spoke on behalf of the Stake of Zion committee to announce that they had identified the place of gathering along the border of the Cherokee Nation, saying that he felt certain God would reveal the exact location when they sent scouts to examine the land. On hearing mention of Cherokees, Bickerton's brother, Alexander, who by then had reclaimed his apostleship, arose and spoke in tongues "for a considerable time and exhibited Indian characteristics very decidedly," William Cadman recorded. Cadman was concerned that members would misunderstand the meaning of the dramatic portrayal of an Indian language and said, "Now brethren; don't you for a moment believe that this ... has anything to do with the procuring of lands." He thought the members might think

15. Martin and Mancini, "History of the Church," 94; Cadman, *History of the Church of Jesus Christ*, 68–69; "Bickerton's Letter," *St. John County Capital*, Nov. 21, 1889.

it authorized them to take advantage of the Homestead Act, and the church would disperse to the four winds. The demonstration probably "referred to something of more importance," he suggested, and Felix McCune confirmed that it implied "nothing, more or less, than a renewal of the Indian Territory Mission."[16]

Bickerton himself had received another revelation on the topic: "While I was at prayer, the whole end of the house seemed open to my view and I saw a multitude of the ancient Fathers above my head looking down upon me. … Especially, I recognized Jacob at the head and I saw that he would be a ministering spirit to this Church in bringing about the purpose of God."[17] The elders formed another committee, this time to "devise ways and means for carrying out the will of the Lord" in establishing Zion.[18] Something definite would finally be done. The conference commissioned Bickerton and John Neish to travel west and find a location, with support from the members donating two percent of their monthly incomes "for the purpose of defraying the expenses of the Church" during this period. The call for a percentage of their income contradicted the 1864 decision that "tithings are contrary to [the] Gospel," that the church should survive on "free will offerings" rather than taxes. But it would be a temporary measure, borne of necessity. It had been six years since Bickerton, Cadman, and Meadowcroft had journeyed west, and Bickerton was enthused about being able to be on his way again.[19]

The truth was, he felt inadequate. "I was no farmer," he confessed, and did not know what good farmland looked like. He decided to see if he could get assistance from members of the Wheeling branch. While staying at his brother Arthur's home, this brother having also

16. Cadman, *History of the Church of Jesus Christ*, 69; Cadman, *Religious Experiences*, 9.

17. Martin and Mancini, "History of the Church," 97; Cadman, *History of the Church of Jesus Christ*, 69–70.

18. The committee members were Charles Brown, William Cadman, James Louttit, Benjamin Meadowcroft, William McDonald, William Menzies, and William Reader.

19. Martin and Mancini, "History of the Church," 66, 95–96; Cadman, *History of the Church of Jesus Christ*, 69.

reclaimed his apostleship, Bickerton studied a map of Kansas and became convinced "by the power of God when I touched the map that Stafford county was the place the Lord wanted me." When he had returned home to Pennsylvania, he received another spiritual confirmation, this time in the West Elizabeth church, at which "my wife and her sister went through the [meeting] house shouting and praising God, giving the word of the Lord that I had done what the Lord had required of me."[20]

At the October conference, held at the Little Redstone branch, the members resolved that they "not entangle ourselves with worldly affairs." They needed to extricate themselves from ties to Pennsylvania and "hold ourselves in readiness to gather to the place where the Lord may appoint." Bickerton was so pleased, he could barely contain himself. Then the Lord put a stamp of approval on the decision, saying, "I have promised unto this people a land, a good land, a glorious land, flowing with milk and honey." The message was impactful, to the extent that "the glory and power of God came down and sealed the promise," the secretary wrote. The branches were requested to take up collections to help finance the journey to Kansas.[21]

As part of the 1874 fall conference, Joseph Smith's Civil War prophecy was read to the delegates, probably because the mission to the Indians was considered a validation of that prophecy.[22] Now that the war was almost a decade behind them, its effects lingered on. On its heels came an economic boom that transformed the North and West but left the South in ruins. It had been eight years since Appomattox, and railroad companies had repaired damaged tracks and laid an additional 35,000 miles of rail lines beyond what had existed before the war. This created a demand for coal, iron, and steel production. It opened new areas in the West to farming and increased the influence of Midwestern cities like

20. Bickerton, "Testimony, June 1903," 2, 3, 11.

21. Martin and Mancini, "History of the Church," 98; Cadman, *History of the Church of Jesus Christ*, 70–71; Entz, "Paradise on the Plains," 158–59.

22. Martin and Mancini, "History of the Church," 98.

Chicago and Kansas City. All of this absorbed the nation's investment capital and left the credit-hungry South short of funds.

Before the war, settlements had not extended very far beyond the Mississippi River. By 1880 the population of the Dakotas, Kansas, Minnesota, and Nebraska had grown from 30,000 in 1860 to over two million. The federal government came to see its responsibility to the Plains Indians to be that of persuading them to give up their religion, nomadic way of life, and communal ownership of land in exchange for Christianity and an agricultural lifestyle on reservations. The Indians stood in the way of railroads and American expansionism, meaning that Indian subordination and assimilation into white society were necessary for the realization of Manifest Destiny. The tyranny against the Indians sparked violent reactions, and the US military responded with such tactics as destroying the buffalo herds that formed the basis of the Indian economy. In 1871 Congress withdrew recognition of Indian tribes as sovereign nations. Railroad companies imported Chinese and Mexican labor rather than hire Indians. When federal troops vacated the former Confederacy, Jim Crow laws ruled the South. Then the final blow to the country's progress was the economic panic of the 1870s, which was the longest uninterrupted depression in American history. It was bad for workers, good for capitalists. Out of the turmoil—low wages, the formation of monopolies, and violent union strikes—somehow the country transformed itself into an economic powerhouse. When Charles Francis Adams, ambassador to Great Britain, returned to the United States in 1868, he and his wife stood in amazement: "Had they been Tyrian traders of the year B.C. 1000, landing from a galley fresh from Gibraltar, they could hardly have been stranger on the shore of a world, so changed from what it had been ten years before," their son Henry Adams wrote.[23]

It was just as Joseph Smith had predicted, that slaves would "rise up against their masters" and Indians would "marshal themselves, and shall become exceedingly angry, and shall vex the Gentiles" (D&C

23. Foner, *Reconstruction*, 460–64, 512–16.

87:4–6). The ideas Bickerton held about the last days were familiar to any Latter Day Saint. The assemblage of believers near Indian lands prior to the second coming of Christ lay at the heart of Mormon eschatology from the beginning. Bickerton explained in 1889 that his intent was to facilitate the inevitable. "Our removal to the west had no bearing on the general gathering of Israel, but to be near the Red man, that when the covenant went to [the scattered tribes of] Israel we should be near the borders."[24] Bickerton understood that his church's role was first to preach to the Indians and establish a gathering place for the righteous. Then God would call a Choice Seer from among the Indians to translate hidden ancient records, thereby confirming that "which shall have already gone forth among them." Bickerton wanted to gather the righteous gentiles who would help the "remnant of Jacob," the tribe of Manasseh (Indians), build the New Jerusalem (2 Ne. 3:11; 3 Ne. 21:23–24).

Smith began the outreach to Indians over forty years earlier in September 1830, only a few months after he organized the Church of Christ. A revelation for his friend and second elder, Oliver Cowdery, commanded him to "go unto the Lamanites and preach my gospel unto them; and … cause my church to be established among them." The Lord gave Cowdery a hint as to where the New Jerusalem would reside. "And now, behold, I say unto you that it is not revealed, and no man knoweth where the city Zion shall be built, but it shall be given hereafter. Behold, I say unto you that it shall be on the borders by the Lamanites" (D&C 28:8–9). Indian Territory in Joseph Smith's day lay just across the border from Missouri. That was where the federal government was relocating the eastern tribes, so Cowdery, along with Ziba Peterson, Parley Pratt, and Peter Whitmer Jr., traveled there, stopping in Independence, Missouri, on the far edge of the state.[25]

A year later, in July 1831, Smith himself traveled to Independence. Cowdery had done his best to reach out to the Indians across the

24. Bickerton, *St. John Weekly News*, Aug. 16, 1889.
25. Bushman, *Rough Stone Rolling*, 122.

Missouri River, but without success. Smith wondered what it meant. When would the day come when the Indians would be converted and Zion built? When would peace reign on earth for a thousand years, he wondered, indicating that he saw a connection between the two: the New Jerusalem and the Millennium. Here are Smith's own words: "When will the wilderness blossom as the rose? When will Zion be built up in her glory, and where will Thy temple stand, unto which all nations shall come in the last days?" As he meditated on this, he received another revelation confirming that "the land of promise, and the place for the city of Zion," was Jackson County, Missouri (D&C 57:1–3). It was the "land flowing with milk and honey, upon which there shall be no curse when the Lord cometh" (D&C 38:18).

In the Bible, John the Revelator had described the New Jerusalem "coming down from God" (Rev. 21:2), while the Book of Mormon clarified that the "remnant of the house of Joseph" would "build up a holy city unto the Lord" before the actual New Jerusalem "should come down out of heaven." In any case, in that day the Lamanites would "no more be confounded, until the end come when the earth shall pass away" (Ether 13). In the spring of 1832, Smith received a revelation that brought new meaning to this future utopia, given as an addendum introducing a new word, "stake," into the church's vernacular. It was derived from Isaiah's view of the expansion of Israel, when Isaiah wrote, "Enlarge the place of thy tent, and let them stretch forth the curtains of thine habitations: spare not, lengthen thy cords, and strengthen thy stakes" (Isa. 54:2). What Joseph Smith was told was that "Zion must increase in beauty, and in holiness; her borders must be enlarged; her stakes must be strengthened; yea, verily I say unto you, Zion must arise and put on her beautiful garments" (D&C: 82:14). This meant that Independence was not the only gathering place. To expand on the imagery, the tent, Zion, had cloth walls—one might say curtains—stretching out, supported by stakes driven into the ground. Independence would be the site of the New Jerusalem, but other cities would be part of Zion. They would be located in

Ohio, Illinois, and, as Bickerton saw it, Kansas. In the Mormon consciousness, Missouri's preeminence was not challenged, it was simply augmented by satellite sites.[26]

Like Joseph Smith, the prophet in West Elizabeth saw Zion as a place, a theocracy, and an era—all three. The church, "the kingdom of God," was the physical embodiment of Zion. The physical Zion would exist at a time when all people, mortals and immortals together, would find they could coexist in harmony and live under divine law. Even the animals would live in peace during the zionic era, which was synonymous with the Millennium. It would occur after Jesus Christ returned to earth and, as Smith declared in 1830, reveal himself "from heaven with power and great glory, with all the hosts thereof." Thereafter, Christ would "dwell in righteousness with men on earth a thousand years, and the wicked shall not stand" (D&C 29:11). During this time, the Jews would occupy the land of Israel again, and the Indians would reside in the Americas, but the scattered tribes could live in either one place or the other, or elsewhere throughout the world. God would also fulfill his covenants to the righteous gentiles, and they too would dwell in peace in Zion.[27]

Explaining this in a letter to a local newspaper in Kansas in 1889, or rather in explaining why the church had moved to that state, Bickerton referenced several revelations (D&C 63, 84, 101) and concluded that "anyone can see that Missouri was to be the place appointed for the gathering of the Saints." The reason the church was forced to leave was because of "transgression" on Smith's part. Bickerton's real target, however, was Brigham Young, because Bickerton wanted to "show that Salt Lake City, Utah, was never appointed by the Almighty, as

26. Ibid., 175–76; Erickson, *Thief in the Night*, 93–121.

27. It appears Bickerton understood that those who accepted Christ before the Second Coming would be resurrected or transfigured and live on earth in an immortal state, while those who converted after the Messiah's appearance in glory at the Mount of Olives would continue on earth in the flesh. That would come after the conversion of the Lamanites, the building of the New Jerusalem, and the translation of additional ancient scripture and before the onset of the Millennium. This is not, however, the official stance of the Church of Jesus Christ today.

a gathering place for His Saints."[28] Since Smith died, God appointed another gathering place for the Saints, he explained. It was not Utah. Whether he thought Independence remained the promised site of the New Jerusalem or whether he thought the Lord had moved that location farther west to the new "land flowing with milk and honey" in Stafford County is unknown.[29]

In 1874 Bickerton was still uncertain if he could identify good farmland without the advice of those who knew what to look for. He may have wanted witnesses too. After all, the Bible asserted that by "two or three witnesses shall every word be established" (Deut. 19:15; 2 Cor. 13:1). When he and John Stevenson, who had replaced John Neish as his travel partner, arrived at the edge of Kansas in late fall 1874, they found two newly baptized members from Wilson County who said they would accompany them to the interior of the state. Bickerton and Stevenson met with the Saints in that area in the town of Parsons, Kansas, only thirty-five miles from Missouri. Stafford County, which was their tentative destination, was another 230 miles to the west. James Taylor and one other church member, whose identity has not survived, helped fit out a springboard wagon for the four of them to travel in to Wichita, where they chartered their way farther west over terrain that was rugged, through a country that was at that time largely unsettled. In fact, the Kansas legislature had just created Stafford County four years prior. Arriving on a Saturday in an uninhabited area, and aware they were in a region plagued by tornadoes, they knelt down on a ridge six miles north of where the town would be founded, and there Bickerton asked God to bless the land that no tornado would ravage it as long as a band of faithful Saints resided there.[30]

Afterward the men walked south and, wary of coyotes and wolves, gathered buffalo bones that were strewn across the prairie and built a

28. "Bickerton's Letter," *St. John County Capital*, Sept. 12, 1889.

29. Bickerton, "Testimony, June 1903," 3, 11; Cadman, *History of the Church of Jesus Christ*, 70.

30. Cole and Reuber, *No Cyclone Shall Destroy*, 4–6; "Bickerton's Letter," *St. John County Capital*, Oct. 17, 1889.

five-foot-high corral to sleep in. When dawn arrived, they looked across the valley toward Rattlesnake Creek and walked two miles "to the spot, or very near it, where our county seat was afterwards located," Bickerton explained at a later date. At that location, the prophet "drove a stake in the ground which we named a stake of Zion," illustrating in a symbolic way the fulfillment of ancient prophecy. The area would be called Zion Valley.[31] Once they had fastened the stake, "We stood up four of us … and asked the blessing of God upon the land, and prayed that the time would soon come that we should go to the Lamanites. This was the Sabbath morning about sunrise."[32] The first days in Stafford County became a holy convocation for the four men. Over a century later, a writer at the *Wichita Eagle* recounted Zion Valley's founding and included Bickerton's prayer to protect the settlers from tornadoes, commenting that since then "many a tornado has come close to the county seat's borders, but none has done damage."[33]

Excited about the decision on where to settle, Taylor traveled twenty-five miles north to the town of Great Bend and informed the newspaper of their intention. People were aware that the land in that area would be good for cattle if someone was hardy enough to try it, but no one paid serious attention to the pretension to establish a town there.[34] This indifference would not last long, but the Saints would not be met with overwhelming opposition either.

Bickerton returned to share what he and Stevenson had accomplished. In a church meeting on January 2, 1875, he said he found the land to be "as good in quality" as one could hope for, although "destitute of timber, and its mineral resources of course unknown, because

31. "Bickerton's Letter," *St. John County Capital*, Oct. 17, 1889; Bickerton, "Testimony, June 1903," 11.

32. In Bickerton's 1903 testimony, he wrote that he drove a stake in April 1874, evidently forgetting that they had not arrived until the late fall, unless he meant another stake driven into the ground when the Saints emigrated in the spring of 1875.

33. Bickel, "St. John Has Little-known History," *Wichita Eagle*, Aug. 13, 2010.

34. *Great Bend Register*, Nov. 12, 1874; Entz, "Paradise on the Plains," 160.

unexplored." He said "it had been made known unto him that it was the place of gathering, and he had dedicated it to that purpose." The Saints welcomed the report and thanked "Brother Bickerton for his faithfulness in fulfilling his duties," and "fully endorsed" his findings.[35]

"We tell you by the power of God, that the Lord is going to move this Church in righteousness," Bickerton said at a meeting two days later. "I tell you in the name of the Lord that this is the Lord's word." He read a revelation of November 1874 about the location of the temple, which would be the focal point of the community. On finishing, his new wife, Charlotte, stood and said, "Hearken unto the word of God that has been given for I have opened a door and no one can shut it." The members rose to their feet to give thanks "to Almighty God for His goodness for having led and guided our Bro. Bickerton to the location and made known His will." The entire congregation was overcome, several people spoke in tongues, and "a power of confirmation came down upon the whole assembly such has not been witnessed by this Church upon any previous occasion," the secretary wrote.[36]

The next thing Bickerton needed to do was to visit the West Virginia congregation. He had previously "told them we were intending to locate in western Kansas," and "they all agreed to locate with us" until a rumor circulated that he intended to create a theocracy and practice polygamy like in Salt Lake City. In Wheeling they "held a meeting at George Baker Sr.['s] house," and Bickerton noticed that the members "hung their heads" until Eli Kendall stood up and said, "Verily thus saith the Lord, this people will not do as they are doing in Salt Lake in their abominations." George Kendall endorsed this, and with that having been established, the group retired to an area outside the house where "the spirit of the Lord came down, and we had a general

35. Cadman, *History of the Church of Jesus Christ*, 74–75; Martin and Mancini, "History of the Church," 100.

36. Martin and Mancini, 101–02. The text of the November 1874 revelation is not extant.

rejoicing in the orchard of Geo Baker."[37] In support of the prophet, George Baker and Eli Kendall agreed to move to Kansas.

Moving quickly to make preparations, the prophet issued a public notice in February 1875 that the members were organizing a company called Zion Colonization Society, with him as president, and would move in the early spring. Church members had subscribed a total of $20,000 ($450,000 today), and outsiders were welcome to invest, he wrote. He explained that "although it was a church movement, yet individuals who were not members of the church had equal rights as others."[38] This benefited families like Jane Glackin's, whose husband, Hugh, was a non-member. She was a midwife whose skills would be invaluable to a new colony.[39] Members agreed as part of the by-laws that there would be "no swearing or drinking of intoxicants" and "no immoral act." The society would operate a communal store. Of the initial $20,000, about a third ($6,000) had been personally subscribed by Bickerton, based on his property value. "I sold some of my property and mortgaged the rest," he wrote, and received help from William Cadman to finalize the sales. For a small church, this was a major undertaking.[40]

There was a problem in that many of the members remained reluctant to cut themselves free from the East and sell their property. Even though they contributed funds, the total amount fell short of what was needed. "When it came to selling properties, none but myself, Brother Charles Brown, and Arthur and Alex Bickerton would sell," Bickerton noted. Some of them, like William Cadman, made other

37. "Bickerton's Letter," *St. John County Capital*, Oct. 17, 1889; Bickerton, "Testimony, June 1903," 3.

38. "Zion Colonization Society," *Monongahela Valley Republican*, Feb. 18, 1875; "Bickerton's Letter," *St. John County Capital*, Nov. 14, 1889.

39. Robinson interview, 1998, n.p.

40. "Bickerton's Letter," *St. John County Capital*, Nov. 14, 1889; Bickerton, "Testimony, June 1903," 3; *Elizabeth Herald*, Feb. 13, 1875; Entz, "Paradise on the Plains," 162. The officers of Zion Colonization Society were William Bickerton, president; James Louttit, vice president; Joseph Astin, financial secretary; William McDonald, corresponding secretary; Benjamin Meadowcroft, treasurer; and a twelve-member board of directors: John Neish, William Menzies, Joseph Menzies, Charles Brown, William Cadman, Eli Kendall, A. Love, William Skillen, and four unnamed persons.

preparations to support the colony. Cadman constructed a boarding house in Elizabeth to raise money and "show his faith in the work." Bickerton wanted the town they were establishing to operate on a communal basis like in the New Testament (Acts 4:32–35) and as had been practiced for a time by the Latter-day Saints in Ohio and Missouri (D&C 51, 78, 104). Charles Brown was concerned that at least no one would be neglected, and suggested that James Louttit be "bishop over the poor in the 'Land of Zion.'"[41] They must not have been bothered by the fact that the Mormons, like the early Christians, had abandoned their collectivist program due to inherent difficulties. Bickerton viewed the model as a noble cause that merited another attempt. In his plan, the church would maintain a storehouse and charge up to six percent interest for items loaned to settlers. "I had three houses that had not yet been sold," he explained, "so I appointed a committee to sell the remainder of my property and give it to the Church, thus I carried out what we read about, having all things common." His funds would presumably be used to purchase goods for the storehouse. This was actually in line with a longstanding American tradition of utopian societies that had begun to appear already in the eighteenth century, so that by 1860, 137 had come and gone in the United States.[42]

It made sense that some members would stay in the East and support the first wave of settlers. The call for colonists was something else and mostly fell on deaf ears. Even James Louttit, the bishop-elect, changed his mind about actually moving to Kansas. The more he thought about it, the less he wanted to live "in a cellar or cave in the ground," he said. He doubted some of the revelations, so his apprehensions were probably a rationale for prior misgivings. Increasingly other members questioned the quality of the soil in Stafford County, for instance. Some of the Saints traveled there and did not find it to their

41. Martin and Mancini, "History of the Church," 101. See also Doctrine and Covenants 42:32–33; Bushman, *Rough Stone Rolling*, 181–83.

42. Bickerton to *Elizabeth Herald*, Jan. 13, 1877; "Bickerton's Letter," *St. John County Capital*, Nov. 14, 1889; Bickerton, "Testimony, June 1903," 3; Bushman, *Rough Stone Rolling*, 165; Fogarty, *Communal and Utopian History*, xxiv.

liking, or as Bickerton said, they "did not like the locality" at all. Bickerton had faith that God would bless them, despite hardships, and that this would nullify the reservations the naysayers had. In the future, he would become more bitter about this and say that Louttit was deserving of an accident that befell his family because of his bullheadedness.[43]

By the end of February, Bickerton was ready, even if others were not. The geopolitical boundaries had changed, so that Stafford County no longer existed. With so few settlers, the legislature decided to divide it up among Barton County to the north, Pawnee to the west, and Pratt to the south. Zion Valley would now find itself in Barton County under the jurisdiction of Great Bend.[44] In addition, a surveyor and carpenter, James Miskin, with wife, Amelia, and infant daughter, had moved near the location where the Saints were headed. The Miskins proved to be a blessing. In response to rumors that "a colony was on their way to locate from Pennsylvania, most of them being miners," the Miskins urged a wait-and-see approach. As Amelia remembered, "One of our neighbors came in great haste and excitement and told my husband that this colony was composed of Mormons, and that … they were a bad lot and had to be driven from Missouri." James thought this over and said, "Let them come and prove themselves first. Maybe they are better than we are."

James had heard about polygamy, but "did not think they had any religion." Amelia thought otherwise because, as she remembered from an article in *Harper's Weekly*, they were portrayed singing a hymn with the line, "We are not ashamed to own our God." That had made her wonder if it should not be the other way around, "whether God is not ashamed to own them." The Miskins seemed grateful to be getting some neighbors, either way.[45] Before long, the Saints arrived in Wilson County to the east, where the Kansas converts helped the men buy horses, oxen, and wagons. Bickerton bought "thirteen yoke of oxen,

43. Bickerton, "Testimony, June 1903," 3.
44. Entz, "Paradise on the Plains," 165–66.
45. Miskin and Miskin, "Notes on Our Early Life," 2.

ready for work," to arrive later, along with "two wagons, and one team of horses." The members witnessed two miracles while procuring supplies. A child of John Rankin fell to diphtheria and was instantly healed. Another child, the six-week-old baby of Samuel Nutting, suffered from "chokeing in its throat" and "refused to take the brest for the space of 24 hours." An elder anointed the child, and it "took the brest again." The vanguard company of mostly male members of some forty households loaded five wagons with supplies and headed westward in March.[46]

On April 3, 1875, they arrived at the designated place in a snow storm. Accustomed to a higher standard of comfort, they had to adapt to living in "tent houses" for the time being. "Only two or three women had arrived as the men wanted to build before sending for their families," Amelia recollected. "At this time we were 28 miles from a railroad or any store and my nearest neighbor live[d] more than a mile away."[47] The first item of business for the settlers was to apply for a registered site at the land office thirty miles to the west. While there, they petitioned for a post office and individual homestead claims. Their request for mail delivery was granted, the name Zion Valley being approved, "with mail twice a week." Almost immediately there was a problem because someone had to put down their name to claim the town site. Duncan Bell had agreed to do this, but somehow it ended up in the name of George Brickenridge. After a brief dust-up, the misunderstanding was straightened out. As they started to define their lots and build houses, they had "good spiritual meetings at all times, all members doing duty, no drinking or bad habits of any kind, and we could hear the prayers of the saints going up from each homestead," Bickerton said.

They ordered lumber from Chicago. On May 17 the oxen arrived. "Each two men had a yoke of oxen" and "each yoke broke seventy acres," Bickerton recalled. They planted corn. For the moment, they

46. "Bickerton's Letter," *St. John County Capital*, Nov. 14, 1889; Bickerton, "Testimony, June 1903," 3, 12; "Council Meetings at St. John," 1:3; Entz, "Paradise on the Plains," 165–66.

47. "Bickerton's Letter," *St. John County Capital*, Nov. 14, 1889; Bickerton, "Testimony, June 1903," 12; Miskin and Miskin, "Notes on Our Early Life," 2–3.

were not yet able to think about visiting Indian Territory. They did visit the nearby towns to preach to the gentiles. Bickerton wrote that "the people of Great Bend were very kind to us, and showed it in various ways," one of which was to allow Bickerton the use of a schoolhouse on Sundays to preach.[48]

When they first met their neighbor James Miskin, it was because he and someone from the colony, possibly Bickerton, were on their way to Great Bend at the same time and Miskin's horse became lame. Climbing up onto the wagon, Miskin listened to the grave older man talk about religion, telling him that "angels had [recently] visited the earth" and that "Joseph Smith had been visited by God, the Father, and his Son, Jesus Christ, after seeking in prayer to know which church he should join." This made Miskin curious about the people's other beliefs. Amelia reported that her husband was "very much interested and surprised at hearing something different from what he had ever heard before and promised to come to hear them preach at the blacksmith's home the next Sunday." She was equally interested but had a sick baby to look after. "You go," she told her husband. "If they preach from the Bible, I will go next Sunday, if all is well." James attended the service, after which the Saints asked him what he thought of the sermon. "It was all Bible doctrine," he told them, "but he thought they were a little one-sided in not offering him the sacrament." They asked if he would be interested in knowing more about their doctrines, including that of the closed communion, and loaned him a copy of the Book of Mormon. Before long, he and his wife both had "earnestly read the book" and had become converted.[49]

In Pennsylvania, Benjamin Meadowcroft had been appointed to preside over the eastern church with counselors William Cadman and James Louttit. In late spring the eastern presidency sent John Neish, a member of the colony's board of directors, to audit the financial books. When he arrived in Kansas, he was welcomed by Bickerton,

48. Bickerton, "Testimony, June 1903," 11–12.
49. Miskin and Miskin, "Notes on Our Early Life," 3.

who thought everything went well. "Mr. Neish came out here during the time I was acting superintendent," he remembered, "and examined the books and said they were all correct."[50] Back in Pennsylvania, Neish gave a less rosy report. He said the books were not being kept in good order, probably out of neglect but possibly in a way that was to the superintendent's advantage. As far as he could see, "the Almighty has [not] had any part in directing the Saints to the locality of Zion Valley, . . . a barren prairie, a county of sand hills, occasionally interspersed with narrow valleys, containing (with the sand) a slight admixture of soil." The colonists were convinced, he said, that the "droppings of birds and buffaloes" would fertilize the ground. It was only "within the last fifteen years [that] grass first began to grow in that region." After a few years of planting crops, Neish predicted, the settlers would "exhaust the productive qualities of these valleys, and the droppings of birds and buffaloes would all be transformed into vegetable productions, and the supply being very limited would soon be exhausted." Then "the hapless inhabitants would be found in great destitution and want; and the country would revert to its natural and original state, comparable, apparently, only to Sahara," where even "a crow would not be able to pass across that country without carrying its own rations." He thought the settlers, in their deprivation, had entirely laid aside "the principal of spiritual guidance" and were relying on "the disordered brains of a few professing to possess the perfection of human wisdom."

The trustees were alarmed to learn that they had been misled. Benjamin Meadowcroft, the treasurer, decided to halt further support for the settlement and urge the colonists to return, in order to limit the loss to the investors. It was a devastating blow. The colonists had not yet received much support, but would soon need it to survive until the first harvest.[51] When their supplies were becoming depleted, they were

50. Cadman, *History of the Church of Jesus Christ*, 72; Bickerton to *Elizabeth Herald*, Jan. 13, 1877.

51. Cadman, *Great Bend Register*, Sept. 21, 1876; Cadman, "The Latter Day Saints and Zion Colony," *Elizabeth Herald*, Nov. 25, 1876; Entz, "Paradise on the Plains," 172.

told they would have to fend for themselves. Until June 1875, the emigration company had only sent two checks, one for $125 and the other for $100. In desperate circumstances, Bickerton spent $1,200 he had remaining in personal funds, and the others did the same with what means they had, to make purchases collectively and place building supplies with Eli Kendall and merchandise with Thomas Taylor, the storekeeper, for the common good. Kendall and Taylor disposed of the food and lumber as they were needed. When the goods were diminished toward the end of June and the fall harvest had not yet arrived, they had even "run out of flour." Bickerton had nineteen dollars left "to get provisions for all." Knowing he needed more than that, he borrowed money in Great Bend, delivered food to the colony, gathered some examples of the produce raised in Barton County, and bought a train ticket to Pennsylvania. On June 28 he proceeded east to defend himself and the colony.[52]

On his arrival in Pennsylvania, the church was struggling under the burden of having added 103 new members, not to mention Neish's dim view of the survivability of the colony. To combat the negative report, Bickerton displayed the produce he had brought with him—corn in tassel, potatoes, onions, and beets—by placing the crops right on the pulpit at the July conference "so that they could see with their own eyes." Some of the members came around to his defense, one speaking in the name of the Lord as a revelation. The other leaders attempted to soften the friction and agreed to something unexpected—a conference the next July in Zion Valley. They still demanded a revision of terms for the settlement to protect the investors. Their concern was not so much whether enough funds were being generated to send to Kansas as they were that the profits flow back to Pennsylvania. From now on, they insisted, the farmers needed to share the profits with the investors when they took produce or grain to market. The supplies obtained by the farmer would be "charged as debt" to the corporation. It would be a joint-stock company. Settlers

52. Bickerton to *Elizabeth Herald*, Jan. 13, 1877; Bickerton, "Testimony, June 1903," 4; "Bickerton's Letter," *St. John County Capital*, Nov. 14, 1889.

would be sharecroppers, not members of a commune. Further, the trustees had the authority to sell assets to raise money, whether land, crops, cattle, or machinery. One can imagine that Bickerton did his best to head off some of these measures, but at the same time worried about maintaining peace with the sponsoring company and sparing the colony. The conference agreed to "exonerate the board of directors from all charges preferred against them, and endorse their actions as being the best they could do under the existing circumstances."

Bickerton resigned as president and superintendent of the company, agreeing to "no longer be responsible for the furnishing of supplies." He may have hoped that their future success would mend all wounds and that he would show he had nothing to hide by allowing someone else to make decisions and keep the records. Benjamin Meadowcroft and John Neish likewise submitted their resignations. In their place, William McDonald was made president and superintendent, and John Neish was retained as an assistant. Benjamin Meadowcroft was retained on the board. This meant that opponents of the settlement had now seized its leadership. Later in life Bickerton would regret that the conference "appointed another man as president that was not very honest."[53] McDonald accompanied Bickerton to Kansas in July. On their arrival McDonald took control of the storehouse, telling "each family [to] turn in all the products they had raised" so he could "deal out" what they could keep. He confiscated seventy cattle the colony had received as a gift from the Saints in Wilson County. He also confiscated a number of horses, wagons, and lumber, and with the help of a few colonists Bickerton described as "worthless … of no use in this country" sold the assets at a public auction in Great Bend. The proceeds were distributed to the settlers, with a percentage of the income retained to take back to Pennsylvania, along with the account books for the lumber, cattle, and storehouse. Having spent less than a month in the valley, he left. "Each

53. Cadman, *Great Bend Register*, Sept. 21, 1876; "Bickerton's Letter," *St. John County Capital*, Nov. 14, 1889; Bickerton, "Testimony, June 1903," 4; Martin and Mancini, "History of the Church," 103–04.

person got a share," Bickerton remarked. "I, myself, got a couple of shares" representing a net loss to him of $1,700. Essentially the settlers had been raided when they were in greatest need.[54]

"This was just about the breaking of the Colony," Bickerton later remembered. Without cattle, supplies, or a ripe fall harvest, they were reduced to scouring the prairie for buffalo bones and selling them in Great Bend for six dollars per ton.[55] Bickerton decided to buy another train ticket east to check on his property, which he had left in the hands of a committee. Later he said, without hyperbole, "I have done all I could for the work of God." He had been thwarted at every turn, and now he would feel ambushed again to learn that the building he had donated to the West Elizabeth branch had been put up for auction, the leadership deciding the branch could meet in William Cadman's home for a while and make a profit on the sale of Bickerton's gift. He intervened and stopped the auction by placing a bid that was unusually high. A few days later, the property sold anyway. "If I had intended to make money out of it, I could have left it to my children," he lamented. The October conference in Monongahela City tried to placate Bickerton by promising to donate part of the proceeds to the colony. Bickerton was not buying it. In any case, the branch would not have another chapel until 1882.[56]

The flash sale of the settlers' property in Zion Valley put an end to the communal experiment and created a breach between the eastern and western members. The colonists still believed that Zion Valley was divinely appointed. They were determined to continue on "the best we could," Bickerton said, considering that "a great number of [them were] miners from Pennsylvania and Ohio who knew very little about

54. Bickerton, "Testimony, June 1903," 4, 13; Bickerton, *Elizabeth Herald*, Jan. 13, 1877; "Bickerton's Letter," *St. John County Capital*, Nov. 14, 1889.

55. The bones were pulverized and sold as fertilizer, as an additive for livestock and poultry feed, and for filtering sugar-cane juice and other liquids. See, for instance, Delbert and Ruth Trew, "Recycling on the Plains: Buffalo Bones for Fertilizer," *Farm Collector*, Aug. 2007.

56. Bickerton, "Testimony, June 1903," 3, 4, 10, 12; Martin and Mancini, "History of the Church," 76, 104; Cadman, *History of the Church of Jesus Christ*, 86.

farming and as to working oxen we knew as little about that as they did of us." They were left with some oxen and a few teams of horses that allowed them to break ground and sow 300 acres of wheat by the first day of October. When they built new houses, it was "almost as by magic," one newspaper reported, and by November had more than a dozen buildings finished. "Winter did not check the ardor of these people," the reporter noted after seeing plans to construct a schoolhouse in the spring. They kept warm by "burning corn stalks and buffalo chips," according to Bickerton, who admitted that "I have been nearly frozen to death in the country."[57]

In Pennsylvania, William Cadman had grown tired of hearing complaints about Kansas from the officers of the company, William McDonald, John Neish, and Benjamin Meadowcroft. In December 1875 he held a council meeting in his home to be briefed on the state of the colony, upset to realize that the seizure of assets had left the colony in dire straits. "Any neglect on our part to reinforce them," he said, stating the obvious, "cannot possibly be attended with other than disastrous and ruinous results." The report he and others heard "created with us an alarm of a general character for the welfare of Zion." The council concluded that McDonald and Neish had condemned Zion Valley "without sufficient reasons." Meadowcroft, Neish, and McDonald had further created chaos by vetoing the proposal to hold a general church conference in Zion Valley in July 1876, and were soon advertising an alternative conference to be held in Coultersville, Pennsylvania. They were also suggesting settling in South America.

Wondering what to do about this, the council was blessed with a "wonderful shower of divine glory." One person spoke in tongues and three people received the same interpretation, that Zion Valley was "to be a choice land, a good land, and that it was the place of gathering; and that the Saints would gather to it, and none but the Saints, and that there should be no speculation there, and that it was a

57. "Bickerton's Letter," *St. John County Capital*, Nov. 14, 1889; "Zion Valley," *Great Bend Register*, July 27, 1876; Bickerton, "Testimony, June 1903," 4.

spiritual gathering and not a temporal gathering." Cadman beseeched those planning to attend the January 1876 conference to "revers[e] the erroneous conclusions" of the Zion Colonization Society officers and "let us for once obey the voice of revelation and place this people near the border of the Cherokee Nation, that the Deliverer may go out of Zion and turn ungodliness from Jacob; or else be candid and confess to all men that we do not believe in what we have been teaching these many years, namely the principles of immediate revelation." If anyone objected to this, he said, speaking for the council, then they wanted the vote of the council to be recorded "positively against them, both now and forevermore."[58]

Cadman wrote to assure Bickerton of their support and to warn him that they might see a "considerable" spring immigration. Cadman requested that Bickerton prepare "a comprehensive account of the colony to [deliver to] the Conference of January." "Express yourself firmly," he requested, "on the quality of both land [and] water; and, also, describe climate, whether natural grasses are nutritious, and if there is material for making brick, and to what extent, and, in short, a general outlook of the prospect of building up a colony." Regarding the more central issue of the settlement's spiritual claim, "give a truthful account … and express yourself concerning [the] locality being appointed of God," he advised. The assumption of some of the Pennsylvania members was that a convert from Kansas had influenced Bickerton. Cadman asked the prophet to affirm that the settlers were unified. McDonald and Neish claimed "that it is only a faction or click that professes enjoyment," including spiritual fulfillment. Cadman also suggested that Charles Brown and other influential Saints sign their names to Bickerton's account. Then with a warm closing remark, Cadman reminded Bickerton, "I remain your ever affectionate, and, will endeavor to be, your ever trustworthy brother."[59]

58. Cadman, *History of the Church of Jesus Christ*, 74–75; Cadman, *Great Bend Register*, Sept. 21, 1876. Cadman said "received" rather than "recorded."

59. *Great Bend Register*, Sept. 21, 1876.

Six months before the scheduled conference in Zion Valley, another conference was held in January 1876 at the Little Redstone branch. When Benjamin Meadowcroft was asked to explain his campaign against the colony, his response was found to be unsatisfactory. He asked for forgiveness and it was granted. The same could not be said of William McDonald, who three months earlier had proposed that the church move to Carbondale, Pennsylvania, to work in the coal mines, and had leased a mineshaft and engaged a boarding house without general approval, informing the membership that they had until January 8 to take advantage of this opportunity. Unimpressed, the conference quashed the plan. In his view, the church had fallen into a pit of romanticism and thrown fiscal responsibility to the wind. In response to complaints about how he had handled the Zion Colonization Society, he resigned his position as president and superintendent. His replacement was James Louttit.[60]

As promised, the church began sending more settlers and supplies in February. A journalist in Pennsylvania told readers that "a couple of families left this place this morning for the Mormon colony, in Barton county, Kansas. Charles Miller late clerk in O'Neil's store will leave with his family for the same place next week." The reporter was informed that "a great many more families will go west to the colony as soon as they get the means to go with." Even though "the colony is twenty miles from the railroad," they had been promised a branch line in the near future.[61]

It did not go well for some of the new settlers. Some were less the pioneering type than the first wave of colonists. Miller stayed two months and quit, and he was not the only one who felt the hardship and wondered if it was worth it. During an April council meeting, it was candidly reported that several of the settlers were "not enjoying themselvs very well."[62] A conference that month in Monongahela City

60. Martin and Mancini, "History of the Church," 107, 109–10.

61. "West Elizabeth Letter," *Elizabeth Herald*, Feb. 12, 1876.

62. "Council Meetings at St. John, Kansas," 1:16; Entz, "Paradise on the Plains," 182.

saw another attempt by the colony's opponents to relocate the conference now three months away. Their main purpose for doing so was to secure control of the church finances and revoke Bickerton's fiscal role. As president of the eastern church, Meadowcroft agreed to the plan to meet in Coultersville. That created a rift between him and Cadman, who called the Coultersville conference illegal and refused to attend. He continued to endorse the conference in Zion Valley. Although he would not be able personally to travel to Kansas, he sent a letter as a representative of the West Elizabeth branch. Other leaders boycotted the Coultersville meeting as well.[63]

The Saints in Zion Valley knew they had little time to plant crops, build houses, and get everything ready for the upcoming inspection. With warmer weather came a renewed enthusiasm. One of the colonists, Thomas Taylor, wrote to the *Great Bend Register* in May that "our Valley is filling up very fast. A new house is built every few days. … About 20 persons settled here this week, and we are looking for about 30 persons from Wilson county, this State, this week." The immigrants were traveling to Great Bend by rail, so their arrival had been noticed. "We have a blacksmith shop in running order," Taylor wrote, "and H. H. Kidder, of the Bend, talks of starting a branch store here. A good store will do a splendid business here." In addition to that, the "wheat crop looks well," he persisted. "I never saw as fine wheat grow in any country. We had wheat that measured three feet high the first day of May. Oats looks well and so does corn that is up." He invited people to come and see their town and attend a Sunday service. "It will do you good to come down to one of our meetings and hear the Doctrine of Christ and his apostles preached by Inspiration and hear the gift of tongues and Interpretation of tongues, prophesy, &c., as on the day of Penticost." Although the letter was promotional, the Saints had in fact plowed an additional 700 acres of crops and finished construction of the schoolhouse by the end of July.[64]

63. Cadman, *History of the Church of Jesus Christ*, 72–73.

64. "West Elizabeth Letter," *Elizabeth Herald*, May 6, 1876; Taylor, "Zion Valley," *Great Bend Register*, May 11, 1876; Entz, "Paradise on the Plains," 183–84, 186.

After enjoying some success in planting crops, the colony hosted the visitors for its July 1876 conference, aware that the rival conference was being held simultaneously in Coultersville, although with minimal support from the Fayette, Monongahela, and even Coultersville members. Those attending the eastern conference appointed Meadowcroft church president and James Louttit and John Neish counselors. Bickerton's letter condemning their insubordination was read in the conference. In response, John Neish and William McDonald were asked to go to Kansas to "investigate matters and seek to bring about a reconciliation, and if possible to keep the Church, 'one.'" As was evident from their choice of ambassadors, however, they may have lacked sincerity, or at least diplomacy, in sending such vocal opponents of the colony. In conjunction with the conference, Louttit held a colonization meeting in his home and notified the board that he would never call for another meeting. He considered the company "busted" and therefore dissolved. McDonald and Neish were instructed to tell Bickerton that they held him personally responsible for the better half of the company's debts.[65]

In Zion Valley, too, there was evidence of tension. The colonists demanded that proceeds of the sale of church properties be sent west, especially since past sales were a result of so many members relocating to Kansas. A group of six men, including Bickerton, was appointed to travel east to assure that this would happen, and to ship the church's movable property to the colony. The conference addressed the membership status of Joseph Menzies, who had left the colony with unpaid debts. The result was that he was excommunicated for "rascality" and "dishonesty."[66]

At the Zion Valley conference, Zebedee Kendall spoke on July 2 about the future of "Jerrusulum and of Zion," prompting Bickerton to ask how many in the congregation were satisfied with the progress

65. Cadman, *Elizabeth Herald*, Dec. 9, 1876; Cadman, "The Latter Day Saints and Zion Colony," *Elizabeth Herald*, Nov. 25, 1876; McDonald, "Communications," *Elizabeth Herald*, Dec. 2, 1876; Martin and Mancini, "History of the Church," 111–12; Cadman, "The Zion Colony Matter," *Monongahela Valley Republican*, Nov. 23, 1876.

66. Bickerton, *Elizabeth Herald*, Jan. 13, 1877; "Zion Valley Minute Book 1876–1877," 6; Cadman, "The Zion Colony Matter," *Monongahela Valley Republican*, Nov. 23, 1876.

of the colony. Sixty-six men and women stood up—all but four of the adults present—including some non-members. He asked how many believed they were building a place of gathering. Forty-seven stood, and at that point "such a cloud of glory that came down I never experienced before," the secretary remarked, "and they all gloryfied the God of Israel." It is not certain what the secretary may have meant, in this instance and others, by a "cloud of glory," but it conveys the enjoyment of some sort of hyper-spiritual experience. For instance, Alexander Cherry said he had a vision, although its details were not recorded, pointing "to this work and to the gathering." Arthur Bickerton related that the day before he had seen in vision "a woman," presumably an angel, stacking "large piles of bread to feed the saints uppon." Thomas McManaway testified that the treeless plain was "as the tree of life" to him. He said further that in 1874 he dreamed he saw Bickerton shadowed by "two white swans," and in asking about them, Bickerton said they were angels that had "followed him all the way around when he was looking for the land."[67]

The next day the prophet told the conference he wanted to appoint twelve councilors to serve as judges. They needed to be "men of sound Judjemen[t] for the purpose of settleing dificulty that may arise in the Church," possibly to balance the authority of the colony's trustees and to satisfy those who considered him an autocrat seeking glory. This council of judges also resembled Joseph Smith's high council of twelve high priests responsible for "settling important difficulties which might arise in the church" (D&C 102:2). The conference gave its approval. Now all they had to do was await the visit of McDonald and Neish, the colony's overseers, later that month. There was some feeling that the colony should not welcome them and should break free of their control. During a patriotic service on July 4, including an address that reminded hearers of the War of Independence, emotions ran so high that Bickerton suggested they too should free themselves from the yoke of tyranny imposed by McDonald and Neish. "We have power to duel with them,"

67. "Zion Valley Minute Book 1876–1877," 6–7.

he said, calling for their excommunications. George Kendall concurred, calling McDonald "a wolf," and the crowd agreed. They decided John Neish should be suspended from office. Feeling empowered, the conference endorsed a letter to the Quorum of Twelve Apostles—specifically addressing William Bacon, Cummings Cherry, James Louttit, Benjamin Meadowcroft, William Menzies, John Neish, and William Skillen—requesting "that they lay down their weapons and become obedient to the will of god or they will be dealt with according to the laws of the Church." These apostles were either holding doubts about Zion Valley or were "fi[gh]ting against the location of the gathering."[68]

Bickerton wielded a firm hand when McDonald and Neish arrived in Zion Valley in late July. Before the pair met with the prophet, the Saints held a council meeting and voted not to receive them. The colony, the council decided, was not in need of reconciliation, the two visiting usurpers were. The colony was "perfectly reconciled" with its prophet, while the ambassadors were attempting to steal the church out from under them.[69] Bickerton himself chose to meet with McDonald and Neish to inform them that if they were there to talk business, the colony was "ready for a settlement." The colonists wanted out. Bickerton was irritated by their officiousness. "They wasted" his time by trying to persuade him "to receive them as delegates or members sent by a pretended Conference held at Coultersville by a few individuals who were trying to break down our church." He let them know they had been "suspended from the church for misconduct," then sent them back to Pennsylvania.[70]

Insulted, the two vowed to do everything they could to thwart the colony and dethrone Bickerton. At another rival conference, this one in early September 1876 at Mt. Vernon, a community across the Youghiogheny River to the southwest from Coultersville, they returned

68. Ibid., 7–10; Astin, "Minutes of the General Conference Held at West Elizabeth, Oct 7th, 1876," *Great Bend Register*, Nov. 9, 1876.

69. "Zion Valley Minute Book 1876–1877," 12.

70. Cadman, "The Zion Colony Matter," *Monongahela Valley Republican*, Nov. 23, 1876; Martin and Mancini, "History of the Church," 115.

the favor by excommunicating the prophet himself. McDonald issued a statement that read:

> Be it known unto all men here and everywhere else, that Wm. Bickerton, formerly of West Elizabeth, Pa., and now of Barton county, Kansas, has been disrobed of all authority, and suspended from the church of Jesus Christ by a general conference of the same … for the crimes specifically set forth of *superstition*, *idolatry* and *blasphemy*, and the church here and everywhere else is hereby warned to take no notice of him hereafter as a teacher, but to treat all attempts on his part to act the role of a teacher with that supreme contempt which the baseness of his conduct alone merits.[71]

Few of the Saints regarded McDonald's accusations as valid, and to protect Zion Valley, Thomas Taylor published an announcement in the *Great Bend Register* warning citizens against allowing McDonald or Neish to collect money on behalf of the colonists. He notified readers that McDonald "was cut off from the Church for … misrepresenting this country [Kansas] for the purpose of keeping members of this Church from coming here." McDonald had also been drunk, Taylor said, and Neish too "has been suspended from Church privileges for one year." Taylor wanted readers to know that Bickerton had contributed $2,500 to the association since they broke ground in Kansas, while McDonald and Neish themselves had "not put in anything" at all.[72]

Stunned by the attack on Bickerton, the eastern Saints decided at the fall conference to endorse the excommunication of McDonald and suspension of Neish and sustained Cadman as president of the eastern church, replacing Meadowcroft. They "resolved to treat the Saints misled" by the conference in Coultersville "with the utmost forbearance and endeavor to induce them to return to their Father's House." Voicing determination "to abide in the faith of the gathering," they promised to "work in unity with our Brethren in Zion's Valley and locate ourselves with them as soon as possible." Despite the conspiring of

71. McDonald, "Communications," *Elizabeth Herald*, Nov. 18, 1876.
72. Taylor, "Zion Valley," *Great Bend Register*, Sept. 21, 1876.

McDonald and Neish, the church had turned itself around and stood united in support of Zion Valley.[73]

The immediate problem in the West was putting food on the tables and countering accusations by McDonald that confused the non-member residents in both Barton and Allegheny Counties. To survive financially, they sent six men 200 miles east to Osage County to dig in the coal mines for the time being.[74] It was not long before their nemesis, William McDonald, responded to Thomas Taylor's newspaper article with increased polemic, threatening to sue Bickerton over what he said was owed to the society, claiming Bickerton had taken $6,000. The number must have been derived from the amount Bickerton originally subscribed, based on the presumed value of his property, which sold for a little less than $4,000. It was the amount he intended to contribute, not how much he withdrew. Since McDonald had the account books, it would not be easy to refute the accounting. McDonald went on to say that when Bickerton resigned in July 1875, it was an admission of guilt. Prior to doing business with him, people should first consult Neish, McDonald advised, adding that "we are not of those [type of personality] that will sit with folded arms and see our people robbed that a few scoundrels may grow fat on their credulity." It may have been easy to portray Bickerton, already suspected by outsiders of being a charlatan, as someone who might prey on people's naïveté for the sake of personal gain.[75]

This unrestrained tirade incited an editorial battle in both Kansas and Pennsylvania. Probate judge E. L. Chapman of Barton County took offense at McDonald's and Neish's less than flattering view of Kansas, calling their remarks on the suitability of the land for farming "the ravings of insane men." The land produced excellent grain, he assured readers. Samples from Zion Valley had represented Kansas at

---

73. Astin, "Minutes of the General Conference," *Great Bend Register*, Nov. 9, 1876.

74. "Zion Valley Emigrating," *Great Bend Register*, Nov. 2, 1876; Entz, "Paradise on the Plains," 188–89.

75. McDonald, "Communications," *Elizabeth Herald*, Nov. 18, 1876.

the Centennial Exposition in Philadelphia. On the other hand, the contention that McDonald and Neish had been drunk was ironic, he wrote, since it was nearly impossible to find alcohol in Zion Valley, at least he personally had found whiskey to be "very scarce" in the area. The community consisted of a "quiet, sober and religious people, and the merchants and citizens generally are always glad to see them and often refer to them as an industrious go-ahead people." At a religious service he attended, he "had never seen a more attentive and earnest people than I saw on the bright Sunday morning." In short, the settlers had been "grossly misrepresented."[76]

None too pleased, McDonald wrote that the judge must be some kind of fool for siding with Bickerton, "a man whose own family had denounced [him for] being crazy. He had his mind destroyed … while on a mission to the Indian Territory, and has never been right since." The reference to Bickerton's family was probably to his brother, Thomas, who left the church after his suspension from the Quorum of Twelve Apostles in 1869.[77] This latest invective drew the attention of William Cadman, who was finally fed up with this turncoat rhetoric and wrote his own letter to the *Elizabeth Herald* and *Monongahela Valley Republican* to inform readers that McDonald had "lately been excluded from our society for bad conduct, and now he wishes to make it appear that we are no better than himself." Cadman had known Bickerton "for nearly twenty years. … He has always been strictly honest and upright in all his dealings." Anyone who knew Bickerton knew that, he said. Regarding McDonald, he thought that "if this vile creature who is now endeavoring to stain [Bickerton's] reputation" tried instead to "emulate his virtues," he would find himself much improved. "There is as wide a contrast, in my judgement, between the accused and the accuser, as their is between virtue and vice, or light and darkness."

Cadman then addressed McDonald directly, reminding him of Bickerton's centrality within the church and the importance of the

76. Chapman, "Communications," *Elizabeth Herald*, Nov. 25, 1876.
77. McDonald, "Communications," *Elizabeth Herald*, Dec. 2, 1876.

mission to Kansas. "Now you may talk or write until the skies turn green, and that matter will still remain as it is," he wrote. "William Bickerton, myself, and many others (before your time) associated ourselves together as a religious people, and were organized and incorporated. ... We have since spread ourselves into various states, and wherever our people are found they exist as branches of the parent stem, and the largest and most influential of these branches is now located in Zion Valley." He denounced the unauthorized conference in Coultersville as "childish" behavior.[78]

Bickerton followed with his own letter to the *Elizabeth Herald* pointing out McDonald's duplicity and assuring readers that despite the setback, the settlers had begun to prosper. "We have plenty to eat and to wear, and plenty of fuel, and think when we get another harvest that we will be able to pay all the debts that we owe," at least locally, even if they were not able to immediately repay everyone who had subscribed to the emigration company. Looking on the bright side, they had "about 1000 acres of wheat that looks well. We also have good health, good land and good meetings, and we invite all good Saints who want a good house, to come to Zion, and enjoy the blessings of God—as we have them in our midst."[79]

In the end, McDonald's diversionary measures were unsuccessful in bankrupting the project or usurping the church's leadership. The confusion was momentary. It slowed the rate of progress for a time, and that was all. When he ranted against the prophet, it persuaded the members that he was disloyal and that he did not have the best interests of the church in mind. Nor would he succeed in leading his own faction much longer. He, Louttit, and Neish would never rejoin the church. Benjamin Meadowcroft, on the other hand, eventually returned and was accepted back into full fellowship.[80]

After two years of heartache and hard work, Zion Valley started to

78. Cadman, *Elizabeth Herald*, Dec. 9, 1876.
79. Bickerton, *Elizabeth Herald*, Jan. 13, 1877.
80. Cadman, *History of the Church of Jesus Christ*, 73.

show signs of self-sufficiency. In the spring of 1877, the editor of the *Great Bend Register*, A. J. Hoisington, traveled with Barton County's mail carrier, N. H. Ritchie, on one of his biweekly deliveries to the valley. Hoisington wanted to see, for an article, how the colony was faring. The men visited the postmaster, Bickerton, and sat with him "for a good dinner which was heartily relished," Hoisington stated. "Mr. Bickerton is one of the foremost men and farmers in our county and has a residence doing much credit to Zion Valley. … The crops look beautiful and especially the winter wheat … can not be exceeded in western Kansas. Zion Valley is a superior farming region and with the energetic, industrious class of people who have located therein, cannot fail in a few years to be a perfect garden." He admired the character of the settlers.

> These people are mostly from western Pennsylvania and West Virginia and Wilson county, Kansas. They are mostly 'Saints' or what the 'gentiles' call 'Mormons'—not the Brigham Young class. They are honest hard working people and strictly moral, earning their living by the sweat of their brows and not inclined to speculate or engage in merchandising. They have endured much privation, but the day of prosperity seems to be near at hand and they all are hopeful of not only temporal but spiritual success in the near future.

In April, Zion Valley had a population of almost 200 people. More were expected the coming year. The reporter held no misapprehension about the settlers' religious view of their valley as a gathering place, but it did not matter to him. He wished them well and hoped it "may be indeed to them all the 'Land of Promise.'"[81]

Facing the coming harvest of 1,000 acres, Bickerton and George Baker invested in a Wood's Self-binding Harvester.[82] It was so effective, others purchased the harvesters until there were seven in operation, James Miskin noted. The Saints helped other settlers with the harvest.

---

81. Hoisington, "To Zion Valley," *Great Bend Register*, Apr. 26, 1877.

82. With this harvester, invented in 1874, "one man, with a team of two or three horses, can cut and bind twelve to eighteen acres per day," the promotional material claimed. A sheaf of stalks was cut and bundled with wire every ten feet. *Walter A. Wood Mowing and Reaping Machine Co.* catalog, 1878, 3–5.

Jasper Davis planted a large hedge to fence in cattle. Jacob Beitler, a German emigrant from Wilson County, constructed a granary for storing wheat. As the living conditions stabilized, Bickerton's thoughts turned to how he could move his family to Kansas from Pennsylvania. Charlotte visited the valley to attend the July 1876 conference, but returned home until the settlement had reached a better stage of completion. For an unknown reason, when she returned home she stopped attending church. One could speculate that it was a reaction to how she and her husband had been treated, financially and otherwise. Still, in January 1877 the ministry addressed her negligence by suspending her "from all church privileges." Hearing about this, Bickerton thought it was time for her to join him. At the end of summer 1877, she boarded a train and headed west.[83]

It may be that she was accompanied by the church leadership on their way to the summer conference, where they intended to appraise the condition of the settlement and receive further guidance from Bickerton. The conference appointed replacements for six of the apostles: James Louttit, Benjamin Meadowcroft, William Menzies, John Neish, James Nichols, and William Skillen. All six were formally separated from the Quorum of Twelve Apostles, and William Cadman was sustained president of the quorum. The new men called to fill the vacancies were: Alexander Cherry, Eli Kendall, George Kendall, Paul Lathorpe, W. H. Reader, and George Shawver. Each new apostle, after his ordination, was given a special blessing. Cherry was told he would have "great power to speak to the Gentiles." So too the Kendall brothers, who were told that they would (Eli) "speak to Ephram in his language" and (George) that "Kings and princes shall fall before you by the Power of God." Drawing a metaphor from the agricultural setting, Lathorpe and Shawver were promised they would "bring many sheaves into Zion." Bickerton's counselors were also given blessings. First counselor Charles Brown was told he would "take Abraham by the hand, and see Isaac & Jacob, and see the triumph of Zion." Second

83. Entz, "Paradise on the Plains," 198–99; "Church of Jesus Christ in the East," 1:4, 9.

counselor Arthur Bickerton was promised to "see the lame walk, and the blind to see, and the deaf talk." At the end of the installations and blessings, William Bickerton announced that "the Devil is defeated and the Church is set in order." Charles Brown promised that the apostles would "see Satan fly like lightning before you, and ye shall see the Heavens opened and Angels decending and ascending."[84]

At the close of the year, Bickerton filed with the Kansas secretary of state to reincorporate the Church of Jesus Christ, now headquartered in Zion Valley, with Charles Brown and Arthur Bickerton as trustees.[85] On paper the church had become securely anchored in Kansas. In reality, there was no church in Kansas—not a physical headquarters. The main task for 1878, they decided, was to build one. The members had met in individual homes, at the Great Bend courthouse, and in the schoolhouses of nearby towns. With a call for donations, they raised $800 of the estimated $2,000 needed to construct the edifice, which was enough to start construction. Some of the contributions came from non-members who were thanked in the *Great Bend Register*. The newspaper, in turn, thought the chapel would "be a credit" to the community. The location was "a rise of ground commanding a fine view of the Valley," the newspaper explained. It was the same place where Bickerton had driven a stake in 1874.[86]

In February 1878 businessmen from a nearby town began constructing a store in Zion Valley. Emigrants from Pennsylvania were giving the valley a generally better assessment now. "I like this country very well," apostle Joseph Astin wrote to the *Monongahela Valley Republican*. He found the environment to be healthy. "It is a good country for stock raising and farming, our wheat looks well … and people are … astonished to find such a lovely place as this is." He could not imagine why people would continue working in the coal mines, "groveling

84. Martin and Mancini, "History of the Church," 115–19.

85. *Great Bend Register*, Dec. 6, 1877.

86. *Stafford Citizen*, Feb. 1, 1878; *Great Bend Register*, Feb. 7, 1878; *Great Bend Inland Tribune*, Feb. 9, 1878.

for a bare, scanty living," when they could be a farmer in Kansas. He was equally enthusiastic about the religious trappings of the colony. "We are hauling lumber to build a meeting house … and the people are sending for us to go and preach the everlasting gospel both east, west, north, and south. There will be preaching in the Court House at Great Bend Sunday and I also expect for several days," he informed his readers in Pennsylvania.[87]

Bickerton shared *The Ensign* with the newspaper in Great Bend, and the editor borrowed from its publishing a history of the Church of Jesus Christ in three installments through July. In August, aided by a loan of $700 from Jacob Beitler, a convert from Wilson County, the church completed construction of the church headquarters. David Carduff was proud to see a structure the size of a barn emerge, holding what he said was a capacity of about five hundred people. That was an exaggeration for a building 36' x 50', although its footprint was almost twice that of the Red Brick Store (23' x 41') in Nauvoo, for instance, where some of the early Mormon rituals were performed. The dedication ceremony was held on August 11. The church was seen as a symbol of the settlers' success.[88]

Not everyone was impressed. Charlotte Bickerton, for one, could not take the dust and heat and returned to Pennsylvania sometime before the end of October 1877. William entreated her to stay, but to no avail. Details are scant, but she had become disenchanted with the church and distanced herself from her husband and Zion Valley forever. Just a few years prior to this, she had been an ardent supporter of both.[89] She

87. *Great Bend Register*, Feb. 21, 1878; Astin, "Latter Day Saints—The Monongahela Colony in Kansas," *Monongahela Valley Republican*, Feb. 21, 1878; Entz, "Paradise on the Plains," 200–01.

88. Bickerton, "The History of the Church of Jesus Christ of Latter Day Saints: A Memorial to All People," *Great Bend Register*, June 20, 27, July 4, 1878; *Great Bend Inland Tribune*, Aug. 3, 1878; *Stafford Citizen*, Mar. 29, 1878; Entz, "Zion Valley," 114. The building was the size of a four-horse barn, or a five-car garage.

89. "Mormons established first church in county," *St. John News*, 1940; US Census, Allegheny County, Pennsylvania, July 1870; *William Bickerton vs. Charlotte Bickerton*, May 25, 1880.

agreed to leave her thirteen-year-old son, William Alma, with his father. However, on October 4 the boy accidentally discharged a shotgun and the pellets grazed his forehead, stripping his skull bare for several inches. "If the shot had struck two inches lower[,] the top of his head would have been blown off," the newspaper reported. "It was a narrow escape" and would "leave an ugly scar," was the prognosis. As a result of this, William Alma returned to Pennsylvania to be with his mother. The absence of his wife and young son was heartbreaking for a man who remained committed to his visions but sorely missed his family. At least one of his children from his previous wife was part of the colony for a while.[90]

Nearly four years after the Saints had migrated to Kansas, the town had transformed itself into an important commercial center that attracted locals from nearby towns and migrants from around the United States. Between 1878 and 1879, the valley received many new Bickertonite and non-member settlers. The town at the center of what had been Stafford County was a convenient hub for anyone in the general area. Those living in the settlement formed an organization called Zion Valley Town Company to appeal to the governor, John P. St. John, to restore the original county and make Zion Valley the county seat. People in and near Zion Valley signed a petition supporting the proposal. When word reached the *Great Bend Register*, people in that part of Barton County were displeased with the attempt to divide tax revenue and political influence, but they did not actively resist it.[91]

Wanting to become recognized as a town, whichever way the county configuration went, Thomas Taylor, secretary of Zion Valley Town Company (as well as Bickerton's church secretary), began looking with others in February 1879 into acquiring a forty-acre town site. They discovered the company needed $200 to buy and survey the land. As they worked on securing a loan, news reached them that an April session of

90. "Nearly Fatal," *Great Bend Register*, Oct. 10, 1878; Entz, "Paradise on the Plains," 206–07.

91. "The Stafford County Petition," *Great Bend Register*, Nov. 28, 1878; Entz, "Zion Valley," 115.

the Kansas Supreme Court had decided the legislature's action four years earlier in dissolving Stafford County had been improper. The county was therefore reinstated, with nearly the same boundaries. The county seat was yet to be determined,[92] and there was competition from the town of Stafford, twelve miles west of Zion Valley. This prompted Zion Valley Town Company to reorganize itself into a joint-stock company and sell shares for $5, whereby they quickly raised $2,000. Frederick Hawkins agreed to sell his land surrounding the meeting house for the town's business center. C. B. Weeks suggested they change the name of the town in honor of Governor St. John, which was done. Then they applied for incorporation.[93]

No sooner had the town been approved than political control began slipping through the fingers of the original settlers. The Bickertonites were becoming a minority in the community they founded. Every month the population increased. When it came time to appoint the first county commissioners, the governor named four non-Saints, even though he was pleased to designate St. John the county seat, named after him. Bickerton stayed mostly aloof from politics and business, finding that his ambitions lay elsewhere. He never mentioned that he was disappointed by the influx of non-members. In fact, he seemed to be pleased by this evidence of prosperity that contradicted the predictions of his opponents. "The suburbs of St. John are covered with michinery now, to take care of our present wheat crop," he wrote in 1903. "All the farmers in Stafford County are getting rich. I feel the blessing of God in this."[94]

Although William Cadman had hoped that Zion Valley would be only a gathering place for the Saints, and "that there should be no speculation there, and that it was a spiritual gathering and not a temporal gathering," neither Bickerton nor Cadman could do anything about the large influx of settlers that continued to stream into town. Like

92. Taylor, "Zion Valley," *Great Bend Register*, Mar. 6, 1879; Entz, "Zion Valley," 115.
93. Entz, 115–16.
94. Ibid., 116; Bickerton, "Testimony, June 1903," 12.

nearly all settlements that began as a communal society or religious refuge, Zion Valley eventually succumbed to the influence of secular life and commercial enterprise.[95]

Beginning in July 1878, a year-long drought drew people's attention to the town's foremost religious leader, Bickerton, who led the populace in prayers for rain. Some people buckled under the pressure of the drought and abandoned the area, including James and Amelia Miskin and even the town's former promoter Thomas Taylor. For a short time, the Miskins migrated to southeastern Kansas so James could work in the coal mines. Taylor ventured in the opposite direction to Colorado in search of gold. Both families returned in 1880.[96] As for the remaining Saints who withstood the elements, they did better in subsequent years. Bickerton relinquished his position as postmaster to C. B. Weeks in order to devote himself full time to preaching.[97] He wanted to finish what he had started and make inroads into Indian country.

95. Cadman, *History of the Church of Jesus Christ*, 75; Cadman, *Great Bend Register*, Sept. 21, 1876.

96. Cole and Reuber, *No Cyclone Shall Destroy*, 8; Miskin and Miskin, "Notes on Our Early Life," 4; Entz, "Zion Valley," 116.

97. *Great Bend Register*, July 17, 1879; Entz, "Zion Valley," 116–17.

ELEVEN

THE RIFT

1879–84

"God, Almighty, told me to tell the Church to set a match to that paper, that contains the charges, and Burn it up, that the smoke may go up before the Almighty as a lie, and if the Church would not do it for me, to go ahead and build up the Church."

—May 1, 1880

Despite losing his chance to make Zion Valley a communal haven, Bickerton stayed focused on his primary but long-delayed mission to preach to the American Indians. Dissatisfaction among the members and whatever personal failings Bickerton had, even if only inattention to the effect his actions had on other people, were obstacles to thwart his overall quest. All along, his plan had been to make Zion Valley a base from which to send missionaries west into Indian Territory. Nor did the secularization of Zion Valley into St. John impede the immigration of Saints to the hub from which they would operate as they awaited the arrival of the Choice Seer. In 1879 it finally appeared that Bickerton would be able to accomplish his goal, and then once again, the nearer he approached it, the more it receded.

His family life had not improved either. He tried to convince Charlotte to come back to Kansas, expressing his desire to remain devoted to her. The reality was that he had lost not only the company of his wife, he had lost a spiritual partner who championed his vision of the conversion of Native Americans.[1] The church was his home, the

1. *Bickerton vs. Bickerton*, May 25, 1880; "Church of Jesus Christ in the East," 1:4, 9.

Saints his family. That single-mindedness would soon backfire and turn his life upside down.

His closest associates, William Cadman, for instance, would come to disagree with him about fundamentals such as whether the Millennium and Zion were to be the same event, which in a way contradicted Bickerton's main purpose for migrating to Kansas, to prepare a gathering place for the righteous in anticipation of the imminent Second Coming. It appears that Cadman did not draw much attention to his eschatological beliefs at first, possibly not wanting to create another controversy over Bickerton's prophecies. Yet he would ultimately choose to call into question the prophet's understanding of the end times.

He came out in open disagreement in early 1879, at the same time the postal designation Zion Valley was changing its name and identity to the incorporated town of St. John. From the comfort of Pennsylvania, Cadman expressed his thoughts in six letters to the *Elizabeth Herald* titled "Pre-Millennial." Writing to non-members as well as to the faithful, he interpreted the biblical prophecies to show that the United States was "the last important political power that will arise on the earth previous to the Kingdom of God." Where the Old Testament prophet Daniel saw ten nations arise out of the former Roman Empire and a "little horn … pluck up" three of them "by the roots," Cadman understood this to refer to the colonization ventures of England, France, and Spain, over which the United States would eventually prevail. The little horn would have "eyes like the eyes of man, and a mouth speaking great things," which Cadman interpreted to be the American principles of freedom and rule of law. However, the U.S. would fall and be replaced by a holy kingdom overseen by a righteous leader Daniel called the Ancient of Days, someone with hair like "pure wool" and garments as "white as snow" who would sit upon a throne that "was like the fiery flame." A "fiery stream" would emanate from his presence, he would be transported on "wheels as burning fire," and he would rule over a hundred million ("ten thousand times ten thousand") subjects (Dan. 7:8–10). Cadman saw in this the Choice

Seer foretold by the Book of Mormon—the American Indian Moses. "Now we wish it to be understood that this is not the coming of the Savior," Cadman penned, "but it is the building up of the kingdom of God upon some part of the earth prior to his coming." After a long duration of peace and harmony in the flesh, which would be the era of Zion, the Choice Seer would deliver his kingdom to Christ. That would inaugurate the Millennium. Those who had lived in Zion in the flesh would be transfigured "in the twinkling of an eye" (1 Cor. 15:52) to live as kings and priests in the Millennium for a thousand years, joined by all those who had ever lived and died righteously, who would now be resurrected to an immortal body.[2]

It is unclear what Bickerton's precise thoughts were about Daniel's prophecy, but it is certain that he believed the time was short, that unlike Cadman's interpretation, Jesus Christ would soon return to earth to inaugurate the Millennium. It would not occur after the Ancient of Days ruled for a long period of time over the peaceable kingdom of Zion. The Millennium and Zion were synonymous, the Choice Seer would help establish the New Jerusalem, and when it was ready for him, the Savior would return. In other words, according to a plain reading of the Book of Mormon (3 Ne. 21:23–25), there was no time to waste. Christ would soon descend to earth with the "power of heaven" to assist in the gathering, and the Millennium/Zion would commence. For Cadman, there was less need for urgency.

The newspaper editor became unhappy with Cadman's interpretation of Daniel and canceled the series. Newspaper clippings and documents that have survived were published by the Bickerton church some eighty years later as a pamphlet.[3] It appears the prophet refrained from commenting. Whether or not he cared about a difference of opinion about eschatology, he must have noticed that the president of the

2. Cadman, *Pre-Millennial*, 7–16. A modern understanding of Daniel's vision was that it had to do with the Syrian (Seleucid) kingdom of Antiochus Epiphanes, a reading that Benjamin Scolnic affirms "all modern scholars agree with." Scolnic, "Antiochus IV and the Three Horns in Daniel 7," 1.

3. Cadman, *Pre-Millennial*, 1.

Quorum of the Twelve was willing to publicly contradict his friend and church president on a key issue, and still Bickerton seems to have let the matter pass without making an issue of it.

The Saints in Kansas were dealing with the drought. On March 1, Bickerton said in a council meeting that even though "every thing looks Black and dark," and there were "poor prospects of any Crops," it was also true that Kansas was not the only place where there was "pestelance and famine." That kind of misfortune was "abroad in various lands," he pointed out. They needed to pray to be spared this deterrent, not for their own sake, but to be allowed to keep their promise to the Indians. If "we did our duty in what the Lord our God commands us," he assured the council, the Lord "would change the seasons for our good and bless us abundantly."[4]

In April, Samuel Campbell reported that some of the members "can't endure the trials," despite the generally "good feeling" that existed among most of them. Bickerton worried that they were being punished for delaying the mission to the Lamanites and perhaps for abandoning their communal society. "The Savior would not accept the Church unless they had all things common at his coming," his revelation had confirmed. People were already under stress, but the pressure to abandon St. John and its leadership would increase exponentially in June 1879 when James Taylor dropped a bombshell in the middle of the community and accused Bickerton of having had an affair with his wife, Tryphena—specifically for not "walking according to the Gospel," implying an illicit relationship.[5]

The Taylors were from Tennessee and had converted in 1873 in Wilson County, Kansas, during one of John Stevenson's mission tours. They moved to Zion Valley two years later. James was ordained an evangelist and Tryphena was ordained a deaconess. On one occasion

4. Martin and Mancini, "History of the Church," 135; "Church of Jesus Christ in the East" 2:46.

5. Martin and Mancini, "History of the Church," 135–37; "Church of Jesus Christ in the East," 2:47, 49.

when she became ill, she was thought to be near death, and Bickerton gave her a healing blessing. He explained it like this:

> Mrs. Taylor was taken very sick with lung fever, so there seemed no chance of her living and she gave up all hope[.] She bade her husband and all the brothers and sisters farewell and told them what to do with the children, I went to the edge of the creek and felt by the spirit of God that she would be healed, I came up to the house and found all standing around her bed, I asked her if she had faith in Christ, she said yes; I took her by the hand and commanded her to arise and be made whole, [and] she arose and went through the house gloryfying God, and from that time was healed.[6]

Sometime thereafter, her "youngest child … was at the gates of death" and was similarly "made whole by the gift of healing."[7] Through these events, Tryphena developed a strong bond with the prophet, and Bickerton was apparently not troubled about being alone with her and other female members as he gave spiritual counsel, contrary to Victorian social etiquette prohibiting close contact with anyone of the opposite sex who was not a family member.[8] The impression that he was overly friendly with women had surfaced before. It may have been a problem in his marriage. However, we might suspend that question for now to simply recognize that he crossed a line of propriety, most likely because he was so obsessed with his work, he was unconcerned about appearances. But whatever occurred, it was a devastating blow to be so accused and would for a time block his ability to proceed with his plans for the church.

When he traveled back to Pennsylvania in 1875 to check on the sale of his property, Bickerton met privately with another deaconess, Frances Hunt, in Allegheny Park, where they were seen by someone who informed the ministry. He confessed to this impropriety at an October council meeting, where they accused him of not keeping "his

6. "Bickerton's Letter," *St. John County Capital*, Nov. 14, 1889.
7. Ibid.
8. Edwards, *New Spirits: Americans in the Gilded Age*, 130.

promise to the Church in regards to Sister Hunts company." After hearing him out, the council decided "the accusation against Bro Bickerton and Sister Hunt being seen together in Allegheny Park, there is nothing wrong in it. As he has a right to treat her as a sister in the Church," they found no evidence of transgression. Although they were not entirely comfortable with the prophet's behavior, he had never condoned philandering among his adherents.[9]

At the same time, it looked bad, especially four years later when he found himself before another council meeting defending himself against involvement with Tryphena. When a secretary penned that they were "reconciled"—"Bro William Bickerton and Sister Taylor and Bro Taylor, … the Blessing and power of God accompanying," it would seem that this would be the end of the controversy, but that would not prove to be the case. What was behind it? With Charlotte in Pennsylvania, maybe William, now sixty-four, was flattered by the attention he received from a twenty-eight-year-old woman, and having gone two years without female companionship, he could have been tempted. No more is known about it.[10]

If it seemed like a low point in Bickerton's life, the year 1880 would be worse, leaving an indelible stain on his life and the church's history. At the start all seemed well to Bickerton as he expressed his usual high aspiration for the future. At the January conference, he declared that "the spirit had been" with them to the extent that they expected to see "the Prophet Moroni coming and delivering the sealed records unto this Church, along with the Urim and Thummim, also the breast plate of Judgement, that this church may be fully armed to fight the Devil in all his strong holds." Such an announcement must have stirred the audience's attention, as thirty-three people arose to express hallelujah. It would mean that Zion was near. No more details were given, so it must have been meant to occur in the future rather than in subsequent weeks.

9. Martin and Mancini, "History of the Church," 106.

10. Ibid., 137; "Church of Jesus Christ in the East," 2:49; Entz, "Bickertonites," 9.

One thing was clear enough. If the sealed portion of the gold plates were to be translated, it was high time to convert the Indians, the conference concurred. Samuel Work was assigned to accompany Bickerton south to Medicine County, and as they were given blessings by the laying on of hands, James Taylor, who saw "the Glory of God upon Bickerton's head," professed that he had a testimony of the prophet's goodness and leadership. It seemed like all was forgiven and forgotten. Bickerton appointed Eli Kendall to preside over the church in St. John in his absence, and the conference elected John Williams to preside over the Quorum of Seventy, a position otherwise held by Work. Someone prophesied that Williams would "see the Triumphs of Zion and the Strong holds of Satan torn down and the Sons & Daughters of Zion go forth in the dance with Israel." The minutes of the January conference were sent to Pennsylvania. When they were read aloud, William Cadman and sixteen others stood up to show their support. Everyone was anxious to learn more about the mysteries of God contained in the sealed portion of the gold plates.[11]

Before departing, Bickerton tried to meet with every Saint in Stafford County to request their full support for the church's Indian mission. In an unexpected twist, he asked his friends James and Tryphena Taylor to accompany him, and for three weeks Bickerton and the Taylors trekked together across west-central Kansas to see all the members in their homes. James prophesied several times that the angel Moroni would soon visit the prophet.[12] Bickerton appreciated his friend's support. It must have been gratifying to share this kind of amicable feeling toward each another in light of the previous year's controversy. Then something triggered Taylor's jealousy again, and on April 3 he made a formal complaint at a church council meeting, accusing Bickerton of "knowingly bringing a separation in his family and also for bringing division into the church," this time explicitly accusing

11. Martin and Mancini, "History of the Church," 140; "Church of Jesus Christ in the East," 2:57; Weeks, *St. John County Capital*, Aug. 18, 1887.

12. Weeks, *St. John County Capital*, Aug. 18, 1887.

Bickerton of adultery. Not knowing what to do, the council adjourned for two days to investigate and take time to form a course of action.[13]

The council asked Bickerton's first counselor, Charles Brown, to preside over the investigation, assisted by apostles Eli Kendall and George Shawver. Brown spent Monday through Wednesday, April 5–7, hearing testimony from church members. A Brother Wilson testified "that he lived near Bro and Sister Taylor and he thought he never saw people more happy than they seemed to be." Mary Glackin remembered that during one conversation with Tryphena, the accused said, "I do not know what I would do if Mr. Taylor was of a Jealous nature or disposition." On the third day, James Miskin, who thought Bickerton was innocent, related three dreams, the content of which was not recorded. The council was then adjourned for ten days to give the accused time to prepare a cross-examination.

What developed when the hearing resumed on April 17 was a revelatory contest, continuing into the next month. Charles Brown opened the session, followed by John Williams uttering a sharp rebuke in the name of the Lord, saying "the Spirit … Wm. Bickerton was possessed of was not of God." The secretary taking the minutes agreed that Williams was right. The next session was held two weeks later on May 1. When Eli Kendall opened the meeting and expressed his support of James Taylor, Bickerton countered by dramatically declaring: "God, Almighty, told me to tell the Church to set a match to that paper, that contains the charges, and Burn it up, that the smoke may go up before the Almighty as a lie, and if the Church would not do it for me, to go ahead and build up the Church." This was endorsed by four brethren: Jacob Beitler, David Carduff, Thomas McManaway, and Samuel Work. Kendall and others shot back that it was a self-serving and "pretended revelation" and made a motion that the prophet "be suspended from all Church privileges, until he repents, and makes a

13. Martin and Mancini, "History of the Church," 141; "Church of Jesus Christ in the East," 2:58–59; Cadman, *History of the Church of Jesus Christ*, 1, 77; Cadman, "Notice," *St. John Advance*, July 10, 1880.

public acknowledgement of his faults, in the charges made by Bro Taylor." Eighteen people voted their assent to that proposition. The fact that no contrary votes were registered indicates that Brown and others may have walked out.[14]

That may also explain why Kendall conducted the subsequent proceedings, holding another session a week later on May 8 that was attended by only fifteen people, and of those only one supported Bickerton. The lone wolf was Samuel Work. When asked the opinion of the officers who were missing from the proceedings, Marion Campbell offered that "Jacob Beitler said he would not acknowledge" the legitimacy of the proceeding. John Williams confirmed that "Bro & Sister Beitler Said they would stand by Wm Bickerton." William Moore had visited Charles Brown, David Carduff, and his wife, and they also denied the council's standing. Joining in, Samuel Work arose and stated that "he answers for himself and wife and also for sister [Tryphena] Taylor, that if we would accept of the revelation given last Saturday, by Bro Wm Bickerton, as the word of God, he would go with us, but if we reject it, he would not go with us." The council scoffed at this proposal. John Williams and Harrison Baker suggested that anyone who took such a position should be "suspended from their offices, and also from membership, and all the priviledges of the Church," which the council, such as it was, agreed with. All those who spoke in Bickerton's behalf would thereafter be condemned.[15]

Kendall's faction held another council meeting on June 8, at which apostle Joseph Astin said "in the name of Jesus Christ, that William Bickerton be seperated from the Holy Priesthood of the Son of God. Also Charles Brown and Arthur Bickerton and all the rest of those Elders who have taken part with William Bickerton." Kendall was gaining support, marginalizing those of the other camp and consolidating his

14. Martin and Mancini, "History of the Church," 141–42; "Church of Jesus Christ in the East," 2:59–60.

15. Martin and Mancini, "History of the Church," 142–43; "Church of Jesus Christ in the East," 2:60.

control of the church.[16] However, even as he placed his thumb on the scales in opposition to the prophet, there was the inconvenient fact that the council as a whole had not come to a consensus and had broken apart in disarray. For his part, Bickerton and counselors Charles Brown and Arthur Bickerton went ahead as if nothing had happened and announced in the *St. John Advance* that a church-wide conference would be held in July. It was a discreet rebuff of Kendall's authority.[17]

To complicate matters, William Cadman, the acting president of the church in the eastern area, followed the reports from St. John and advised Kendall to try to persuade Bickerton to repent. This must have seemed like a sharp insult when Bickerton learned that his friend had sided with the opposition and believed Bickerton was guilty of adultery. For his part, Kendall followed instructions and went to see Bickerton at his home in the company of John McKewan and Samuel Campbell. Bickerton professed innocence and denounced his accusers, saying his visitors lacked authority to try him, and sent them off itching to answer his rebuff.

On June 26 the *St. John Advance* published, in response to the June 19 notice of a forthcoming conference, a letter from Kendall, McKewan, and Campbell stating that Bickerton and counselors could not preside over a church conference because they had all been "suspended from the church … until they become reconciled, or further actions be taken and others put in permanently." To explain how the founder and his counselors could be removed from their own organization, they explained that "this church is just like it used to be; Paul withstood Peter, especially when Peter was to blame, and sometimes William [Bickerton] withstands John [McKewan] when John is to blame and again James [Taylor] withstands William [Bickerton] when William is to blame." As it would happen, when Cadman arrived in St. John to attend the July conference, he and Kendall would meet by

16. Martin and Mancini, "History of the Church," 143.
17. Bickerton, Brown, and Bickerton, "Conference," *St. John Advance*, June 19, 26, 1880.

themselves, or with as many members as they could persuade to join them, but not in concert with the prophet.[18]

Before Cadman's arrival, McKewan became aware that the members who had been reprimanded for supporting Bickerton's outburst were still going to "stand for William Bickerton." Unless there was a guilty verdict, the actions of the council would appear arbitrary. When the day came for the conference, Bickerton presided over a typical church convocation. Missionaries were called, business was conducted. However, some had opted to stay away and gathered instead with Kendall and Cadman at a meeting devoted to addressing the adultery scandal.[19] Between sessions, Cadman visited Bickerton's representatives on July 5 at the schoolhouse and offered to conduct a new investigation. It was agreed that if both sides chose three men each to serve as the jury, and if Cadman, rather than Kendall, presided, it would be a workable solution. Cadman relayed the terms to Kendall's group, who rejected them. They would "allow Bro William Cadman to examine the charges," and if Bickerton wanted to present a defense, that was fine. However, they would not allow Bickerton's supporters to serve as judges.[20]

Kendall and Cadman returned to the schoolhouse to present the counter-proposal to the Bickerton sympathizers, who were immediately indignant. Their suggestion quashed, they refused to give any more ground. Cadman, in turn, became angry and decided he had faced enough of this rebellion and withdrew from further negotiation. Two days later, on July 7, he and Kendall announced their determination, "in as much as William Bickerton will not acknowledge his faults after the law of the Church has been fulfilled upon him, but still

18. Kendall, McKewan, and Campbell, "St. John, June 22, 1880," *St. John Advance*, June 26, 1880; Cadman, "Notice," *St. John Advance*, July 10, 1880; Entz, "Bickertonites," 10–11.

19. Martin and Mancini, "History of the Church," 143; "Church of Jesus Christ in the East," 2:61; Entz, "Bickertonites," 11.

20. Martin and Mancini, "History of the Church," 144; "Church of Jesus Christ in the East," 2:62.

persists in trampling under foot all the law and order, That the Priesthood and all his callings be taken from him and also his membership and all, that he be seperated from the Church of Jesus Christ." Next, the conference passed several resolutions excommunicating every individual who had assisted Bickerton in his defense, including his counselors, Charles Brown and Arthur Bickerton. The next day John Williams and James Taylor nominated William Cadman to be the general church president, which was approved by the small group meeting in St. John. Eli Kendall and Cummings Cherry were elected first and second counselors. The elders washed Cadman's feet, anointed his head with oil, and ordained him. On July 12, Eli Kendall spoke in God's voice saying, "Now I have established my Church and the powers of darkness shall not prevail against it."[21]

The conference requested Cadman to write to the *St. John Advance* to explain their proceedings, "setting forth our actions against Wm Bickerton and why they were taken." The new president chose to address the founder personally.

> You and the public are hereby respectfully notified that charges of a very grave character have been preferred against you by the church in this place, namely: "you have wilfully and knowingly walked in such a way as has brought a division in the family of Bro. James Taylor, also a disgrace upon the family, also a reproach upon the church of Jesus Christ and a disturbance among the Saints." Also, you have walked in such a way that you have put a hindrance in the way of the work of God in this place, and have caused some of the Saints to err and some to do things causing their separation from the church. You are notified also that said James Taylor complained of your conduct and requested you to discontinue it, both

21. Martin and Mancini, "History of the Church," 144–46; "Church of Jesus Christ in the East," 2:63–64. The new church faction needed a local leader, as well, and elected George Kendall to replace Eli Kendall as president in the Kansas area. Cadman, *History of the Church of Jesus Christ*, 85. When Cadman, Kendall, and Cherry became a presidency, they were separated from the Quorum of Twelve Apostles, meaning that at least three new apostles would have to be called. Other officials decided to go with one faction or the other, resulting in further restructuring as time went on. Martin and Mancini, 145; "Church of Jesus Christ in the East," 2:64.

> alone and before witnesses, also summoned you before the authorities of the church in accordance with the laws of Jesus Christ, all of which you blindly and madly rejected, which drove the church to the unpleasant necessity of suspending you from all the privileges of said church, or, as the Saviour said, "treat you as a publican and a sinner."[22]

If Cadman was right, at least to the extent that Bickerton had been blind to the hurt he had caused, or if the prophet had resisted being treated like a regular member, it was equally true that Cadman had overstated his case by putting all the blame on Bickerton, accusing him of "unaccountable perverseness." "If you considered yourself wronged," Cadman suggested, "you should have appealed to our conference for redress according to our laws and you will bear me witness that I urged this course upon you as your only lawful course, only to be disregarded by you." What Cadman failed to mention was that the proceedings had fallen apart before he arrived and had given way to a crowd mentality, that Bickerton had been tried by a revelatory contest by both sides rather than solely on the testimony of witnesses—on as much "spectral evidence" as anything.[23] Not only that, Kendall had taken over the hearings from Brown. Nor was a final verdict reached until after Kendall's side had barred any known Bickerton sympathizer from serving on a jury.

Bickerton chose not to respond to what must have felt like a smear on his personal reputation, and one can only imagine the embarrassment as he went about his life in St. John, as someone whose identity was defined by his adherence to a strict moral code, knowing that everyone who saw him wondered if he were guilty. The somewhat eloquent message from Cadman belied other attributes such as Cadman's quick temper, brashness, and overconfidence, characteristics that drew him to Bickerton in the first place, making Cadman an asset to the

22. Martin and Mancini, "History of the Church," 145; "Church of Jesus Christ in the East," 2:65; Cadman, "Notice," *St. John Advance*, July 10, 1880.

23. Spectral evidence came from supernatural sources—spirits, visions, revelations. In Salem, Massachusetts, in 1693, its suitability as evidence in court was debated back and forth and finally allowed on a limited basis. Hoffer, *Salem Witchcraft Trials*, 78–79.

church—aspects of his personality that were nevertheless a challenge to anyone who crossed him. For someone who had been a longtime close associate of the prophet and had defended his character in the past, Cadman's change of allegiance was surprising and leads one to suspect whether Cadman had begun to take his own counsel, believing he was capable where Bickerton was not. He may have also relied on what he knew previously about Bickerton's dalliances with women—possibly an emotional involvement with selected female members of the church or failure to tamp down the awe he was held in by female followers, which would be a problem even if both sides were innocent.

The Saints who still supported Bickerton were jarred by Cadman's about-face. Two of them, Robert Cardwell and Duncan Bell, rallied to the prophet's defense with a public reply in the *St. John Advance*. Pointing out that it was unfair to charge an otherwise upstanding citizen of "a crime that is not becoming to any good citizens," they assured readers that in the ten years they had known Bickerton, they had "never known him to say an ill-begotten word to any lady and wherever he went to preach the gospel he always found favor with the people, both men and women and aided the church accordingly." It was a shame that people had jumped to conclusions, they wrote, and that in this case Cadman had unconscionably left Bickerton "to the mercy of the public." They noted Cadman's recent proposal for a public meeting to let members and non-members decide about Bickerton, although the meeting would have no final bearing on the judgment of the church. This would amount to a public shaming, they pointed out. It would be a chance for people to ridicule a revered leader. "To call a public meeting is entirely out of place."

Wanting to appear reasonable, the two defenders of Bickerton admitted that they were "not prepared to say which side is right," only to point out that an unsubstantiated accusation in the newspaper, before an audience of strangers, was unacceptable. "There is no telling where it may end," they wrote. They suggested that since Cadman's faction had met "in conference for several days" to discuss the case, they should "give us all" the information they had "and not keep the public in the dark." Most likely, Cardwell and Bell suspected, the minutes would show how the church founder had been railroaded out of office by aspiring competitors.[24]

This made Cadman even more determined to stage a public hearing and prove once and for all that Bickerton was guilty. On July 15 at 10 a.m., he welcomed the public and suggested that they elect a chairman and secretary, which they did, putting two individuals who were unaffiliated with the church into those positions. The chairman, William R. Hoole, "made a few appropriate remarks" to acknowledge the "grave and serious charges that had been prefered against the head of the Mormon church, and he hoped the meeting would be conducted with due decorum," the newspaper reported. As the prosecutor, Cadman called twenty witnesses who lived near Bickerton. For about eight hours, the jury consisting of non-church members listened to arguments from Cadman and considered the witnesses' testimonies. At 6:30 p.m., the examination ceased, and to ensure an unbiased decision "all who were interested in the church" were asked to retire. After thirty minutes of deliberation, the jury issued their verdict:

> We, the undersigned citizens of the county of Stafford, and State of Kansas, after giving due consideration to all the testimony, and all extenuating circumstances, would most respectfully submit the following as our true verdict: While we do not believe that Wm Bickerton and Mrs. James Taylor have been guilty of any criminal intimacy, still we *do* believe that said William Bickerton has acted in such a manner as to cause a division of the family of James Taylor, and disturb the society in this neighborhood.[25]

It must have been a disappointment to Cadman that he was unable to obtain a clear decision. The jury confirmed that Bickerton had violated social etiquette, contrary to his stature as a religious leader and community father. The point was valid. The fact that Bickerton's

24. Cardwell and Bell, "Ed. Advance," *St. John Advance,* July 17, 1880; Cadman, "Notice," *St. John Advance,* July 10, 1880.

25. Cox and Hoole, "Ed. Advance," *St. John Advance,* July 24, 1880.

relationship with Tryphena incited jealousy in her husband was reason enough to criticize him. It may be that Bickerton's personality was such that he would not be denied friendship with a woman simply because her husband was overly protective.

The seeming indifference Bickerton granted the proceedings was belied by a fervent attempt to defend himself to his friends. He agreed to his own public hearing conducted by his first counselor, Charles Brown, who opened by stating that in "thirty years" he had never heard "anything of an immoral character" come from the prophet. Brown said he was personally "satisfied that charges like these, coming from such a source, must fall to the ground," comparing the suffering of Bickerton to Jesus. Even with such a partial officiator, however, Bickerton himself was unable to get a judgment that wholly cleared his name. He received a tie vote, which he then stated was in his favor since those who voted to exonerate him did so by the Spirit, while those who cast votes in the negative relied on their own judgment. The *St. John Advance* reported this remarkable outcome, preceded by Bickerton's defense on the stand in which he denied that there had been discord in the Taylor family. He asked four witnesses in the audience to verify this, which they did—at least that there had been no discord during the time Bickerton and the Taylors were friends. He claimed "the whole fabric, the whole foundation of the charges, [was] attributable to 'jealousy, corroding every thought and blasting all love's paradise.'" He said he would "humbly bow to God's will in this matter" but could not succumb to the "authority of a handful of imposters." When the proceeding was over, "the vote stood two for, and two against. The first two by a majority without any manifestation of the power of God, and the next two in his favor, the power of God [having come] down and testified he was justified, [and so] he was justified," the report read. Bickerton explained that "it is well known that in the church of Jesus Christ—when there is no competent witnesses[,] things must be proven by revelation." This was endorsed by Brown, who ruled that Bickerton was therefore innocent of the charge.[26]

26. "Wm. Bickerton's Answer," *St. John Advance*, July 24, 1880.

The fact that Bickerton discounted the revelations his detractors received and accepted the revelations his supporters dictated reveals another reason the prophet may have been losing support from formerly loyal adherents. He had become irrational. He was angry that his good name had been sullied, frustrated that he was unable, try as he may, to rectify it. For Tryphena, the historical record is practically silent. For the time being, she stayed married to James, while remaining loyal to the Bickerton faction, according to Samuel Work, even as her husband switched sides to join with Cadman. The latter took a hard line on Tryphena's membership status, relegating her to the standing of a former member and excluding her from her husband's chosen society of believers.

After Cadman had completed his business in St. John, he traveled back to Pennsylvania to gather support from the members there. Bickerton, encouraged by the fact that two separate investigations had been unable to determine him guilty of adultery, worked equally hard to secure the allegiance of the Saints in both Kansas and Pennsylvania. He sent a copy of the minutes for his July conference to the ministry in the East, and they were read at a special conference held in West Elizabeth on July 31, 1880, although Cadman, apparently disgusted by this, or maybe just withdrawing while the conference deliberated, left the room during their airing. The eastern leadership ruled that Bickerton's conference was illegitimate. Cadman's wife, Elizabeth, agreed, declaring in God's voice, "Verily, verily, they are rejected of me, saith the God of Heaven." Others joined in too, speaking in tongues and supporting a resolution that "he whom God rejects, we reject." They would henceforth refuse to recognize as members anyone who supported Bickerton. Through the entire ordeal, it appears that both Cadman and Bickerton thought that they were following proper protocol. Bickerton saw it as another attempt by Satan to keep him from reaching Indian Territory. By this point, he may not have cared that the tide had turned and a majority of Saints in the East and a small cohort in Kansas sided with Cadman. He still had the support of the main body of believers in

Kansas and a small group in the East. Regardless, the church had been rent in two. After he had carefully fostered the church for twenty-eight years, it had fallen apart; Bickerton's twenty-one-year friendship with Cadman was fading to memory.[27]

For over a century, Cadman's version of events has been the official church history. In 1945 his son, William H. Cadman, the church historian, preserved his father's interpretation of the scandal in the first authorized chronicle of the church. The assumption of William H. was that Bickerton had gone down the same path as Joseph Smith, Sidney Rigdon, and Brigham Young, their pride leading them to sin, and their sin leading to apostasy. The historian copied a section of the church minutes in which the scandal was discussed, along with some evidence he believed supported his father's side of the story. The significance of his account is not in determining who was right or wrong but in showing how the members at the time viewed their cast-off leader.

William H. said he was "quite young" when he heard his father tell of Bickerton's fall from office as church president. As William H. remembered what his father told him, it began with an 1870 meeting in West Elizabeth involving several men of the church. "After arising from bed on a Sunday Morning," the son remembered, his father, William Cadman, "felt impressed to go to Bro. Wm. Bickerton's home. Upon arriving there, he found that several other Brethren of prominence from other Branches of the Church had been prompted as he himself had, that is, to go to Bro. Bickerton's home. Thus a number of the Brethren having obeyed their promptings found themselves mysteriously gathered together on a Sunday Morning, not knowing for what purpose." All of a sudden Bickerton spoke in tongues, the interpretation being that if he "was not careful he would lose his calling and that the Lord already had chosen another to take his place." At about the same time, Bickerton had begun making wine from a vineyard he planted. "The drinking of it had caused a reproach to come upon the

27. Cadman, *History of the Church of Jesus Christ,* 78; Entz, "Bickertonites," 15–16.

Church; not that Bro. Bickerton was drinking of it, but because he was the owner of the Vineyard, and also the position he held in the Church." Bickerton had learned to augment his meager wages as a coal foreman by raising grapes and investing in real estate, according to the historian's understanding. Word spread that Bickerton had fostered, albeit unwittingly, imbibing and lascivious behavior. According to the older Cadman, Bickerton admitted that it was wrong to facilitate sin and "asked the Brethren not to record this matter, promising that he would rectify the situation." This was "before his move to Kansas in 1875," insinuating that the prophet had veered from the path of rectitude even before becoming involved with the Taylors in Kansas.[28]

There are a few problems with the story. As far as is known, no one else documented this "mysterious" meeting, and as William H. admits, he recounted it "to the best of my memory" long after the fact. William H. Cadman was born six years after the alleged meeting, and he composed his history nearly seventy years later.[29] He may have been right, but he also may have misunderstood the discussion of adult themes when he was young. Even at that, Bickerton is not accused of misbehavior per se, only that the wine may have had a bad effect on other people. To bolster the legitimacy of his father's reaction to the charge against Bickerton in Kansas, William H. included in the church history a dream related by Susannah M. Trump. He placed her dream immediately after his discussion of Bickerton's excommunication, giving credence to the accusation against him. Susannah said she dreamed that she and some other Saints were traveling, and

> my attention was attracted off to the right by a company of people. They were singing and seemed to be having a Camp meeting. I inquired who these people were and the two women told me they were Saints of our own kind. I felt a desire to go to this meeting but my friends bade me go with them and not to fear. We then turned to the left and traveled on. Then we saw a very large and furious beast coming toward us. … I

28. Cadman, *History of the Church of Jesus Christ*, 71.
29. Ibid.; United States Census, Jefferson Township, Allegheny County, June 4, 1900.

> observed that on the beast was a person … endeavoring to control the beast and restrain its violence. When it came close to us, I recognized the person as Bro. Cadman. "Why," I said, "That is Bro. Cadman. I am not afraid of him. He will not hurt me." But my companions told me it was not he, but the beast that was seeking the destruction of the Saints and that it would not hurt [us] as long as he could control it.

Eventually "the [skin of the] beast fell to the ground … [and] left standing as if she had been in the midst of it a beautiful, innocent-looking woman." Cadman smiled and said, "Now you see what it is."[30]

William H. thought the meaning was self-explanatory and did not offer further commentary. It would have been clear enough to supporters of his father, and in his father's day they must have imagined that it portended well for their side. Bickerton's group might have interpreted such a dream differently, though, showing Cadman provoking the beast. In the dream, it was not Cadman alone who prevailed, but Susannah Trump through the "prayer of faith and the power of God." It was the triumph of a common member—a woman, in fact—who had come to the rescue when her leader was locked in a grueling, perhaps unnecessary, battle. It is significant that Susannah had this dream in 1880 as everyone was choosing sides.[31]

About sixty years after Cadman's history was written, a subsequent church historian, Larry Watson, suggested that Bickerton may not have been fairly treated. When charged with adultery, Bickerton responded with a denial and was never found guilty.[32] In 2006 non-Bickertonite historian Gary R. Entz came to the same conclusion, but showed more gumption in writing of the injustice to Bickerton of having his legacy stolen by Cadman, compounded by Cadman's son when he "wrote William Bickerton and the western branch in St. John out of much of the Church's chronicles. The result has been that the memory of Bickerton has become obscured within

30. Cadman, *History of the Church of Jesus Christ*, 79–80.

31. Ibid.

32. Watson, *History of the Church of Jesus Christ*, 2:50; see also Watson, "Church of Jesus Christ," 194–95.

his own church."[33] What Cadman and his supporters failed to realize was that, like the Taylors, Bickerton's struggle to keep his own family together had been undermined by these rumors and exaggerated responses. If one were to look at Bickerton more sympathetically, the accusation of infidelity tore his family apart and his defensiveness might have been well founded. Charlotte Bickerton, for reasons we may only guess at, left him in 1877 and refused to return at a time when he not only wanted her company but needed her support. When he did not get it, he filed for divorce. His attorney, C. B. Weeks, petitioned the Ninth Judicial District Court of Stafford County on his behalf on May 25, a few weeks after Eli Kendall's faction accused Bickerton of adultery. It was bad timing, and Bickerton must have known it would taint him in the eyes of anyone trying to ascertain his guilt or innocence. Either way, he had lost his patience after waiting three years for his wife to return to him. She had, no doubt, heard about the scandal and may have believed there was something to it. His attorney explained that Charlotte had "refused and still refuses to live with your petitioner" and that "there is no hope of a reconciliation."[34]

Rightly or wrongly, Bickerton may have expedited the divorce in an attempt to protect his assets. His attorney asked the court to annul "all and such further relief" the wife might request, meaning alimony. Bickerton said later he had worried ever since he moved to Kansas that Charlotte might try to take control of the West Elizabeth property they had granted to the church. When he visited Pennsylvania, he decided he would "make the deed so my wife could not take any advantage of the Church house." He had not anticipated that his rivals would auction the house for cash. Through all this, it is not insignificant that 1,100 miles lay between St. John and West Elizabeth. Later it appears he felt he had acted rightly in trying to salvage his marriage and then to

33. Entz, "Bickertonites," 44.

34. *Bickerton vs. Bickerton*, May 25, 1880.

protect himself through divorce.[35] Maybe his suspicions and defensiveness signaled a lack of trust that made matters worse.

He probably knew that his divorce would look like a plan to elope, and it may be why the petition attested to his faithfulness. "During the time your Petitioner and Defendant lived together," the attorney wrote, "he provided for the wants of said Defendant in manner in keeping with his circumstances in life, and your Petitioner further alleges that he was to Defendant a kind and dutiful husband." If Bickerton thought this could be handled discreetly, he must have been surprised by the requirement to publish a public notice of his intent, as he did May 29, 1880, in the *St. John Advance*, with a line informing Charlotte that she had sixty days to answer or demur. Bickerton mailed a copy to her as well. She made no attempt to appear "in person or by attorney" or to plead her case, having resolved to abandon Bickerton. On August 27, 1880, the court granted the divorce.[36] Thereafter, Bickerton was a solitary soul, surrounded by supporters but living alone in self-imposed exile on the plains of Kansas.

There was more disappointment to come, as Bickerton's and Cadman's factions fought over the church building in St. John. Cadman's people sued for possession in August, and Jacob Beitler, a Bickerton supporter who had advanced $700 to build the church, called in his loan. This was during the drought that overshadowed everything. The paltry harvest left the members meeting in a building for which they could no longer afford the mortgage payments. The court ordered the building sold on November 3 at a public auction, where Beitler himself won possession and announced that he was moving the building closer to the town's central square, which he did in April 1881.[37] The irony was not lost on locals, who remembered that the previous spot was

35. Ibid.; Bickerton, "Testimony, June 1903," 12; "Bickerton Party Minute Book 1882–1887," 11–12.

36. *Bickerton vs. Bickerton*, May 25, 1880; *Bickerton vs. Bickerton*, Affidavit, Aug. 16, 1880; *Bickerton vs. Bickerton*, Hearing, Aug. 27, 1880; *St. John Advance*, May 29, 1880.

37. Beitler was loyal to the prophet, so he allowed Bickerton's Saints to continue holding services in the building, until he sold it the following year.

where Bickerton had driven the stake into the ground. "Despite all the prophesies heretofore," the *St. John Advance* observed, "the church of Jesus Christ, so long a land mark on the hill north of town, has been moved down nearer the square and will be repaired and strengthened."[38]

Petty quarrels continued. In January 1881, Cadman's faction held a conference in St. John where they discussed what they considered an affront due to Cadman sending a card to Bickerton's followers in an attempt to reach out to them. He had sent an identical card to the loyal church members, and they wanted to know why, "after all the action that has been taken against them (he, Cadman) still acknowleges them."[39] As far as they were concerned, rapprochement was not an option.

At a Bickerton conference that spring, the prophet explained the history of the Latter Day Saint movement and why God had given him a prophetic mantle to perpetuate the Restored Gospel. The conference was "numerously attended" by his followers, "some of them traveling two hundred miles to be present," the *St. John Advance* reported. Bickerton assured those unfamiliar with the church that they did not associate in any way with the Utah Mormons and did not accept polygamy. "This branch of the organization refusing to adopt that part of the belief, chose a leader of their own, and have numerous church organizations throughout the land." The congregation "appeared to be thoroughly in earnest in their belief and adhere very strictly to their religious vows. As a class they are intelligent, law abiding, peaceful citizens, they do not attempt to force their religion on any person, but are very firm in the opinion that their's is the only true faith, and the only hope for salvation lies inside the portals of their church." Even so, the journalist applauded them, writing that "their religion although somewhat singular, is their own by right and is not interfered with by the community. They always extend a cordial invitation to all classes to attend their meetings, and are very courteous in their treatment

38. Entz, "Bickertonites," 16; "Town and Country," *St. John Advance*, Apr. 8, 1881.

39. Martin and Mancini, "History of the Church," 147; "Church of Jesus Christ in the East," 2:68.

of strangers. Their meetings are often very interesting and would well repay any one for attending them."[40]

Again, Bickerton captured more generous attention from the community than from his own church as long as a majority in the East sided with Cadman. In an effort to "gather together the Latter Day Saints," Bickerton wrote, he and his brother Arthur traveled to Pennsylvania, although not to meet with Cadman. Their mission was to bolster their followers and try to persuade others to join them. Cadman, in turn, journeyed to Kansas to strengthen the rapport with his followers there, both sides working against each other.[41] When the court validated the sale of the chapel to Beitler, Cadman's followers appealed the decision. The *St. John Advance* weighed in on November 25 that "they should settle this matter by compromise of some kind, and not drag any more of their private scandals before the public."[42]

The animosity continued in July 1881 when Cadman's faction excommunicated James Miskin and apostle Alexander Cherry for fraternizing with Bickerton. In another brisk move, they suspended apostle Joseph Astin in August for giving the church's records to Jacob Beitler, as he had done for safekeeping. Now they prepared to sue for custody of the books.[43] The final decision upholding the sale of the church building came in June 1882, and Beitler decided to sell it to Elijah and Frank Swartz of Ohio. The building was moved yet again, this time to the very center of town, renovating it into a hardware store. Then they constructed a house on the previous property. "The old church has probably reached its final resting place now, on the corner north, opposite Rohr's, where Swartz Bros. will convert it into a first class hardware store," the *St. John Advance* announced. Rohr's

40. "The Annual Conference of the Church of Jesus Christ," *St. John Advance*, May 6, 1881.

41. William Bickerton, "To All Whom It May Concern," *St. John Advance*, May 6, 1881; Entz, "Bickertonites," 17.

42. "Town and Country," *St. John Advance*, Aug. 19, Nov. 25, 1881; Entz, "Bickertonites," 17–18.

43. Martin and Mancini, "History of the Church," 147–48; "Church of Jesus Christ in the East," 2:64, 71–74.

was a two-story mercantile establishment built by Henry Rohr in September 1879. The amount of material that had been brought to the former property for construction of the house and "unloaded on the old church block, give it the appearance of a full grown lumber yard."[44]

It must have been demoralizing for church members to see their chapel dismantled and turned into a retail establishment. The embarrassment they felt seemed to be shared by the community generally. "Are we spiritually digressing?" the *St. John Advance* provocatively asked. "It looks that way. A church was the first building ever erected here, but the rush of business has necessitated its conversion into a business house." It had been a symbol for the town; the paper called on people to erect another, regardless of denomination. "Nothing would tend more to indicate intelligence, civility, good society, and thrift than a church, even though it be small," the editorial continued. The Swartz brothers offered to contribute to any such undertaking. "We hope to see some one take an interest in this question, and not let this be the last heard of it," the paper added.[45] Disgruntled and disunited, Bickerton's and Cadman's factions met in private homes and in the town hall.

The Taylors seemed to have weathered the storm until it was reported at the July 1882 Bickerton conference that Tryphena had been "keeping company, walking, and driving around with another man," attorney E. S. Hadlock, even though she had "a man of her own." The ministry did not want to rush to judgment, considering what she had already endured, and assigned Jacob Beitler and James Miskin to visit with her, after which she was invited to an afternoon council. When the allegation was read aloud, she admitted "she had no power to [do] any thing else" and did not even consider it wrong. She would not quit associating with the attorney, she said. Bickerton implored her to reconsider, but "she got angry and would not listen." When he entreated her further "to humble herself," she "walked out," the

44. Entz, "Bickertonites," 18; "Town and Country," *St. John Advance*, Sept. 21, 1882; Cutler, *History of the State of Kansas*, s.v. St. John.

45. "A Church," *St. John Advance*, Nov. 2, 1882.

secretary recorded. The council resolved "that Sister Taylor be seperated from the Church of Jesus Christ for unworthyness in keeping company walking & driving around with Mr. Hadlock ... showing her conduct to be contrary to the scripture."[46] Shortly thereafter she went to court to divorce James. Equally surprising was that Hadlock was her attorney, which caused a commotion in town. The divorce rate had skyrocketed in the 1870s and 1880s in the United States, but a woman initiating divorce was still shocking, especially in a small town like St. John.[47] People considered it a public humiliation of her husband. It was known that Taylor had previously run his wife's name into the ground, and this was seen as possible retaliation. The divorce trial became public entertainment, reported in the *St. John Advance* on December 28, 1882, as "the much talked of Taylor vs. Taylor divorce case," with "some rich developments." Those attending the trial "were not entirely disappointed," although "the custody of two bright and attractive little girls" was a tragic element. The hearing lasted two days "and was the largest and most interesting divorce case ever tried in this county—if not the largest case of any kind."

Divorce was granted, and guardianship of the girls went to Tryphena's brother, Adolphus Singleton, with "the privilege [granted] to defendant [James] of seeing them at all reasonable times." Tryphena's brother was probably considered more financially able to care for the children. It was nevertheless an insult to James and not a complete victory for Tryphena. She would legally remain the girls' mother, but under her brother's supervision.[48]

It is ironic that Bickerton was involved in excommunicating Mrs. Taylor, if the action is seen as a defense of the husband, who was Bickerton's accuser. If Bickerton had been involved with Tryphena, her reaction might be interpreted as contempt for hypocrisy. With a

46. "Bickerton Party Minute Book," 7–8.

47. Edwards, *New Spirits: Americans in the Gilded Age*, 135–37. In the late nineteenth century, social standards were in flux, with more rights being granted to women, but the perception that a wife was the property of her husband was still common, even under the law.

48. "Town and Country," *St. John Advance*, Dec. 28, 1882.

suspicious eye, one could imagine Bickerton exploiting a situation to redeem his reputation. More likely, though, it appears that Bickerton had in mind the good of the church and the individuals in question. Even if he wavered slightly in his friendship with Tryphena, he saw something more nefarious at work in her association with the man who was not a church member. She may have thought her reputation (a prized possession in Victorian America) was ruined and so why not associate with whomever she wished.

Then there was the Indian mission. The adultery scandal delayed it, but it was impossible to destroy Bickerton's resolve. Sometime before 1883, accompanied by Samuel Work and Silas Busby, he headed west to proselytize among the Cherokee. They preached in schoolhouses and homes. They sometimes worked together and other times they went different directions to cover more ground. "I had the privilege to meet in a school house where they had an organ[,] and an Indian Squaw played it during services," Bickerton recalled. "They were very prejudiced when I first began teaching the Book of Mormon; but by the time I had finished with my discourse, they were very kind, as the Lord worked upon them in his own way. Some asked me to dine with them. I showed them the Book of Mormon and told them it was their Father's Bible before them, and I showed them that their forefathers came from Jerusalem, and that they were the promised seed from that place."[49]

Some of the people they encountered remembered Bickerton from his mission about fifteen years earlier. In one instance, he had "left a pair of spectacles and a hymn book, and they had taken the best of care of them until my return." He was especially touched by this, since he had only met them once and they had been convinced by his message to the extent they had retained their belief in their ancestors' history being in the Book of Mormon. One day the missionaries

49. Bickerton, "Testimony, June 1903," 5; Entz, "Bickertonites," 19–20. It is possible to date the trip because Samuel Work was suspended in January 1883 and would not return to full fellowship until 1891. See "Bickerton Party Minute Book," 10–11; "Cherokee District Conference," Jan. 17, 1891.

encountered a family anticipating the death of a child. "They thought there was no hope for the child, and the house was full of people." Asking the mother if she had faith, and receiving a positive reply, he "took the child in my arms, and Brother Busby anointed it, and I asked the blessing of God upon it, and the dear little one was healed. Everybody was astonished."[50]

Bickerton visited the African Americans he and his previous mission companions had converted. "[We] returned back to where Brother Cadman and I had been years before in some colored folks house, and we all felt that we had never spent a better day in the work of the Lord." They preached to a racially mixed congregation, "a crowded house, whites, and Indians, some of whom had been in the Union army," Bickerton wrote. "I stayed there after Brother Work and Brother Busby had gone home, and I got quite well acquainted with the Indians in that locality. One large family of Indians I tought to say the Lord's prayer and sing the hymn, 'Oh, stop and tell the red man,' and I rejoiced in the spirit to look upon their red faces."[51] The mission undoubtedly gave emotional relief to the man who had endured so much heartache in the past fifteen years.

Busby met and married an Indian woman and moved near Caney, Kansas, on the state's southern border with Oklahoma. Bickerton and Work returned to St. John and found employment managing the City Hotel on the town square in a building that had been moved there from somewhere else in the county in 1879, the matter of dissembling and reassembling wooden structures having been somewhat common at the time. Another building in the downtown area, owned by John Fish, had also been moved there. The hotel was owned by John Askew,

50. Bickerton, "Testimony, June 1903," 5.

51. Ibid., 5–6. This hymn by William W. Phelps was sung in Joseph Smith's time and was included in the first Latter-day Saint hymnal. It has not, however, stood the test of time with its reference to Indians as people who "lived by hunting, instead of work and arts," along with a message for them to "quit their savage customs, to live with God at home." Smith, *Collection of Sacred Hymns*, 83–84.

although before long Bickerton acquired it and left Work to be the manager while Bickerton served a mission to far-off New Mexico.[52]

The shadow of rumor continued to follow Bickerton in unexpected ways. On May 21, 1883, James Miskin arrived at a council meeting thinking they were going to help reorganize the church's leadership and resolve the issue of Bickerton's divorce, or more specifically address a revelation Bickerton had received to countenance his divorce. Miskin had apparently told three people he was prepared to assist, having received a revelation about the matter, or "the spirit of the presidency." When he arrived at the meeting, he found instead that they wanted to discuss his aspiration to take over the leadership of the church. He was dumbfounded. The confusion embarrassed Bickerton, who lectured Miskin, saying, "You have got nothing to do with my case, this is your trial and even if I did get a divorce that does not give you the spirit of the presidency." Bickerton asked him if he had the spirit now. Not understanding what was happening, Miskin said it "seemed like a trap." Yet when the council pressed him, he said he had probably erred and received his revelation "from the Devil." In any case, the secretary recorded, he "promises not to Broach the matter again."[53]

In another unexpected turn, Eli Kendall was suspended from William Cadman's faction in 1884. Released in August 1884 from the apostleship and presidency he had been serving in as Cadman's first counselor, a year later in July he was excommunicated.[54] Within three years, he would join the Utah church and become a leading opponent of Bickertonites of all stripes.

Bickerton had not lost his ability to sway an audience. If he was reluctant to admit failings in private, he was open about his spiritual ups and downs the minute he stepped in front of a congregation, and this trait allowed him to impart to followers the thrill of inspiration

52. Entz, "Bickertonites," 20; Cutler, *History of the State of Kansas*, s.v. St. John.

53. "Bickerton Party Minute Book," 11–12.

54. Martin and Mancini, "History of the Church," 151–52; "Church of Jesus Christ in the East," 2:90.

and comfort of belonging to a society of believers. At the July 1882 conference, he had uttered a heartfelt prayer that especially touched the members, a secretary writing that "Bro. Wm. Bickerton followed by prayer[,] and the gift of prayer and intercession fell upon him and the spirit of prayer fell upon each one in councel, so we had a refreshing shower from the Lord and this giveth us strength." There was a greater "faith in the lord, yea we feel as if the turning point had come on behalf of the church," the minutes continued.[55]

Bickerton dearly wanted to find a turning point in his life and for the church, and instead the scandal continued to weigh him down like an anchor. It may have been almost refreshing to his followers to see him troubled by the vicissitudes of life the rest of them faced when they were falsely accused, their virtue or lack of it being no guard against a tainted public opinion. The mission into Indian Territory would remain Bickerton's main focus. He imagined that in his lifetime he would meet the Choice Seer and ordain him. Whether he realized it or not, his personal scuffle with Cadman had weakened both of their factions to the point that they were unable to make much progress, and only plowed the ground and planted the seeds for the Utah Mormons to bring in a plentiful harvest when they returned to the East. The battle for primacy among believers in the Book of Mormon in Pennsylvania and Kansas had just begun. Surprisingly, the contest would not be primarily between Bickerton and Cadman.

55. "Bickerton Party Minute Book," 8.

TWELVE

CONFRONTATIONS AND DEFECTIONS

1885–90

"Mr. Bickerton, good morning sir. On the rampage again, are you?"
—William Cadman, Aug. 11, 1887

At the age of seventy, Bickerton saw the bitter fruit of discord ripen, going back to the defection of his counselor George Barnes in 1872. Two of the men who joined Barnes in Coal Valley, Pennsylvania, were John E. Baxendall and Charles Price. By 1885 they had become converted to the Doctrine and Covenants as a divinely inspired text and contacted the president of the Utah church, John Taylor (Brigham Young died in 1877), to request more information. Taylor forwarded their message to William Moroni Palmer, president of the LDS Northwestern States Mission, who sent Victor Emanuel Bean and William W. Allen from Indiana to Pennsylvania to meet with Barnes's group. Bean and Allen found not only one congregation but others that looked ripe for picking.[1]

Upon their arrival in Western Pennsylvania in December 1885, they heard from Barnes about the more recent breach among the Bickertonites and decided to contact the two major factions.[2] First, on December 9, they met with Thomas Bickerton, who had parted ways in 1869 to start his own church. From him they learned that "if it were not for [polygamy], they would gladly be one with us." Undeterred, the

1. Entz, "Bickertonites," 20; Bean and Allen to Palmer, Dec. 14, 1885.
2. Bean, Journal, 4:1–11.

missionaries tried to meet with William Cadman, who was in Europe conducting some sort of real estate transaction. His wife, Elizabeth, and five other women were willing to converse. After the missionaries had collected information "concerning that sect, we arose to leave," when the women "broke out against Poligamy and went so far as to say that the licentious practice of the world is far above Mormon Plurality of wives." The missionaries "answered their statement by quoting them scripture," according to Bean, "to show that ... Plural Marriages was honored and commanded by God in ancient times."[3]

Bean and Allen were able to see Thomas Bickerton's brother Arthur on December 10. He had recently moved back to Pennsylvania and associated with Cadman's group. He talked about the adultery allegation against the prophet and said that, in Kansas, Cadman's group had filed lawsuits to obtain the building and records. "And so they are split upon religion here," Bean wrote in his journal.[4]

That evening William Bickerton's oldest son, James, met the Mormon missionaries to defend his father's convictions. He "came in with his wife and being introduced to us he began arguing against Poligamy, and failing to gain his points either by scripture or reason, he then became enraged and left the house." Arthur, though, wanted to hear more. The next day he told the missionaries he thought they should preach in Elizabeth Township and that he would help them find a venue. He was surprised to discover the degree of animosity among acquaintances who told him they would not tolerate a lecture from Mormons. "Everywhere he would mention Salt Lake Mormons he would get into a debate," Bean found, and it was because three days earlier, in his annual message to Congress, US President Grover Cleveland had mentioned what he considered to be the danger of polygamy. American homes, the president said, were "sanctified by parental love," and that was absent from "the homes of polygamy." Continuing to hammer his point, the president added that the ideal mother reflected

3. Ibid., 3–6.

4. "Bickerton Party Minute Book," 15; Bean, Journal, 4:6–7.

"true womanhood, unperverted and unpolluted," in contrast to the "cheerless, crushed, and unwomanly" motherhood seen in polygamy. So too an American father, "undefiled with plural marriage, is surrounded in his single home with his wife and children [and] has a stake in the country which inspires him with respect for its laws and courage for its defense." Cleveland announced his intent to "approve such further discreet legislation as would rid the country of this blot upon its fair fame."[5]

The president's address was discussed during the evening of December 11 in George Barnes's home. Barnes was unfazed by it and asked the missionaries to accompany him four miles the next day to anoint a sick woman in McKeesport. At first Bean and Allen "were much in doubt as to the authority of Bro. Barnes as he was baptized into the Bickerton church after Bickerton had apostatized" from the Mormon Church, but decided to accompany him because, as they said, Bean needed a new pair of pants and thought they could find a tailor in McKeesport. When they arrived, the sick woman was "so low that she could not sit up." Barnes requested them to do the honors in performing a healing ordinance, which they did, and were afterward invited by the family to stay for dinner. They were gaining the confidence of people on the fringe of the Bickerton movement, although they also learned that those of Cadman's faction were speaking in "very bitter terms against us and denounced the Utah people."[6]

Two days later Bean and Allen wrote to their mission president that "on arriving here we found things so tangled up that it was necessary for us to visit quite a number of the older settlers … in order to be able to give you a proper understanding of the origin and continuation" of the Bickerton church. It would be possible, they had determined, to find converts among the splintered branches of the sect. The uncertainty about their "prophet, seer, and revelator," they said, began "soon

5. Bean, Journal, 4:7–8; *Journal of the Senate of the United States of America … Forty-Ninth Congress,* (Washington, DC: Government Printing Office, 1885), 40.

6. Bean, 4:8–13.

after the church [in Green Oak] was burned down." Bickerton and two others had gone to "Indian Territory to preach to the Lamanites but all got sick and had to return." This "caused many of his followers to disbelieve in him." It was a simplified version of the story, told from the perspective of the dissenters and filtered through the eyes of the missionaries, but nonetheless instructive of how those in the Barnes and Cadman circles perceived Bickerton.

Regarding Barnes, the missionaries informed Palmer that he "drew away from the Bickerton organization" and was willing to entertain the idea that the Utah Twelve were properly commissioned and those chosen by Bickerton were not. Barnes was a "prominent man and a preacher [who] yielded a considerable influence among the people," the missionaries explained. They went on to tell of Bickerton's "revelation that he should go to Kansas and build up a Zion. Accordingly he and as many as would, went to St. Johns, Staford Kansas but many of them refused to go. … And, after going to Kansas, he (Wm. Bickerton) got into adultery with his neighbor's wife which caused a separation I believe in both families. For this crime, Bickerton was cut off the church and formed a separate body with the few that still upheld him and they still held the books, or church revelations and records, etc."

Cadman's group did not fare better in the missionaries' report. They "meet every Sunday and also meet in conference every 3 months at which time they sustain Cadman as their President until they can do better. Some thinks he is the man for that position and others of the same branch is wanting him removed." Summing up, Bean wrote, "I would say that after Bickerton went to Kansas, the church scattered in all directions and was split in many pieces."[7]

Palmer saw a potent enough opportunity to convert entire congregations that he informed Bean he would accompany him the next year on a second trip to Western Pennsylvania. Accordingly, the two arrived in Coal Valley and held a meeting on May 23, 1886. Three days later Palmer obtained a copy of Bickerton's pamphlet, *The Ensign*, and

7. Bean and Allen to Palmer, Dec. 14, 1885.

found it intriguing. That same day, he met with the Miller family, some of whom were affiliated with the Bickerton or Cadman faction. After talking "a great deal to them," Agnes, Helen, Helen Jane, and Mary Miller, along with their acquaintance Annie Gardener, agreed to baptism by Bean. A few days later the missionaries baptized George Barnes in the Monongahela River. On Sunday, May 30, President Palmer ordained Barnes an elder and appointed him to preside over the New England, Pennsylvania, branch.[8]

At this time, Bickerton was trying his best to reclaim lost members in Kansas, promising to receive anyone with open arms who wanted to rejoin. Some did. Elder J. S. Weeks left Cadman in 1885 and reunited with Bickerton. On December 6, Weeks was ordained an apostle. The next day Joseph Astin, who had denounced Bickerton during the adultery scandal, rejoined him, as his wife had done in November. It pleased Bickerton to mend these broken friendships. At a council meeting on February 27, 1886, he confessed he had not done enough to save souls. He had let the splintering of the church impede his ability to reach people and make an impact in the world. They had the exclusive key to prepare for the Millennium, he reminded the elders, and were not doing enough in that regard. "There was just one voice to warn the world and that was the voice of Joseph Smith," he said, "and this Church has had the voice." Rather than emphasize his view that Joseph Smith died a fallen prophet, for the moment he spoke of Smith's standing prior to his fall. Bickerton was once again intent on completing the church's mission. To do so, he would need to pick up the pieces after the secession of Cadman's group and staff the positions that had become vacant. The council voted unanimously to support him in these endeavors.[9]

He decided in April to address the charge that he too was a fallen prophet. For those who had been "shaken by the burning of the House at Greenock," he explained, "the promises of God were not to the

8. Palmer diary, May 23–30, 1886.
9. "Bickerton Party Minute Book," 15–17.

Lumber & nails in the Church … but were to the … Church of Jesus Christ," to the congregation itself. That was the "House of God" that was protected. He knew the Saints in the East "doubted the wisdom and propriaty of the Saints [living] in the west," so he called on the conference to "testify to all Saints" that God had "order[ed] his Church to … the Land of Zion." Standing firm on the premise that they had not erred, Bickerton's group asked J. S. Weeks to write a letter to "the Church back East asking them to report either by person [or] by letter to the Church here at general Conference," warning them that a "failure to comply with this request" would result in them being "dealt with as the Spirit of God designates."[10] They expressed their desire to the entire splintered church, including George Barnes's group and other dissenters, that they wanted to reunite.

Some responded favorably to the call. Alexander Bickerton reported from West Virginia that he had remained faithful and would have attended the conference if he had had the means. He "hope[d] we shall all join that Great Assembly of the holy & noble men & women of all [time] who have gone up through tribulations[,] who have washed their robes in the blood of the Lamb[,] and to spend that thousand years of millennial rest where the glory of God shall cover the earth as the waters cover the Great Deep."[11] The members of the Little Redstone branch responded similarly. Alexander Cherry reported that "he intended to do the will of God and uphold the church." Arthur Bickerton asked to renew his membership. For their loyalty, these three men, Alexander and Arthur Bickerton and Alexander Cherry, were sustained as apostles. On the other hand, Joseph Astin left Bickerton's group again. At the summer conference when Bickerton had imagined a reunion of many former members, they instead withdrew the priesthood from ten leaders of the opposition, excommunicating George Barnes and William Cadman.[12]

10. Ibid., 18–19.

11. Ibid., 25–26.

12. Ibid., 20–23. The ten men were Joseph Astin, George Barnes, William Cadman, Cummings Cherry, John Dixon, Eli Kendall, George Kendall, Paul Lathorpe, George Shawver, and William Skillen.

The only response from Cadman's group was to instruct its trustees on August 9, 1886, "to take the necessary steps to prevent William Bickerton and others from infringing upon the rights of our Charter, and also to take from them all properties belonging to Said Church." It irritated Cadman that Bickerton's followers had purchased a seal in Kansas with the incorporation insignia on it and had retained possession of some of the church's records and real estate.[13]

One unexpected response came from the Utah mission president, who decided that because of the success they had experienced among the Bickertonites in Pennsylvania, they should see what the situation was in Kansas. On a reconnaissance mission to St. John in November 1886, after visiting with Bickerton, President Palmer had the impression the area was a hornet's nest that could be profitably disturbed. He set about organizing a dedicated campaign to proselytize. Before leaving, he wrote to John H. Morgan of the First Council of Seventy in Utah to request "2 experienced Elders" to be sent to St. John "at once to stir them up."[14]

For a while a thin aura of contentment surrounded Bickerton's group. James and Amelia Miskin opened their home on Christmas Day 1886 to church members and neighbors. J. S. Weeks reported to the *St. John Sun* that the dinner table was filled with ham, turkey, cakes, and pies. He found "the dinner was in every way a success, and the visitors enjoyed themselves to the utmost." After the meal, Bickerton "called the house to order and opened a religious meeting by singing and prayer, and gave for a text the proclamation of the angels at the birth of Christ: 'On earth, peace and good will to men' from which he spoke for a while with feeling and power." Miskin, Weeks, and James Ross spoke after Bickerton, "awaken[ing] deep feelings in all present, and all seemed glad because The Almighty Father had seen fit in his infinite wisdom to send such a glorious message to the fallen sons and daughters of Adams race." There was "a Christmas tree … standing

13. "Church of Jesus Christ in the East," 2:92; "Bickerton Party Minute Book," 19, 21–22.
14. Palmer diary, Nov. 25, 1886; Entz, "Bickertonites," 21–22.

in one corner of the parlor and was well filled with gifts for the little ones," Weeks commented.[15]

In the spring of 1887, Miskin "felt that the Lord called him to go down to the Indian territory." Weeks gave him a blessing, promising that he would find God "around him on every side." Miskin's family moved with him to the Caney area, where they knew Silas Busby lived. Miskin wrote to the *St. John Advance* in May to report that they had baptized three people. Those three were the former missionary Silas Busby, who had drifted away and wanted to rejoin the church, Busby's Indian wife, Mary, and an Indian man named George Washington. Miskin re-ordained Busby an elder and ordained Mary a deaconess.[16]

In mid-1887 the LDS Church in Utah added Kansas to the Northwestern States Mission, freeing William Palmer to send Elders D. E. Harris, J. O. Swenson, and Elder Candie to St. John.[17] Bickerton warned his members, advising them "not to let the Salt Lake Mormons, as the L.D.S. Missionaries were called … in their homes."[18] J. S. Weeks went to the press to let people know the missionaries were not Bickertonites but were polygamists. "Many of the citizens know that as a people we do not believe in the doctrine of a plurality of wives," he explained. If people chose to speak to the "three Mormon Elders here now," they would "easily discover that there is a wide gulf between us and those who live in Utah." As "a church," he continued, "we do not believe that Joseph Smith ever taught or practiced polygamy, and we would not believe the doctrine to be from God if he did." They believed in "the 'Mormonism' of 1830," he asserted.[19]

That letter ended up being the stick that beat the hornet's nest. John Williams could not resist following up with a public letter calling

---

15. J. S. Weeks, "St. John, Kansas, Dec. 27, 1886," *St. John Sun*, Dec. 30, 1886.

16. "Sand Hill Farm," *St. John Advance*, May 5, 1887; "Bickerton Party Minute Book," 31; Miskin and Miskin, "Notes on Our Early Life," 4–5.

17. Entz, "Bickertonites," 22–23; Palmer diary, July 12, 1887.

18. Astin, "Synopsis of the Life of Joseph Astin," 2.

19. Weeks, "St. John, Kansas, June the 21, 1887," *St. John Sun*, June 23, 1887. See also Weeks, "A Letter," *St. John County Capital*, June 24, 1887.

Bickerton's followers imposters: "I wish to notify the public," the Cadman follower wrote, "that the above named party, presided over by William Bickerton, is not the Church of Jesus Christ, whose charter is filed on the records in this county. … William Bickerton was lawfully expelled according to the laws of the above named church, for disorderly conduct." Williams resurrected the warning that "any business transacted by that party since that time in the name of the Church of Jesus Christ is illegal and without any authority whatever." He added a disingenuous note, "Now I don't make this statement because I wish to contend or quarrel with any one, I do it to defend ourselves and to keep the public from being imposed uppon."[20]

The Mormon missionaries were making their way through town, joined by President Palmer on July 12. Palmer stayed with Eli Kendall, the man who had been first counselor in Cadman's church. As Palmer talked with the Kendall family, he learned that "several parties were investigating" the claims of the Utahns. That evening Palmer held a meeting at the local schoolhouse, Blake's Hall, where he preached "on the gathering of Gods people in the Last days proving … that [the] place spoken of by the prophets is Utah." He attempted to show "geographically from the prophicies of Isaiah Jer[emiah] Ezeakal & others" that "west from Jerusalem at the farthest end of the earth from there [was] the highest [peaks] of the [Rocky] Mountains."[21]

The next day he received an opportunity to preach twice and elicited sympathy in his first sermon about how oppressive the 1887 Edmunds–Tucker Act had been in disincorporating the church, seizing the emigration fund, and appropriating real estate not directly used for religious purposes. This was in fulfillment of the prophecies of Ezekiel, he said. In the evening he preached about "the Eternity of the Marriage covenant" to a crowded house of attentive listeners.[22] This attracted the attention of the newspaper. "Several elders of the Latter

20. Williams, "A Letter," *St. John County Capital*, June 30, 1887.
21. Palmer diary, July 12, 1887.
22. Ibid., July 13, 1887; see also Ludlow, *Encyclopedia of Mormonism*, 1:52.

Day Saints, have been preaching in Blake's school building," the article read. "Among them are some very smooth and pleasant talkers, and they have been greeted by fair audiences." However, "as to their success in the shape of new converts," the *St. John Advance* continued, "we have not learned of any thing worth mentioning."[23] That would not remain so. Already on July 14, Palmer had taken Eli Kendall, George Kendall, and Hiram Smith and their wives to Rattlesnake Creek to baptize them into the Western church. It was a resounding success for the Utah Mormons, a heavy blow to Cadman's group.[24]

Bickerton's people thought if they educated the public about Latter Day Saint history, it would strengthen their position and protect them from such defections. J. S. Weeks provided three newspapers with a clarification of Bickerton's connection to Joseph Smith. He added that although it had not been "the custom of the church of Jesus Christ, of Latterday Saints, since its location in this country, to publish" the content of its conference proceedings in the newspaper, it would in this instance. This gave Weeks an opportunity to respond subtly to Williams by suggesting the longevity and continuity of the Bickerton faction.

Weeks rehearsed the history of "Joseph Smith, the Martyr." After Smith, Young had usurped the church leadership and introduced polygamy, and "the world knows the result," he suggested. "Sidney Rigdon, by virtue of his calling and ordination, had the only authority of presidency ... but because he stood in the way of those wicked men who were determined to get control of the church, in order that they might gratify the lust of the flesh, he was rejected by a large number of those who called themselves saints." Before long, Rigdon succumbed to "age and other causes" of senility, and Bickerton, who had been a member of Rigdon's Quorum of Seventy, stepped forward, as called on "by the Holy Spirit," to be "Rigdon's successor." Bickerton taught the same doctrine "as was taught by Joseph [Smith]." He had legally incorporated the church in Pennsylvania in 1865 and in Kansas in

23. *St. John Advance*, July 19, 1887.
24. Palmer diary, July 14, 1887.

1877. At the general conference in 1876, "the Lord did, by his spirit, accept the church and all present felt the divine glory and approval of God." Bickerton possessed a prophetic mantle that God had sanctioned, Weeks argued.

Weeks then took a jab at Bickerton's rivals. "Internal discussions which were brought about by men who were not stable in doctrine, and who have since fallen away from the church, prevented the proper growth of the church and for some years not much progress has been made," he claimed, although "of late the Lord has manifested to us that the time to favor Zion had come and that he would build us up."[25] This was a provocative, even biased statement that was bound to create controversy. It did not tell the whole story, and when Cadman read it, he became incensed. Weeks had been a close associate. Ready to spill more ink, Cadman picked up his pen in August for his most impassioned rebuttal yet, saying that "for some time" he and his followers had been "suffering abuse and misrepresentation from one Wm. Bickerton and some associates of his." Since "the public were being imposed upon by [Bickerton's] announcements and pretentions," he "thought it proper and necessary" to respond. The recent letter by J. S. Weeks was notable only for its "evasiveness and falsehood," Cadman wrote. "Now sir!" Cadman retorted, "if you [Weeks] had any desire to act the part of a man, why do you endeavor to evade an investigation of the abominable conduct of the man you are endeavoring to defend, as your letter indicates, from beginning to end."

Cadman characterized Bickerton's life as one of "scandal and disgrace," an embarrassment to "every person … worthy of the name of a Latter Day Saint." By investigating Bickerton's conduct in 1880, the public would only discover "his foolish and fanatical presumption and ignorance." At the conference Cadman attended in 1880, the members had condemned Bickerton. In saying this, Cadman, like Weeks, left out important information. He failed to mention that the only people

25. Weeks, "A Letter," *St. John County Capital*, July 28, 1887; Weeks, *St. John Sun*, Aug. 4, 1887; Weeks, *St. John Advance*, Aug. 10, 1887.

who attended the conference in question were Bickerton's rivals, and he neglected to mention that a later public hearing he presided over ended in the prophet being acquitted.[26] Nonetheless, Cadman chided, "if you can successfully defend his conduct, you have only another to defend, which is the Devil." Not satisfied with that as his final blow, he added that "all your talk sir, about spiritual blessings etc, is the merest bosh and nonsense."

Cadman went on to call Weeks's comprehension of Latter Day Saint history into question, for instance regarding polygamy. "Now sir, it is of no use lying about these matters. The evidence is now conclusive that Joseph Smith authorized spiritual wifery and polygamy," based on statements by Isaac Sheen and William Marks in the RLDS *Herald*, where "they admit fairly and squarely that [Smith] gave the revelation, but afterwards repented and declared it was of the Devil. For further particulars I refer you to David Whitmer, one of the three witnesses to the book of Mormon." For Bickerton being "ordained successor to Sydney Rigdon and duly recognized as such, by a general conference of the church [in 1862]," Cadman wanted to know "on what authority" Weeks made that claim. "Where was you at that time? I never saw you there." Aside from the fact that Weeks had not used the word *ordained* to describe the recognition Bickerton received in 1862, one could well question when and how Bickerton had assumed the role. At a minimum, it became gradually understood and was not a single event. For instance, sometime in late 1845 or early 1846 Rigdon ordained Bickerton a "prophet, priest, and king," but Rigdon ordained other men to the same office. In 1859 members of Bickerton's ministry ordained him a "prophet," and yet again there were others in the church who were recognized as such. It was the same when Bickerton was anointed "prophet, seer, and revelator" in 1863; before long others in

26. Nevertheless, the jury did indicate that Bickerton's actions had incited James Taylor's jealous rage, causing a division in his family and a disturbance in the community, see Cox and Hoole, "Ed. Advance," *St. John Advance,* July 24, 1880. Another public hearing conducted by Charles Brown ended in a hung jury, see "Wm. Bickerton's Answer," *St. John Advance*, July 24, 1880.

the church shared the same title. "I perceive sir, that Wm. Bickerton is using you as a little penny whistle, to blow through, and he blows through you whatever he wishes to. In the case under consideration he simply blowed a falsehood through you, as nothing of the kind has ever before been expressed to my knowledge, and I am certain, was not expressed at that time."

Cadman was not done yet. Turning his attention to Bickerton himself, he wrote, "Mr. Bickerton, good morning sir. On the rampage again, are you?" He raised the issue of Bickerton's ordination as prophet, priest, and king as evidence of his pretension, a sticking point in any case because Cadman believed the Millennium would come at the end of the era of Zion, making someone's designation as priest and king a sign of clinging to a false eschatology. Cadman got in another jab by accusing Bickerton of exercising "kingly prerogatives in … immitation of … King David in the case of Bathsheba" (adultery). The writer had an overall poor opinion of Rigdon, too, who he said "sank as far in religious fanaticism as any other man that ever lived." He lectured Bickerton that "associating his name with your bad conduct don't help you one bit." In case anyone was unaware, he added, Bickerton had associated with Brigham Young as well, so his choice of associates had not been the best. To sum up his thoughts, Cadman said the letter from Weeks was "a silly attempt to evade answering the church, and also the public, for your disregard of the laws of both God and man."[27]

Bickerton was stunned. Not only had he been libeled by a former friend, the letter left one wondering what Cadman believed at all. It was the last straw for a man who determined he would no longer tolerate such abuse. Bickerton filed suit against Cadman for libel.[28] His mood was no doubt influenced by the news he had just received hours earlier that his long-time loyal friend Charles Brown had died.

27. Cadman and Taylor, "An Answer," *St. John Sun*, Aug. 11, 1887; *St. John County Capital*, Aug. 11, 1887.

28. *Bickerton vs. Cadman and Taylor*, Aug. 1887.

Weeks notified the newspaper that "Father Time has swung his scythe with resistless stroke, and an aged man has fallen before the grim old reaper. Elder Charles Brown died at his home last night [August 10] at about 10 o'clock." After reading Cadman's barbed letter, Bickerton attended the funeral and paid tribute to his departed friend. "It was truly touching to see the aged Elder whose looks have grown white in the service of his Master, standing by the casket which contained the remains of his fellow laborer, to deliver the funeral oration." As Bickerton spoke, "tears came in his eyes, and for a time emotion almost checked his utterance."[29]

Then Weeks took pen in hand and rebuked what he considered Cadman's impudence. Where Weeks claimed those in Bickerton's camp had exercised restraint, having "mentioned no names and g[i]ve[n] vent to no spleen … [or] spirit of malice," he found it uncharitable to be personally slandered. "I have resided here for nearly 5 years and to my positive knowledge neither Wm. Bickerton or his associates have made any public attack either directly or indirectly on Mr. Cadman or his associates," he stated with indignation. He had apparently forgotten or did not know that the prophet in 1880 had called his accusers "ungodly christians" and "imposters." In any case, why did this antagonist not leave Bickerton's fate to God? Weeks wanted to know. "For if we are not of God[,] we will fall, and if [it] so be that we are of God[,] your sarcasm and railing will only bring condemnation on your own head."

"Now sir, as you have befouled Joseph Smith, and Sidney Rigdon, and made sport of Bickerton's calling and ordination, and have spoken sneeringly and with intent to cast odium upon him, will you be kind enough to tell the public where you got your authority, (if you have any?)," Weeks asked. "Now sir I was not there, as you suggest," he quipped, "but I am told that you was baptised in 1859 under the authority of William Bickerton, that you received all your ordinances under the same authority, that you was ordained an Apostle by Wm. Bickerton, and also by him ordained as president of the Twelve. I am

29. Weeks, "St. John, Kansas, August 11, 1887," *St. John County Capital*, Aug. 18, 1887.

also told that … as late as 1868, you accompanied Bickerton and Meadowcroft on a mission to the Indian Territory." Cadman had indeed supported Bickerton for over two decades. "Did you not indorse Wm. Bickerton as late as 1875 … in coming to this country [Kansas]?" Also, why did James Taylor and his ex-wife accompany Bickerton on a tour of Stafford County in 1880 if Bickerton had fondled the woman?[30]

The next thing that happened was that Bickerton eventually withdrew his lawsuit. Either he was satisfied by this public response or wished he had not gotten involved in such a polemic and wanted no more of it. He sent Weeks to Indian Territory for the winter. The Utah Mormons sent a new missionary to St. John in 1888, Heber Bennion, who held discussions in the local courthouse about the "schisms among the Latter Day Saints." Bickerton attended one of them, and the newspaper reported that an "exciting" debate ensued. Eli Kendall claimed Bickerton was "violent in his denunciation of Elder Bennion, the latter described him as literally foaming at the mouth and at one time he thought he intended making an assault on him but he managed to satisfy himself with a volley of imprecations." Bickerton's attempts to thwart the Mormons ended up helping them by making himself look intemperate. By contrast, Bennion had a gift for connecting with people. He was likeable.[31]

Standing aloof from the controversy, Joseph Astin lay on his sick bed in the spring of 1888 at the age of sixty-two. He was not displeased when Elder Bennion visited him, although Astin's wife was unhappy. She "coolly escorted" Bennion to the bedroom past two teachers from Cadman's group, who said, "Well, the Devil has gotten in this house, so now we must leave." Bennion remained with Astin for an extended period, making everyone in the house curious to know what they had talked about. As the son, William, recalled, "Mother went into the bedroom" after Bennion departed. "Much to her surprise she found

30. Weeks, "St. John, Kas., Aug. 13th 1887," *St. John County Capital*, Aug. 18, 1887.

31. Entz, "Bickertonites," 27–28; "Home News," *St. John County Capital*, Apr. 13, 1888; Eli Kendall, "The Other Side," *St. John Weekly News*, July 19, 1889.

Father overjoyed and delighted. ... 'They have the truth, that's what I've been looking for,'" he said. When the Astins moved twenty-one miles west of St. John to a farm near Macksville, the Mormons went to great lengths to keep in touch. "One can appreciate how difficult it was for the Elders to visit us," said William. They had to "travel from St. John to Macksville by train and hire horses to ride the remaining 7 miles to our home" using "burlap sacks" for saddles. On May 13, 1889, the missionaries obtained a wagon and team of horses and lifted Astin into it, with only hay and a quilt to rest on. They hauled him "over rough uneven roads a distance of five miles to the nearest stream, Rattle Snake Creek, where he was baptized by Elder Eli Kendall." The convert died in August, but his family followed him into the LDS Church, relocating to Salt Lake City in 1893.[32]

Others drifted over to the Mormons. James and Amelia Miskin had suffered such trials in Indian Territory, it made them question their calling. Their daughter, Emma, died of sickness. Their cattle contracted Texas Fever. They moved back to St. John and lost Amelia's father to malaria. As Amelia concluded, "The Lord did not seem to smile on this gathering." When they encountered the Mormon missionaries, they were prepared to listen. Amelia remembered that "as soon as we were able, we went to hear them (the Salt Lake Elders, as they were called)" and became acquainted with Elder Gunn. After engaging in "several gospel talks," James attended the Mormon services. He said to the missionary, "I have been to several of your meetings. Now come to one of mine next Wednesday." The missionary did so and was treated to a sermon by Miskin himself. He liked the content. "You did fine, Brother Miskin, I have seldom heard better on the topic," Elder Gunn said. Then he asked a provocative question. "You said the work was on earth never to be taken away. Where was your church from the time Sidney Rigdon died to when William Bickerton started his?" Gunn was misinformed about the details, since Rigdon would not die for another twenty-four years after Bickerton's church was established in 1852, but

32. Astin, "Synopsis of the Life of Joseph Astin," 3; Entz, "Bickertonites," 29.

there was a gap of five years between the collapse of Adventure Farm and Bickerton's decision to succeed Rigdon. The more Miskin thought about it, the more he realized he was stumped. In addition, Bickerton's prior membership in the Mormon Church complicated the picture of a smooth succession.

Amelia remembered that her husband "walked the floor in a very excited manner" all night, thinking about this, and finally said he was "convinced the Salt Lake Elders, as we called them, belong to the right church, and I am going to the fountainhead. The reason we have so much confusion and splits and bitter feelings is because this is just a side show." He was fed up with the backbiting between the Bickerton and Cadman factions. Amelia was not so sure. There were other denominations, such as the Josephites (RLDS). "I don't see much difference in the preaching," she said. "We all believe in the restoration of the gospel and that Joseph Smith was a prophet of God." Eventually Amelia became converted to the doctrine of baptism for the dead. "I felt [the Mormon] church had more light," she decided. Having recently lost her father and daughter, she was comforted by the idea that she could do something for them. The Miskins were baptized by the fall of 1889 and soon moved to Salt Lake City.[33]

The *Stafford County Rustler* observed that the Mormons continued to hold lectures to introduce themselves to the locals, but that the number of meetings was outpacing the number of "people who attended them."[34] Bickerton did not find it amusing that people still considered Latter Day Saints of any stripe to be cut from the same cloth. He penned four letters to the *St. John Weekly News* in mid-1889 entitled "Saints vs. Mormons." Referencing passages from the Doctrine and Covenants, future LDS apostle Charles W. Penrose's 1884 pamphlet, *Blood Atonement*, and articles from the LDS *Millennial Star*, he attempted to contrast his church's beliefs from those of the Mormons.

33. Miskin and Miskin, "Notes on Our Early Life," 4–6.

34. "Local, Personal, and Otherwise," *Stafford County Rustler*, May 30, 1889; Entz, "Bickertonites," 30.

In the first letter he discussed polygamy, quoting from LDS Doctrine and Covenants Section 132, the document authorizing plural marriage, saying it was "of suspicious origin, … fostered in secret and shielded in falsehood." Echoing President Cleveland, he condemned the institution that "turns home into a hell and heaven into a harem. … If these things reflect the character of God and his works, we are at a loss to know how we shall ever identify the devil and his institutions."[35]

The second doctrine he contested was blood atonement. Brigham Young had said "there are sins which men commit for which they cannot receive forgiveness in this world or in that which is to come," and for which they must have "their blood spilt upon the ground." The doctrine was "nothing less than [license to] murder," Bickerton concluded, "and ought to be rejected by all honest people. There is no place between the lids of the Bible, where man is justified in shedding his [or others'] blood for the remission of his sins." The Bible says that "whosoever sheddeth man's blood, by man shall his blood be shed."[36]

The third doctrine he critiqued was Brigham Young's Adam–God concept, that "when our father Adam came into the garden of Eden, he came into it with a celestial body, and brought Eve, one of his wives with him. He is Michael the Archangel, the Ancient of Days, about whom holy men have written and spoke. He is our Father and our God, and the only God we have to do [with]." By eating the "fruits of the earth," they produced offspring who were mortal, so the teaching went, and it was Adam–God, not the Holy Ghost, who impregnated Mary, the mother of Jesus. Bickerton dismissed it, saying it was "simply idolatry, and needs no comment."[37]

He wanted to assure people that he was not intending to assail the character of the missionaries. "We have no desire to interfere with the character of men, but are only dealing with principle," he wrote. However, he did want people to be aware that the missionaries "preach

35. Bickerton, "Saints vs. Mormons," *St. John Weekly News*, June 7, 14, 1889.
36. Ibid., June 14, 1889.
37. Ibid.; Turner, *Brigham Young*, 232.

here what they call the first principles of the gospel, but as they tell you, you will have to go to Utah to know it ALL."[38] He invited anyone interested in corroborating his statements to "view the books which we have quoted from." He finished by relating Joseph Smith's discovery of the Book of Mormon, the main tenets of the Book of Mormon, a defense of Sidney Rigdon as the rightful successor to Joseph Smith, and his own church's beliefs.[39]

In July, Bickerton published another discourse, this one with the provocative title, "The Difference," contrasting the doctrines of the "Salt Lake Mormons" with those of the Church of Jesus Christ overseen by him. After the article appeared, Heber Bennion suggested that Eli Kendall write a response. When the editor of the *St. John Weekly News* gave the Mormons space for a series titled "The Other Side," Kendall devoted his attention to denigrating Sidney Rigdon's and Bickerton's spiritual authority.[40] Rigdon "had been known for some time among the Apostles to be[,] at heart[,] recreant to the cause of God; but among the people who had been so often electrified by his marvelous gift of oratory, much sympathy was felt for him," Kendall wrote. Even Joseph Smith had wanted Rigdon removed from the church presidency. "I have thrown him off my shoulders and you have placed him back again," Smith complained at a church conference that voted to retain Rigdon. According to Smith, the Twelve Apostles held keys of leadership as well. Smith had made this clear when he said that "where he (Joseph) was not[,] 'there is no First Presidency over the twelve.'" Smith had "rolled the burden of the keys of the kingdom … upon the shoulders of the Twelve Apostles," Kendall quoted Smith as saying.

If that was not evidence enough, Kendall continued, people in Nauvoo, after Smith's death in 1844, saw the "direct manifestation

38. Bickerton, "Saints vs. Mormons," *St. John Weekly News*, June 14, 1889.

39. Ibid., June 21, 28, 1889.

40. Bickerton, "The Difference," *St. John Weekly News*, July 12, 1889; Kendall, "The Other Side," *St. John Weekly News*, July 12, 1889.

of the power of God resting upon President Brigham Young." When this happened, Young's "voice and entire visage seemed transformed into that of Joseph." That Rigdon would "reject and fight against such testimonies almost surpassed human credulity," Kendall suggested. In fact, Brigham Young's transfiguration into Joseph Smith was a bit of folklore that originated in Utah and had not been in circulation very long. As historian Richard Van Wagoner found, there are "no known contemporary record[s] support[ing] a supernatural occurrence." The contemporary accounts relate that Young's manner of speaking was similar to Smith's and that the "mantle of the prophet" fell on Young, meaning there was a general sense of authority or even a halo around his head. This gradually evolved into the tale of "an explicit transfiguration, a physical metamorphosis of Brigham Young into the form and voice of Joseph Smith." Van Wagoner found that the "earliest detailed accounts ... did not begin to surface until long after the Saints were settled in the Great Basin."[41] Kendall relied on second-hand accounts rather than his own personal experience.

He went on to say that Rigdon "was a well-known adulterer," which was entirely spurious. Kendall referenced the Adventure Farm fiasco to indicate that if "the fruit of a tree is [found to be] worthless[,] it may be known at once that the branch on which it grew is impure," meaning that in Kendall's mind Bickerton's attempt to salvage the tree was misguided. He claimed that Bickerton had once admitted that Rigdon's conduct was "so shameful, and his loose immorality so manifest," that Bickerton "dissolved all connection with him and stood by himself." This was a fabricated tale, either misunderstood or deliberately miscommunicated in the writer's zeal to score points. Kendall then asserted that Bickerton's followers "preach and baptize in an unorganized and desultory manner. The smallest grain of reason or consistency should have taught them that if the church had gone astray and were without authority, they themselves were equally destitute of that essential ingredient, without

41. Van Wagoner, "Making of a Mormon Myth," 14–16.

which it is sheer blasphemy to minister in gospel ordinances." Piling on additional criticisms, he added that Bickerton "had acted hastily in rejecting a principle [plural marriage] he had never fully examined and understood, and thereby placed himself under condemnation." Kendall said Bickerton became even more hardened against polygamy in 1857 when the Mormon elder Samuel Woolley traveled through Pennsylvania and informed Bickerton of his excommunication.[42]

This skewed version of church history rankled Bickerton. Try as he did to ignore it, saying he "would have taken no notice" if possible, in August he decided "it contained so many bare-faced falsehoods, that we could not feel justified without refuting them." What he wrote was a sharp rebuttal, pointing out that Kendall had only known him "about sixteen years," and yet the editorial covered a period of "about fifty years," nor could Kendall find anything more substantial to engage in, such as the "difference in the doctrines," than to "vilify" Bickerton's character with misinformation and lies. "At the death of Joseph Smith, Sidney Rigdon was right-hand counselor, and was in good standing up to that time," Bickerton countered, and Kendall wanted to "make him an adulterer of which there is no proof." And this coming from the Utah polygamists! he thought. It could not be taken seriously, originating with people whose claim to authority was "mere moonshine and of no worth." He posed a rhetorical question to "the people of Stafford Co." whether the characteristics Kendall ascribed to him were true or not. "And as all of our meetings are open to the public, we leave you to judge."[43]

In addition to responding to criticisms, Bickerton thought it was time to write a thorough history of his church for the benefit of the public. The extensive chronicle he produced was serialized in eleven issues of the *St. John County Capital.* He hoped the information he imparted would stem the persistent controversy.[44] As part of the history,

42. Kendall, "The Other Side," *St. John Weekly News*, July 12, 19, 1889.

43. Bickerton, *St. John Weekly News*, Aug. 16, 1889.

44. The installments were published under the title, "Bickerton's Letter," the first one addressed to "Mr. Editor, Sir," in the *St. John County Capital*, Aug. 15, 22, 29; Sept. 5, 12; Oct. 3, 10, 17; Nov. 14, 21, 28, 1889.

he offered a partial disclosure of his own past. Some of it was dismissive. "We have been charged from time to time as having connection with the Salt Lake Mormons, on account of a similarity of name," he wrote. "We declare, therefore, unto all people, that we are entirely a separate organization and have no connection with them, neither one way or another." "They ask us why are we so few," he added. "Because they have never known the difference between Salt Lake Mormons and Latterday Saints, and we have to bear the reproach." In response to former members of his church who, from time to time, attempted to besmirch his character, it reminded him of the persecution of Jesus. "The Savior was just as much the Christ when he hung on the cross as when they wanted to make him a king," he reasoned.[45]

Not because of his letters, but more likely due to the departure of Heber Bennion in July 1889 and Kendall's move to Salt Lake City in March 1890, there was a reprieve in animosity in 1890. By May, there were enough immigrants to Utah that a former Cadmanite told the *St. John Advance* he had "met several members of the St. John colony in Salt Lake City." All were "doing well," he reported.[46] Kendall estimated that eighty people had been converted from the "scattering-division-breeding proclivities of Bickertonism" in Pennsylvania alone, not including Kansas.[47] He may have exaggerated, but the number must have been large enough to deserve comment.

Bickerton kept an ear to the ground for news from Indian Territory. Older now, seventy-five years of age, he was more frail and had lost his right eye.[48] With no sign of the Choice Seer or the angel Moroni, he still anticipated these events, believing that each passing day brought them closer to fulfillment rather than closer to confirming that he had been wrong. He trusted that the Lord would mend the church's breach and allow him to facilitate the gathering of the lost tribes. Despite his

45. Ibid., Nov. 21, 1889.
46. Entz, "Bickertonites," 34–35; *St. John Advance*, May 1, 1890.
47. Kendall, "The Other Side," *St. John Weekly News*, July 19, 1889.
48. Bickerton, "Testimony, June 1903," 8–9.

fragile health, he needed to preach to the Indians. In September 1890, the *St. John Weekly News* reported that "Rev: Wm. Bickerton left for the Indian nation Wednesday. He will remain there about six months."[49] In the heart of Oklahoma and along the plains of Kansas, he would await the signs of the approaching Millennium.

49. *St. John Weekly News*, Sept. 18, 1890.

THIRTEEN

AMONG THE LAMANITES

1890–99

"We held meetings in different parts of that country, and I never felt more of the power than while preaching the gospel of Christ in that country."

—June 1903

For many Latter Day Saints, 1891 was a prophetic year of epic proportions. Back in 1835, Joseph Smith had predicted that Jesus would possibly return to earth in that year, ushering in the promised glories found in the scriptures, and Smith repeated something similar in 1843: "I was once praying very earnestly to know the time of the coming of the Son of Man, when I heard a voice repeat the following: Joseph, my son, if thou livest until thou art eighty-five years old, thou shalt see the face of the Son of Man; therefore let this suffice, and trouble me no more on this matter" (D&C 130:14–15).[1] Smith was born on December 23, 1805. Therefore, the Second Coming was thought to be scheduled for 1890–91. Expounding on the revelation, Smith stated that he was unsure whether it meant that Jesus would "make his appearance" on earth that year "or I shall go where he is."[2] He was murdered in 1844, yet people held to the conviction that 1891 would see the Second Coming.

1. The official LDS history quotes the February 14, 1835, prophetic reference to "the coming of the Lord, which was nigh—even fifty-six years should wind up the scene." Smith, *History of the Church*, 2:182.

2. Bushman, *Rough Stone Rolling*, 489.

In a way, Bickerton was no different. If he did not literally believe Christ would return in 1891, at least he assumed the era of the gentiles was ending and it was time for the American Indians to rise up and prosper. He understood the prediction in the Book of Mormon to have come true, that in "that day … the Gentiles shall sin against my gospel … and shall be lifted up in the pride of their hearts above all nations … and shall be filled with all manner of lyings, and of deceits, and of mischiefs, and all manner of hypocrisy, and murders, and priestcrafts, and whoredoms, and of secret abominations; … and then will I remember my covenant which I have made unto my people, O house of Israel, and I will bring my gospel unto them" (3 Ne. 16:10–11). Bickerton's own church had been torn apart by pride, lies, deceit, and so on. He thought the Mormons had perverted the Restored Gospel. So he would become an itinerant prophet, or a tool in the master's hand, spending months at a time over the next ten years in Indian Territory awaiting the arrival of Joseph, the Choice Seer. This Indian Moses would lead his people out of captivity. To Bickerton, all indications were that the Millennium was nigh.

With the Civil War twenty-five years behind them, one would think its significance as a predictor of the end times would fade. Not in Bickerton's mind, however, who saw it as the cataclysmic event foretold by scripture. The aftermath of the war showed a continuing decline in social conditions, from his perspective. For instance, in the hotly contested 1876 general election, Republican Rutherford B. Hayes promised to withdraw federal troops from the South, guaranteeing a bleak fate for African Americans.[3] The Indians did not fare any better. Between 1867 and 1887, the federal government implemented the policies of the "Reservation Era," during which Native Americans were *transformed* from free-roaming hunters and gatherers to self-sufficient farmers and ranchers. Forced onto reservations where the living conditions were unhealthy, still susceptible to disease, their

3. Foner, *Reconstruction*, 575–87, 604.

total population was reduced from a onetime high of 1.5 million to less than 250,000 by 1890.[4]

Looking for hope, Indians turned to the messianic deliverance foretold in the Ghost Dance Religion initiated in 1870 by Tavibo, a Paiute Indian in Nevada whose messages from the Great Holy Force Above were that the Indians would soon be delivered from their white oppressors. After Tavibo's death, his son, Wovoka, proclaimed that since white people had killed Jesus, there needed to be a second incarnation of Jesus, and Wovoka was that messiah. He revamped his father's religion by promoting self-restraint, ritual bathing, abstinence from alcohol, and pacifism. They no longer needed to mourn the dead because the departed would soon resurrect. Before long, "the living and dead Indians would be reunited in a restored world where all would live in happiness, free from misery, death, and disease," he said. The grass would flourish on the prairies, buffalo would roam freely. At Indian gatherings lasting five days each, his adherents would meditate, chant, and dance in order to see visions and receive revelations.

Native Americans came from California, the Pacific Northwest, the Southwest, the Great Plains, and Indian Territory to meet Wovoka. He explained that God had sent the Europeans to punish them for their sins, and that the day of deliverance from oppression would be in 1891.[5] Surprisingly, this concept of Indians being overrun by Europeans, "scattered" and "smitten," then gathered and redeemed, correlated with the Book of Mormon and Joseph Smith's prophecy about the Second Coming (1 Ne. 13:14; 3 Ne. 16:4–5). Leaders of the Mormon Church, including President Wilford Woodruff and first counselor Joseph F. Smith, saw it as providential timing that the Ghost Dance occurred at the very time they themselves anticipated the millennial onset. Joseph F. Smith thought the Indians were seeing immortal Nephites who roamed the earth without dying. At the Sanpete stake conference in August 1890, Apostle Anthon H. Lund announced, "We

4. Gibson, *American Indian*, 443–44.

5. Ibid., 476–78.

need not say—'our Lord delayeth his coming!' … We can be sure it is in the near future, because the Lord told Joseph Smith … that if he lived to be a certain age, he should see His face, which points to [18]91." On May 29, 1890, LDS apostle Lorenzo Snow predicted during a meeting with the Quorum of Twelve Apostles: "You brethren will live to behold the savior, you shall not die, death shall have no power over you. You have a great work to perform. … Be faithful and you shall never taste death." Seeing the advent of the Millennium coming closer, John H. Morgan, a president of the Seventy, revealed a sweeping belief that "missions would necesarily be short; that the end is very near and the Elders about to be called home."[6]

To protect the LDS Church from Congress, President Woodruff issued his Manifesto on September 24, 1890, publicizing that the church would stop polygamy. It was to be a temporary solution, the Mormons believed. Apostle Moses Thatcher and others said they supported the decree because the Millennium was near and everything would be restored.[7] Some of the leaders continued to sanctify new plural marriages in secret, also with the Millennium in mind. When Woodruff presented the Manifesto to the October conference in Salt Lake City, he spoke these words of reassurance about the fulfillment of prophecy:

> I will say to the Latter-day Saints, as an Elder in Israel and as an Apostle of the Lord Jesus Christ, we are approaching some of the most tremendous judgements God ever poured out upon the world. You watch the signs of the times, the signs of the coming of the Son of Man. They are beginning to be made manifest both in heaven and earth. … We are approaching these things. All that the Latter-day Saints have to do is to be quiet, careful and wise before the Lord, watch the signs of the times, and be true and faithful; and when you get through you will understand many things that you do not today.[8]

---

6. Erickson, *Thief in the Night*, 202–03.
7. Ibid., 204–05.
8. Ibid., 207.

Bickerton may not have entirely understood the cross-currents of influence competing for the attention of Native Americans, but he clearly saw their plight and desperation, what he believed to be their desire to regain their former status as leaders of nations. On January 17, 1891, Bickerton held a Cherokee district conference at the house of Samuel Work, a colleague who now lived in Indian Territory. The prophet spoke of his belief in the imminent fulfillment of prophecy. Work's wife, Phebe, said, "Verily Verily thus Saith the Lord, my Servant William Bickerton Shall live to ordain the Choice Seer, who is the Shepherd[,] the Stone of Israel, and lay the government on his Shoulders. Verily Verily, thus Saith the Lord this is my word Stand ye to it, the work wich is going on among the Indian is by me Saith the Lord Amen." The "Spirit bore a powerful witness to nearly all present," the secretary noted, "and we did but little but bear witness praise god and Speak to one another about the mysteries of God." It appears the Saints may have been aware of Joseph Smith's prophecy regarding 1891 and believed, like the Mormons, although without having left explicit evidence of it, that the current year carried epic significance.

Excited over the day's events and "conversing about the Red man" with Silas Busby, Bickerton suddenly uttered a prophecy and repeated it twice: "The Lord will give us power to prevail over the government, yea over Benjamin Harrison and his cabinet, in favor of the Red man, for his god is our god and the god of the Jews and the ten tribes of the North."[9] Bickerton could see for himself the burden of living under the federal government's authority. Three weeks earlier on December 29, 1890, federal troops had massacred 146 Lakota Sioux—men, women, and children—at Wounded Knee in South Dakota. As the Sioux, who had come under the influence of Wovoka, performed the Ghost Dance, it appeared to be a prelude to war, in the eyes of white observers, and the attempt by the Seventh Cavalry to disarm them resulted in bloodshed. President Harrison dispatched 3,500 troops to quell what he assumed was an all-out Indian revolt. This captured not

9. "Cherokee District Conference," Jan. 17, 1891.

only national attention but the sympathy of the missionaries in Indian Territory. Bickerton's revelation was a reaction to Wounded Knee.[10]

In a meeting two days later, January 19, Bickerton discussed the prophecies about the Urim and Thummim, the stones Joseph Smith had used to translate the Book of Mormon, and the sealed record he had prophesied would come forth. "We felt by the Spirit of god, that it was the will of god, for us to have the Urim and Thummim," the secretary recorded him saying. Presumably they would be delivered by an angel because "the Spirit—also testified that god would Send Moroni to deliver the Sealed Records to Bro William Bickerton."[11] "Come unto me, O ye Gentiles," the Book of Mormon impleaded, "and I will show unto you the greater things, the knowledge which is hid up because of unbelief. Come unto me, O ye house of Israel, and it shall be made manifest unto you how great things the Father hath laid up for you, from the foundation of the world; and it hath not come unto you, because of unbelief" (Ether 4:13–14).

As Bickerton labored among the Indians, William Cadman's group struggled in Pennsylvania, the West Elizabeth branch reporting in October 1890 that they had become "few in number," although they had "good meetings when we meet together." In Coal Valley there were "few [who] meet," and the report from Coultersville was, "We cannot meet together often." They occasionally received defections from Bickerton's membership, Alexander Cherry changing sides around 1890, for instance. In April 1892 the Lucyville branch was asked to sign an agreement verifying that they would stand against Bickerton and the Mormons. "A goodly number has signed it already," the secretary noted.[12]

It was a relatively quiet decade, punctuated at times by such surprises as the *St. John Weekly News* running a farcical account of the town's founding, told by local resident Bob Wilson in May 1892.

10. Gibson, *American Indian*, 479.

11. "Cherokee District Conference," Jan. 19, 1891.

12. Martin and Mancini, "History of the Church," 163, 165; Cadman, *History of the Church of Jesus Christ*, 1:90.

The first colonists, Wilson said, were a bunch of "plum dandies" who were Mormon but sensitive about being called that, even though they "banked hard on Joe Smith and the book of Mormon." Unlike the Utah Mormons, though, the settlers did not have "concubines." Nevertheless, "their big medicine man claimed to be the only original head of the church and with a commission to hold onto the keys of heaven ... the same as Saint Peter did, and whenever any of the saints bucked he'd threaten to club 'em off the golden stairs." Of all the colonists, the leader was himself "a plum dandy and no mistake. His name was Bill Bumbleton [William Bickerton], and he had the e[d]ge over everything in that valley for a long while."

"Old Bill had a revelation that they was to settle ... [and] drove a wagon spoke down in the top of a hill to mark the place where they was to build a church." Continuing in that vein, Wilson informed the paper that "Old Bill run the thing mostly his own way, for whenever he wanted to do anything, he had a revelation that it was to be so, and the other saints had to knock under. There was nothing in the rules of the church to keep any of the rest of 'em from having revelations, but Old Bill was the boss revelator of the outfit, and the other saints' revelations didn't count for much."

When it came time to settle and build a church, "they couldn't find their stake ... [and] fell to prayin' to the Lord for Him to show 'em where the hill was with the stake onto it. They prayed 'round fer three or four days and they didn't find no stake right quick, and then they set to having revelations and dreamin' dreams about where that wagon spoke was." One of them, an "enterprising rooster of a saint what hadn't had any revelation or dreamed a whole lots, got an old wagon spoke and slid over to a little raise on the prairie and he druv 'er down tight and fast." Then "this enterprising saint ups and tells 'em that he'd had a revelation tellin' him where the stake was, so he takes 'em over to where he had drove the wagon spoke the night before, and sure enough, there it was." "This didn't please their old high man because it showed there was a better man at the revelation business than he was," Wilson quipped, "so he falls to and has a boss big revelation that the Lord had pulled up the stake and kept it a while to fool 'em and try their faith."

"Besides dreaming dreams and having revelations and seeing visions and s[u]ch monkey business as that, they spoke in unknown tongues," Wilson remarked, gradually drifting from good-natured humor to more raw sarcasm. "I heard Old Bumbleton cut 'er one day. He was a preachin away like a prairie fire and all to once he stopped and yelled: 'Tunee waddle opee sockee ty tunee popi sockee, socke popi too, tishomingo whack.' And then some old saint ups and says, that means that there warnt going to be any more rainfall on the crops of the gentiles what had come into the valley, and that the hot winds would blow on the gentile's crops and pass over the saints' and the gentiles would have to vamoose. ... You want to take notice that when the hot winds did come ... the saints' corn curled jist the same as the gentiles." One day "Old Bumbleton ... had a revelation ... that his old woman was accursed and she had to prance back east. Then the old man got to cavortin around among the saintesses and the he-saints gittin down on him started a dream and revelation trust and cornered the market on dreams and then proceeded to revelate him out of the church. I tell you ... they shore fired him." Wilson concluded that "Old Bill busted the church up and they aint got any any more."[13] Bickerton did not respond to the slapstick history, although it must have been a dagger to the heart to know that the adultery allegation still dogged him.

William Cadman, who similarly believed the latter-day prophecies were unfolding, told the church's April 1894 conference at the Lucyville branch that he wanted to renew his mission to Indian Territory. He had accompanied Bickerton to Indian lands in 1868 and supported the church's unsustained outreach to the Cherokee Nation from 1886 to 1889, but had never felt good about the abandoned mission. Not to mention, Bickerton had intensified his proselytizing in the West, providing more contested ground on which to vie for converts. Cadman's

---

13. Benton, "'Them Old Times': A Bit of Local Fiction That Is Not Wholly Fictitious," *St. John Weekly News*, May 27, 1892.

followers agreed that it was "God's Will that such should be done." Even so, they were not sure about the when and how, so they decided to postpone making a final decision until July. Before they closed the April conference, a letter from the Bickerton faction, composed by J. S. Weeks, was read asking if the Cadmanites would support a united front in reaching the Indians. This was probably part of the stimulus for Cadman's renewed interest in Oklahoma. Whether the communication from Weeks is seen as bold or naïve, it was an unexpected olive branch.[14]

By July, Cadman had published a pamphlet titled *Daniel's Little Horn* expounding on the 1879 letters he had written to the *Elizabeth Herald.* He repeated his belief that the "little horn" mentioned by the prophet Daniel represented the United States. He did not explain who the "Ancient of Days" was, but he had previously identified him as the American Indian Moses, the Choice Seer of the Book of Mormon prophecy who would oversee the government of Zion.[15] The conference endorsed the pamphlet and Cadman's proposal to reopen the Native American mission without Bickerton. Their enthusiasm continued at their October conference. The Lord expressed his pleasure, although in a backhanded way: "Thus Saith the Lord, I have taken my displeasure from off you, because of disobedience[,] and I have chosen you and ordained you, [and affirm] that this revelation is true and faithful." In considering what to do, they assumed the members in Kansas would be the ones to launch the mission. They were therefore disappointed to hear from Marion Campbell about a decrease in membership to only "12 Brothers and a number of sisters" remaining in the Cadman faction in Kansas. More of Cadman's followers had drifted back to Bickerton's congregation over time.[16]

---

14. Martin and Mancini, "History of the Church," 167; Cadman, *History of the Church of Jesus Christ*, 91. William H. Cadman wrote that his father spoke of the Indian mission at the January 1894 conference, but Martin and Mancini, "History of the Church," placed the conference discussion in April.

15. Cadman, *Daniel's Little Horn*, 12–14; Cadman, *Pre-Millennial*, 14–16.

16. Cadman, *History of the Church of Jesus Christ*, 91; "Church of Jesus Christ in the East," 1:118; Martin and Mancini, "History of the Church," 167; Entz, "Bickertonites," 38–39.

Alexander Cherry was assigned to respond to Campbell. In an affectionate letter that mostly offered encouragement, he opted not to mention the Indian mission, allowing them to learn for themselves from the enclosed minutes that the topic was reported.

> Well Breathren & Sisters i am very hapy to have the opertuneity to Wrighte you and get aquainted With Saints Whom i never saw and to Tell you that We had an Excelent Confernce[.] The Power & Blesing of god Was With us and Made us to rejoice[.] I Might Say that We have come thrue a great Deal of Truble hear the Last few years and still have a little, but We Will have as Long as Life remanes[.] We still trust in the promises of god to Direct us and help us to the End of the race[.] We fe[e]l very Well in Teaching the Gospel to the World and have Som Converts now and again and good Deal of invatatins to Teach in Strange parts[.] The Lucyville Branch has Bin very prosper[ous] for some Time[.] ... I think [we] have about Thirty in all Elders and members[.] The other party has Tried hard many Times to over throw us But the Lord has come to our rescue and has Deliverd us and We fe[e]l there is a Beter Day a head of us if We Will Doo Wright and Observe the Spirite of god and live in the Bonds of Love and peace and have Confidence in Each Other and hold one another up Before the Throne of Grace[.] Humblenes is the grater part of val[o]r in this Fight for the Kingdom[.] He that Wins the Batle Reaps the reward when he or She get[s] to the end[.] Tharefore May god Bles you all and keep you all Faithfull and Walking in the Light the Butyfull Light and Liberty of the Gospel of our Lord & Saveour[.] Tho i have never seen sume of you Still i Love you because Jesus first Loved Me. We have all Drank of the one spirite and have Eaten from the same Table the feast of Fat things for the ritches preparing Day by Day as We Live for it. tharefor Breathren i pray god May spread the Light to the honest in heart. Let us live that he May Direct the Church aright.[17]

To Bickerton, the hope that Jesus would return, despite his failure to do so in 1891, remained strong. "But of that day and hour knoweth no man, no, not the angels of heaven, but my Father only," the Bible had cautioned. "Watch therefore: for ye know not what hour your

17. Cherry to Campbell, Oct. 15, 1894; Martin and Mancini, "History of the Church," 168.

Lord doth come" (Matt. 24:36–42). The founder continued to preach, for instance, in August 1894 on the imminence of the sealed portion of the Book of Mormon being translated.[18]

Bickerton seemed unusually content when he spoke in June 1895, remarking on "the goodness of God" in "meeting with us at all times wether their are many or few." The number of people who had remained faithful, and the divided state of the church, were more a concern to the members than to the leaders at the moment. C. E. Dansen insisted that "each Bro. Make it a matter of prayer that the Lord will break down division and vindicate his work." Why should the Bickerton and Cadman factions not unite in reaching the Indians? they wanted to know. They voted unanimously to back Dansen's recommendation, in stark contrast to Cadman, whose members had resolved in October 1894 that they had "the Gospel as it was revealed to Joseph Smith, in its purity and power; that these other churches, called Saints, ha[d] adulterated the Gospel as revealed to Joseph Smith, and the Lord commands that none other Gospel than that, shall be taken to his Anoint[ed]–Covenant people."[19] The way Cadman saw it, Bickerton's group was like the Mormons, the RLDS, and any other Latter Day Saint denomination that had deviated from the true path. His was the only denomination worthy to preach to the Indians.

At the conference for the Bickerton faction, Dansen suggested that they retrieve the land where Bickerton had driven his stake in 1874. The problem was that there was now an LDS chapel on the property. At Dansen's request, the congregation petitioned God to "open up the way" for them "to get the house and lot on the corner of the old Church."[20] However, that would not happen. The history of the property is worth reviewing. Early in 1895 the Utah Mormons purchased the lot, as well as a chapel from the United Brethren which they moved

18. "Bickerton Party Minute Book 1882–1887," 4. The minutes for July 1892 through June 1895 occupy only three pages in the typescript.

19. Martin and Mancini, "History of the Church," 168–69.

20. "Bickerton Party Minute Book," 4–5.

to the location for an instantly produced church ready for worshipers. It was soon nicely furnished, eliciting from the *St. John County Capital* the comment that when it came to places of worship, it was "second to none in the city." The Mormons had not meant to honor Bickerton's revelatory acumen, but rather to subtly co-opt his legacy. According to Joseph Astin's son, William, "the L.D.S. Missionaries were enjoying considerable success in making converts, especially from among the Bickertonites. They soon had so many converts that it became apparent they needed a place of worship of their own. I do not know when or how it happened but when a location was selected for the erection of their new chapel they chose the exact site dedicated [by Bickerton and again later] by Father [Joseph Astin] and George Baker."[21]

The dedication of the church in September 1895 was a grand affair. Edward Stevenson of the LDS First Council of the Seventy and Andrew Kimball, president of the Indian Territory Mission, were both on hand. Kimball preached. A large choir composed of Mormons and other locals sang hymns. During the following days, visiting missionaries played baseball against the St. John Nine, while others gave presentations to farmers about irrigation. The *St. John County Capital* found that "the Elders and others present conducted themselves in a highly gentlemanly manner, and all were courteously and pleasantly treated by our citizens." People were smitten by the attention of these outsiders, and before long the town became the hub of Mormon activity in the region. In the fall of 1895, Mormons added a pipe organ to their chapel and began holding recitals. A violin concert in December 1895 attracted a large crowd. For Christmas they decorated their meetinghouse with Chinese lanterns, eliciting a comment from the press that they were providing "everything that tickles the public palate,"

21. Entz, "Bickertonites," 36; "The Mormons," *St. John County Capital*, Sept. 13, 1895; Astin, "Synopsis of the Life of Joseph Astin," 2, 4. William Astin stated that before his father converted to the LDS Church, he and George Baker had rededicated this exact plot of land. "The urge was so overpowering," William reported, "that, without hesitation, they obeyed the impulse and promptly dedicated the plot."

showing themselves to be "hustlers." If that was slightly pejorative, it did not matter because the locals were thrilled.[22]

While the Mormons provided entertainment (Utah actor Philip Margetts visited in December), the Cadmanites still talked about how to even the score with the Bickerton faction, not seeing that the ground had shifted beneath them. Bickerton himself was in Indian Territory and left the debate for others to decide. Because of the confusion over so many Latter Day Saint groups in town, Bickerton's adherents began referring to themselves as the Stafford County Saints and issued public invitations to their services but otherwise kept a low profile, although for three consecutive days in October they offered lectures at the court house on the "difference between the Latter Day Saints church of Stafford county and the Utah church."[23]

The prophet's most recent excursion into Indian Territory ran from November 1895 to July 1896. He told the *St. John County Capital* on his return that he had "good meetings and good success. The Lord has crowned our efforts by bringing some few honest souls" to the church. Not able to resist a dig at the Mormons, he said the impediment to conversion was the "stigma" of being "connected with the Utah Mormons." He was "laboring hard to break down the prejudice," he explained, and was "intending to return again soon." He was well "cared for both by Saints and strangers. I have not wanted for anything. They were all very kind to me. We present Primitive Christianity to the people and there is no argument, as they cannot gain say it. We have the gifts, among the[m] Prophecy, tongues and interpretation and gifts of healing."

Enumerating further, he explained that "Sister Faulkner that lives in Fish Creek who has lately been baptized has had [performed] some wonderful gifts of healing." Clearly the women were still conducting faith healings. Bickerton himself healed a Mrs. Haden, who afterward was baptized in the Caney River. "She was a praying woman," Bickerton

22. Entz, "Bickertonites," 36–37; "The Mormons," *St. John County Capital*, Sept. 13, Dec. 27, 1895.

23. Van Lieu, *St. John County Capital*, Oct. 18, 1895; *St. John County Capital*, July 24, 1896.

wrote, "and the Lord revealed to her in a dream that he would send one of his servants to administer the ordinance and ... when she saw me at the Indian Smoke she said she knew I was the man." She was paralyzed on one side of her body and had cut her head and ear in a fall. Her husband "lifted her arm up and I anointed it, and I likewise anointed her ankle and foot and her head and ear where she struck the stove. She testified that the pain had left her rightaway." Two days later he anointed her again and she began walking without a crutch. "Until she was anointed her husband had to dress her like a child."[24]

Bickerton's spirituality earned him friends in Indian Territory, although his overall success was still predominantly among white people. His devotion impressed the Cadman faction in St. John so much that, in a stunning turnaround after sixteen years of separation, the Kansas branch decided to rejoin Bickerton's denomination at the July 1896 conference. Both branches met together and the visitors were accepted back into full fellowship if they simply attested that the Bickerton faction was "the Church of Alma," organized at Green Oak, Pennsylvania, in 1862. And just like that, the two factions came back together—although in Kansas only, not in Pennsylvania. When put to a vote, the conference unanimously acknowledged Bickerton as a prophet, seer, and revelator.[25] It had taken the mission to Indian Territory to convert friends and neighbors in St. John. Now that they were reunited, they wanted to send a letter to Cadman to suggest the same in Pennsylvania. They chose Solomon Van Lieu, Joseph Kennedy, and David Lynch to write a letter proposing unification. The first two had once been elders in Cadman's faction.[26]

Their expectation of finding a sympathetic ear in Pennsylvania was

24. Bickerton, "From the Indian Territory," *St. John County Capital*, July 17, 1896. When Bickerton arrived back home, he was visited by B. H. Roberts of the Utah church's First Council of Seventy. Roberts learned that Bickerton had succeeded Sidney Rigdon and that he had organized "a 'First Presidency' of three, himself the chief," and followers "in Pennsylvania and Kansas," but that "the organization as such amounted to nothing." Bergera, *Autobiography of B. H. Roberts*, 206.

25. William Bingham and David Carduff became Bickerton's counselors.

26. Minutes of the Church of Jesus Christ of Latter Day Saints, July 16, 17, 20, 1896.

dashed when the letter and minutes of the combined conference in St. John were read at the October gathering of Cadman's faction. The news that they had lost their satellite branch in Kansas must have been difficult for them to process. Cadman thought it was best to "ignore" Kansas, even though he wrote to Bickerton's people "to notify them of [the] same," telling them he did not recognize the spiritual authority of their new church.[27] Aside from his stubborn resolve, there may have been another reason he hesitated to negotiate with the competition. According to his son, in June 1896 he had a dream that "the floor of my house at its southwest corner was sunken." He "examined it and observed that the deficiency existed all along the edge of [it]." As he related, "I found the sill entirely rotted about the corner and the studding without any support. I cleaned out the rotted wood and found the foundation entirely good." When he awoke, he realized "the southwest corner represented Kansas" and "the House represented the Church." When he presented the dream and his interpretation of it to the conference in the summer of 1896, Alexander Cherry offered his concurrence in tongues and John Grimes added that this probably explained why he had heard the words while lying in bed, "We are true men." In his view, this was confirmation of Cadman's dream and a repudiation of the Kansas Saints.[28] It appears that Cadman did not consider whether the dream also verified the importance of the southwest foundation, only apparently the need to clear away the "rotted wood."

The dream made him feel resolute, not only in Pennsylvania but in competing in Indian Territory as well. He must have been encouraged when George Washington, an Indian who had once associated with Bickerton, converted to the Cadmanites in October 1897. A year later when Washington was ordained an elder in Monongahela City, someone spoke in tongues, interpreted to mean, "A chosen vessel to carry my Gospel to his people. I will be with him."[29] This not only confirmed

27. Martin and Mancini, "History of the Church," 173.
28. Ibid.; Cadman, *History of the Church of Jesus Christ*, 93.
29. Martin and Mancini, "History of the Church," 177, 179.

to the Cadmanites that they were right in supporting missionaries in Oklahoma, it assured them that they were the ones with authority to do so. They continued to delay their expedition while they formulated plans, and during that time Bickerton made two more trips to Oklahoma, totaling four since 1880. He paid little attention to Cadman's threat of competition while he enjoyed an additional four months with the Indians.[30]

His most cherished memories came from that time and place. "The greatest power I felt while on mission to the red man was in a little village named Shatts. I circulated ten pamphlets of David Whitmer's letter,[31] gave one to the Chief Judge of [the] Cherokee tribe and some to some Indian store-keepers." The Indians spoke of their desire for self-rule. "They said they were waiting for the Lord to deliver them," he wrote. "They were splendid men and spoke with tears in their eyes. They were getting weak in the faith because the Lord had not interfered in their behalf." Bickerton told them they were descendants of the Israelite tribe of Joseph and his son Manasseh. He was quick to point out the distinction between his church and the Mormons. "The red man is thoroughly convinced that he is the chosen people of God," Bickerton remarked, "but the Salt Lake Mormons have no foothold there as the red man will not go near them."

"I traveled two hundred miles to cotton creek to reach the home of Brother [Silas] Busby," he continued, "and we had a glorious meeting there upon my arrival, and many were brought in" the church. "We held meetings in different parts of that country, and I never felt more of the power than while preaching the gospel of Christ in that country." There "were several white people baptized in the Indian nation who had gone to Oklahoma." One European American named

30. *St. John County Capital*, May 7, 1897; *St. John County Capital*, Feb. 18, 1898.

31. *An Address to All Believers in Christ: By A Witness to the Divine Authenticity of the Book of Mormon*, 1887. Bickerton no doubt passed out Whitmer's pamphlet in Oklahoma because Whitmer agreed that the Choice Seer was not Joseph Smith, but rather an American Indian Moses who would rise up and help convince the Native Americans of their Israelite heritage, 84–88.

Smith "was a member of a quaker church, and they do not believe in baptism [or the] Lord's supper, and not much of anything else, but he went to Brother [William] Binghams meetings … and he was convinced of the gospel, but would not submit to baptism." Several times he felt the Holy Spirit and "resisted" it until he "went home [and] became completely paralyzed." Stunned, he called for Elder Bingham "to come and baptize him." Four men carried the 200-pound man into the water. "They got a wagon and took out the endgate and backed it to the door [of his house]. They put him in, and when they reached the water, several helped to carry him" to the stream. Emerging out of the water, "he was made strong and well, and spoke in the gift of tongues." Soon he was ordained an elder.[32]

Although Bickerton was in his twilight years, he continued to trudge through miles of harsh landscape to preach. One time, he said, "I had two meetings twelve miles apart. There were many streams to cross, and you may know I had hard struggles, for I had to take off parts of my clothes to cross." After wading half naked through water on this occasion, a herd of Texas cattle stampeded behind him. "I thought they would put an end to me," he said, "but the Lord was with me," so that the cattle turned at the last moment and avoided trampling him. While he was "in the Indian nation … four different times, about twenty-five Indians were baptized," he related.[33]

When he returned to St. John, he and his followers established another visible foothold in town. Since 1882 they had been without a permanent meetinghouse. Unable to purchase their original plot now occupied by the Utah Mormons, they collected enough money to buy another plot on West Second Street. In 1899 they completed a small, wood-frame structure on the property, and even though it was not dedicated with the fanfare the Mormons had arranged for the dedication of their building, it indicated that the Bickerton faction intended to stay in Kansas. It was still the founder's conviction that this community

32. Bickerton, "Testimony, June 1903," 4–7.

33. Ibid., 4, 6.

would be the zionic headquarters for other communities extending throughout Oklahoma.[34]

Meanwhile, Cadman sought to validate his recent entrance into Indian Territory by publishing a new pamphlet in 1899 with the title, *Religious Experiences and Expectations.* In it he related some of the church's history and revelations regarding Indians, as well as why God had called his church above all others to preach in Oklahoma. Less nuanced than the title, the pamphlet avowed that Cadman's church "had the Gospel purer than any other people," and that "our glorious God proclaims our superiority (by divine revelation) as compared with all other Latter Day Saints."[35] God had called them to Oklahoma to finish what Bickerton started in Kansas. Bickerton's first mistake was theological, Cadman asserted. At the July 1874 conference, Bickerton had preached "that we were Israel, and that the covenants made to Israel were ours. I had a very distinct and powerful operation of the Spirit of God that morning; 'that we were not Israel … and that we would not be incorporated with Israel until we had carried the Gospel to Israel.'" If Bickerton on that occasion emphasized anything other than that European Americans were gentiles and the Indians were a lost tribe of Israel, it would have been out of character. Usually he preached that the gentiles would take the gospel to the Indians and that when the time came the Indians would take over from there. The gentiles could be adopted into the House of Israel, Bickerton sometimes mentioned.

"I do not mention this matter for the purpose of reproaching William Bickerton," Cadman wrote, "but for the purpose of correcting an error, which evidently has been with latter day saints from the beginning in all their schemes of gathering. They have been encouraging themselves by the promises made to Israel, under the covenants, and have neglected the first step in that direction, which is preaching the Gospel to the seed of Jacob."[36] In saying this, he left out a few details,

34. Entz, "Bickertonites," 39–40; *St. John County Capital,* May 7, 1897; Feb. 18, 1898.
35. Cadman, *Religious Experiences and Expectations,* 11–12.
36. Ibid., 8.

such as that the greater part of Bickerton's ministry had been devoted to gaining a foothold in Kansas, from which to launch a mission into Indian Territory, and that Cadman himself had written to Bickerton in 1876 assuring him "that you can depend upon this branch [West Elizabeth] to sustain the original position of the gathering [to Kansas]; and, also, to raise considerable of a Spring emigration."[37]

Cadman criticized other things Bickerton had done. Traveling by train to Kansas in 1874, Bickerton had spoken with three Choctaw Indians who wanted him to accompany them to the Choctaw Nation. Bickerton declined, saying that once his people "got moved and fixed up a little, they would come right down into their country and preach the Gospel to them." As Cadman explained, "I have long since concluded that this was the error of the Kansas affair; placing the temporal before the spiritual." The greatest impediment to the Indian mission had actually been the contention between the two factions. But in Cadman's mind, the church was

> similar to the ancient Israelites. They approached the borders of the land; became frightened through their blind unbelief, and were driven back into the wilderness forty years, until all the unworthy unbelievers were dead. Our period in the wilderness has only been thirty years; wandering hither and thither, vainly searching for a resting place; in every case disappointed; evidently because we were not seeking this favor and blessing within the channel the Almighty promised to bestow it.[38]

For all the talk of finishing the work Bickerton had failed to complete, the pamphlet had little to say about any progress from the Cadman faction in Oklahoma.

The movement Bickerton founded remained splintered as the churches stood on the cusp of the twentieth century. The founder had twice attempted to reconcile with his former friend, but Cadman would not hear of it. The reunion of the branches in St. John had gone smoothly. All Bickerton required was a simple oath affirming a

37. Cadman, *History of the Church*, 74–75; Cadman, *Great Bend Register*, Sept. 21, 1876.
38. Cadman, *Religious Experiences and Expectations*, 9–11.

foundational principle for the former dissidents to be accepted back into the fold. Sometime after mid-1886, Arthur Bickerton joined the RLDS Church and stayed until July 1898, then joined the Cadman church. His affiliation did not dampen his enthusiasm for his brother's spiritual authority, though, and he told a conference in April 1899 he believed his brother would one day receive the sealed portion of the Book of Mormon. He went on to endorse the idea of reconciling the two factions. Cadman "condemned" him for suggesting such a thing. Bickerton was the problem. Bickerton needed to repent and reconcile himself to the church, Cadman said. He asserted that the angel Moroni would not be giving Bickerton the sealed record, and the church had "to be very careful in the future if we would avoid the errors we fell into [in] the past."[39] If any prophecies were to be fulfilled, they would be fulfilled by Cadman and his followers, he believed. If there were to be a reconciliation, Bickerton would have to give up the church presidency, relinquish his role as prophet, and accept Cadman's leadership. In other words, Bickerton would have to swallow his pride if he wanted to preserve his legacy. Eventually the aging seer would realize it was the only medicine that would keep the church intact.

39. Cadman, *History of the Church of Jesus Christ*, 94–95; Martin and Mancini, "History of the Church," 178–80.

FOURTEEN

RECONCILIATION

1900–05

"I feel like Job[,] that the balance of my life I will wait until my change [death and resurrection] comes."

—Jan. 20, 1905

William Bickerton's brother Arthur was not the only one in Cadman's faction who wanted the church to reunite. In July 1900 some of Cadman's followers expressed at their conference "that we are not satisfied with the disorganized condition of the Church."[1] It was twenty years since the adultery scandal, and people had grown tired of the power struggle to the point that the ministry convinced Cadman to travel to St. John to meet with Bickerton. He did so, meeting privately with the prophet and with a council of Bickerton's followers to try to jump-start his own church's Indian mission.

It is unknown what the two leaders said to each other, only that when Cadman returned, he informed the October conference that his trip had been unsuccessful, that Bickerton was "as yet standing aloof from the Church." He had made some inroads among Bickerton's followers, however, who in fact "wished to unite with us."[2] What the members actually wanted was for their leaders to come together, while realizing that Cadman, nearly two decades younger than Bickerton, was more likely to carry the church into the future. There was too much bad blood between the men for either one to yield. For Cadman

1. Martin and Mancini, "History of the Church," 182.
2. Ibid.; Cadman, *History of the Church of Jesus Christ*, 95.

to relinquish the presidency would be to acknowledge that he had mistreated the founder, and for the founder to submit would be to say that Cadman had been right about the adultery charge. Despite their complicated relationship and cold rendezvous, Cadman had at least reached out, and in doing so had gotten to know what his rival's followers were thinking. It would be among the adherents of Bickerton that the first real steps toward reconciliation would be made.

What they decided to do was join Cadman's church on his terms, although without repudiating the founder's legacy. They agreed "that hereafter we will endever to conduct ourselves, and this branch of the Church of Jesus Christ, in accordance with the principals of righteousness, the laws of the Church and of God."[3] It would take some time, but the eighty-five-year-old Bickerton could not hold out much longer, and with his adherents defecting to Cadman, his entire legacy was at stake. He would have to decide between his pride and the church, and it was the latter that tugged more at his heart.

Cadman saw himself as more competent with a better education and business background. He was surprised when he arrived in America in 1856 to be drawn to a backwater denomination, but was so touched by the spirit he felt in Bickerton's presence and by the rationality of the prophet's theological positions that he could not resist. At the January 1902 conference, the ministry asked Cadman to write about marriage addressing especially divorce, adultery, and polygamy. When *Faith and Doctrines of the Church of Jesus Christ* was published, it had a broader scope, with a reminiscence of his early life and first contact with the church prior to his conversion. He included his earliest unfavorable impressions of Bickerton. He thought then, as he did now, that Bickerton was an incompetent administrator. For instance, Cadman asked him what should be done about an immigrant convert who was "imposing" on local members. Cadman framed the question in a scriptural context, quoting Proverbs 25:17, "Withdraw thy foot from thy neighbor's house; lest he be weary of thee, and so hate thee."

3. Martin and Mancini, "History of the Church," 182–83.

Bickerton's breezy response was, "Oh, our people are very kind." This vacuous answer upset Cadman. "I knew that they were kind, which was the reason I despised his [the immigrant's] conduct so intensely in taking advantage of their kindness." Cadman told Bickerton it was his "duty to correct this man," but the church president apparently felt he had more important concerns to address.[4]

At a time when the members of both factions were on the verge of reuniting, Cadman was quick to remind them of other incidents in the past illustrating Bickerton's weaknesses as a leader. For a July 1902 celebration of the fortieth anniversary of the church's founding, Cadman's followers had asked their leader to write a brief history, but when the summer conference arrived he had not written anything. He instead "made some remarks about things that transpired years ago that was not very pleasant History."[5] A problem for Cadman was that the early history was all about Bickerton, and instead of complimenting the deposed leader's accomplishments during that period, he reinforced the idea that the founder was an apostate.

As open as he was to reunification, Cadman believed he was not the one who needed to compromise, especially with Bickerton growing older and more frail. Bickerton's brother Arthur died in 1901, and William himself was eighty-seven. The thing to do, Cadman resolved, was to send a friendlier face to St. John, and he settled on the fifty-year-old Alexander Cherry, a former apostle in Bickerton's administration, and armed him with a concrete proposal.[6] Cherry met with the founder and suggested that he resign, renounce his prophetic office, and submit to Cadman's leadership. In turn, "the past would be forgiven, and all would go heart and hand in the work of the Lord, and be subject to the Authority of the Church in all things." Worn down from years of contention, and pleased to see that the accusation of adultery would be erased from the record, Bickerton consented. His followers signed

4. Cadman, *Faith and Doctrines*, 2:12.
5. Martin and Mancini, "History of the Church," 186.
6. Ibid., 188; Cadman, *History of the Church of Jesus Christ*, 96–97.

a resolution stipulating the terms. In November they transferred the church's assets to Pennsylvania. Bickerton settled into his new position as a common elder.[7] Twenty-two years of heartache had transpired, so it must have felt good to put the unpleasantness behind him, although it probably also left a bittersweet taste in the mouth.

In fact, before long, the bitterness overwhelmed the sweetness. In the beginning everything went smoothly. In January 1903, Bickerton was named presiding elder of the St. John branch. He was soon invited to attend the July conference as a delegate. But when the summer arrived and he was not feeling up to a long trip, he decided to recite a short history of his life to a friend, who transcribed it for him, and send a copy of it to the summer conference to be read and considered for publication as a church tract.[8] He admitted in his narrative that he had been premature in thinking the Second Advent would come on the heels of the Civil War. He conceded that he had been wrong to think he would be the one to translate the sealed portion of the Book of Mormon. "We have learned since [then] that the Indians would not be brought in until the work of the Father commences," he said. Still, he would continue his mission to the Indians and "intend[ed] to go to Oklahoma this fall, if the Lord permits."[9]

He found himself in the same predicament as Christ's original followers, who thought the Savior would return within their lifetimes. The gospel writer John declared in the first century that it was "the last time" they would experience persecution before Christ's return. The apostle Peter thought "the end of all things is at hand," as did Paul, who wrote that "the time is short" (1 John 2:18; 1 Peter 4:7; 1 Cor. 7:29). All Bickerton could say was that he had done his "best for the work of God, and with God's help, I will so continue in the future."[10] He had thus confessed what he considered to be his faults, but Cadman could not

7. Martin and Mancini, "History of the Church," 189; Cadman, *History of the Church of Jesus Christ*, 98.

8. Martin and Mancini, 189; Cadman, 98; Bickerton, "Testimony, June 1903," 1, 14.

9. Bickerton, 4, 6.

10. Ibid., 14.

see in the account even the slightest acknowledgment of moral transgression or apostasy, Bickerton portraying his life and the history of the church as an unbroken continuum, without mentioning the rift. Cadman assumed the founder had returned to the church as a penitent. That was not how Bickerton saw it. In his view, he had carried on the work of God unabated while being persecuted on all sides. Bickerton had thought that with reconciliation "the past would be forgiven," the challenge to his good name and membership in the church written out of the history. He made this disclaimer: "Don't think I am trying to throw any reflections on any one, as I am only trying to give you all a brief sketch of my own experience with God, feeling the blessing in doing so, not knowing whether or not it will be acceptable to all." It was his way of trying to place any controversy aside. As the "organizer of this Church," he wrote, "it is only right to present to you the history."[11]

When the conference secretary in Pennsylvania read the manuscript out loud to the assembled branch representatives on July 4, 1903, an animated discussion ensued. Apparently some of the ministry objected to having the history read at all or considered it wholly inappropriate to publish. Unable to reach an agreement in the morning session, they decided when they reconvened at 7:00 p.m. to endorse the portion that dealt with Bickerton's life and ministry up to 1880, "so far as he was a member in good standing in the Church," and reject the portion of the autobiography having to do with Bickerton's post-1880 activities. However, if they thought this would satisfy all sides, it upset Bickerton. Apparently all had not been forgiven and forgotten, he realized. He saw in this that Cadman had won a decisive battle for control of the church's narrative, and that he would be portrayed as a prodigal son who had sinned and remained out of fellowship until he repented years later and returned to the fold. The vote of the conference of 1903 was a vote to rewrite history.[12]

---

11. Martin and Mancini, "History of the Church," 189; Bickerton, "Testimony, June 1903," 13–14.

12. Martin and Mancini, 190; Cadman, *History of the Church of Jesus Christ*, 99. The way Bickerton felt might be summed up by his request that Job 19 be read at his funeral.

Cadman tried to move on, while Bickerton continued to feel betrayed. During the years of scuffling, Cadman had left some of the church offices vacant, indicating that on some level he did not yet feel commissioned to assume the role of naming men to high office. At the conference of January 1904, when the ministry suggested they fill up the Quorum of the Twelve, he opened the floor to nominations and let the ministry propose candidates. They elected eleven men on that occasion: J. L. Armbrust, William H. Cadman (William Cadman's son), Marion Campbell, Alexander Cherry, Thomas Dixon, William Lynch, W. T. Maxwell, James Skillen, Thornton Welch, John Williams, and Allen Wright. Someone in the congregation spoke in tongues and Thomas Sloan interpreted it to mean, "Verily, thus Saith the Lord. this is my work, this is my will."[13]

In July, Cadman ordained the men, beginning with Cherry, and then Cherry assisted him in ordaining the other new apostles. It was decided to keep the church presidency within the quorum, something Cadman had been thinking about since 1900 when he began to express doubts that there should be two competing quorums at the top of the church hierarchy. Now in the current structure, Cadman and his two counselors, Cherry and Wright, would remain in the Quorum of Twelve Apostles.[14]

Bickerton may have been pushed to the sidelines, but his rival continued to see him as a threat who was capable at any moment of disrupting the church. The antagonism was contained but still evident enough that the ministry felt it needed to present a motion for "Bro. Cadman, and all saints [to] be declared out of order when bringing up past difficulties in the Church."[15] If there had not been peacemakers within the ranks who refused to allow the animosity to be expressed openly, the fragile peace was apt to have crumbled.

13. Martin and Mancini, 191–92.

14. Ibid., 182; Cadman, *History of the Church of Jesus Christ*, 99–103. In July 1908 the hierarchy would be reorganized again, with the presidency standing outside of the Quorum of Twelve Apostles; see Cadman, 119.

15. Martin and Mancini, "History of the Church," 192.

For his ninetieth birthday, Bickerton wrote a reminiscence for the *St. John Weekly News* reminding readers that his people were "not Mormons" but "Stafford County Saints, who have come here from Pennsylvania, West Virginia, Ohio and Eastern Kansas." He expressed gratitude to the people of Kansas for their hospitality: "We love the people of Kansas and especially those of St. John as they have never interfered with our view of christianity." He once more related the central concept of the Book of Mormon, that the Indians came from "a colony of Israel [that] came to this country from Jerusalem about 600 years before Christ was born." He said he was pleased to see that his birthday in 1905 was on a Sunday, as had been the recent Christmas and New Year's, which he found "very peculiar and showed that there is an order in it." It was God's way of indicating that he had fulfilled a divine purpose. At ninety, he might well be forgiven this bit of self-indulgence. He was still aware that people were skeptical of his spiritual authority. It made him "feel like Job[,] that the balance of my life I will wait until my change [death and resurrection] comes." He was ready to go, however, having lived a full life, with "no enemy that I know of, and only pity the poor souls that do not believe in christianity." His identification with the Old Testament luminary Job was part persecution complex and part realization that life is hard and one's convictions will be tested. Job lost everything and had everything restored to him, "twice as much as he had before" (Job 42:10). Bickerton lost not only material goods, but also his reputation, and that was something that, try as he may, he could not recover fully. Unlike Job, he felt an anguish that only death could remedy.[16]

It came sooner than anyone would have guessed. On a cold February night, Bickerton took a heated stone and placed it at the bottom of his bed to keep his feet warm. By morning it had ignited the bed and produced a blazing fire that the volunteer fire department extinguished, saving Bickerton and his home. As the *St. John Weekly News* reported, "the shock was almost too much for [Bickerton] and … he

16. "Elder Bickerton Writes," *St. John Weekly News*, Jan. 20, 1905.

is in a very feeble condition." A few days later, on February 17, 1905, he died in the home of his friend, apostle Allen Wright, who had taken him in to convalesce. "'Uncle Billie' Bickerton is dead," a journalist commented, "called to His Long Rest." Allen Wright conducted the funeral the following Sunday.[17]

Bickerton died with his reputation in disrepair. He had stayed quiet when the church discreetly tucked away his autobiography. While still alive, his cries for redress had been muffled by rivals. He uttered a *cri de coeur* from the grave by requesting that the nineteenth chapter of Job be read at his funeral. His kindred spirit, the "gentile prophet" from the Land of Uz (Job 1:1), conveyed his own feeling of betrayal as well as any Jewish prophet in the Bible could have expressed it:

> How long will ye vex my soul, and break me in pieces with words? These ten times have ye reproached me: ye are not ashamed that ye make yourselves strange to me. And be it indeed that I have erred, mine error remaineth with myself. If indeed ye will magnify yourselves against me, and plead against me my reproach: Know now that God hath overthrown me, and hath compassed me with his net. Behold, I cry out of wrong, but I am not heard: I cry aloud, but there is no judgment. He hath fenced up my way that I cannot pass, and he hath set darkness in my paths. He hath stripped me of my glory, and taken the crown from my head. He hath destroyed me on every side, and I am gone: and mine hope hath he removed like a tree. … He hath put my brethren far from me, and mine acquaintance are verily estranged from me. My kinsfolk have failed, and my familiar friends have forgotten me. They that dwell in mine house, and my maids, count me for a stranger: I am an alien in their sight. I called my servant, and he gave me no answer; I intreated him with my mouth. My breath is strange to my wife, though I intreated for the children's sake of mine own body. Yea, young children despised me; I arose, and they spake against me. All my inward friends abhorred me: and they whom I loved are turned against me.

17. "A Small Blaze," *St. John Weekly News*, Feb. 17, 1905; "Wm. Bickerton," *St. John County Capital*, Feb. 23, 1905; "A Pioneer Gone," *St. John Weekly News*, Feb. 24, 1905.

Like Job, Bickerton had pleaded for judgment and was unable to receive a satisfactory verdict. He had lost his glory in the eyes of his friends and wife, who had abandoned him. He was despised by those who had once esteemed him a prophet. Nevertheless, he felt touched by God for a greater purpose:

> Have pity upon me, have pity upon me, O ye my friends; for the hand of God hath touched me. Why do ye persecute me ... and are not satisfied with my flesh? Oh that my words were now written! oh that they were printed in a book! That they were graven with an iron pen and lead in the rock for ever! For I know that my redeemer liveth, and that he shall stand at the latter day upon the earth: And though after my skin worms destroy this body, yet in my flesh shall I see God: Whom I shall see for myself, and mine eyes shall behold, and not another; though my reins be consumed within me.

Those final words of Job's lamentation were Bickerton's last testimony, indicating his steadfastness in belief despite having been ridiculed and accused. The seemingly shallow charge that he had betrayed his calling had interfered with his ability to perform his mission, and that had frustrated him more than anything else. The injustices remained, and he had received not so much as a warm greeting from his former friends, let alone an apology. He had been wronged by men he had led by the hand. When they had the chance, they had not given him the benefit of the doubt, but took the opportunity to ridicule him. He carried on, believing it would be sorted out on the other side of the veil. When the trumpet sounded and he was vindicated, he believed, he would spend a thousand years in Zion with his Indian friends and converted Jews and gentiles who had proven themselves worthy, black elders, and female deaconesses. All these would live under the watchful eye of Christ after he descended through the sky to the Mount of Olives and assumed his throne in the New Jerusalem.

EPILOGUE

The William Bickerton headstone at Fairview Park Cemetery reads, "Dear father rest in peace." That is the reward for a man who repeatedly sacrificed his own tranquility for the common good—the respect of his children at least. The day he died, another church leader passed: John Williams, an apostle who had been loyal to Cadman. Indicating the peace that now reigned in the church, apostles J. L. Armbrust and W. T. Maxwell composed notes of sympathy for both families. Nine months later, William Cadman died at seventy-one years of age, having led the reunited church for three years.[1] Almost as soon as the factions had reconciled, Bickerton and Cadman both went to their graves, ushering in a new era for those left to carry the church forward.

As a testament to the founder's choice to place the health of the institution above his own well-being, the Church of Jesus Christ continues today, more than a century and a half after its founding, with over 22,000 members in twenty-three countries.[2] In Greensburg, Pennsylvania, seventeen miles east of Greenock (formerly Green Oak),

1. Martin and Mancini, "History of the Church," 198; Cadman, *History of the Church of Jesus Christ*, 103–04. "A paralytic stroke received some time ago hastened his death" on November 6, 1905, Cadman's obituary reported. Alexander Cherry conducted the funeral service. Interestingly, he read verses 23–24 of Job 19, part of the same passage read at Bickerton's funeral: "Oh that my words were now written! oh that they were printed in a book! That they were graven with an iron pen and lead in the rock for ever!" According to the obituary, "As our departed brother's remains lay peacefully in full view, the calm countenance seemed to say that were he still alive he would write of the Lord's greatness and goodness and have his excellencies graven, as it were, in the hearts and lives of his brothers and sisters." "To His Reward," *Gospel Reflector*, Dec. 1905.

2. Paul Palmieri, "150-Year Anniversary of the Church of Jesus Christ," *Gospel News*, Oct. 2012, 3; church records, Dec. 31, 2015, www.ripsystem.org.

the World Operations Center is an impressive complex. The mystery and controversy surrounding the founder may remain, for some, a blemish on the memory of the church's history, but they are no longer issues that divide the members.

The attempt to distance the church from its founder was unsuccessful; the prophet's memory remains alive in the popular nickname *Bickertonites*. In addition, the priesthood authority in the church is derived from the founder's vision of the mountain and chasm: "I was on the highest mountain on the earth: [God] told me if I did not preach the Gospel, I would fall into a dreadful chasm below, the sight there was awful."[3] Bickerton was the only man who could build up God's kingdom on earth, the vision revealed.

Sometime before his death, Bickerton summed up why he had accepted the gospel as taught by Joseph Smith: "I was a miner all my life and never had any chance of learning or never was at school. During all this time I belonged to the Methodist church, up to 1845 when I went to Limetown, Washington county, Pa., to hear the Saints preach. As soon as I went in amongst them I found that they had more [enlightenment] than I had, and I wanted to have all that the Gospel promised."[4] He spent the balance of his life teaching his followers they could receive the full power of the Holy Ghost. They could prophesy, speak in tongues, see visions, and interpret dreams. He himself led the church through his visionary power and revelations of God's word as a prophet among prophets, encouraging others to develop the same spiritual gifts; and he judged his rivals by the same standard.

Zion Valley became the quiet town of St. John, Kansas. There is little to indicate that the first settlers envisioned it as a future millennial capital. Occasionally believers visit Bickerton's grave to pay their respects, but of the sixty-seven Bickertonite congregations in the United States, only a few members reside in St. John or even in Kansas. In the 1990s the presiding elder in Kansas, Alexander Robinson, placed

3. Bickerton, *Ensign*, 5.
4. "A Pioneer Gone," *St. John Weekly News*, Feb. 24, 1905.

a memorial next to the grave—a lectern and book, open like a pulpit Bible, with the engraved words, *Successor to Joseph Smith. Noble, visionary, generous, forgiving. All speak of him. He walked with God.* For members of Bickerton's church, it has been an appropriate epitaph.

APPENDIX

TESTIMONY OF WILLIAM BICKERTON

1903

Bickerton sent this autobiographical reminiscence to the conference in Pennsylvania in the summer of 1903. If he had appeared in person, he would have had to travel 1,100 miles, and at eighty-eight years of age he was not feeling up to it. The church quietly tucked away the document, and it has never been published. To preserve its historical integrity, I have retained the idiosyncrasies of original spelling, grammar, and small factual mistakes, but also silently corrected major misspellings to facilitate comprehension.

St. John, Kansas
June 1903

My beloved in Christ, I herewith hand you a history of my life from the time I came into the Church of Jesus Christ; or in other words, since I obeyed the gospel down in to the present day, I hope this will be read in the General Conference. I was baptized under the orginization of Sidney Rigdon in June 1845. I was confirmed, received the Holy Ghost by the laying on of hands, and was ordained an Elder shortly afterwards and set apart by washing and onnointing. I was ordained into the seventies, and also ordained prophet, priest and king.

I can testify that Sidney Rigdon had the power of God. He was the right hand councelor of Joseph Smith and Brigham Young. The rest of the twelve rejected him and they had no president for eight months. Sidney

Rigdon was the best orator I have ever heard in classing the scriptures together. He went wrong after he came to Pittsburgh, wanting to make a gathering in the Emlenton Valley of the Allegheny Mountains.[1]

At this same time we organized a school of the prophets, or solemn assemblies, and many things were revealed to us, showing things were going wrong. No one followed Sidney Rigdon from that Branch, because we knew by the spirit that he was going wrong. He sent two of his apostles to stop our assembly of the school of the prophets. The object of the school of prophets was to learn the young Elders to know the teachings of the spirit; and many things were revealed that came to pass. After Rigdon went wrong all that followed him fell away, and I was left alone, seeking to know what course to pursue. My house was a resting place for many of those who had followed Sidney Rigdon. At that time I was a boss in a coal mine. I had great understanding of the Latter-Day Saint doctrines. At this time Rigdon published a paper in Pittsburgh called the "Messenger and Advocate." We appointed a committee of five to expose the false doctrines of Brigham Young, P. P. Pratte, and Orson Pratt. In their paper it was published that a woman had no eternal salvation unless she had a husband; and they appointed Mothers in Israel to teach young women to be married in the Priesthood; and they succeeded in their undertaking to a great extent. Thus, I had had a good chance to see where they took advantage of the gospel in its purity. I had a chance to get acquainted with some of the Danite Band. The mountain meadow massacre was committed by, or through these false teachers of my acquaintance, as the Elders from that time, on down to the present, must obey the orders of their superior officers.

Because I lived true to God and his interests, I was carried away in the spirit and placed on a high mountain with just room enough for me to stand. The Lord told me unless I would go ahead and preach the gospel, I would fall and be torn into bits. I moved with fear, having no education, and having the Salt Lake mormons in the way. I was left alone. I held outdoor meetings sometimes in the market place,

1. He meant the Cumberland Valley.

sometime in public houses, on streets or any other available place. The first meeting I held was beside the ferry, at a store house door. A lady passing at the time, testified to the gospel, and was baptized in McKeesport. I held these outdoor meetings and many were convinced, and several were baptized. I then went to Allegheny City, had good meetings there, also had a church there. I baptized a family, on the hills opposite Pittsburgh, and also baptized a good many at Six-Mile Ferry; and had a good many members at Pine Run.

In 1861, when the war began, the Utah people sent missionaries out and scared a good many away to Salt Lake City. At the same time we had Conference within a half mile of the Salt Lake people's Conference. We had no apostles at that time, but in that Conference the Lord revealed to us that He accepted this Church as the Church of Alma. Thirty people stood up and testified to the revelation. Alma never received any ordination; and while King Noah was establishing a "many wife doctrine," Alma was forced to flee before King Noah. King Noah wrote down what Abinadi had to preach. Alma fled to a thicket of timbers, and there was what they called the Waters of Mormon. About two hundred followed him, and Alma asked them if they had any objections to being baptized. They clapped their hands, declaring that was just what they wanted. Alma and Heleman went into the water, and Alma declared he had the authority from God to baptize, and they both went down under the water; and were filled with the Holy Ghost. And they took all and baptized them, having received the authority from God.

I wish to give a short sketch of the gathering of the saints. I did not want to come myself, feeling weak in the line of education, but I was always willing to do what God had for me to do. While I was in Brother Arthur Bickerton's house in Wheeling, West Virginia, I looked at the map of Kansas, and was directed to Stafford County, Kansas. On returning home, there was a wonderful gathering in the meeting house at West Elizabeth, and my wife and her sister went through the house shouting and praising God, giving the word of the Lord that I had done what the Lord had required of me. Twenty thousand dollars was subscribed to move a colony of saints west. I set my name to six thousand dollars of my own money, and they were to back us up, here in this country, until we would be able to make our own living. I sold some of my property and mortgaged the rest. William Cadman was with me and helped me to sell and mortgage my property, but when it came to selling properties, none but myself, Brothers Charles Brown, and Arthur and Alex Bickerton would sell. The following spring I came my way of Eastern Kansas, bought thirteen yoke of oxen, ready for work, two wagons, and one team of horses. We did not get the oxen untill May 17, 1875. I reserved one hundred dollars only, the balance I shared with the brethren. Every two families had two yoke of oxen and a plow, and I shared with all, all being on a common level. Many of the Eastern Kansas brethren had teams and some cattle. Five teams landed here on the third of April, 1875. Each yoke of cattle broke about seventy acres of land the first season. The balance of the people that would not sell their property stayed in Pennsylvania in different places.

Brother William Cadman began building a boarding house at Elizabeth, while we were on our journey west, to show his faith in the work. I had three houses that had not yet been sold, so I appointed a committee to sell the remainder of my property and give it to the Church, thus I carried out what we read about, having all things common. James Louthet declared he would never come to this place and live in a cellar or cave in the ground as we did in early days, and he almost lost all of his family. This, several Brothers and Sisters professed, was a judgement of God sent on him. Some did not like the locality, and this divided the Church. I went to West Virginia, and the people there reported we were going to start another Salt Lake Church.

Eli Kendall gave the word of the Lord that these people would not do as they had done. Eli Kendall, his family, his father's family, and the Baker family came here. As I have said before, we had to support the Colony until they could support themselves, and by the 28th day of June we had run out of flour. I had nineteen dollars to get provisions for all, so I went back to Pennsylvania and told them I would no longer be responsible for the support of the Colony. I gave up my position as president of the colony, and they appointed William McDonald in my place.

I took back with me a sample of the products of Kansas. They had a conference at this time at Coultersville, so I put the samples in the pulpet to show. At this time two brethren came from the east and made a change in the conducting of the Colony. The conditions were that each family turn in all the products they had raised, and the Superintendent was to deal out what it would take to keep each family. This would have brought endless trouble, which never would be settled. At the same time we had seventy head of cattle brought by the Brethren from eastern Kansas, and Cherry hearded them. William McDonald came the second time and sold all the cattle at auction. Each person got a share. I, myself, got a couple of shares. This was just about the breaking of the Colony. Each family was forced to do the best it could, and had it not been for the buffalo bones at six dollars per ton, we would have experienced much hard times, and this was God's blessing to the saints in Kansas. I have been nearly frozen to death in the country, and have had to spend the winter burning corn stalks and buffalo chips. I have been in the Indian nation several months at a time four different times, delivering the Gospel to the red man. About twenty-five Indians were baptized. We have learned since that the Indians would not be brought in until the work of the Father commences. The greatest power I felt while on mission to the red man was in a little village named Shatts. I circulated ten pamphlets of David Whitmer's letter, gave one to the Chief Judge of the Cherokee tribe and some to some Indian store-keepers. They said they were waiting for the Lord to deliver them. They were splendid men and spoke with tears in their eyes. They were getting weak in the faith because the Lord had not interfered in their behalf. The red man is thoroughly convinced that he is the chosen people of God; but the Salt Lake Mormons have no foothold there as the red man will not go near them. I had the privelege to meet in a school house where they had an organ and an Indian Squaw played it during services. They were very prejudiced when I first began teaching the Book of Mormon; but by the time I had finished with my discourse, they were very kind, as the Lord worked upon them in his own way. Some asked me to dine with them. I showed them the Book of Mormon and told them it was their Father's Bible before them, and I showed them that their forefathers came from Jerusalem, and that they were the promised seed from that place.

I then went to where Brother Cadman and I had previously been to on this trip. I had left a pair of spectacles and a hymn book, and they had taken the best of care of them until my return. Their fathers and mothers were dead, but they were strong in the faith. Brother Busby and Brother Work were with me, and there was a couple who had an infant child sick. They thought there was no hope for the child, and the house was full of people. I went to the Mother and asked her if she had faith. She said she had, so I took the child in my arms, and Brother Busby annointed it, and I asked the blessing of God upon it, and the dear little one was healed. Everybody was astonished.

I returned back to where Brother Cadman and I had been years before in some colored folks house, and we all felt that we had never spent a better day in the work of the Lord. We baptized three, and I believe if we had made our mission to the colored race instead of the red man, we would have had better success. I speak positively by the operation of the Holy Ghost. As I was the senior of the three, I went officially to Downing, the Chief of the Cherokee tribe, but he refused to receive us as God's people on mission to the red man. I saw a black cloud come between him and me, which gave me to understand that when the time does come, we shall speak their own language. I do not believe in sectarian interpretation. God's way is perfect, for that was my faith that we should speak the Indian language. At that moment I felt as if I had run against a rock. I then returned to Chief Naze and presented the Book of Mormon to him, and showed him the witnesses to it. He was a gentleman, fairly well educated, and he did not make any objections to the book. We took dinner with him. It was very rough weather, late in autumn, and we gave out an appointment for Sunday at a little Indian school house. We had no shelter, but the Lord opened the way, and sent a man to invite us to his house. We remained there for several weeks. The Indians have the life of General Lee, which has caused them to become cold towards the mormons, as they called us.[2] We had a meeting with a crowded house, whites, and Indians, some of whom had been in the Union army. I stayed there after Brother Work and Brother Busby had gone home, and I got quite well acquainted with the Indians in that locality. One large family of Indians I tought to say the Lord's prayer and sing the hymn, "Oh, stop and tell the red man," and I rejoiced in the spirit to look upon their red faces. I helped them the next fall in their cotton gathering. Cotton is a fine plant, and it is delightful to see the red man in his toils, knowing he is of the chosen race. I had two meetings twelve miles apart. There were many streams to cross, and you may know I had hard struggles, for I had to take off part of my clothes to cross, but the Lord never forsakes his own. I had to travel through a large herd of Texas cattle, and I thought they would put an end to me, but the Lord was with me, so I now finish up on this mission.

I traveled two hundred miles to cotton creek to reach the home of Brother Busby, and we had a glorious meeting there upon my arrival, and many were brought in. We held meetings in different parts of that country, and I never felt more of the power than while preaching the gospel of Christ in that country. Afterwards I came to Kansas, and held meeting in Montgomery County. There were several white people baptized in the Indian nation who had gone to Oklahoma, and we also have members in the new addition to Oklahoma. We have two Elders in this new addition, Brother Bingham and Brother Smith. They hold meetings every Sabbath, and the writer of this article and myself, intends to go to Oklahoma this fall, if the Lord permits, for we have saints there who are strong in the faith. I wish to speak further of Elder

2. In commanding the Confederate armies, Robert E. Lee, an Episcopalian, partnered with the Indian Cavalry Brigade led by General Stand Watie, who was also chief of the Cherokee Nation. The Bickertonites were mostly Yankees.

Smith. He was a member of a quaker church, and they do not believe in baptism, and Lord's supper, and not much of anything else, but he went to Brother Binghams meetings that he held in his own house, and he was convinced of the gospel, but would not submit to baptism. He resisted the spirit at several meetings, and when he went home he became completely paralyzed, so that he could not move. He was a man who weighed about two hundred pounds, so he sent for Brother Bingham to come and baptize him. He, and three others helped to carry him to the water. They got a wagon and took out the endgate and backed it to the door. They put him in, and when they reached the water, several helped to carry him in. When he came up out of the water, he was made strong and well, and spoke in the gift of tongues. This happened about five years ago. We had a visit from Brother Bingham recently, and he carries the blessing of God with him. We intend to organize another branch in the Brother Bingham's locality, for there are twenty-two members there.

We will now show the promises of God to the [ancient] Church of Philadelphia, that he has set before us an open door, that we might go in and out and find pasture, which has been fulfilled, and would give us the Key of David, which means the work of the Father. This is the only Church of the seven Churches of Asia which is now standing. In 1852 we held a Conference in my house, and there was a Bow of the glory of God in rainbow form that stood over me at that Conference. I felt by the Power of God that I was as a rock, and if a cannon ball would strike me it would not affect me, being protected by the Power of God, (Read John 1st Chapter 42nd verse.). About this time Orson Pratt went to Washington, and layed before congress the revelation of Plural marriage, and plurality of Gods, too, and as far as I can judge, he published this to show that this was their faith and salvation, and to show that the constitution of the United States allowed every man to serve God according to the dictates of his own self, so that they would not be molested by the government. Now you will see by this false revelation that they were rejected and that we were accepted, having the Keys of Peter. I called a meeting the same day I read Orson Pratt's pamphlet. There was a Latter Day Saint that was on his way to Nauvoo, but was delayed on account of the river freezing and did not reach his destination that winter. Several nights he heard singing in the air of the line of Zion, and he thought he would follow the sound to where it would lead him, and he traveled about one hundred miles, and he landed at my house. He did not know there was a Latter Day Saint anywhere near, only by the spirit. We could tell a great deal to show we were in the purposes of God, but it would take too much writing, but we feel the Power of God from moment to moment. We want to show we always had the Power of God in this Church.

There was a woman who had been confined to her bed for five years, and the last two years she was perfectly helpless. We carried her down to Peters Creek in her bed, and it took four of us to baptize her, and when we brought her up out of the water the blood flowed from her mouth. We carried her home, confirmed her a member of the Church and attended the ordinance on her, and she was healed sound and well. She also bore children afterwards. Brother Brown, who did not profess anything, told us he would give us credit for healing her. We have given you this statement to show you that God has acknowledged us as the Church of Alma. We oppose the Salt Lake people, just as Abinadi opposed King Noah. It will continue to be the Church until the Saviour comes again on the earth. I will now give you a vision I had of John the Baptist. It was not a dream, but a vision. There was a coffin without a lid appeared in my room, and I was in the spirit, and it was revealed to me that it was John, the Baptist. He was about six feet tall and he had a fine head of hair. There was a pair of scissors put into my hand, and I was to go around the bottom of his hair and clip it around the back of his neck. I went around with scissors, but did not clip any hair off. I lifted up his hair, and oiled and perfumed it. This was an open vision, and I can testify it was given by the Power of God. This is the end of the vision. I was very much concerned about it as I did not get the interpretation of it for about two weeks, but it was given in Sabbath meeting two weeks after.

It was that as John the Baptist was a forerunner of His first coming, so I should be a forerunner of HIS second coming. Five witnesses bore evidence to the truth of this, namely, William Bingham, Ellen Harris, David Lynch, Jannett Carduff, David Carduff, and myself, and it stands so on the church books. Testified: William Bickerton. When I awoke in the morning, I had a vision and revelation. I was carried away in spirit to Deliah Hawkins, who resided about three hundred yards from my house, and in a moment I was sitting in her house. Sister Glasscock and she were speaking about me in a spiritual way. Deliah said the Lord had called me to be a prophet, Seer, and revelator. They both sanctioned it. In a moment the holy ghost fell upon me there at my house, right on my breast, and I had never spoken to either of these sisters as to this calling. As to the truthfulness of it, I can lift my hand toward heaven and say it was given by the Power of God. I lost one of my eyes a few days after, and also had a hard spell of the grippe. I would likewise say that Brother Charles Brown in 1849, gave the word of the Lord, that I was to be a prophet to lead this people. He annointed me with oil, and this people should go in and out and find pasture.

When we landed in Parsons, Kansas, there was a good bit of fault found concerning me, claiming I had never fulfilled what I had promised. As you can see, I have been among the Indians three times, hunting for three Indians of my acquaintance of years ago, but could not find them. So now we will look upon church building for awhile. None of our church buildings were paid for when we dedicated them. We confess that was a fault of the church. It was decided to build the Greenock house a year before it was built, and the proposition was that each brother should lay it before the Lord to say what he should give to help erect the building. We were to work in a body, both Brothers and Sisters. My gift, or donation was two hundred dollars. A good many of the brethren were faithful, but when the time came to pay, there was a good many not faithful, and did not pay what they had promised. The money had to be paid to the builders. It was in war time, and as I was President of the Church, the Sheriff served papers on me, and

I was sued. We had dedicated the house before this, and because of war times, the builders would take nothing but gold, which made my subscription cost me four hundred dollars that I paid on the Greenock Church. About the Little-Red-Stone Church there was a mistake somewhere, as I was charged with building it with the consent of the Church as a body. I will refer to Brother William Bacon. We labored together and had a membership of eighty-four and had members in Troytown and various other places. I also refer to Frank Lederer, and many other brethren in your country. Where I have done wrong, I am willing to acknowledge it if shown to me. These two that I refer to will likely be in July Conference, and they can speak for me. We were to blame here in Kansas when we built the first church house, and dedicated it as soon as it was done, owing Brother Beitler $700. He got a Sheriff's deed and the house was closed on account of indebtedness. We will now speak of the Church I bought at West Elizabeth for our people. We had been meeting from house to house and many found fault and wished to have the meetings discontinued at private houses, and as there was a division at that time between the North and South, according to a revelation given by Joseph Smith, I inquired of the Lord if I should buy a house for a church, and while I was inquiring in the afternoon, I heard the song of "Home Sweet Home" being sung by voices not visible but far superior to human voices, and it brought such glorious blessings to me that I took it for granted that I was to stay in the East. I went the next day and purchased the house. I gave two hundred fifty dollars for the building. About this time I saw a vision of a table spread with no end to it as far as I could see, and I saw the saints feasting on all sides of the table, and all were rejoicing. I did not take notice where it was for looking at them. I drew my mind back and found myself sitting at the head of the table. That night I baptized three, and I never slept that night on account of the glory of God that I experienced, it lasting the whole night. I was feasting on heavenly food. No one knows without the experience. No tongue can express the peace and rest of a soul wrapt in Jesus' love.

Our Church house became too small for us to meet in, and there was a brick schoolhouse that became too small for the borough. I gave one hundred fifty dollars for it. I seated it up, and it cost $60.00 more. There was not a member that helped me pay for anything, except my Brother furnished two stoves. It was at the commencement of the war. There was no work to be had, and I sent my oldest son, 17 years of age to war. I was over age for a soldier, so I went and worked at sawmill run. I baptized six that winter in a strange locality. I baptized them in the Ohio River. There was such a stagnation that there was no work to be had. My Brother sent me word that my wife had no provisions, and I sent her ten dollars, so you can see what I have done for the work of God. I made many sacrifices. I gave three buildings to the church for meeting houses. I have done all I could for the work of God. When I went to Kansas I turned the buildings over to the General Church for Church purposes. As I have referred to Brother Bacon in pages of this letter, I will also refer to Brother Stimmel. He had a good property in Troytown with coal near his house. He had loaned some money on the Church at Little-Red-Stone and made a demand for it, although he did not need it. He died shortly after. It is worth while for you all to notice this. Was it not God interfering that caused his death, for he was the cause of the church being sold?

When the Church was organized at Greenock in 1862, I gave the word of the Lord, and gave Brothers Brown and Cadman commission to go above Brownsville to preach in Virginia. They had good success and baptized thirty in a short time. You have the account of it. There was a man took a fit while Brother Brown was preaching. He left the pulpit, took the man by the hand, raised him up and the fit left him. It was said that he never got relief in less than two hours before. Brothers Arthur Bickerton and John Stevens from Wheeling were successful, and they brought in many souls. Two Elders were sent into Ohio, but they did not agree with each other and did not do much good. There also were two sent to Brownsville, and from there to Mt. Pleasant, and then down the Youghiogheny River, and then back to Brownsville. In after years there was eighty-four members brought in at Fayette City and other places visited by these two Elders. I am giving this to show that it was the word of the Lord that was given as there were more than two hundred members brought in through following it. The Greenock Church was built according to the plan of God, both in Greenock and Coultersville. There was scarcely a week passed without baptisms, and if the Church was organized according to the word of the Lord, the question might arise, "what is the highest authority of the Church?" As the Church was organized upon the word of the Lord, there can be no higher authority, and when the word of the Lord was given six or seven bore witness to the revelation of God. So this Church is on a better foundation than other latter day saint churches. It has been mentioned that I was undecided where I would locate when I first went to Eastern Kansas. The reason was I was no farmer, and there was brethren there whom I wished to come with me when I was in Wheeling. There was a map of Kansas presented to me, and I felt by the power of God when I touched the map that Stafford county was the place the Lord wanted me. I landed here and drove a stake on the 3rd of April, 1874, and we named it Zion's Valley.[3] We stood up four of us, after we drove the stake, and asked the blessing of God upon the land, and prayed that the time would soon come that we should go to the Lamanites. This was the Sabbath morning about sunrise. We slept in a correll made of buffalo bones about five feet high, and we drove the stake within one half mile of where St. John now stands. We petitioned for a Post-Office, and requested the name of Zion's Valley, which was granted with mail twice a week. We were very strict in the moral character of all the saints. We landed here in April 1875 with five teams. It was very rough weather and snowing. Many of the brethren came from the East, and we lived in tent houses. We had good spiritual meetings at all times,

3. William Bickerton evidently forgot that he drove a symbolic stake into the ground at Zion Valley during the late fall of 1874. However, it is possible that he drove another stake into the ground when he and the Saints immigrated to Zion Valley in the spring of 1875. Bickerton could have accidentally written the wrong year.

all members doing duty, no drinking or bad habits of any kind, and we could hear the prayers of the saints going up from each homestead. The people of Great Bend were very kind to us, and showed it in various ways. We had preaching at Great Bend in the school house, also in other localities, and were well treated by all. The first school house built here, we held meetings in twice a week, glorious meetings with the saints. As we could only get one claim to locate a town site, we appointed a committee of seven to go to Larned to take claims for that purpose. [D]uncan Bell agreed to take a claim and hold it for a town site, but George Brickenridge, one of the seven turned traitor, and went, unknown to the others, and took the claim for his own use. I want to impress upon you that this is one of the smallest counties in the State, and it is the most prosperous of the 105 counties in the State, for God is with his people. The suburbs of St. John are covered with machinery now, to take care of our present wheat crop. All the farmers in Stafford County are getting rich. I feel the blessing of God in this.

I want to say a little more about the Church of West Elizabeth. I made a gift to the Church of the meeting house, and I never intended to have it sold. I thought I would make the deed so my wife could not take any advantage of the Church house, but when I went back from this country, they had the building advertised for sale. Was it McDonald, or who was it that offered it for sale? When I was ready to come back, it was auctioned off to the highest bidder, and I made a bid of $999 dollars, and that stopped the sale, but as soon as I came back to Kansas they sold the house. I would like to know who gave them the right to do so, or who they gave a good deed for the property. If I had known in time, I would not have given a deed, and that church would have stood as a monument of my generosity, but as a shepherd of the sheep, they underminded me, while I was trying to show the care I had for the Church of Christ, but they acted as if they did not want any property left there belonging to the Church. If I had intended to make money out of it, I could have left it to my children. That is all I will say about the Church building at present.

William McDonald was made president of the colony, and he sent a few worthless members, who were of no use in this country, instead of the heads of the Church, who know how the Church should be governed. There were a few officers that came here, and they had been in a general conference, and they left a few that kn[e]w about it. They were in the majority, and things went different. In speaking to the Eastern Kansas saints, they were not all able to support themselves except three or four, and the West Virginia saints were able to keep themselves. The Church of Greenock was organized by the inspiration of God, and it is to be perpetuated by continual revelation, as it was said to Peter, and the highest authority of the Greenock Church was the word of the Lord, and all important cases of any difficulty of settle, the Lord would bare witness to the Elders of the Church to the end, that this Church should not be led astray. This church is organized differently from any other faction of latter day saints church. The Utah Mormons profess to have the melchisedec Priesthood, so no one can condemn their authority. I am not writing to justify them, for they profess that others outside of them knows God's will, so that closes the door that any doctrine they preach is from God, such as the multiplicity of Gods and women. The Church would never have gone into these false doctrines, and would never have suffered so many to follow them. The Josephites are upon the same platform. The Catholic Church has closed the door against their false doctrines, which you know for yourselves, and this is the reason why I show that we may not be led astray. So I want everybody to understand that we are not as a reed shaken by the wind. Of the Church I've been speaking of, there was an angel of God came in while my wife was sweeping out the house, with a crown of twelve stars in his hand, and said, "This crown is for this church." (see Rev. 12 Chapt.) We know from what we have learned from God that Church is the only true church upon the face of the earth. Man may fall away, but God is the same. We know that this is the last dispensation, and Christ will soon set his feet upon Mount Zion, and will sit on the throne of David to reign for ever and ever Amen and amen (so be it).

Dear Brethren, Don't think I am trying to throw any reflections on any one, as I am only trying to give you all a brief sketch of my own experience with God, feeling the blessing in doing so, not knowing whether or not it will be acceptable to all, though I did my best for the work of God, and with God's help, I will so continue in the future. I think by sending an Elder here from your Conference there would be much good accomplished. There are twenty-four members scattered through the additional [region] to Oklahoma, and I think we ought to have a branch of the Church there, for there would be more good accomplished by getting more in a body. All the school houses are open for services, and much good could be done if we had a missionary there. I have had a pure motive in having this article written, and have felt the blessing from time to time. Every church has a history of its own, and I was the organizer of this Church. It is only right to present to you the history and our claim from the Almighty God, as we fear and serve him day and night. I have been speaking to the editor here in regard to getting this history printed, to send to all the members of the Church. By sending Brother Cherry here, and the conditions of our mind was to carry on the work as it was in 1862. I would like to have been present at Conference, but was not able to come, but hope I will be able to come in the near future. In conclusion, I send my love to all, both Brothers and Sisters, and hope you will all prove faithful and stand by the Church.

Your humble Brother in Christ,
Elder William Bickerton

BIBLIOGRAPHY

Books, Articles, and Pamphlets

Addams, R. Jean. "The Church of Christ (Temple Lot): Its Emergence, Struggles and Early Schisms." In Bringhurst and Hamer, *Scattering of the Saints.*

Ashton, T. S. *The Industrial Revolution, 1760–1830.* New York: Oxford University Press, 1969.

Bagley, Will, ed. *Pioneer Camp of the Saints: The 1846 and 1847 Mormon Trail Journals of Thomas Bullock.* Spokane: Arthur H. Clark Company, 1997.

Basler, Roy P., ed. *The Collected Works of Abraham Lincoln.* 9 vols. New Brunswick, N.J.: Rutgers University Press, 1953–55.

Bates, Samuel P. *History of Franklin County, Pennsylvania.* Chicago: Warner, Beers, and Company, 1887.

———. *History of Pennsylvania Volunteers, 1861–65.* 5 vols. Harrisburg: State of Pennsylvania, 1870.

Beecher, Maureen Ursenbach, ed. *The Personal Writings of Eliza Roxcy Snow.* Salt Lake City: University of Utah Press, 1995.

Bergera, Gary James, ed. *The Autobiography of B. H. Roberts.* Salt Lake City: Signature Books, 1990.

Bickerton, William, et al. *The Ensign: Or a Light to Lighten the Gentiles.* Pittsburgh: Ferguson and Company, 1863; 2d ed. 1864.

Bowman, Matthew. *The Mormon People: The Making of an American Faith.* New York: Random House, 2012.

Bringhurst, Newell G., and John C. Hamer, eds. *Scattering of the Saints: Schism within Mormonism.* Independence, MO: John Whitmer Books, 2007.

Brodie, Fawn M. *No Man Knows My History: The Life of Joseph Smith.* New York: Alfred Knopf, 1945.

Burnley, James. *Two Sides of the Atlantic.* London: Simpkin, Marshall, and Company, 1880.

Bush, Lester E. Jr. "The Spaulding Theory: Then and Now." *Dialogue: A Journal of Mormon Thought* 10, no. 4 (Winter 1977): 40–69.

Bushman, Claudia Lauper, and Richard Lyman Bushman. *Building the Kingdom: A History of Mormons in America*. New York: Oxford University Press, 1999.

Bushman, Richard Lyman. *Joseph Smith: Rough Stone Rolling*. New York: Vintage Books, 2007.

Butler, Jon. *Awash in a Sea of Faith: Christianizing the American People*. Cambridge, MA: Harvard University Press, 1990.

Cadman, William. *Daniel's Little Horn*. 2nd ed. Monongahela, PA: Church of Jesus Christ, 1950.

———. *Faith and Doctrines of the Church of Jesus Christ*. Roscoe, PA: Roscoe Ledger Print, 1902.

———. *Personal Observations of William Cadman*. Monongahela, PA: Church of Jesus Christ, 1970.

———. *Pre-Millennial*. Monongahela, PA: Church of Jesus Christ, 1960.

———. *Religious Experiences and Expectations*. Pittsburgh: By the author, 1899; 3d ed. Youngstown, OH: United Printing Company, 1962.

Cadman, William H. *A History of the Church of Jesus Christ*. Monongahela, PA: Church of Jesus Christ, 1945.

Cohn, Raymond L. *Mass Migration under Sail: European Immigration to the Antebellum United States*. New York: Cambridge University Press, 2009.

Cole, Clelland, and Helen Malin Reuber. *No Cyclone Shall Destroy: The Story of St. John, Kansas*. Ardmore, PA: Dorrance and Company, 1981.

Conrad, William. *Conococheague: A History of the Greencastle–Antrim Community, 1736–1971*. Chambersburg, PA: Robson and Kaye, 1971.

Cutler, William G. *History of the State of Kansas*. Chicago: A. T. Andreas, 1883.

Daniell, Mortlock, ed., *Hymns Sung at Broad Street Church*. Ramsgate, UK: W. Thiselton, 1851.

Deseret Sunday School Song Book: A Collection of Choice Pieces for the Use of Sunday Schools, and Suitable for Other Occasions. Salt Lake City: Deseret Sunday School Union, 1894.

Dinger, John S., ed. *The Nauvoo City and High Council Minutes*. Salt Lake City: Signature Books, 2011.

Edwards, Rebecca. *New Spirits: Americans in the Gilded Age, 1865–1905*. New York: Oxford University Press, 2006.

Entz, Gary R. "The Bickertonites: Schism and Reunion in a Restoration Church." *Journal of Mormon History* 32, no. 3 (Fall 2006): 1–44.

———. "Paradise on the Plains: The Development of Cooperative Alternatives in Kansas, 1850–1900." PhD diss., University of Utah, 1999.

———. "Zion Valley: The Mormon Origins of St. John, Kansas." *Kansas History* 24, no. 2 (Summer 2001): 98–117.

Erickson, Dan. *As a Thief in the Night: The Mormon Quest for Millennial Deliverance*. Salt Lake City: Signature Books, 1998.

Fehrenbacher, Don E., and Virginia Fehrenbacher, eds. *Recollected Words of Abraham Lincoln*. Palo Alto, CA: Stanford University Press, 1996.

Fogarty, Robert S., ed. *Dictionary of American Communal and Utopian History*. Westport, CT: Greenwood Press, 1980.

Foner, Eric. *Reconstruction: America's Unfinished Revolution, 1863–1877*. New York: Harper and Row, 1988.

Foote, Shelby. *The Civil War: A Narrative*. 3 vols. New York: Random House, 1958.

Fox, Arthur B. *Pittsburgh during the American Civil War, 1860–1865*. Chicora, PA: Mechling Bookbindery, 2002.

Freese, Barbara. *Coal: A Human History*. Cambridge, MA: Perseus, 2003.

Gibson, Arrell Morgan. *The American Indian: Prehistory to the Present*. Lexington, MA: D. C. Heath, 1980.

Grandstaff, Mark R. "Having More Learning Than Sense: William E. McLellin and the Book of Commandments Revisited." *Dialogue: A Journal of Mormon Thought* 26, no. 4 (Winter 1993): 23–48.

Gregory, Thomas J. "Sidney Rigdon: Post Nauvoo." *BYU Studies* 21, no. 1 (January 1981): 51–67.

Grow, Matthew J., et al., eds. *The Joseph Smith Papers: Administrative Records; Council of Fifty Minutes, March 1844–January 1846*. Salt Lake City: Church Historian's Press, 2016.

Hall Florence Howe. *The Story of the Battle Hymn of the Republic*. New York: Harper and Brothers, 1916.

Hansen, Klaus J. *Mormonism and the American Experience*. Chicago: University of Chicago Press, 1981.

Hastings, H. T. *Songs of Pilgrimage: A Hymnal for the Churches of Christ*. Boston: Scriptural Tract Repository, 1886.

Hayden, Amos Sutton. *Early History of the Disciples in the Western Reserve*. Cincinnati: Chase and Hall, 1875.

Hoffer, Peter Charles. *The Salem Witchcraft Trials: A Legal History*. Lawrence: University Press of Kansas, 1997.

Howe, Daniel Walker. *What Hath God Wrought: The Transformation of America, 1815–1848*. New York: Oxford University Press, 2007.

Howe, Eber D. *Mormonism Unvailed*. Painesville, OH: By the author, 1834.

Hyde, Orson. *Speech of Elder Orson Hyde, Delivered Before the High Priest's Quorum, in Nauvoo, April 27th, 1845*. Liverpool: James and Woodburn, 1845.

Hymns of the Church of Jesus Christ of Latter-day Saints. Salt Lake City: LDS Church, 1985.

Jessee, Dean C., ed. *The Papers of Joseph Smith*. 2 vols. Salt Lake City: Deseret Book, 1989–92.

Jessee, Dean C., Mark Ashurst–McGee, and Richard L. Jensen. *The Joseph Smith Papers: Journals, Volume 1, 1832–1839*. Salt Lake City: Church Historian's Press, 2008.

Jordan, John W., ed. *Genealogical and Personal History of Western Pennsylvania*. New York: Lewis Historical Publishing, 1915.

Keller, Karl, ed. "'I Never Knew a Time When I Did Not Know Joseph Smith': A Son's Record of the Life and Testimony of Sidney Rigdon." *Dialogue: A Journal of Mormon Thought* 1, no. 4 (Winter 1966): 15–42.

Kenney, Scott G., ed. *Wilford Woodruff's Journal*. 9 vols. Midvale, UT: Signature Books, 1983–85.

Kleinberg, S. J. *The Shadow of the Mills: Working-Class Families in Pittsburgh, 1870–1907*. Pittsburgh: University of Pittsburgh Press, 1989.

Langland, Elizabeth. *Nobody's Angels: Middle-Class Women and Domestic Ideology in Victorian Culture*. Ithaca, NY: Cornell University Press, 1995.

A List of Immigrants Who Applied for Naturalization Papers in the District Courts of Allegheny County, PA, 1856–1869. Pittsburgh: Western Pennsylvania Genealogical Society, 1978.

Little, James A. *Jacob Hamblin*. Salt Lake City: Deseret News, 1909.

Linn, William Alexander. *The Story of the Mormons: From the Date of Their Origin to the Year 1901*. New York: Macmillan, 1902.

Ludlow, Daniel H., ed. *Encyclopedia of Mormonism: The History, Scripture, Doctrine, and Procedure of the Church of Jesus Christ of Latter-day Saints*. 5 vols. New York: Macmillan, 1992.

Mason, Richard Lee. *Narrative of Richard Lee Mason in the Pioneer West, 1819*. New York: C. F. Heartman, 1915.

Martin, Joseph. *A New and Comprehensive Gazetteer of Virginia and the District of Columbia*. Charlottesville, VA: By the author, 1835.

Mather, Cotton. *Magnalia Christi Americana*. Hartford: Silas Andrus, Roberts, and Burr, 1853.

McCauley, I. H. *A Historical Sketch of Franklin County, Pennsylvania*. Harrisburg, PA: Patriot Publishing Company, 1878.

McPherson, James. *Battle Cry of Freedom: The Civil War Era*. New York: Oxford University Press, 1988.

Miner, Craig. *Kansas: The History of the Sunflower State, 1854–2000*. Lawrence: University Press of Kansas, 2002.

Nead, Benjamin M. "The History of Mormonism with Particular Reference to the Founding of the New Jerusalem in Franklin County." In *Papers Read before the Kittochtinny Historical Society*, 9:411–27. Chambersburg, PA: Franklin Repository Press, 1923.

Peterson, John Alton. *Utah's Black Hawk War*. Salt Lake City: University of Utah Press, 1998.

Piston, William Garrett, and Richard W. Hatcher. *Wilson's Creek: The Second Battle of the Civil War and the Men Who Fought It*. Chapel Hill: University of North Carolina Press, 2000.

Prince, Gregory A. *Power from on High: The Development of Mormon Priesthood*. Salt Lake City: Signature Books, 1995.

A Prophecy by Joseph Smith: Revelation and Prophecy Given by Joseph Smith on December 25, 1832, [which] was recorded in our record in October of 1874. Monongahela, PA: Church of Jesus Christ, nd.

Quinn, D. Michael. "The Mormon Succession Crisis of 1844." *BYU Studies* 16, no. 2 (Winter 1976): 187–233.

Rice, Otis K. *West Virginia: A History*. Lexington: University Press of Kentucky, 1985.

Richards, LeGrand. *A Marvelous Work and a Wonder*. Salt Lake City: Deseret Book, 1967.

Reynolds, David S. *Waking Giant: America in the Age of Jackson*. New York: HarperCollins, 2008.

Rogers, Jedediah S. *The Council of Fifty: A Documentary History*. Salt Lake City: Signature Books, 2014.

Roy, Andrew. *A History of the Coal Miners of the United States: From the Development of the Mines to the Close of the Anthracite Strike of 1902*. Columbus, OH: J. L. Trauger Press, 1907.

Scolnic, Benjamin. "Antiochus IV and the Three Horns in Daniel 7." *Journal of Hebrew Scriptures* 14, no. 2 (2014): 1–28.

Shipps, Jan, and John W. Welch, eds. *The Journals of William E. McLellin 1831–1836*. Provo: BYU Studies, 1994.

Smith, Emma, comp. *A Collection of Sacred Hymns*. Kirtland, OH: F. G. Williams, 1835.

Smith, Joseph Jr. *History of the Church of Jesus Christ of Latter-day Saints*. 7 vols. Salt Lake City: Deseret Book, 1950; first printing 1902.

Smith, William. *An Emigrant's Narrative; or a Voice from the Steerage*. New York: E. Winchester, 1850.

Speek, Vickie Cleverley. "From Strangites to Reorganized Latter Day Saints: Transformations in Midwestern Mormonism, 1856–79." In Bringhurst and Hamer, *Scattering of the Saints*.

Spencer, Orson. *Letters Exhibiting the Most Prominent Doctrines of the Church*. 6th ed. Liverpool: William Budge, 1879.

Stimson, A. L. *History of the Express Companies and the Origin of American Railroads*. New York: By the author, 1858.

Strong, James. *The New Strong's Exhaustive Concordance of the Bible*. Nashville: Thomas Nelson, 1990.

Thomas, David. *Travels through the Western Country in the Summer of 1816*. Auburn, NY: David Rumsey, 1819.

Thurston, George H. *Pittsburgh and Allegheny in the Centennial Year*. Pittsburgh: Anderson and Son, 1876.

Turner, John G. *Brigham Young: Pioneer Prophet*. Cambridge, MA: Belknap Press of Harvard University, 2012.

Van Noord, Roger. *Assassination of a Michigan King: The Life of James Jesse Strang*. Ann Arbor: University of Michigan Press, 1997.

Van Vugt, William E. *Britain to America: Mid-nineteenth-century Immigrants to the United States*. Champaign: University of Illinois Press, 1999.

Van Wagoner, Richard S., ed. *The Complete Discourses of Brigham Young*. 5 vols. Salt Lake City: Signature Books, 2009.

———. "The Making of a Mormon Myth: The 1844 Transfiguration of Brigham Young." *Dialogue: A Journal of Mormon Thought* 28, no. 4 (Winter 1995): 1–24.

———. *Sidney Rigdon: A Portrait of Religious Excess*. Salt Lake City: Signature Books, 1994.

Walker, Ronald W., Richard E. Turley, and Glen M. Leonard. *Massacre at Mountain Meadows*. New York: Oxford University Press, 2008.

Watson, Larry. "The Church of Jesus Christ (Headquartered in Monongahela, Pennsylvania), Its History and Doctrine." In Bringhurst and Hamer, *Scattering of the Saints.*

Watson, Robert A., et al., eds. *A History of the Church of Jesus Christ.* Monongahela, PA: Church of Jesus Christ, 2002.

Wiley, Richard T. *Elizabeth and Her Neighbors.* Butler, PA: Ziegler Company, 1936.

Woodward, Grace Steele. *The Cherokees.* Norman: University of Oklahoma Press, 1963.

Young, Brigham. *History of the Church: Apostolic Interregnum.* Vol. 7 of Smith, *History of the Church.* Salt Lake City: Deseret Book, 1950.

Documents and Manuscripts

CHURCH OF JESUS CHRIST ARCHIVE, GREENSBURG

Bickerton, William. "Testimony, June 1903."

Bickerton, William, Charles Brown, George Barnes, William Cadman, and Joseph Astin. "The Ensign: or a Light to Lighten the Gentiles, in which the Doctrine of The Church of Jesus Christ of Latter-Day Saints, is Set Forth, and Scripture Evidence Adduced to Establish it," 1863. Typescript.

"A Book of Record of the Revelations Given unto the Church of Jesus Christ of Latter Day Saints."

"Cherokee District Conference of [the Church of] Jesus christ—of Latterday Saints," minutes, 1891.

Cherry, Alexander, to Marion Campbell, Oct. 15, 1894.

Humphrey, Ishmael. "Biography of William Bickerton and His Brothers in the Organization of 1862, Greenoak, Pennsylvania."

Martin, Idris A., and John E. Mancini, eds. "The History of the Church of Jesus Christ: May 25, 1851, thru October 7, 1905, along with commentary by Idris A. Martin—Assistant General Church Historian."

Minutes of the Church of Jesus Christ of Latter Day Saints, July 16, 17, 20, 1896.

Pilgrim, Joyce Bickerton. "Descendants of Thomas Bickerton." Typescript.

William Bickerton vs. Charlotte Bickerton. Petition for Divorce, Hearing for Divorce, and Affidavit of Mailing Petition, Ninth Judicial District Court, Stafford County, Kansas, May 25, 27, Aug. 16, 1880.

William Bickerton vs. William Cadman and James Taylor. Amended Petition, Ninth Judicial District Court, Stafford County, Aug. 1887.

LAMB FOUNDATION ARCHIVE, ALBUQUERQUE

typescripts by John E. Mancini

Bean, Victor Emanuel, and William W. Allen to William Moroni Palmer, Dec. 14, 1885.

Bickerton et al., *The Ensign: or a Light to Lighten the Gentiles,* 1864 (photocopy).

Bickerton Party Minute Book 1882–1887.

Church of Jesus Christ in the East, October 7, 1876 to July 6, 1895.

Council Meetings at St. John, Kansas, April 24, 1875–May 26, 1877.

Greenoak Revelations, Visions, Dreams, February 1865 to November 1870.

A List of Branches and Members Names and Blessings 1859, 1860, 1862, 1876.

Record of Church under William Bickerton before Incorporation, May 25, 1851–January 29, 1859.

Redstone Valley Branch, March 11, 1871 to October 25, 1873.

West Elizabeth Branch, June 19, 1863, to July 24, 1868.

Zion Valley Minute Book, 1876–1877.

LDS CHURCH HISTORY LIBRARY, SALT LAKE CITY

Astin, William B. "Synopsis of the Life of Joseph Astin," n.d., typescript.

Bean, Victor Emanuel. Journals, 1884–89.

Brothers, William. Family register, 1871.

Journal History of the Church, 1830–2008. Online scan of CR 100 137 available at churchhistorylibrary.lds.org.

Miskin, Arthur R., and Amelia L. Moore Miskin. "Notes on Our Early Life."

Palmer, William Moroni. Diary, 1880–87. Online scan of MS 9463 available at churchistorylibrary.lds.org.

"Way Paved for the Honest in Heart to Receive the Gospel," 1957.

NATIONAL ARCHIVES, WASHINGTON, DC

Naturalization Petitions for the US District Court, 1820–1930, and Circuit Court, 1820–1911, for the Western District of Pennsylvania. NAI 3, M1537, online at *Ancestry.com.*

Registers of Vessels Arriving at the Port of New York from Foreign Ports, 1789–1919. Microfilm M237, roll 14.

US Federal Census, Marshall County, West Virginia, 1850; Allegheny County, Pennsylvania, 1850, 1860, 1870, 1900.

OTHER ARCHIVES

Hands, William Oscar. "The Life of William Oscar Hands," n.d. Community of Christ Historical Archives, Independence, Missouri.

Robinson, Alexander. Interview conducted by Gary R. Entz. St. John, Kansas, Apr. 6, 1998. Transcript, Special Collections, J. Willard Marriott Library, University of Utah.

———. "The Passing of the Torch: William Bickerton." Unpublished manuscript in author's possession.

Stevenson, James C. "History of the Pennsylvania Volunteers, 1861–1865: Record of the Men of the 100th PA Infantry." Lawrence County Historical Society, New Castle, Pennsylvania; online at www.ancestry.com.

Newspapers

INTERNET ARCHIVE DIGITAL LIBRARY (HTTPS://ARCHIVE.ORG)

Frontier Guardian, 1851; *Journal of Discourses*, 1861; *Latter Day Saint's Messenger and Advocate*, 1844–45; *Latter-day Saints' Millennial Star*, 1848; *The Saints' Herald*, 1887; *The Seer*, 1853; and *Times and Seasons*, 1841.

KANSAS HISTORICAL SOCIETY, TOPEKA (MICROFILM)

Great Bend Inland Tribune, 1878; *Great Bend Register*, 1874, 1876–79; *St. John Advance*, 1880–82, 1887, 1890; *St. John County Capital*, 1887–89, 1895–98, 1905; *St. John News*, 1940; *St. John Sun*, 1886–87, *St. John Weekly News*, 1889–90, 1892, 1905; *Stafford Citizen*, 1878; and *Stafford County Rustler*, 1889.

SENATOR JOHN HEINZ HISTORY CENTER, PITTSBURGH (MICROFILM)

Elizabeth Herald, 1875–77; *Monongahela Valley Republican*, 1871–73, 1875–76, 1878; *Pittsburgh Christian Advocate*, 1844; *Pittsburgh Daily Gazette and Advertizer*, 1844–45; and *Protestant Unionist*, 1845.

UNCLE DALE'S READINGS IN EARLY MORMON HISTORY (WWW.SIDNEYRIGDON.COM)

Commercial Journal, 1844; *Lehigh Register*, 1852; *People's Organ*, 1844; *Pittsburgh Morning Post*, 1844; and *Washington Reporter* (Pennsylvania), 1847.

Photographs and Illustrations

A highway for riverboats and barges running from Pittsburgh to the coal fields in West Virginia, the Monongahela River is shown here from the hills overlooking the towns of California and Newell, twenty miles south of Elizabeth. *Courtesy California Area Historical Society*

This early likeness of Sidney Rigdon was based on a photograph by Irving Saunders, whose photo studio was located in Friendship, New York. Rigdon was Bickerton's spiritual mentor. *Courtesy Wikimedia Commons*

The West Elizabeth branch was growing so fast that Bickerton had no sooner purchased a new meeting house in 1862 than it was too small to accommodate the membership. He had to buy the school pictured here and convert it into a chapel. *Reprinted from Robert A. Watson's* History of the Church of Jesus Christ, *2:66*

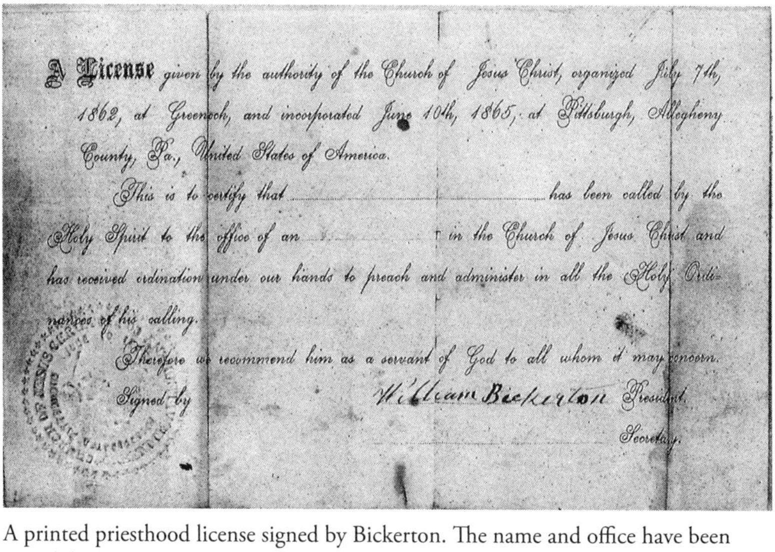

A License given by the authority of the Church of Jesus Christ, organized July 7th, 1862, at Greenock, and incorporated June 10th, 1865, at Pittsburgh, Allegheny County, Pa., United States of America.

This is to certify that ________ has been called by the Holy Spirit to the office of an ________ in the Church of Jesus Christ and has received ordination under our hands to preach and administer in all the Holy Ordinances of his calling.

Therefore we recommend him as a servant of God to all whom it may concern.

Signed by William Bickerton President.

Secretary.

A printed priesthood license signed by Bickerton. The name and office have been erased, but one can still faintly read *Joseph Astin* and *Apostle. Courtesy LDS Church History Library*

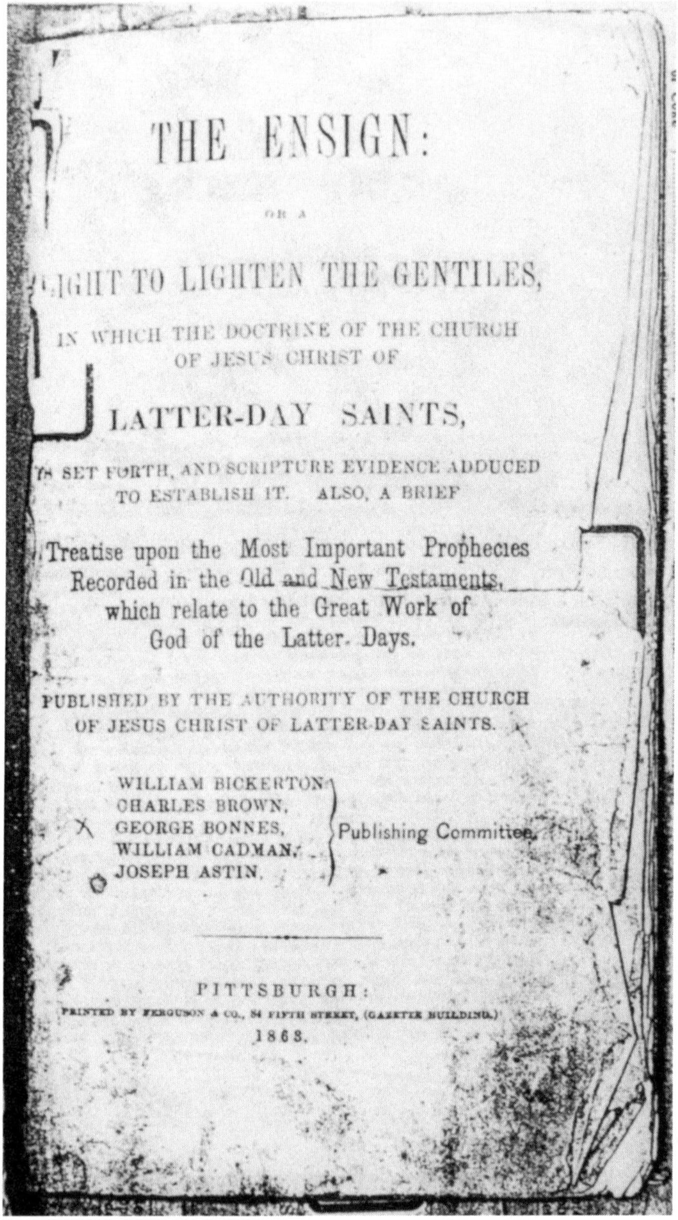

THE ENSIGN:

OR A

LIGHT TO LIGHTEN THE GENTILES,

IN WHICH THE DOCTRINE OF THE CHURCH
OF JESUS CHRIST OF

LATTER-DAY SAINTS,

IS SET FORTH, AND SCRIPTURE EVIDENCE ADDUCED
TO ESTABLISH IT. ALSO, A BRIEF

Treatise upon the Most Important Prophecies
Recorded in the Old and New Testaments,
which relate to the Great Work of
God of the Latter Days.

PUBLISHED BY THE AUTHORITY OF THE CHURCH
OF JESUS CHRIST OF LATTER-DAY SAINTS.

WILLIAM BICKERTON,
CHARLES BROWN,
GEORGE BONNES,
WILLIAM CADMAN,
JOSEPH ASTIN,
} Publishing Committee.

PITTSBURGH:
PRINTED BY FERGUSON & CO., 84 FIFTH STREET, (GAZETTE BUILDING.)
1863.

No copies are known to have survived of the 1863 *Ensign*, the first missionary tract published by the Church of Jesus Christ. However, a typescript and partial photocopy of the pamphlet still exist. *Courtesy John E. Mancini, Lamb Foundation Archive*

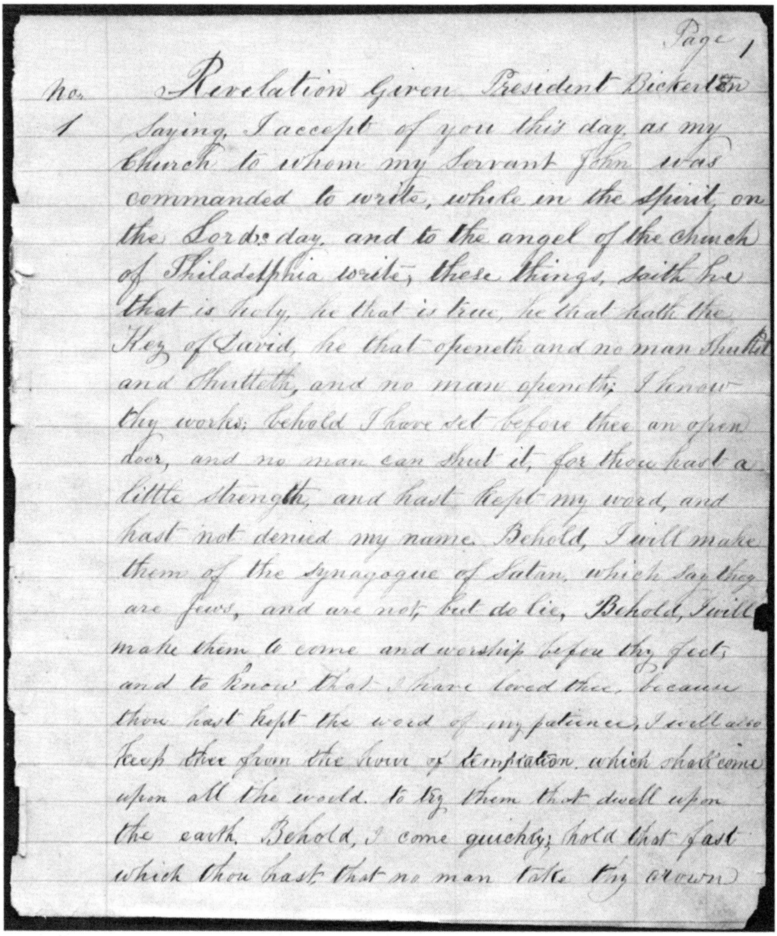

Page 1

no. 1 Revelation Given President Bickerton
Saying, I accept of you this day, as my
Church to whom my Servant John was
commanded to write, while in the Spirit, on
the Lord's day, and to the angel of the church
of Philadelphia write; these things, saith he
that is holy, he that is true, he that hath the
Key of David, he that openeth and no man shutteth
and shutteth, and no man openeth; I know
thy works; behold I have set before thee an open
door, and no man can shut it, for thou hast a
little strength, and hast kept my word, and
hast not denied my name. Behold, I will make
them of the synagogue of Satan, which say they
are Jews, and are not, but do lie, Behold, I will
make them to come and worship before thy feet,
and to know that I have loved thee, because
thou hast kept the word of my patience, I will also
keep thee from the hour of temptation, which shall come
upon all the world, to try them that dwell upon
the earth. Behold, I come quickly; hold that fast
which thou hast that no man take thy crown

The first page of the revelation book begun by Bickerton's church in 1858. Here the Lord tells "President Bickerton" to "hold that fast which thou hast, that no man take thy crown." *Courtesy Church of Jesus Christ Historical Archive*

The Bickerton family in the late 1860s. Seated are William and Charlotte. In the back are *(l–r)* Eliza Ann, James, and Clara Virginia, and in front *(l–r)* Angeline Ann, Florence, and Josephine. *Courtesy St. John News*

The Little Redstone congregation promoted a racist doctrine in 1872 that was quickly quashed by the headquarters ministry. Their meeting house was dedicated a year later. *Reprinted from William H. Cadman's* History of the Church of Jesus Christ, *1:70*

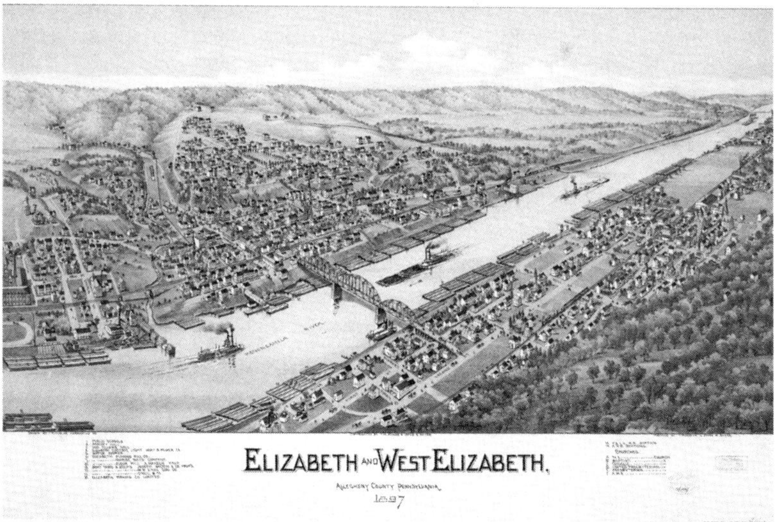

This bird's-eye view of Elizabeth, Pennsylvania, was drawn in 1897 by Thaddeus Fowler and James Moyer, showing real-world details for each house and building. *Courtesy Library of Congress Panoramic Maps Collection*

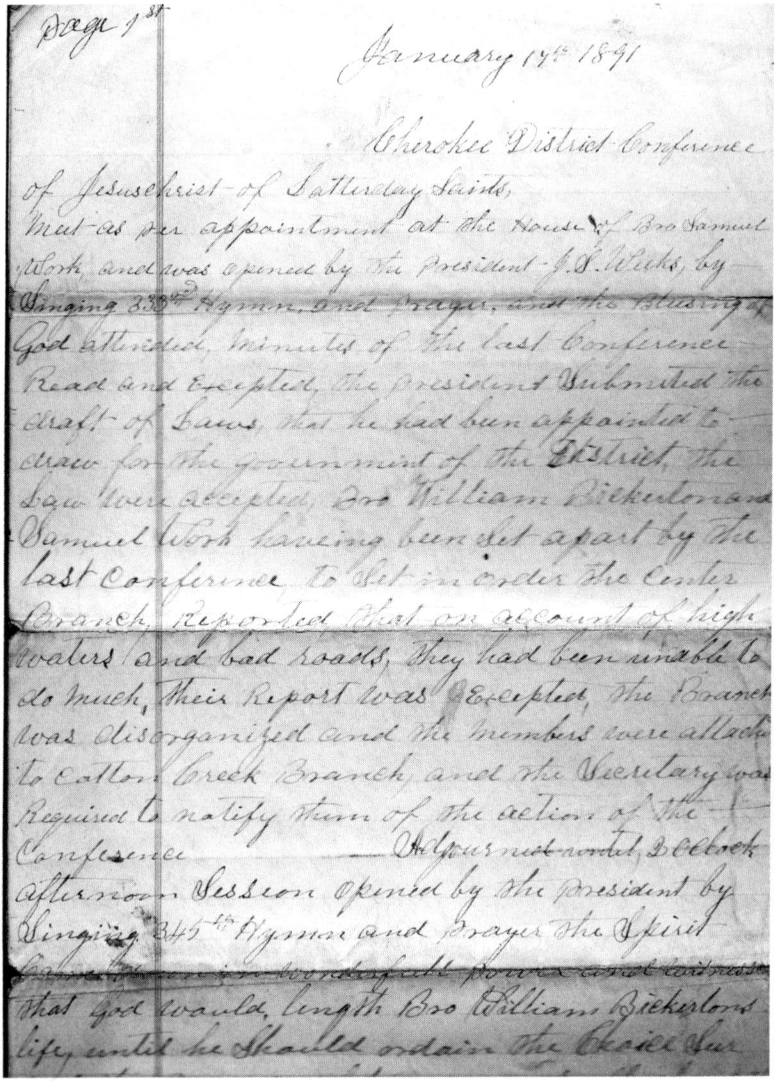

Page 1st

January 17th 1891

Cherokee District Conference
of Jesuschrist of Latterday Saints,
Met as per appointment at the House of Bro Samuel
Work, and was opened by the president J. S. Weeks, by
Singing 33rd Hymn, and Prayer, and the Blessing of
God attended, minutes of the last Conference
Read and Excepted, the president Submitted the
draft of Laws, that he had been appointed to
draw for the government of the District, the
Law were accepted, Bro William Bickerton and
Samuel Work haveing been set apart by the
last Conference to set in order the Center
Branch, Reported that on account of high
waters and bad roads, they had been unable to
do much, their Report was Excepted, the Branch
was disorganized and the members were attach
to Cotton Creek Branch, and the Secretary was
Required to notify them of the action of the
Conference — Adjourned until 2 o'clock
afternoon Session opened by the president by
Singing 345th Hymn and Prayer the Spirit
[illegible] wonderfull power and witness
that God would length Bro William Bickertons
life, until he should ordain the [illegible]

The minutes of the Cherokee District Conference, held in January 1891 on the Oklahoma border, a month after the massacre in South Dakota at Wounded Knee. Bickerton prophesied that "the Lord will give us power to prevail over the government, yea over Benjamin Harrison and his cabinet, in favor of the Red man." *Courtesy Church of Jesus Christ Historical Archive*

Lewis Downing was a young man when the Cherokees were moved from Tennessee to Indian Territory in 1839, to what is now Kansas/Oklahoma. He attended a Baptist mission school, became a chaplain during the Civil War, and tribal chief in 1866, two years before William Bickerton, William Cadman, and Benjamin Meadowcroft visited him. *Courtesy Wikimedia Commons*

Some of the branches met in members' homes or in rented halls. For this 1902 gathering in Jefferson, Pennsylvania, a tent was pitched so that neighbors could be invited. The guests included William Cadman and Alexander Cherry. *Reprinted from Robert A. Watson's* History of the Church of Jesus Christ, *2:55*

Even though the branch in Kansas had long since ceased communal practices by 1899, the members still met occasionally for a meal together. Bickerton is seated to the far right, displaying the Bible and Book of Mormon. *Courtesy Alexander Robinson*

W. R. Gray took this picture in 1905 and identified the unnamed individuals as being from the "Bickerton Colony" in St. John. *Courtesy Gray Studio Glass Plate Negative Collection, Stafford County Museum and Forsyth Digital Library*

Sidney Rigdon's disciple Stephen Post was sent to Pittsburgh in 1863 to convert the Bickertonites. A later mission assignment, accompanied by his wife, Elder Jane Post, was to Manitoba. *Courtesy Wikimedia Commons*

When the church lost its property in St. John, Kansas, in 1882, the two congregations met in private homes and public buildings for seven years until Bickerton's followers constructed a second meeting house. It remains there today on West Second Street. *Photograph by author*

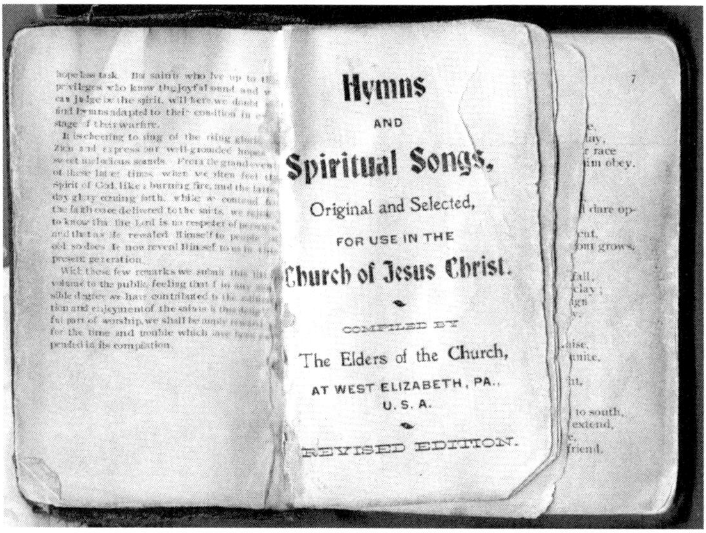

The church published hymnbooks in 1855, 1864, and the edition shown here that was released by Cadman's faction sometime toward the end of the century. *Courtesy Church of Jesus Christ Historical Archive*

This United Brethren chapel purchased by the LDS Church in 1895 was moved to where Bickerton had driven the stake into the ground two decades earlier, indicating the future site of Zion. *Photograph by Dillian M. Zimmerman, courtesy Jan Zimmerman and Jill Budge–Bowden*

James Nichols was an original apostle who lost his position in 1877 for opposing the Zion Valley colony. *All images on this page reprinted from Cadman's* History of the Church of Jesus Christ.

Alexander Cherry was ordained an apostle in 1877. After drifting from one faction to the other, he became instrumental in uniting the two groups and became the church's third president.

William Skillen became an apostle in 1865, replacing an apostle who had asked to be released. After Skillen opposed the Zion Valley colony in 1877, he too was dropped from the quorum.

William Cadman was baptized in late 1859. He became a member of the original Quorum of Twelve Apostles two and a half years later. In 1880 he began presiding over his own faction, and continued as president in 1902 after the church was reunited.

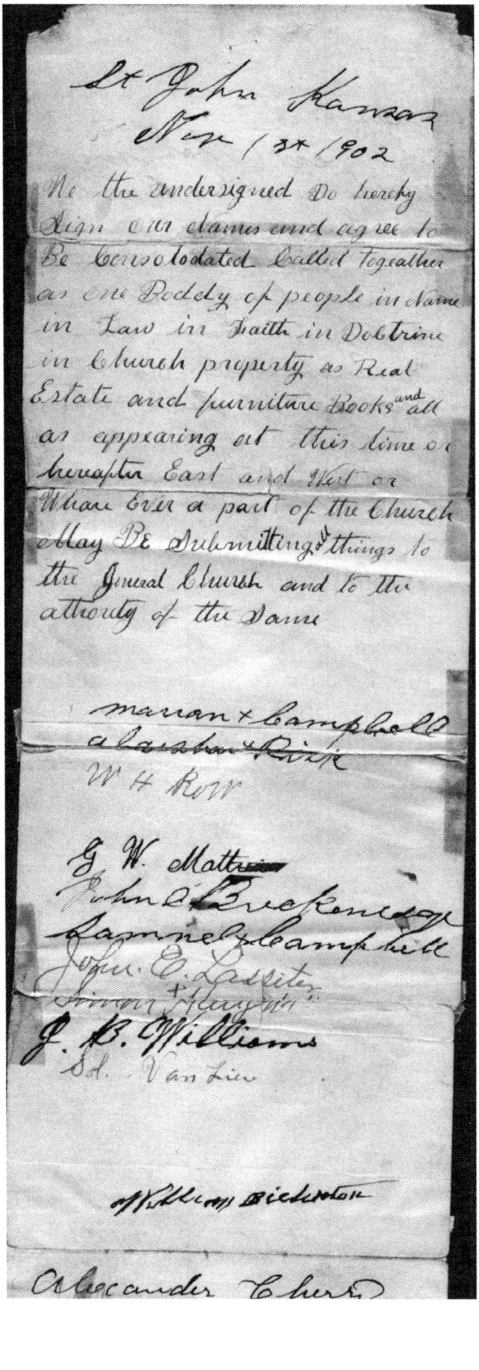

St John Kansas
Nov 1st 1902
We the undersigned Do hereby
Sign our names and agree to
Be Consolodated Called Togeather
as one Boddy of people in Name
in Law in Faith in Doctrine
in Church property as Real
Estate and furniture Books and all
as appearing at this time or
hereafter East and West or
Where ever a part of the Church
May Be Submitting all things to
the General Church and to the
athority of the Same

marian + campbell
W H Ross
G. W. Matt
John C Breckenridge
Sammuel Campbell
John C. Lassiter
J. B. Williams
William Bickerton
Alexander Cherry

This reconciliation document brought the Bickerton and Cadman factions back together in 1902. Bickerton's tiny autograph is the second-to-last on the page, above the signature of Alexander Cherry. *Courtesy Church of Jesus Christ Historical Archive*

In about 1900, William Cadman (6) attended this church gathering in Jefferson, Pennsylvania, forty miles south of Elizabeth. He was accompanied by his son William H. Cadman (7) and apostles Alexander Cherry (5) and William Lynch (3), along with former apostle Arthur Bickerton (4), among others. *Reprinted from Robert A. Watson's* History of the Church of Jesus Christ, *2:54*

In this formal studio portrait of William Bickerton taken in 1905, photographer W. R. Gray wanted to avoid the right side of the subject's face because of his missing eye. *Courtesy Church of Jesus Christ Historical Archive*

George W. Baker in 1905. A convert from West Virginia, he was among the first immigrants to St. John, Kansas. He is ninety years old in this photograph. *Courtesy Gray Studio Glass Plate Negative Collection, Stafford County Museum*

This memorial was erected next to Bickerton's gravestone around the turn of the twenty-first century by Alexander Robinson, the area's presiding elder at the time. *Photograph by author*

The top panel of the Bickerton gravestone reads, "BICKERTON: DIED FEB. 17, 1905, AGED 90 YRS. 1 M. 2 DA" (referencing his January 15, 1815, birth). The lower panel reads, "Dear father, rest in peace." *Photograph by author*

INDEX

ALSO FROM SIGNATURE BOOKS

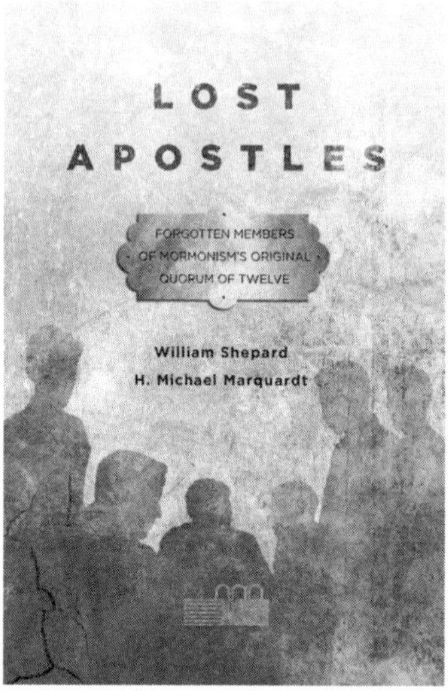

Lost Apostles: Forgotten Members of Mormonism's Original Quorum of Twelve
William Shepard and **H. Michael Marquardt**
400 pages | hardback

Sidney Rigdon:
A Portrait of Religious Excess
Richard S. Van Wagoner
640 pages | paperback

The Nauvoo City and High Council Minutes
John S. Dinger, ed.
700 pages | hardback

"God Has Made Us a Kingdom": James Strang and the Midwest Mormons
Vickie Cleverley Speek
396 pages | hardback

ALSO FROM SIGNATURE BOOKS

Natural Born Seer: Joseph Smith, American Prophet, 1805–1830
Richard S. Van Wagoner
600 pages | hardback

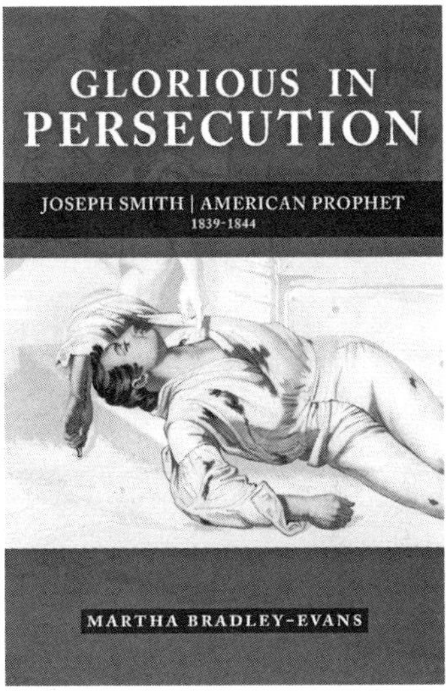

Glorious in Persecution: Joseph Smith, American Prophet, 1839–1844
Martha Bradley-Evans
664 pages | hardback

Brigham Young, Colonizer of the American West: Diaries and Office Journals, 1832–1871
George D. Smith, ed.
forthcoming: 2019
2 vols. | 1,500 pages | hardback

The Pre-Nicene New Testament: Fifty-four Formative Texts
Robert M. Price
1,248 pages | hardback

Daniel P. Stone is a PhD candidate studying American religious history at Manchester Metropolitan University in England. He has BA and MA degrees from the University of Florida and Florida Atlantic University, has worked as an archivist in Detroit, and has taught history at the University of Detroit Mercy. He has published in the *Journal of the American Revolution* and *Journal of Mormon History*. He is a deacon in the Church of Jesus Christ that William Bickerton established.

At last a comprehensive and objective biography of William Bickerton. Daniel P. Stone has written an insightful, detailed, and readable narrative of a man more Latter Day Saints should become familiar with. Not only is his story interesting and unique, but because Stone was granted access to archival documents of the Church of Jesus Christ (Monongahela, Pennsylvania), he is able to provide copious never-before-seen details, including quotations from Bickerton's revelations and accounts of miraculous healings and other spiritual manifestations. The third largest of the six major denominations to emerge intact from the Fragmentation Era, the Church of Jesus Christ and William Bickerton are crucial to a broader understanding of the Latter Day Saint movement. Succeeding Joseph Smith's counselor Sidney Rigdon, Bickerton emerged as a prophet with keen spiritual insight. His biography is a must-read!

—**Steven L. Shields**, World Church field minister (ret.), Community of Christ; guest columnist, *Korea Times*; author of *Divergent Paths of the Restoration: A History of the Latter Day Saint Movement*

I learned about William Bickerton and the Church of Jesus Christ (Bickertonite) quite by accident. Around 1996 I was at the University of Utah researching a British socialist colony that settled in 1870s Kansas. My dissertation advisor wanted me to bring in other groups for comparison, and it happened that I discovered a religious colony active in Kansas in the 1870s known as Zion Valley. This was William Bickerton's group. As I delved deeper into it, I was surprised to discover that the colony was associated with the third-largest denomination in Joseph Smith's Restoration movement. And yet, so little had been written about it that even Roger D. Lanius and Linda Thatcher, in their notable anthology, *Differing Visions: Dissenters in Mormon History*, did not include it. This oversight has now been corrected through this comprehensive biography—a welcome and much needed addition to the scholarship surrounding the Latter Day Saints. Stone's book is engaging, informative, and an example of scholarship at its best. His research represents the first time the Church of Jesus Christ has opened its archives to a scholar. They chose well. Stone's ability to weave fragmented evidence into a sympathetic, and yet straightforward, narrative is impressive. Historians and casual readers alike will find Stone's biography enlightening. It restores a long-missing piece of the Restoration back to its rightful place in history.

—**Gary R. Entz**, PhD, history, University of Utah; author of *Llewellyn Castle: A Worker's Cooperative on the Great Plains*

In this finely crafted and vividly executed biography of William Bickerton, Daniel Stone has done far more than chronicle the life of a single individual or even of a single denomination. In Bickerton's life, Stone has discerned and explored crucial ideas about how religions work. As a historian of religion, I am most intrigued by his ability to explain how revelation can function as dissent, a concept that was foundational to Joseph Smith's original religious project and enshrined itself within the various Latter Day Saint traditions to produce both instability and adaptability. As Stone so deftly makes clear, Bickerton benefited from and suffered from both sides of that coin. His life is the story of the inextricable links among individual personalities on one hand and how religions form, change, grow, decline, and situate themselves in varied geographical settings on the other. For these reasons, and many more, Stone's work will be of interest not only to scholars of the Latter Day Saint traditions but also those seeking a better understanding of the complexities of cultural/religious interactions in the American context. The author's unprecedented access to the archives of the church, as well as his deep commitment to the subject matter, and his skill as a researcher and writer, have coalesced in the production of one of the most important biographies ever to be written about any Latter Day Saint leader.

—**Stephen C. Taysom**, Associate Professor of Philosophy and Comparative Religion, Cleveland State University; author of *Shakers, Mormons, and Religious Worlds: Conflicting Visions, Contested Boundaries*

William Bickerton became known for his revelations and visions after Charles Brown anointed him with oil in 1849 and prophesied that "this people should go in and out and find pasture," and again ten years later when Brown washed Bickerton's feet, as in the New Testament, and anointed him a "prophet and seer."

It therefore seemed right for jacket designer, Aaron Fisher, to portray this spiritual leader in the same way artists of the Byzantine period portrayed the saints of the Bible, with an illumination about their heads and a Christian sign of benediction formed by their fingers.